The Adventures

of a

Young Merchant Sailor

D1361796

James Scott Bernard

-Dedication-

The Adventures of a Young Merchant Sailor is dedicated to

My loving wife Cherie,

My patient mother, who never gave up on me,

And, to all

Those who go down to the sea in ships.

Psalm 107

-The First Voyage-

My seagoing days began in May 1946. I had just reached my sixteenth Birthday. My father died when I was thirteen. My mother went to work to support my younger sister and me. Needless to say without the supervision of a father, and a mother at work, foot loose and fancy free I qualified as a true juvenile delinquent; skipping school, drinking, and stealing cars—a mother's true heartbreak and nightmare. I was too young to join the Army or Navy, but at sixteen with a parent's permission, I could join the Merchant Marines. When I suggested it, it didn't take my mother long to agree.

The documents to serve in the Merchant Marines are issued by the U.S. Coast Guard. There are three separate departments that serve on a merchant vessel: The Deck, Engine, and Steward Departments. I chose the Deck Department, where I would begin as an ordinary seaman.

Once I received my documentation I was required to join the Sailor's Union of the Pacific. The union hall was located at 3rd and Burnside in Portland, Oregon. It's now occupied by the Gospel Mission. Right next door to the union hall was the Anchor Inn, a tavern that catered to merchant sailors on the beach (sailors between ships). Beer sold for ten cents a glass.

The union issues each mariner seeking a ship a dated card with their name on it. Openings for positions on a ship are posted daily on a large blackboard. At predetermined times the union office called out the jobs listed. Those interested turned their dated cards in. The ones with the oldest dated cards received the position.

I started making daily visits to the union hall and on several occasions I would frequent the Anchor Inn for a glass or two of ten-cent beer. Although the legal drinking age was twenty-one they rarely checked identification. After visiting the union hall on another day I went with a friend to Sailor Jack's Tattoo Parlor where each of us had swallows tattooed on our right shoulders. We thought to be a true sailor we had to have at least one tattoo.

Finally in mid May 1946 they listed the following positions for *Great Isaac*, a sea going tug:

(1) Bos'n (Boatswain, the one in charge of the deck crew.)

(3) ABS (Able Bodied Seaman)

(1) OS (Ordinary Seaman)

Other positions had already been filled from a previous voyage. The normal crew for a merchant vessel is as follows:

Deck Department:

Captain

1st Mate

2nd Mate

3rd Mate

Radio Operator

Purser

Bos'n

Carpenter

(6) ABS (Able Bodied Seaman)

(3) OS (Ordinary Seaman)

Engine Department:

Chief Engineer

1st Assistant Engineer

2nd Assistant Engineer

3rd Assistant Engineer

(6) Oilers

(3) Wipers

Steward Department:

Steward

Cooks

Mess Man

Bedroom Stewards

The total crew would usually number forty souls.

The Merchant Marine serves in time of war and peace to carry cargo and ammunition—troops during war, cargo and passengers during time of peace. Unfortunately, because of union contracts, the U.S. Merchant Marines were the highest paid in the world and consequently the most costly to operate. As a result, now the majority of ships are all under foreign registry which permits fewer crew and regulations.

On that day at the union hall I threw my card in and to my surprise got the job as an ordinary seaman on the MV *Great Isaac* (Motor Vessel). The majority of vessels in those days were SS (Steam Ships). My ship was powered by diesel not by steam.

In May 1946 my first voyage as an ordinary seaman began. My mother and sister drove me to Northwest Portland where my ship was docked. *Great Isaac* was about 175 feet in length and white in color. I didn't know anything about ships and had never been aboard one.

After a tearful good-bye, which I was convinced was more out of joy on their part than sadness in seeing my departure, I boarded *Great Isaac*.

The crew was mostly old-timers with nicknames like, Suit Case Larson, and Popeye. The old timers waited for a vessel like *Great Isaac* as it was considered easier duty because of its size—unlike larger ships which carry cargo and would require rigging booms, battening down hatches, and so forth. I was both surprised and pleased that this salty crew of old timers seemed to accept and respect me.

Aboard the ship, duties of the Deck Department are divided into four-hour shifts from midnight to 4 AM, 4 AM to 8 AM, 8 AM to noon and so on. I was assigned to the eight to noon watch. In addition to me, there were two able bodied seamen on my watch.

During my four-hour watch I would be a Helmsman steering the ship for an hour and twenty minutes and then on standby for another hour and twenty minutes. As a Helmsman I would be given a compass course to steer by. Ships in those days had magnetic compasses which record course and direction based on the magnetic north pole (which is not true north) and a gyro compass which shows true north. The magnetic compass is used as a backup in case the gyro compass, electronically activated, fails. The magnetic compass is subject to error by variation and deviation. Variation at any place is the difference between true north and magnetic north. This can vary depending on the location of the ship. The amount of variation is recorded on charts. Deviation very simply is a deviation of the compass from its magnetic north caused by magnetic materials aboard the vessel.

I was to learn that ships are navigated by terrestrial navigation which relies on land site bearings, such as light houses and buoys and by celestial navigation which relies on sighting of the sun and stars by use of a sextant which measures the angle of the sun or stars relative to Earth. When land or heavenly bodies are obscured by clouds or fog, the ship is navigated by dead reckoning. This is the advancement of the ship's position on the chart from its last known position based on compass heading and vessel speed. Also taken into consideration are two additional factors: set and drift. Set is the direction in which the current is flowing and drift is the velocity of the current measured in knots (a knot is 1.15 MPH).

Crew quarters on a ship are called the foc'sule. In earlier days the crew quarters were in the bow of the ship—the least desirable location with the greatest motion and pounding into the seas, hence foc'sule was derived from fore castle. Crew members usually share quarters with two other crew members. My quarters were with two able bodied seamen. The quarters consisted of two sets of bunk beds, a bathroom, lockers for clothes and a desk and chair. On the outboard side there was a large port hole, which when the weather was calm could be opened for ventilation. During rough weather, or to darken the quarters there was a heavy, metal hinged cover that could be securely dogged down. Heat for the quarters came from a radiator. Being the newest and least ranked crew member I was assigned to the top bunk.

We left our berth in Portland, Oregon later that morning. Our voyage took us from Portland down the Columbia River which requires a special river pilot to Astoria, Oregon which is a distance of about 90 miles. At Astoria the river pilot would be relieved by a bar pilot who would guide us across the infamous Columbia River Bar, the most dangerous bar in the world, claiming a record for the most loss of lives and ships.

In later seagoing days I wrote the following poem:

-The Columbia River Bar-

I'm heading for the Columbia River Bar.
I've been there many times before.
But friend, it'll never be a bore
One minute calm, the next its war.

I'm heading for the Columbia River Bar.
I've been there many times before.
The Buoy's moan, the frothing foam,
Make ya wonder why you roam.

I'm heading for the Columbia River Bar.
I've been there many times before.
If the sea could talk, we'd probably get out and walk.
For the tales that could be told, of the
Frightened and the bold, of ships laden with gold
How far beneath the cold.

I'm heading for the Columbia River Bar.
I've been there many times before.
With the South Jetty on my stern,
I know some day I'll return—I'll be heading
For the Columbia River Bar.
I've been there many times before.

Jacob Ladder

A Jacob ladder, rope holding together wooden steps, was lowered over the side of our vessel.

Our trips down the Columbia and crossing the bar were uneventful but always beautiful and engaging. The Columbia River Bar with a west wind and strong outgoing tide can cause seas to build to as much as 30-40 feet in height. On a later voyage on a 600 foot T2 tanker crossing the bar we took green water clear over the foremast. Cape Disappoint Coast Guard Station at the mouth of the Columbia is the only rough water training school for many countries in the world.

Lightship *Columbia*

Cape Disappointment Search and Rescue Boat

After crossing the bar we headed in a southwesterly direction approximately 8 miles to *Lightship Columbia*, which marks the entrance to the Columbia River. There we rendezvoused with *Pilot Boat Columbia*. A small open boat was launched from *Columbia* with two oarsmen who maneuvered alongside *Great Isaac*. A Jacob ladder was lowered over the side of our vessel. The bar pilot descended into the open launch which took him back to *Columbia*. In rough water, which I experienced on later voyages, this can be a tricky and dangerous event. Several pilots have lost their lives in this transition.

From the lightship we headed south, our destination Panama, to escort three fishing vessels back to San Diego with a stop in Acapulco, Mexico for bunkers fuel. The voyage was beautiful with sunny skies and calm seas. At night while standing my watch on the bow I would see porpoises diving in and out of the water near our bow as if they were guiding our vessel. It was a beautiful sight, because of phosphorus in the water they lit up like green neon signs. During the day the crew would be kept busy by chipping rust, painting, preparing gear, and replacing lines.

We sailed into Acapulco on a warm, sunny afternoon and anchored in the harbor. Acapulco in those days was a sleepy little fishing village. There was one hotel on the cliff overlooking the bay. Even in those days, young Mexican divers would dive off the high cliff into the bay quite a distance. By this time it seemed the crew had accepted me. Although, I was quite young, I had kind of a "cocky-sure of myself" attitude tempered with a desire to learn and a willingness to pull my full share of duty.

By late afternoon, we were given shore leave. I went with other crew members on one of our life boats to shore. As sailors usually do on shore leave they head for the closest Gin Mill, seaman's term for watering hole. Today was no exception. The streets were all paved in dirt and an occasional chicken scratching for food. The buildings were all of stucco or mud bricks.

I saddled up to the bar with a few others and started with a bottle of Mexican beer. Soon two of the most unattractive senoritas came up and put their arms around me. As I recall they said something to the effect of, "We want blonde, blue-eyed baby!" I was blonde and blue eyed, but continued to drink my beer and replied, "Sorry ladies." Soon they moved to another crew member. Prior to arrival in Acapulco our purser had advised us of the potential of venereal disease and to avoid prostitutes. Apparently with a few too many beers and the warm climate I feel asleep on the dock and didn't wake up until the next morning to a rooster crowing and the sun shining on my face. Later I returned to the ship.

That afternoon after taking on fuel, we headed south toward Panama. About a day's journey south of Acapulco we came to the Gulf of Tehuantepec. North and south of this area it can be very calm seas, but as you cross this area there is a wind that blows from the Pacific to the Gulf of Mexico. It's calm one minute and rough seas the next.

Reaching Panama, we docked in Balboa which as I recall is a U.S. controlled city. I went ashore to a military cafeteria with others and enjoyed one of the best strawberry milk shakes I'd ever had! However, on shore leave the next evening unfortunately I had more than a milk shake. We had taken a cab from Balboa across to Panama City often referred to as the Den of Iniquity, and we proceeded into a bar. A small group of musicians were playing and the bar was filled with smoke. After a few drinks I saddled up to the lead musician and asked if he would play, "You Belong to My Heart." He politely obliged and I handed him a couple of Mexican pesos. As it was playing, for the first time I felt homesick. I had also requested, "South of the Border," which he played. Sometime later, after a few more drinks, I felt tired and I'm sure a bit intoxicated. I left the bar and found a cab parked right in front. I hopped into the passenger seat. The motor was running and I waited for the cab driver to return. When he didn't return, for some crazy unbelievable reason, I moved over into the driver seat, put the cab in gear and started down the street. I was going down a one-way street in the wrong direction. All of the sudden I heard the shrill sound of a police whistle. I stepped on the throttle and kept going until shots were fired; one bullet just missed my head. It grazed my right hand and smashed the windshield into hundreds of pieces. Needless to say, at this point I stopped. I was handcuffed and taken to a medical facility for treatment. From the medical clinic I was taken to the most god-awful prison. It was a large cement cell block with small barred windows. The floor was wet with what appeared to be urine. Raggedly clothed prisoners were sprawled out all over the area. I was very tired. Somehow I laid down in all the filth and fell asleep. Early the next morning I was awakened by what I thought was my name being called. I stood up and a guard motioned me towards the door. I was taken from the cell block to a court room. It was a dark day and I could see lightening flash, followed by the roar of thunder. I was totally filled with fright and almost sick to my stomach. It was a day truly made in hell. My charges were read off in the native language. The only thing I understood in English was: "250 days!" I was led back to the cellblock totally depressed. All I could think about was how could I end my life? I was there perhaps two days. On what was probably the third morning, still in a foggy state, I thought I was in a dream, more like nightmare, when I heard "James Bernard" called out. I stood up and looked toward the voice, and standing there next to the guard was the ships purser. I didn't know whether to cry or laugh with joy. I was free! The purser said that they had all but given up on finding me and were prepared to sail without me.

We left Panama later that afternoon escorting three small fishing vessels back to San Diego. My fine was such a large sum that I was given extra work on overtime to help offset the fine.

On the trip back, we put out a fishing line and landed a marlin. The crew pulled in the line by hand. We also landed a large sea turtle. All along the way we spotted flying fish. I'm not sure what species they were, but they would fly out of the water several feet into the air and then splash back into the sea.

We arrived back in San Diego. We left the three fishing boats and proceeded north for San Francisco where the crew was laid off. The crew had to take up an offering to provide me with funds to return home—and so ended my first voyage.

-Voyages from Portland, Oregon to the Orient-

I continued my sea adventures for the next six years advancing from ordinary seaman to able bodied seaman and then third deck officer. Some of the more exciting and interesting events occurred during these years.

On one voyage, from Portland, Oregon to Kobe, Japan, we left Portland February 1 and didn't arrive in Kobe until March 1. Some days the weather was so bad that we actually lost ground. The ship was a 450 foot Liberty ship with a top speed of 13 knots. Liberty ships were built in World War II to haul goods and munitions to war fronts. Many were built in Kaiser Ship Yards, Portland, Oregon. Some were launched in as few as 28 days. When we arrived in Kobe, Japan, after that length of time in rough seas, when we went ashore we'd go this way and that way. We looked like we were drunk. It was difficult to walk straight. Aboard the ship in Japan, the Japanese longshoremen would continually bow down to us, we being their conquers. If one of our crew dropped an almost finished cigarette to the deck, before he could step on it to put it out a Japanese hand would grab it. In those days you could buy a carton of cigarettes at the ships store for only fifty cents. I found that I could trade a carton of cigarettes for a lovely Japanese tea set that came all tightly packed in a nicely made wooden crate. I would bring them back for family members and sell some to others.

On most of these voyages to Japan we would be loaded to Plimsoll with wheat from Oregon. On the return voyage to Portland we would be empty except for enough water ballast to help keep the stern of the ship deep enough to enable the ships propeller to function. In heavier seas when the ship came down off the large swell the propeller would come out of the water causing the ship to vibrate violently. Unless the RPMs of the engine were immediately reduced it could cause damage to the ship. To accomplish this was referred to as the Butterfly Watch manually controlling the RPMs of the ships engines.

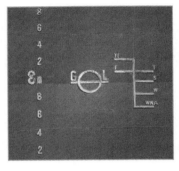

Plimsoll

Samuel Plimsoll, in the 1800s, was successful in passing a law which became international. It required marking on the side of ships showing the maximum depth to which a ship could be loaded. Prior to its passing, ships had been over loaded resulting in loss of lives and ships.

Another problem crossing the ocean in a cargo-less ship is the constant rolling and pitching of the ship. It is like a cork in water. The crew bunks on most ships are thwartships, from port to starboard, left to right. As the ship would make a big roll from left to right you would slide from the bottom edge of the bunk to the top, often banging your head. It was very difficult trying to sleep. In the eating areas, dishes would fly in every direction. The captain and officer's bunks were fore and aft, a bit easier for them in rough seas.

-Scaling the Top Mast-

On another voyage aboard a Liberty Ship to Japan they needed someone to replace the halyard (rope) in the top mast. The top mast is mounted on top of the mizzen mast. The mizzenmast is immediately forward of the wheel house. The mizzenmast is approximately 55 feet in height and the top mast is an additional 20 feet in height. The bos'n, the one in charge of the deck crew, took a look around the mess hall where we were finishing breakfast. I kind of slid behind another crew member to avoid the bos'n's eyes. But to my surprise he walked right over to me and said, "You'll be just the right one for the job." I suppose I was probably the smallest crew member. The task required climbing up the mizzen mast which had steel bar steps and then with the end of the new halyard tucked in my jeans shimming up the top mast which was approximately 15 inches in diameter—without any safety gear. When reaching the top of the mast I was to feed the halyard through a pully and bring both ends back down and secure it at the top of the mizzen mast. I had to brace myself against the top mast as the ship was gently rolling from port to starboard. The entire crew was watching from the deck below so I thought I better at least act like I'm not scared. So up I went, ship rolling and all. My first attempt to put the line through the pully was unsuccessful. I was hanging on to the top mast with one arm, my legs wrapped around the mast, and with the other hand, the rope. I was successful in getting the job done on the second attempt. A little shaky, but with a sense of relief I returned to my shipmates on the main deck. The only purpose for the rigging is to attach a bos'ns chair to the halyard and give a crew member the means to paint the top mast.

Liberty Ship

Can you imagine chiming up the top mast in rolling seas without a safety harness?

Mercy

Breeches Buoy

-Drama at Sea-

Many of my voyages were from Portland, Oregon to Japan with large cargos of wheat, as I mentioned earlier. On one of these voyages, a crew member had an attack of appendicitis. We were in very stormy seas about half way to Japan. His condition worsened and finally his appendix burst. The captain had Sparks, the radio operator; make emergency calls for advice and assistance. Almost like a miracle he made contact with the hospital ship *Mercy*, which was about a two hour distance from our position. The crew member remained in extreme pain. The ship's purser had given him a large dose of morphine.

Finally after two hours, out of a misty, stormy sea we spotted the all white hull of *Mercy*. As it came closer, we could make out the large Red Cross on its side. The seas were very rough. *Mercy* maneuvered within approximately 150 feet of our vessel. A line was fired by a Lyle-gun from our vessel to *Mercy*. The line was rigged with a breeches buoy, a chair like device on pulleys that slides along the rope. The crew member was carefully placed in the chair. Both vessels were rolling and tossing in the seas. A line attached to the breeches buoy from *Mercy* successfully pulled the ailing crew member safely to *Mercy*. All this took place in 20-30 foot seas with winds in excess of 30 knots.

The crew member was treated aboard *Mercy* and taken to a port in Japan where he made a full recovery.

-To the Phillipines · A Scare and an Affair-

My next voyage was to the Phillipines to pick up a load of World War II surplus and return it to San Francisco. The voyage took us to a small island with palm trees and sandy beaches. The name of the island, I believe, was Managani. It is situated south of the main island of Luzon. Shortly after arriving, the crew was given shore leave. It was a warm but pleasant day. With three other crew members we headed for a nearby beach where we rented a native outrigger dugout. We launched the dugout and paddled out into a very warm gentle breeze with an almost flat sea. Talk about a tropical paradise. We must have paddled about a mile or so off shore. I was sitting up in the bow totally relaxed when I started to hear screams from my crew mates. When I turned around I saw the craft was filling with water and sinking. One of my crewmates had accidently pulled the plug in the bottom of the dugout and it sank to several inches below the surface. Only the outriggers kept it afloat. Somehow in all the confusion we had lost the paddles. So, hanging on to the side of the dugout we hung on with one arm and paddled with the other. Shore appeared to be far away. The water was warm—we were not sure about sharks. We paddled frantically and finally, after more than an hour, we reached shore. But to our dismay we were still about a quarter of a mile from the rental facility. So with played out bodies we pulled the dugout along the shoreline to the launching spot, reimbursed the proprietor for the lost paddles and returned to ship for some rest.

After ship duties were completed, the crew would spend time swimming and exploring the beaches. At night the crew would visit a military canteen to drink beer, play cards and shoot pool. I would usually join them and then, at about 10 PM, return to the ship with others. Some of the crew would take off with young Phillipino gals. The next morning at breakfast the crew would share their adventures from the previous evening. One rather macho crew member told how when he was apparently making love to a young Phillipino gal on a hillside and she started moaning, and then the moans turned into screams. He got real excited thinking he was really getting the job done only to find out that every time he pressed on her he was jamming her back side into some sharp rock.

-Duties on Night Watch-

After a three week stay, we finally left the Phillipines with a full cargo of World War II surplus bound for San Francisco. At night time during my period on lookout, which usually was on the bow, my responsibilities were to report any lights which usually would be another vessel, and to keep my eyes open for floating mines which we frequently spotted—following World War II many remained. When I spotted a light I would call the bridge via a phone which was enclosed in a water tight box to report the position of the light or mine. The position, if not dead ahead, would be reported in points. A point is 11 1/4 degrees on the compass, the total degrees of the compass being 360 degrees. Thus the call would go something like this, "A light at approximately (2) 22 1/2 points off the starboard bow." On watch at night, I would often see falling stars and a beautiful sight of the Heavens. The only noise was the restful and peaceful sound of the ship gliding through the water and porpoises darting in and out of the water near the bow as though they were leading the ship.

-Last U.S. Ship to China-

We were the last U.S. ship allowed into Communist China. We had a cargo of UNRA goods (United Nations Relief Aid). We anchored on the Yangzee River at Shanghi China. All around us were families living on Chinese junks. Wooden crafts powered by sail or paddles.

It was interesting to see a mother washing clothes in the river at the stern of the boat and another family member relieving themselves at the bow. Several of us took a water taxi to shore. Shortly after arriving on shore, a large group of Chinese males, as I recall unusually tall, surrounded us. We were frightened not knowing what was going to happen. Finally they demanded money which we readily gave them and they departed. Americans at that time were not looked upon with favor. We continued our walk toward the center of Shanghi. The streets were dirty and covered with lots of garbage and trash. Several dead human bodies were lying near the street decaying. To top it off, a foul smelling wind was blowing dust everywhere including into our eyes. There were street vendors already selling some of our relief supplies. Our only thought at this point was, "Let me out of here!"

From Shanghi we sailed to Hong Kong China. Hong Kong was under British control. What a contrast. The city was beautiful and squeaky clean. The people were all very friendly and receptive to us.

-A Visit to a Japanese Bath House-

From Hong Kong we sailed to Yokohama, Japan. There I was to rendezvous with my brother-in-law, a career Army Officer stationed in Japan. After dining together my brother-in-law took me to a Japanese bath house. A very clean and nice looking facility where it was staffed with young Japanese girls (I'm sure over eighteen year's old.) garbed in white shorts and tee shirts. These bath houses were totally above board and no hanky panky. I was directed to a small bamboo cubicle where a large round tub was already heated, with steam rising off the water. I was instructed to disrobe and enter the tub, which I did, and as the warm water covered my already quite tired body, oh did it relax me. As my hostess began to bath me, I heard screams from a nearby cubical. My brother-in-law's hostess was apparently screaming in response to his unwanted advances.

While in the Phillipines we had run out of American coffee. It had been replaced with coffee from China. It was horrible, made of chicory and I don't know what else but it was ugly. So the next morning after our adventure in the bath house, I was anxious for a decent cup of coffee. We went to a Japanese restaurant and ordered coffee. It was a bit different than I had expected. Instead of a regular coffee cup, it came in a very small demitasse cup. As I peered into it, the coffee was as black as ink. It did have a very pleasant aroma. After a brief taste, I knew that it had to be almost pure caffeine. Very strong and boy did it give me a jolt!

Prior to going to sea I had never drank coffee, but with the late night watches I started drinking coffee to keep awake and alert.

We left Yokohama for a return voyage to Portland, Oregon. One thing I noticed while going to Sea was that about a day from reaching shore I'd start to smell the sweet aroma of land. This was especially true in the springtime approaching the Oregon coast when the cottonwoods were in bloom. While way out at sea the air would be quite sterile, except for the smell of the sea. Approaching each different country, the fragrance would vary, depending on the countries vegetation.

-A Saki Party in Formosa-

On a voyage to Taipei Formosa, shortly after arriving, my crew members and I were invited to, of all things, a morning Sake Party. Sake, as you probably know, is a rice wine served hot in a very small ceramic cup. Well, after several shots of Sake we were returning to the ship when we spotted a big red fire engine being washed in front of a fire station. We all hopped aboard the fire engine. The fireman graciously climbed aboard and allowed us, with siren screaming, to go a short distance. We stopped and turned the truck over to them.

-Crew's Delegate at Seventeen-

Although I was only seventeen years old I did have a fairly assertive way and was reasonably articulate. Consequently the crew on many occasions would elect me to be the ships union delegate. My duty as ship's delegate was to negotiate disputes between crew members and company representatives, which was usually the 1st mate. In many cases it would be a dispute about overtime pay. So there I was, a seventeen year old kid, negotiating with a mature fifty-five to sixty year old 1st mate. On one occasion, I was involved in a negotiation with an older salty 1st mate with an untrimmed beard and the smell of alcohol on his breath. We were at an impass in our negotiations and I think he figured I had outfoxed him. All of a sudden he opened his desk drawer and pulled out a .357 magnum pistol, started waving it at me and said, "You know all men are created equal and for those that are not there's these." He continued to wave the pistol toward me. As he thought about what he had done, he slowly slipped the pistol back in the drawer. We were finally able to come to an agreement.

-One Way Voyage-

Guess What Happened On a Greyhound Bus?

Many of my voyages would be intercoastal going form ports on the west coast of the U.S. through the Panama Canal to ports on the east coast and vice versa. Going through the Panama Canal was always an exciting and interesting experience. It's amazing how the canal was carved in many areas out of solid rock. Reference "Song of the Panama Builders," builders who did the impossible.

It's no secret that Merchant Seaman are known for a considerable amount of drinking. Although no alcohol is sold on Merchant ships, many crew members bring their own supply aboard.

On one intercoastal trip from Long Beach, California to New York City the bos'n, a heavy drinker, had run out of his private stock and started buying Aqua Velva After Shave from the ships store and drinking it. When he'd burp all you would smell was Aqua Velva.

At least once a week, while at sea, it was required that the ship's crew have a fire and boat drill. The ship's horn would blow a distress signal and bell alarms located throughout the ship would ring. All crew members would put their life jackets on and assume their designated places at the fire stations and life boats. In all my seagoing days I experienced only one fire which was quickly extinguished. On this intercoastal voyage we were taking a C2 cargo ship to New York for layup. It was newer, larger and more streamlined than the older Liberty ships.

Early during my seagoing days, a friend of mine started going to sea; he joined me on this voyage.

When we reached New York we were given our final pay and transportation money to return home. My friend and I purchased Greyhound tickets to Portland, Oregon, our home. My friend had always been very gregereous at high school parties. Instead of joining in with the other kids he would be upstairs making advances with one of the kids' mothers.

On this bus trip we had made a brief layover in Pittsburg, Pennsylvania. My friend hailed a cab and asked the driver where he could find some female company. We drove to a crummy looking area; it was starting to get dark. The cab driver stopped and pointed to a second story window, where a red light was flashing and what appeared to be a black woman motioning for the cab's occupants to come up. With great haste my friend took off. He was gone for a little more than a half an hour. We then returned to the bus depot to continue our trip home.

The next day as we were traveling through a rural area of Iowa, all of a sudden my friend started groaning and then almost screaming in pain. He made a bolt for the front of the bus and demanded that the bus be stopped and the door opened. The bewildered driver stopped the bus and opened the door. My friend ran from the bus into some nearby bushes returning to the bus a short time later. After taking his seat beside me he explained that after the previous night episode he applied a prophylactic kit which is designed to avoid venereal disease and that the vibration of the bus had caused an involuntary erection. A bag tied around his penis (part of the kit) started to strangle his penis as the erection occurred and hence the pain.

-Drama between Voyages-

St. Johns Bridge

During a maritime strike, my friend and I took a job painting the St. Johns' Bridge in Portland, Oregon. The bridge crosses the Willamette River near the St. Johns area. During our first days on the job we were painting the insides of the bridge columns. We carried three gallon buckets of paint, climbing metal ladders inside the columns. There was very little ventilation consequently the fumes would cause us to become delirious. On our lunch breaks we would catch pigeons in paper sacks and take them home for our evening supper.

Our final day painting the St. Johns Bridge ended with some real drama. We were painting on electric scaffolding, often referred to as a stage. We were a couple of hundred feet up in the air painting the exterior of the bridge's arches, suddenly without warning my end of the stage started to drop. I hung on for all my life. It dropped about 12 feet and stopped. Here we are hanging catty wompus with one end of the stage up, the other down, paint spilling to the deck below, both of us really scared and hanging on for our dear lives. Spectators below saw our plight and called the police. When they arrived they stopped all traffic. We were fearful of hitting the button that activates the up and down of the stage but finally we hit the down button, and jumping and jerking we were able to safely reach the deck of the bridge. With a little prayer and great haste we went to the job shack and quit.

Shaver Tug

During another Maritime strike I got a job with Shaver Transportation Company, a tow boat operation. My position was referred to as a deck hand, also called a logger—O' how I hated this job. My job was to hitch up the tug to log rafts. This often required walking out on single logs. I have a very poor sense of balance and would fall into the cold winter water of the Willamette and Columbia Rivers, often twice a day. I'd come dragging home damp and cold with a bag of wet clothes. Fortunately the strike ended and I returned to sea.

Shore Leave, Japan

S.S. Augustine Daly

Pusan, Korea May 1952

Yokohama, Japan 1952

Jim and Cherie content at home after the last voyage.

-Drama in South America-

It's amazing to me how few altercations occurred between the ship's crew in all my time at sea. However, one very serious event stands out like a sore thumb. I was on Grace Line's ship, *Clove Hitch*. It was a C1, smaller and less draft than most freighters; this enabled it to service ports from Mexico, Central and South America. (A C1 is a class of merchant ships designed to negotiate smaller harbors.)

We were on a voyage that took us from Long Beach, California to many ports in Mexico, Central America—ending up in Lima, Peru. While in Lima a grievance between a deck crew member and the ships steward came to a head. The crew member was 6 foot 2, with a burley muscular build. He had a hatchet looking face and very sharp features. The steward was just the opposite. He was very small in stature, balding and kind of whimpy looking. He was always whining. The crew members for weeks had been complaining about the food the steward had been serving. On this particular day the crew member had returned to the ship after boozing it up on shore. He came stumbling aboard late in the afternoon, hollering, "Where is that G.D. Steward? I'm going to kill him!" Finally, sad to say, he found the steward and dragged him into one of the foc'sles and proceeded to beat the holy hell out of him. Finally the bos'n and 2nd mate came to his rescue, but by this time the poor fellow was half beaten to death. Blood was spattered all over the room. The steward was taken to the hospital and never returned to the ship. According to maritime law the crew member was placed in irons and put under twenty-four hour guard in one of the ships supply rooms, there he was to remain until we reached a U.S. port where he would be turned over to the authorities.

Lima was a fascinating city with narrow streets and many small interesting shops, purveying silver jewelry, lama blankets, rugs, and much more. I bought a silver charm bracelet, a silver drinking set, a lama blanket, and real puffy lama slippers. After dinner in a small restaurant I registered at Lima's finest hotel. I believe it was The Hotel Boliva which was very plush. I wasn't due back on the ship until late the next day. My room was super elegant with a large canopy bed. As soon as my head hit the pillow I fell fast asleep. When I woke up in the morning I was kind of thirsty and spotted what I thought was a drinking fountain. I proceeded to push a pedal and drank from it. I was to learn later that is was a bidet. Anyway, with thirst quenched I was hungry and I had always wanted to order breakfast in bed so that is exactly what I did.

I was back snuggled up in my canopy bed when there was a knock at the door. It was the bellman with my breakfast. He carefully set the breakfast on a tray across my lap. He left and I proceed to enjoy my breakfast in bed. As I recall it was orange juice, a cheese omelet, toast and coffee. While in Lima I hired a guide, for a carton of cigarettes, to show me around Lima and assist me in making purchases. The day the ship was scheduled to sail late in the day I gave my guide a couple, perhaps three cartons of cigarettes to purchase me a Peruvian blanket. Apparently it was a case of mistaken trust for as we sailed off into the sunset, no guide and no blanket. Oh well.

Sailing north from Peru we stopped at many Central American ports, Nicaragua, Costa Rica, and so forth. Many of us would go ashore and enjoy the beautiful white sand beaches and the breath taking azure blue ocean water.

Before returning to the ship we would purchase whole stocks of bananas. The entire deck of the ship (almost) was covered with hanging stocks of bananas.

We sailed north to San Francisco where the crew was discharged. In seamen's language we were "paid off." I returned to Portland, Oregon by train. I can recall that I almost froze to death as the train traveled over Shasta Pass.

The majority of ships that I sailed on were Liberty ships. But on at least two occasions I sailed on Victory ships, also built during World War II. They were longer, more streamlined, and faster than Liberty ships.

Victory Ship

In November of 1949 I sailed from Portland, Oregon on a Victory ship, *Clarksburg Victory* for Mobile, Alabama, where the ship was to be layed up and the crew paid off. After arriving in Mobile, we were given travel money to get home. I got four of my crew mates to give me as I recall 100 dollars each with the understanding, I would buy a car and we'd drive home. I went to a used car lot in Mobile and bought a black 1940 Packard Limousine, which had probably been either a funeral or a gangster car. It had a roll up window separating the driver's area from the rear seats. It was real sinister looking. I paid 350 dollars for it. All excited about my purchase, I drove back to the ship to pick up my passengers. When I reached the ship I tried to put it in reverse and the engine stalled, the battery was dead and one of the crew yelled out, "Your gas tank is leaking." I had the car towed to a small garage where an older black mechanic worked on the generator and transmission for more then seven hours. His bill was only 18 dollars. I gave him 25 and left. I picked up my passengers and headed for home. The car had no license plates, and it had freewheeling, which has since been outlawed. When you took your foot off the accelerator it went out of gear. The steering was so loose you had to drive fast just to maintain steerage and the only way we could stop the leaking gas tank was to rub the holes with a bar of soap. When we pulled into a gas station we had to keep the engine running to avoid it not restarting. Consequently attendants were afraid to come out and wait on us—five unshaven men in a black limo with the engine running. Finally, we'd get out and coax them to fuel us.

I was afraid to let anyone else drive because of the steering, so I drove three days with only two hours sleep all the way to Portland, Oregon.

I was so grimy from my trip I stopped at a mobile station near our home to clean up a little. The owner became very indigment and asked me to leave.

I put an ad in the paper to sell the Packard. A peg legged fellow from Alaska paid 350 dollars for the car. As he left I had to lift his peg leg onto the gas pedal and he was off to Alaska. He gave me a call from Seattle and said he had the steering checked and only a small cotter pin had kept the steering from going totally out.

1940 Black Packard Lemo

On January 1, 1949 I married my high school sweetheart, Cherie. It was almost like Christmas or even better to get home after a long voyage and be with my Cherie. During our early marriage, our meals would often consist of Krafts Macaroni and Cheese which came in a box and cost only fifteen cents, or we'd have Spam with seasoned catsup sauce.

One day between voyages when I came home from the hiring hall my wife said, "Guess what," and I said, "What?" She said that a cookware salesman was coming by around supper time to give us a demonstration. I said, "No way!" Sure enough, about 5 PM there was a knock at the front door. We immediately dropped to the floor and crawled toward the kitchen on our stomachs. He kept knocking even louder and hollering, "I know you are in there." He made a hasty move to the back door near the kitchen which prompted a crawl on our tummies to the bedroom. Finally, he gave up and left.

Some days I would come home to stacks of encyclopedias or a new vacuum cleaner, which, after a few tears, I successfully returned. Those were the days!

Leaving on another voyage was almost like dying a little. I'd be homesick before I left. But yet each new voyage would be filled with new adventure which helped to mitigate the malady.

-To My Beloved Wife-

November 2, 1949

I'll always Love you, Cherie dear,

With all my aching heart.

You've been my everything,

Since the very start.

While in the far lands of Peru,

My heart beats strong for only you.

And in the distant land of Japan,

My heart ached more than

I could stand.

And now I've sailed away again,

To return, I know not when.

But while upon the seven

Seas I roam,

My only thought is you,

Our son, our home.

So I thought I'd write this rhyme,

While in the passing of my time,

To let you know that

Whether far or near,

I'll always Love you, Cherie dear.

Your loving Husband,

Jim

-North to Alaska-

One of the most sought after positions for those sailing in the Deck Department were ships that had a special union contract that permitted the deck crew to work as longshoreman in port. The deck crew would work loading and unloading cargo to and from Hold 3, which is the cargo hold immediately forward of the wheel house.

Early in 1950 I was successful in getting a job aboard *Sea Fair*, a Liberty ship which had that special contract. At sea my duties would be the same as on other ships, in port, handling cargo. This ship would carry cargo from Long Beach, California to all ports of Alaska. When in the ports of Alaska, the cargo would be worked around the clock. I would work eighteen hours on and only six hours off. It was a grueling schedule but the rate of pay made it quite rewarding, a little over two-thousand a month which in todays' dollars would be over five-thousand a month. In those days there were no cargo containers. All cargo was handled one item at a time. Lumber one stick at a time. Boy how times have changed. This resulted in lots of cargo being pilfered by longshoreman. Even our crew was guilty of pilfering. Our crew's favorite was U-No Bars. Liquor, beer and wine were the only protected cargoes. They were placed in a locked cage.

On a typical voyage we would visit the ports of Valdez, Whittier, Anchorage, and Seward. In Seward they have an interesting event on the Fourth of July. People came from far and wide to take part. It was a race on foot to the top of a mountain right near Seward and back to the bottom. Participants would race to the top and then in many cases, literally throw themselves down the mountain side. The first one to make it up and down in the shortest amount of time was the winner. Needless to say there were many injuries.

While in Seward many of the crew went to nearby streams and fished for Dolly Varden trout. They would bring their catch back to the ship where the ships chef would prepare it for our supper

Serving on the *Seafair* during the winter in Alaska was a bitter cold challenge. Before cargo could be unloaded the crew would have to climb up the mast and chip the ice off the boom sticks. Snow and ice had to be chipped and shoveled off the deck.

The captain of the *Seafair* was much younger than the older, colorful 1st mate. The 1st mate was probably in his seventies, gray hair and scrappy gray beard. When the ship would pound in heavy seas, the crusty old 1st mate could be heard saying, "Easy *Seafair*." Many old timers often talked to their ships as though they were people, and put their juniors down by saying, "I've rung more sea water out of my socks then you've sailed over."

The 1st mate and the captain didn't care much about each other and they often squabbled. On one occasion the 1st mate accidently bumped the binoculars when he put them down. The captain, being picky, admonished the 1st mate for being careless. In response, the mate picked up the binoculars, held them out in front of him and said, "What did you say captain?" He let the binoculars drop to the deck. Their dislike for one another was only to intensify.

-Stowaways from the South-

After leaving Alaska we would often load large rolls of news print paper in Portland, Oregon for ports in California. It took a lot of hussle and muscle to move these large rolls into position in the ships hold. After unloading our paper cargo we sailed to Crockett, California in the San Francisco Bay Area to load sugar for Vancouver, B.C. What a contrast coming from frozen Alaska to the sunny warmth of California. Crockett was in the inner bay so on our way to Crockett we got a great view of Alcatraz.

On the final day of loading sugar in Crockett, the bos'n and other crew members had been ashore enjoying some California brews. When they returned to the ship, apparently feeling no pain, they smuggled three girls aboard with them. They threw the girls shoes overboard to prevent them from leaving the ship. The ship sailed the next morning for Vancouver, B.C. with the stowaways aboard. When the bos'n didn't report for duty that morning, the 1st mate went to the bos'ns' quarters and knocked on the door. When there was no response he opened the door and there was the bos'n asleep in his bunk with one of the girls beside him.

When we docked in Vancouver, B.C. the custom officials came aboard; they found three shoeless U.S. citizens, stowaways without passports. They were taken into custody and then ashore—a sad scene. I never heard what the outcome was.

-Rum and Coca Cola-

Backing up a bit, we were on an intercoastal voyage and on the way we stopped at San Juan, Porto Rico. On shore leave the crew would enjoy one of Porto Rico's major products, rum. In those days a rum and coke cost only 15 cents.

A popular song was, "Drinking Rum and Coca Cola," about a mother and daughter working for the Yankee dollar.

Whipped Cream Dessert

-Officers School-

By December of 1951 I had the amount of sea time required to qualify for my 3rd mate officer's license. Our family had increased in size. We had a son, Kris, who arrived on October 19, 1949 and a daughter, Kim, who arrived on September 17, 1951. I was in Alaska at the time of Kim's birth. Alaska was a military zone and my wife was unable to communicate Kim's arrival to me. Returning from Alaska to Seattle, I called to check on my wife's condition; the baby wasn't due for several weeks. When she said the baby had arrived early, I said, "How great!" I'll be right home. Returning from the phone booth to the ship I shared my news with my crew mates. They said, "Was it a boy or girl?" I replied, "My gosh! I forgot to ask." Back to the phone, "It's a girl." I got a much needed haircut, bought a teddy bear, and flew home.

So in early December 1951 our little family headed by car to Alameda, California where the officers school was located. We were able to rent an almost new apartment which was only a short distance from the officer training facility.

The training course covered navigation, semaphore, cargo stowage, rules of the road, first aid, Morse code, both celestial and terrestrial navigation, ship safety, ship and small boat handling. All this was covered in, as I recall six to eight weeks. My wife helped me with semaphore in the evenings.

One evening we invited my mother-in-law, Millie, who lived in San Francisco, over for dinner. My wife prepared one of my favorites— real whipped cream with mixed fruit—bananas, cherries, pineapple, and so forth. I knew my mother-in-law, who was a great eater, thrived on it. So before she arrived I carefully hid the whipped cream and fruit dish behind some milk and orange juice containers. What does Millie do—coat still on—she proceeds to the refrigerator, paws through the milk and juice containers, gets the large bowl of whipped cream and fruit, sets it in on the table, grabs a tablespoon and starts devouring my special treat. O' how we love mother-in-laws.

After successfully completing the course we packed up for the trip back to Portland, Oregon. We left Alameda late in the afternoon on that same day. We drove straight through to Portland arriving on Sunday morning.

Monday morning, armed with all my acquired knowledge I headed for the Coast Guard office in the Failing Building where I was to be tested. The testing usually takes five to six days. I was somehow able to complete the testing successfully in three days.

-The Perilous Voyage of *S.S. Augustine Daly*-

S.S. Augustine Daly

I had to join the Masters Mates and Pilots Union. I was already a member of the Sailors' Union of the Pacific and the Inland Boatmen's Union. At this time we were at war in Korea. When I went to the hiring hall I could take my pick of ships. There were more ships than officers to fill them. I picked *S.S. Augustine Daly*, a Liberty ship just out of the moth ball fleet being refitted for action. My duties aboard the ship, as 3rd mate included the following: I would stand a watch at sea from 8 AM to noon and from 8 PM to midnight. On my watches, serving with me on the bridge, was a member of the deck department, either an able bodied seaman or ordinary seaman, their job was to steer the ship on a course charted by the captain. I would also have a deck department crew member as a lookout on the bow. Unless the captain was on the bridge, I would be in total charge of the ship.

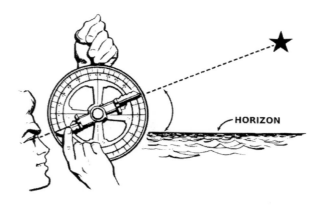

At noon I would join the captain and other deck officers in taking a noon sighting of the sun with our sextants. This would give us a longitude line of position, our exact position moving from east to west. At dusk we would take star sighting with our sextants. Each star sighting would give us a single line of position which would be plotted on the chart.

Plotting several star sighting would cross like this ... ... the center of these, when plotted on the chart, would be our exact position.

Communication with other ships would often be done by blinker light using Morse code. Rarely would it be done by semaphore.

In the event that we were required to abandon ship, I would be in charge of one of the life boats. The life boats were equipped with oars, a sail and an engine, canned food, water, medical supplies, matches, flares, compass, and a jug of oil to pour on a rough ocean to calm it. Also a sea anchor, a canvas bag which when deployed from the bow or stern would help to keep the boat from broaching (turning into the trough of the sea and possibly capsizing).

Some of the pluses of being an officer: I had my own private quarters with a fore and aft bunk. I also got to eat in the officer's salon where I was served my meals by a member of the steward's department.

Later in the voyage, shortly after 9 PM, the captain would retire for the evening. So there I was a young man twenty-one years of age—totally in command and charge of a 450 foot Liberty ship, and its crew of forty souls. It was a heady position to be in. The youngest age at which you can obtain a 3rd Mates license is twenty-one.

My goal at the time was to be the master of my own ship by age twenty-five.

On a cold and cloudy afternoon in early February 1952 I said goodbye to my wife and children and sailed from Portland, Oregon as 3rd mate on *S.S. Augustine Daly*. We traveled down the Columbia River toward Astoria, Oregon which is a distance of 90 nautical miles. I came to the bridge a little before 8 PM for my watch. On the bridge were the helmsman, the captain, the river pilot, and me. We were near Skamokawa, Washington. Skamokawa is an Indian word for "smoke on the water," which was how the Indians described fog, and true to form it was very foggy. We had reduced our speed to slow ahead. Also required in foggy condition is sounding the ships horn at sixty second intervals, which we were doing. Almost out of nowhere, another ship appeared dead ahead in the fog. Immediately the pilot ordered, "Full astern and helm hard left!" Within seconds we collided with the other ship. The other ship was a French vessel which had somehow anchored right near the center of the ship's channel. You could hear the grinding of metal as our ships collided. Neither ship sustained enough damage to endanger sinking. Because of the damage near the bow of our ship we returned to Portland, Oregon for repairs.

What a surprise for Cherie, "Back already?" Repairs took over ten days. In late February 1952 we again left Portland for a destination we'd later receive in secret orders; Pusan, Korea. After crossing the Columbia River bar we sailed over calm seas and beautiful weather in a southwesterly direction. The second day at sea the bos'n was found dead of apparent natural causes in his bunk. Normally the body would be sewn in canvas, filled with iron shackles and a burial at sea. But because of the uncertainty of his death he was placed in the ships freezer.

Beautiful weather and calm seas continued for days, but something very strange was happening. The barometer, which is a predictor of storms, took a dramatic drop way down below 28. The captain, a young Italian on his first voyage as master thought our barometer was faulty and asked Sparks to contact other ships in the area to check their barometers, but no response.

Early the next morning all hell broke loose. Winds had built up to over 120 miles per hour and when I came onto the bridge and saw mountains of seas rising well over 100 feet coming at us, my inner being was filled with fear. In five years of sea time I had never seen or heard of seas like this. The ship would rise into the sea, going almost straight up like climbing a mountain, and then dive straight down on the back side. Finally one high sea completely covered the ship with a huge crash. I was in the chart room making an entry in the ships log and it knocked the original type ink pen from my hand splattering ink all over the deck. The sea had cracked the hull ahead of the wheel house structure, washed part of the deck cargo overboard, smashed the life boat I was in charge of and washed it overboard. The captain ordered Sparks to radio our position and that we had sustained considerable damage and could be in danger of sinking. The fear was so great among all the crew that few ate anything. I was almost paralyzed with fear, couldn't sleep as the gigantic storm continued. Finally in total desperation I got on my knees in my cabin and prayed (As I write this, tears come to my eyes.). "Father, forgive me for my sinful life. Please save me and our ship. I promise I will change my way of life and seek to serve you all the days of my life." The storm continued for another day but I was given a warm feeling of peace. What we had encountered was a typhoon out of the South China Sea. Many smaller vessels and many lives had been lost. When at night fall we reached the harbor of Pusen, Korea, the wind was still howling. The captain said to drop the port anchor. The wind and current were so strong the port anchor chain parted, the captain then said to drop the starboard anchor, which finally held. The ship had taken on a lot of water; lost most of the deck cargo, ventilators smashed in, life boat missing, hull cracked and had a large port list. It made such a sad looking sight that the Pusan paper featured a picture of the ship on its front page. Our cargo was unloaded and repairs were made to the ship. We all thought that we'd be returning to the U.S. shortly but then like a bomb shell had dropped we learned that we would be shuttling ammunition from Japan to Korea for possibly as long as a year. At night we could hear U.S. bombers flying over on their way to North Korea and then we'd hear the thundering sounds of the bombs as they hit their targets. By late April poor Cherie was writing to me saying that she was lonely and missed me and when was I coming home?

The usual voyages were hauling goods and munitions from the west coast to Korea and Japan. A voyage round trip of approximately no more than 45 days, no one had any idea we'd be on a voyage lasting almost a year. So being young, lonely and in love finally an idea came to me, for which, I had to ask for the Lord's forgiveness. I wrote to Cherie and said. "If you want me home, send a telegram saying the following: 'Your wife, Cherie, is very ill. Request you return home immediately. Signed, your loving mother.'" I guess I kind of forgot about it, not knowing if she would really do it. One noon time, just finishing my lunch, I felt a hand on my shoulder, it was the purser. He said, "Jim I have some bad news, your wife is very ill and they want you to come home." I was elated but I thought, Jim, if you ever needed to act now is the time! He continued by saying, "The captain wants to see you right away." When I met with the captain he was pacing back and forth in his quarters and looked at me and said, "I suppose you want to go home?" I responded, "Captain, if it was your wife, wouldn't you want to go home?" He agreed to let me go.

ill and request my return Home
immediately — if you do — I
could show it to the skipper
and ask that I be paid off
over here — it would only
take me about 20 hours —
less than a day to fly home.
— Its O.K. with me if you want
to try it — the sooner I'm
Home with you for keeps the
better. — You might word
the telegram as follows:
"Chris seriously ill. request
your return Home immediately."
                    Love Mom.
Tell them at the telegraph office
that it is an emergency message
— that may speed it up a little.
I will acknowledge it by a
message to you — saying I'm

James B. Bernard
S.S. Augustine Daly
N.R. Chamberlin I Co.
230 California Street
San Francisco, Calif.

mrs. James B. Bernard
9010 N.E. Eugene St.
Portland 16, Oregon,
— U.S.A.

Special

But getting out of a country at war is no easy task. I had to go through the Red Cross, the Korean and U.S. Military. It was a real hassle.

I should mention at this point that there was a stranded 3rd mate who had somehow missed his ship. He was penniless and frantic to find a job. He was hired to fill my spot.

All things work together.

Romans 8:28

Finally with all the documentation and my airline tickets, which cost over a thousand dollars, I boarded a Korean Airlines DC-3. The plane was about to take off when a group of armed Koreans ran toward the plane. They had me get out of my seat and rechecked my papers and left. What a scare! We took off flying over the mountains of Korea for Tokyo, Japan.

-Near Disaster Only Miles from Home-

I had corresponded with my wife's brother, Miles Miller, who was in the army stationed in Tokyo, and he'd agreed to meet my plane. We met and went to a military bar for a beer and then back to the airport where I boarded a Canadian Pacific DC-4. You could still see an almost faded PAA [PAN AM] on the fuselage as it had apparently previously been a Pan American plane. As I looked around the plane all the rest of the passengers were Chinese. In fact, the name of the plane was *The Spirit of Hong Kong*. After the plane was airborne they commenced serving dinner, fish heads and bowls of rice. I thought, "Oh great." But when they got to me they brought me a beautiful filet wrapped in bacon, and a large baked potato. What a surprise and treat! The plane was heading for Vancouver, B.C., with a stop in the Aleutians for fuel.

Navigating in those days was done with a bubble sexton using a dome in the ceiling of the plane for taking sights. As we approached the Aleutians, we were in a big snow storm but landed safely. We fueled and resumed our flight to Vancouver. As we crossed the west coast of British Columbia, I saw Douglas firs. What a beautiful sight!

The flight had taken 17 hours and I hadn't slept for days. After landing, I called Cherie reconfirming my time of arrival in Portland. I took off in another DC-3 for Seattle. In Seattle I boarded the newest plane United Airlines flew, a DC-6B.

DC-3 Commercial Transport

Douglas DC-6B

Shortly after getting airborne, emergency lights came on. We had a top U.S. General aboard, possibly Bradshaw; I'm not sure. The plane may have been sabotaged, but at any rate the engines weren't functioning right. The pilot got on the speaker advising us of an emergency landing. As we approached the landing strip I could see ambulances and fire trucks with lights flashing. I thought of all I'd been through to end up crashing less than 150 miles from home. What a sad way to go. However, we made a safe landing and were immediately put on another plane to Portland. When I got off the plane in Portland I got down and kissed the ground and swore that I would never go to sea again. As I got up I could see Cherie waving from our 1948 Chevrolet convertible, the top was down as it was a beautiful sunny day. We had been apart for almost four months. What a joy to be home! Cherie was as beautiful, if not more so, than ever. We drove up to the top of Rocky Butte where we were finally alone. You can imagine the joy we shared being together again.

It was my last voyage as a Merchant Marine. I have sought to keep my promise to serve the Lord. As a layman I have taught, preached, and written articles—often stumbling but always getting back up. Recognizing that I'm human but not letting my humanness keep me from living a heavenly life.

-Epilogue-

In reflecting back over my early wayward years, my seagoing years, and my life up to this very day, I am convinced that I have been surrounded by angels.

For he shall give his angels charge over thee,

to keep thee in all thy days.

PS 91:11

And that in all my days of trials and triumphs I've been blessed and sustained by the presence of a living and loving Lord.

Finally I think I'm safe in saying that anyone who has spent any amount of time at sea cannot help but see and feel the hand of God as the Psalmist expressed.

If I take the wings of the morning,

if I dwell in the remotest part of the sea,

even there your hand will lead me and thy right hand will hold me

PS 139

Cherie and Jim

-About the Author-

At the age of sixteen Jim Bernard crossed the Columbia River Bar as an ordinary seaman. He received his Deck Officer's license at twenty-one and served during the Korean War.

In college, Jim majored in business, psychology, and religion.

After leaving the sea Jim went on to build an insurance and real estate business in Portland, Oregon. After selling the business, Jim and Cherie moved to Astoria, Oregon where Jim assisted in the management of a Ford dealership.

Jim and Cherie charter fished out of Hammond, Oregon. Jim, until recently, served as a captain and guide at Yes Bay, Alaska taking guests fishing for salmon, halibut and other bottom fish.

Jim served as an elder and teaches in the Presbyterian Church.

Jim and Cherie live in Warrenton, Oregon, less than a mile from the Mighty Columbia River. They are proud parents of four children, fourteen grandchildren, and twenty great-grandchildren. They have been happily married for sixty-six years and have always been blessed by a living and loving Lord.

-Attributions-

-Contact-

For comment or additional information, Jim Bernard can be reached at:

JamesBernard711@aol.com

503-680-2366

James Scott Bernard
Author/Publisher
870 NW Fir Avenue
Warrenton, Oregon 97146
USA

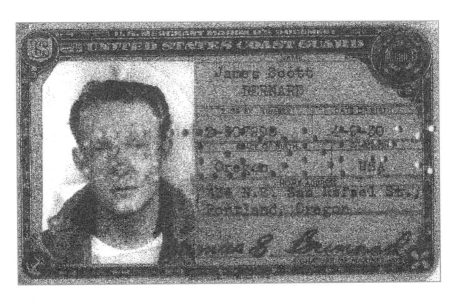

The
Conciliators

The Conciliators

James J. Kaufman

DOWNSTREAM PUBLISHING
NEW YORK · FLORIDA · NORTH CAROLINA

Copyright © 2015 by James J. Kaufman
Cover Copyright © 2015 Downstream Publishing
Cover Design by Erik Hollander Design

Downstream Publishing, LLC
1213 Culbreth Drive
Suite 133
Wilmington, NC 28405
downstreampublishing@gmail.com
ᗡS ®a registered trademark of Downstream Publishing, LLC

Printed in the United States

FIRST EDITION SEPTEMBER 2015

Publisher's Cataloging-In-Publication Data
(Prepared by The Donohue Group, Inc.)

Kaufman, James J.
    The conciliators : a novel / James J. Kaufman. -- First edition.

    pages ; cm. -- (Collectibles series ; book 3)

    Subtitle taken from cover page.
    Issued also as an ebook, an audio CD, and a downloadable audio file.
    ISBN: 978-0-9897571-3-3 (hardcover)

    1. Chief executive officers--Fiction. 2. Conspiracy--Fiction. 3. Women journalists--Fiction. 4. Reputation--Fiction. 5. Helping behavior--Fiction. I. Title.

PS3611.A846 C663 2015
813/.6   2015908678

10 9 8 7 6 5 4 3 2 1

For Patty

In memory of my dear friend, Ann Kalkines

The only person you are destined to become,
is the person you decide to be.

—Ralph Waldo Emerson

∞

Success is not final, failure is not fatal:
it is the courage to continue that counts.

—Winston Churchill

ACKNOWLEDGMENTS

First is Patty, for her love, graciousness, keen eye and ear, and for always believing in what I can do.

Thanks to my agent, Lissy Peace, an amazing talent and wonderful person who makes all things possible.

To my son, Jeffrey: Thank you for your always helpful and insightful input and suggestions.

To my dear friends George Kalkines, Paul Miller, and Dr. Robert Brownlow, who helped make this book possible with their generosity and support.

With deep gratitude, I express my appreciation to the following for their contributions:

• To Jeanne Devlin, for her publishing industry experience, energy, and dedication.

• To Emma Mahn, for her endless patience, exceptional research skills, and contribution to this book.

• To my friend Patricia Roseman, an outstanding person, for sharing her photographic talents in all my works.

• To Erik Hollander and Erik Hollander Design, with deep appreciation for the cover design and artistic expertise.

• To my first reader group, to whom I am indebted for their countless hours of reading manuscripts and their valuable input: Andy Miller, Diana Holdridge, Debra Datesman-Tripp, Brooks Preik, Sarah and Chuck Lee, and Doug Love.

• To Ryan LaSalle, for his administrative assistance and computer skills.

I also thank the members of associations and book clubs with whom I have conversed in person and via Skype throughout the country and those who have taken the time to write to me about *The Collectibles* and *The Concealers*. Your comments have been generously given, instructive, and of immense value.

The Conciliators

PROLOGUE

PRESTON WILSON WOKE EARLY, as was his routine on a weekday. He pulled on a robe, slid his feet into his slippers, and went to get the morning papers. As always, *The New York Times* and *The Wall Street Journal* were waiting for him on the table outside his front door, placed there in the wee hours of the morning by Trump Tower's doorman.

He padded back to the kitchen table where his breakfast waited. In between buttering his toast and drinking his coffee, he proceeded to catch up on the last twenty-four-hour news cycle.

Preston read the front section of the *Times* first, and then did the same with the *Journal*. He was about to put the papers away, when a headline at the bottom of page six of the *Journal*'s financial section caught his eye:

BNA INDICTED IN FRAUDULENT
SCHEME—TWO NY VPs, DEVELOPER,
CFO OF NY AUTO DEALER ALSO NAMED

Preston slowly placed the last bite of toast on his plate. He adjusted his reading glasses and skimmed the article quickly. It seemed to focus on allegations of collusion between Bank North America's real estate department and a developer of residential lots in Long Island. His name did not appear anywhere, though his company's name did, thanks to his old prep school friend and Chief Financial

1

Officer Austin Disley. Preston noted that the story had been picked up from the *Twin Forks Press* via the Associated Press. It carried no byline. If it had, the name would have been one very dear to him. He would never forget his last conversation with his daughter.

> *I've written the story. The question is whether to turn it in. Your CFO is in trouble either way. So are the others. The criminal investigation is ongoing, and my story will add to it. Wilson Holdings will feel the impact. It could bring down your empire. If I don't turn it in, I won't be telling the whole truth. That would be contrary to everything I believe is important about being a journalist. What would you advise me to do?*

At the time, Preston had felt trapped in a box with no way out. His mind had raced back to his childhood when, as a fifteen-year-old boy, he slipped off an Adirondack Mountain trail and fell, subsequently becoming trapped in a crevice.

Preston felt like he was back in a box again. He could not imagine Austin committing a crime, much less one that would threaten his company. He had done nothing wrong, but the chance of him and his business emerging unscathed seemed unlikely nonetheless. Katherine was his daughter. Why could she not pass on this story? Preston understood her commitment, or at least he thought he did. Why should blood not trump principle? When he told Katherine that, she replied, "I don't see why there isn't room for both."

Well, she had made her decision, and now he would have to live with it. He had come too far in earning the love and respect of his newfound daughter to slip backward.

Preston slapped the paper shut. He knew his wife and son would be awake soon, and he knew he was too upset for his wife not to notice. Best to be gone when they woke up.

He tucked the newspaper into his briefcase and headed to the bathroom to shave and shower. If he had had any doubt that the news had rattled him, the three small Band-Aids on his face after his shave said otherwise. This could be the end of all he had worked so hard to build. Marcia was going to be furious.

Preston left a note for his wife on the dresser blaming his early departure on a problem at work. At least that wasn't a lie.

He grabbed his overcoat, hat, and scarf, and headed out to face the dragons. Every neighbor on his floor undoubtedly heard the door slam behind him.

CHAPTER 1

AFTER TWO MONTHS of tension, Preston Wilson could feel an arc of anguish hovering over him. He did not have to wait long for the question he knew would come from his wife.

"How long are we going to have to live like this?" she asked.

"Take it easy, Marcia. I know you're upset. I'm on it. So is Alex. We're going to control the damage. We'll get through this."

"Wake up, Preston. Nothing is getting better."

Preston knew she was right. Things were bad, but at least they could not get worse. Then came the knock at the door.

"I'll get it," Marcia said, putting down her salad fork and starting from the table.

"No, let me," Preston said, welcoming the diversion. But when he looked through the peephole and saw two men he did not recognize in overcoats and hats, he knew he had been wrong.

"Who is it?" he called, concerned.

"FBI," came the loud reply.

The men flashed photo IDs with the FBI logo. Preston slowly opened the door, unprepared for both men to push by him into the foyer. For an awkward moment, the men stood facing Preston, saying nothing.

It was Preston who broke the silence. "It's highly unusual to have someone, especially the FBI, knock on our door at night without notice. We just sat down to dinner."

The taller of the two men spoke first, but he did not apologize. "Special Agent John Bonetti," he said. His tone carried an air of authority as he glanced at the other man. "This is Special Agent Thomas Sullivan. We're here about Austin Disley."

"What about Austin?" Marcia had joined her husband and the look on her face said it all.

Agent Bonetti looked hard at Preston. "Disley's the CFO of your company?" It was more of a statement than a question.

"Yes, he is, but he's on administrative leave until a certain matter blows over."

"How about Teddy Thompson and Stacy Bowers?" asked the other agent. "Do you know them?"

"Thompson works for Bank North America," Preston said. After thinking about it for a moment, "I don't know Bowers."

Preston could tell by the ever-tightening grip on his arm that his wife was becoming agitated. He moved to end the conversation quickly. "Why are you asking me these questions? And why tonight, in our home?" The sharp delivery was not like Preston, even under such circumstances, and he silently chastised himself for it.

Sullivan looked Preston up and down, squinting all the while, making it clear he was the agent in charge. "We're part of a bank fraud investigation team, and it would be helpful for you to cooperate with us. You say you don't know Bowers, but you do know Disley and Thompson. We'd like to discuss both of them with you."

Before Preston could object, both men stepped into the living room, each removing a notepad and pen from his suit coat.

As he and his wife took a seat on the couch, Preston's mind started to spin. The agents remained standing, and Preston was not about to invite them to sit. He was unsure whether he should even be talking to them without his lawyer present. As if reading his mind, Agent Sullivan said, "If you don't want to talk with us without your attorney, that's your prerogative, but it would go a lot better for you if you cooperated with us now. Until recently, you were only a person of interest." He cleared his throat. "What we hear is you're to be named an unindicted co-conspirator."

Marcia jumped up and looked at Preston. "What? Did you know anything about this?"

Preston gave a tiny shake of his head and held his finger over his lips. Marcia seemed stunned, then nodded. She stepped toward the agents and asked to take a closer look at their identification. Each handed his leather-encased badge and identity card to her. She studied them one by one, and then said she would like to speak with her husband privately.

Preston followed Marcia into the office they shared in their Trump Tower apartment. Even after closing the door behind them, when she spoke, it was in a whisper. "Unindicted co-conspirator? What does that mean?"

"I don't know. We need a lawyer."

The strain in Marcia's eyes broke Preston's heart, so he quickly explained what he knew about Disley's situation, covering details he had kept from his wife so she would not be unduly worried about the latest blow his business had taken.

"I'm not overly concerned about Disley. I don't know anything about Thompson and Bowers, but we're going to be okay."

His words sounded shallow even to himself, and he did not believe them. "Marcia, we can talk about this later. We need to get back in there."

Marcia nodded, and Preston followed her into the living room. Standing before the agents, Preston hesitated. When he finally spoke his voice was soft and even, but with an undercurrent of authority. "I'll be happy to cooperate, but this is neither the time nor the place. I would like legal counsel whenever we're together in the future. So, if you gentlemen will excuse us, my wife and I would like to get back to our dinner."

The agents nodded, and Preston and Marcia walked the men out. As Preston closed the door behind them, he realized he still had to deal with Marcia. Before he could say a word, however, his wife looked at him and said, "I don't know about you, but I've lost my appetite. I'm going to bed. Get a lawyer."

CHAPTER 2

PRESTON WOKE AT FIVE in the morning drenched in sweat. He took a shower, shaved, and dressed before he realized he had no place to go. He needed to talk to a criminal lawyer immediately, but he didn't know one. Deep down what he wished was that he could still call Joe Hart, but with his friend long dead now, the best he could do was ask himself, "What would Joe do?"

He slipped out of the apartment, marched past the doorman without their usual exchange, and walked to the Union League Club for an early breakfast. It was not even seven o'clock when he headed downstairs to the phone booths to call Andy Brookfield, his longtime corporate attorney. Preston knew Andy would still be at home, but under the circumstances he found it hard to care.

• • •

Preston entered the iconic Met Life building above Grand Central Station. Passersby could not know that behind his confident blue eyes and powerful stride was a desperate forty-seven-year-old man. Once inside, he looked for the offices of Whitmire & Strowde, the law firm that Andy had recommended. Specifically, he was going to meet Barry Snyder, one of New York City's top defense attorneys specializing in white-collar crime. Although Snyder's services came with a hefty price tag, Preston had no choice but to bear the

one-thousand-dollar-per-hour fee—an obligation he would gladly
pay if Snyder was as good as his reputation. Preston checked the
directory, picked up his visitor's badge from the security desk, and
took the express elevator to the forty-sixth floor. The doors opened
into the firm.

"Hi, I'm Preston Wilson," he said to the receptionist.

The woman smiled briefly, looked down at her list, and asked
him to take a seat. "Someone will be with you shortly, Mr. Wilson,"
she said in an elegant British accent.

Preston took a seat. He was so nervous and anxious that the
Mirós on the wall could have been calendars and the designer
couches, old benches in a park. From the coffee table he picked
up a thick, leather-bound book embossed with the firm's name on
the cover. He flipped through the pages without seeing a thing. His
thoughts drifted to his old friend, Austin Disley. Could Austin actually have done it?

"Sir, if you would please follow me." The request interrupted
his self-generated fog. The new voice belonged to a smartly dressed
woman in her thirties who could have easily been featured in an ad
for a high-end international airline. He followed her down the hall
to a brightly lit, well-appointed corner office. Very impressive, and
all paid for by people in trouble. People like me, he thought.

The assistant guided him to a high-backed, hand-tooled Italian
leather chair opposite a large mahogany desk. The leather desk pad
and other matching accessories included a round pen and a pencil
holder, entirely filled with finely sharpened number two pencils, all
pointing up.

"Mr. Snyder will be with you shortly." With that she stepped
away, gently closing the door behind her and leaving Preston alone
with his fears.

Preston had no more taken his seat than a man in his late forties
entered the office. Snyder's precise appearance, while unassuming
at first pass, was a reflection of his comfort level with detail. He
peered at Preston through his black, wire-rimmed glasses, stuck out
his hand, and smiled broadly.

"Hello, I'm Barry Snyder." Taking a seat, he asked, "Can I get you anything? Coffee? Donuts? Whiskey?"

Preston laughed. "Nothing at the moment, but I'd like to take a rain check on the whiskey." Snyder smiled.

Preston had not expected to laugh during this meeting, and for a brief moment he felt better. Snyder sat down behind his desk, pulled some papers from a tall stack of documents, consulted a folder, and finally addressed Preston. "Is this your first experience with a criminal lawyer—apart from speeding tickets, that is?"

Preston laughed again. "How do you know about the speeding tickets?"

"You're a car dealer, right? Don't you guys generally have lead feet?"

Preston began to relax. This might not be so bad after all.

"I know we both have a lot of questions," Snyder said, again smiling broadly, "so why don't we start with what brings you here, and what I might be able to do to help?"

Preston nodded. "I think I need a lawyer. Two nights ago, a couple of FBI agents showed up at my apartment unannounced at dinnertime. They were asking questions about Austin Disley, my chief financial officer; another banker I barely know; and another person whose name I had never heard before. In the process of scaring the hell out of my wife and me, they indicated that I'm going to be named an unindicted co-conspirator soon, and strongly implied that I'd better cooperate with their investigation. Of course I said I would, even though I had no clue about what they hoped to get out of me."

Snyder leaned forward. "I'm not surprised they came to your home or that it was at night. That's what these guys do. They want to intimidate you."

Preston sat back in surprise. "Well, they succeeded."

Snyder gave Preston a sympathetic nod. "In preparation for our meeting, I had one of my associates do some research." He held up a manila folder. "While gathering information about you, I read what I could put my hands on regarding Austin Disley's arrest, along with the arrest of some officers at Bank North America and a Russian real estate developer. We have a copy of the U.S. Attorney's complaint, which I'll go over with you later."

Preston nodded, impressed—and thankful—that the lawyer had done his homework.

"I need to know everything you know about Austin Disley," Snyder said, "and I mean everything—no matter how long it takes."

The attorney picked a pencil from the leather canister on his desk and pulled a yellow legal pad from a desk drawer. Preston started at the beginning, with his early days rooming with Disley at prep school and how they had become best friends. He took Snyder all the way through their college years. More than once he asked Snyder if he wanted to hear all of the minutiae; the attorney kept repeating that he wanted everything.

After a good hour, Preston said, "We went our separate ways after college, but there came a time not too long ago when Austin asked me for a job, and I brought him in under the guise of helping Casey Fitzgerald, my longtime CFO with—"

"Under the guise?" asked Snyder, interrupting for one of the few times in Preston's monologue. "Did Fitzgerald need help, or was that just an excuse to bring in your friend?"

"In retrospect," Preston said, "it was probably the latter. Casey was a terrific CFO. He came to work with me in '93. He's a smart guy, a Wharton grad, and learned the car business quickly. I made him CFO within a year, and the business ran well until I let things get out of hand a couple of years ago, but that was all in the past, and everything had been great until a few months ago."

Snyder, now on his fifth pencil, raised his eyebrows. "What year did Disley come on board?"

"In 2011—and once he did, one of the biggest mistakes I ever made was not supervising his activities closely enough. Looking back, I see that I was protecting him even though Casey warned me that I'd regret not reining him in."

"Give me an example of what Casey warned you about," Snyder said, and Preston noticed there was a slight edge to his voice.

Preston took a deep breath. "We owed a lot of money to banks, but we had restructured that, and Casey was firm about our keeping up with payments. He saw Austin as sloppy, manipulative, and untrustworthy. Austin was smart, and I thought he'd grow into the job. BNA, in addition to handling our financing for the cars—what we call a floor plan—was also our landlord in Manhattan. BNA wanted information about our business to support the extension of our lease.

"Austin gave them uncorrected operating statements. Casey straightened it out with the bank by submitting the correct information, but he was furious with Austin. It wasn't the first time Austin had been careless. Casey had warned me about Austin's mistakes, so he wasn't too happy with me either." Preston looked away in disgust with what he had to say next. "Right afterwards, Casey told me he was leaving the company."

"How did you feel about that?"

"I was shocked. He's still a shareholder in Wilson Holdings. For that reason, and many others, I'm hoping I can get him back someday."

Snyder checked his notes. He reviewed the allegations against Disley, explaining to Preston that his friend's conduct as an employee could very well put Preston at risk.

"Did you know anything," Snyder said, "and I mean anything, about Disley's activities? If you were at all aware of what he was doing, and took no steps to stop it, you could, indeed, be criminally charged."

Preston looked directly into Snyder's eyes. "I said it before: I knew nothing about what he was doing. What I did know was that he wasn't paying enough attention to certain financial details, and I failed to supervise him adequately; however, I never conspired with him to do anything illegal." Preston inched forward in his chair. "Mr. Snyder, despite my mistakes and poor judgment, I assure you I am not a criminal."

Snyder suggested a short break, after which they resumed discussing Casey, Disley, and Preston's business practices, as well as his legal exposure to the charges of wrongdoing. Suddenly, Snyder changed the subject.

"Let's talk a moment about your wife."

Preston was hesitant to bring Marcia into the conversation, yet he knew he had to answer his lawyer's questions.

"I don't see her listed as an officer," Snyder said. "She's shown as a shareholder in Wilson Holdings. What part, if any, does she play in the business?"

"None, really. She's busy taking care of our two-year-old son, and she's never been involved in the stores." Preston's voice was firmer than at any other time during their intense and lengthy meeting.

Snyder nodded. "Okay, that's it for now." He closed the folder, now many pages of notes thicker. "I advise you not to talk about this case to anyone, except your wife, unless I'm with you and specifically authorize it. That's the only way you retain attorney-client privilege."

"Of course," Preston said, a wave of relief washing over him at the prospect of being able to keep everything about Wilson Holdings and the mess with his friend as private as possible. Disley's arrest had already started the tristate rumor mills churning. It had not escaped him that the first stories in the press had focused on the bank, but the New York media had not been able to resist bringing an icon in the world of luxury cars into the mix. He had hoped the headlines would grow smaller and the stories move to the back of the newspapers, but so far they had just kept coming, with big suggestive headlines.

Preston was already standing when Snyder asked, "Before you go, do you have any other questions?"

Preston sat down. "Yes, one. They say I am going to be named an 'unindicted co-conspirator.' What the hell does that mean?"

Snyder walked over to a wall of books behind him and grabbed one of the tomes and flipped it open. After a few seconds he began to read: "Any person who allegedly agreed with others to violate the law, but who is not being charged with an offense, and who, if not indicted, will not be tried or sentenced for his criminal conduct."

Snyder slammed the book shut. "That's the short answer, and it applies to you based on what I know right now."

"I don't get it. I didn't break the law, and I didn't help anyone else break the law. I haven't been indicted. So what have I done that constitutes criminal conduct? Why have they listed me as an unindicted co-conspirator?"

"I'll tell you why." Snyder settled back in his own chair and sighed. "They want leverage. By putting you on that list, they put you in a position that gives you no choice but to cooperate. Maybe it forces you to become a witness for the prosecution, maybe it discourages you from being a witness for the defense, or maybe it convinces you to just give up and plead guilty. That's why they do it, and you'd be surprised how often it works."

"But I'm not guilty of anything. It's not fair and it's not right."

"It gets worse. In my experience, they could decide to indict you and even under the best scenario, that label will hang over your head until you die."

Preston was speechless. He struggled to maintain his composure. The low-grade anxiety he had come in with had turned to fear. "I hate this. Business problems are one thing, but being treated like a criminal is something else entirely. I've made some mistakes, but I've made them honestly and I've maintained my reputation through it all. Where's the justice? How do we make this go away?"

"We can hope your unindicted co-conspirator classification will someday be dismissed, but that's up to the U.S. Attorney's office. We'll just have to see how this plays out. It's a one-step-at-a-time process. I'm sorry, but no one can predict the outcome."

For the first time, Snyder's face was filled with compassion. Preston knew his lawyer was smart and experienced. Though he had only known the man for less than a day, he felt Snyder was committed to his case.

Preston rose to shake Snyder's hand. "I think I've hired the right guy. Thank you."

The lawyer nodded, handed Preston his card, and escorted him down the hallway and to the elevator. The secretary and receptionist had long since gone home for the day. Preston stepped inside and as the elevator door closed, he heard Snyder say, "I'll be with you every step of the way."

The elevator took him to the ground floor. As he stepped outside, a bracing January wind slapped Preston in the face. It felt like a wake-up call. He was embarking on the fight of his life. Any other time he would have sought out a stiff drink, but there was too much at stake.

Instead, he would go home, face Marcia, and play with his son. Who knew how many more times that would be an option for him?

CHAPTER 3

MARCIA MET PRESTON AT the door with a smile and a kiss on the cheek. She stifled a laugh at the look of shock on his face at what had to have seemed an unexpectedly warm welcome given the trauma of recent events. She did not resist when he pulled her close and kissed her on the lips. As he slowly released her, she saw the devastating smile that had so captivated her the first time they had met all those years ago at Café du Monde in New Orleans. She had been sitting alone when the tall, good-looking guy walked up and introduced himself.

"I hope you don't think I'm out of line," he had said, "but I was about to order a cup of coffee and wondered if you might like to join me. Or me join you?"

She remembered laughing at the word play.

Later, when he had confided that upon seeing her he had lost any desire to look at anyone else—ever again—she had recognized those words as an obvious line, but she had also liked him even more. When he also confessed how charming he found the way she gently daubed her chin after biting into a sugary beignet that had too much blueberry filling, she was a goner. Her intuition had told her Preston would be a challenge, one she had reasoned that would be worth the effort.

It had not hurt that she found him attractive, with his basketball player's physique, dark hair, and penetrating blue eyes. Truth be

17

told, it was not his looks but his quick smile and intelligence she had liked the most.

That day she had listened as he explained he was in town for the National Automobile Dealers Association conference.

"When I first saw you I suspected you were from out of town," she had told him.

"I'm from New York. Now you know I'm a New Yawker," Preston had said, trying on a Bronx accent, "tell me where you're from."

"First of all, Preston, your accent's hardly that of a typical New Yorker. I should know. I live in Manhattan, though I'm originally from Dayton, Ohio."

She had gone on to explain that she was on spring break and visiting the Florentine Art Exhibit at Tulane University.

"Are you an art major?" Preston had asked.

"I'm studying psychology, finishing up my graduate work at Columbia, but I love art."

They had both ordered more coffee, and what he apparently had intended as a half-hour interlude with a young woman ended up a two-hour first date. Nearly a year later, they were married.

Marcia eventually found a teaching position at Columbia University on the Upper West Side of New York City where she made time to take art history courses. She also worked with state educational programs for the mentally challenged.

Always supportive of Preston's aspiration to be a mega-dealer in the U.S. automobile industry, she had long ago discovered his ardor for his dream was unfortunately not matched by his business acumen. He tended to dream big and to chase that dream too quickly. Meanwhile, his attention to detail had often been cursory, at best, and his focus on the bottom line almost nonexistent. The final straw for Marcia had been when the banks insisted that she, as his wife, be named right along with her husband on each of his personal loan guarantees.

Her growing loss of confidence in his ability to care for her, and then the birth of P.J., had created an ever-widening chasm between them. She still loved Preston and prayed things would turn around as they always somehow had in the past. Still, ever since Joe Hart had passed away, it had become increasingly clear Preston was on his own, floundering with no savior on the horizon ready to ride in on a white horse and save the day again.

During the past several months, Marcia had slowly realized her husband was no longer confiding in her. She suspected he did not want to alarm her with the harsh reality of the situation. What he did not know was that instead of his silence restoring her trust in him, it had eroded it. For Marcia, being sheltered by silence was worse than knowing the truth, however unpleasant that truth might be.

Regardless, when Marcia greeted her husband that evening, she was genuinely happy to see him but also determined to get to the truth of their current situation before the night was over. Marcia knew better than to confront Preston; instead, she encouraged him to join her for dinner and to play with P.J. before they gave their son a bath together and put him to bed.

Afterwards, Marcia sat beside her husband on the sofa in the living room, snuggling against him like old times. She kissed him and asked, "Honey, how was your day?"

He groaned. "What a day it was."

"What do you mean?" she asked, hoping that she had eased him into a frame of mind to tell her the true state of his—and ultimately their—affairs, which had been her plan all along.

Preston sat up, moved his arm from around her, and picked up the glass of wine she had poured for him earlier. "I had a meeting with Barry Snyder, the new lawyer I told you about. I like the guy. He obviously knows what he's doing. It was exhausting answering all of his questions—I was with him for almost five hours. Now he has a complete idea of what's happened with Disley, based on what I know, which I wish was a whole lot more."

"Is there anything I can do to help?" Marcia asked. "I hope you know we're in this together, and I don't mean just financially."

Her husband smiled and took her hands in his. "You can't begin to know how much I appreciate your saying that, but I'm still trying to make sense of it all."

Marcia put down her wine. "Who would have thought they could intrude on a family without any notice, here in the land of the free, and *demand* answers to their questions? It felt so wrong for them to show up here like that."

Her speech had become uneven. She had consumed more wine than she was comfortable with, and she was mad at herself for her lack of discipline. Preston threw up his hands in what appeared to be exasperation. "If I had refused to let them in, it would have looked as if I had something to hide," he said.

"Why didn't you get rid of Austin when Casey warned you about him in the first place? If you had, we wouldn't be in this mess. I told you from the start I never trusted him."

"I don't know—and neither do you—that he's guilty. I put him on administrative leave. He deserves to be treated fairly."

Marcia arched her eyebrows. "That's ridiculous. The man's been arrested. Indicted."

"There's such a thing in this country as presumed innocence," Preston shot back.

"My husband, the lawyer." Marcia dismissed him with the wave of her hand before pouring herself another glass of wine.

Finally, Preston heaved a sigh and spoke. "Marcia, there's something I have never told you about Austin. It happened years before I met you, and I've always been too embarrassed to say anything about it because it involves my family, but maybe knowing it would make it easier for you to put your guns back in their holsters."

"I'm listening," Marcia said.

"When Austin and I were at Hotchkiss, my father got into a real mess. He made a down payment on a business deal and couldn't come through with the balance. My mother had already divorced him and wasn't willing to bail him out again."

"And?"

"I knew he had had financial problems, but I'd never seen my father so distraught. Austin figured out something was bothering me and asked me what was wrong. When I told him, he told me he'd talk to his dad to see if he could help. As it turned out, his father knew the brokerage company and was able to assume the entire investment, and my dad was let off the hook. I told Austin I would never forget his help. I haven't."

"So that's why you've been protecting him all this time?" Marcia said quietly.

"Yes. Deep down, I knew he was weak, but he was my friend. He still is. I know that's difficult for you to understand."

"You're right. It is impossible. Especially given the way he's treated you, and the way he has put your company and our family at risk."

"You're not going to make me feel guilty about this, Marcia. One of the things I learned from Joe was the importance of concentrating not on the dark spots but on the intrinsic worth in others."

"I don't think Joe meant that to include criminal behavior, Preston. I have just one more question: Is there anything you haven't told me that the FBI might be trying to pin on you?"

Preston did not answer.

Maybe he honestly had no idea. Exhausted, and with way too much wine in her system, Marcia left Preston on the couch and headed to bed. A short while later, the rustling of the sheets told her Preston had joined her, but neither of them said a word. Too much had been said already.

Marcia did not sleep that night. Once she heard Preston's soft, rhythmic snoring, she went to the kitchen in search of a ginger ale, hoping it would settle her stomach. Her queasiness was not from drinking too much wine but from the difficult choices she would now have to make. Her concerns ran much deeper than any troubles with the business, which, from an operational standpoint, she cared nothing about. No, she was worried about their life, the life she and Preston had made together with P.J. Suddenly, it all seemed at risk.

Marcia thought about how not so very long ago she had had to steal P.J. away to have his hearing loss addressed. Her husband had hoped that his son's hearing would develop as his pediatrician had predicted, but she had known she had to act. Beyond that, he had been keeping business problems from her that could not only ruin the two of them financially but could also possibly land one or both of them in jail.

Preston's withdrawal in the face of a problem was not new—nor was the helpless, disconnected feeling it produced in her. What was going on now, however, was fast becoming more than she could deal with. Preston had put her in an untenable position, and at that moment she was prepared to walk out the door with her son and never return.

CHAPTER 4

PROFESSIONALLY, KATHERINE Kelly's life was on a fast track. With a master's degree in journalism in hand at age twenty-three, she had landed a job as a beat reporter at *Twin Forks Press*, an independent newspaper in affluent Southampton, New York.

Katherine's intelligence and enthusiasm had quickly won the trust of those she interviewed, and they were also the qualities that endeared her to Sol Kaplowitz, her Pulitzer-Prize-winning editor. She often heard him marveling at how, in just a matter of months, she had become an investigative journalist to respect and an asset to the paper.

She prayed the sense of accomplishment such praise engendered would last forever. She was old enough to know that such peaks were only temporary, be they personal or professional. Life was uncertain. It had its ups and downs. Sometimes she could be up professionally and down personally.

Yet who would have guessed her hard-nosed reporting would plunge her into a story that involved her newfound father, Preston Wilson. She could not help but fear their relationship might come to an end as fast as it had started. Her investigative work had already led to the indictment of two bank officers, one of whom was close to her father's business. So far, Preston had not been pulled into the fray, but he could be. Would he tell her if the feds called? He had not spoken to her much since hearing of her decision to file the story.

Beyond that, Katherine faced a new quandary: Austin Disley. As an assistant to the CFO at Preston's Manhattan dealership and later the CFO of both the Manhattan store and Wilson Holdings, he had been named in the New York City papers as a possible participant in a new bank fraud case—one with international ramifications. Katherine knew she was certainly the best qualified reporter at her paper to investigate the developing story, and she believed it was her responsibility to do so, no matter where or how the ax fell—even if, once again, it fell on her father. She also knew she faced at least the appearance of a conflict of interest, and that was why she was headed to a meeting with Sol.

Unexpectedly, Sol's decision was immediate but comforting, given that it was consistent with her own concerns. "I'm sorry, kiddo, but you're way too close to this story. I've also noticed you've been on edge lately, and I think you need a break. I'm going to have to give it to someone else, if we even work it. You need to take things a little slower or you'll burn out—I've seen it before in reporters older and more seasoned than you."

Katherine did not protest—she knew her boss was doing the right thing. She was, indeed, both too close to the story and burning the candle at both ends. She had been increasingly short with her colleagues and for no good reason. She had even put on a few pounds, another result of living on junk food and rarely leaving her cubicle.

She spent the next week working a few mundane stories in the Hamptons to please her supervising editor, Chuck Bumgardner, who relished the paper's new crackerjack reporter having been brought down a peg, even if only for a while.

His happiness would be short-lived. Finishing up a local run-of-the-mill feature, Katherine answered her phone only to find Alice Hawkins, a charming, elderly lady from Braydon, South Carolina, on the line. She had met Alice the previous year while visiting the area to learn more about her father's mentor and benefactor, Joe Hart. Alice had been Joe's legal secretary, and the two women had struck up an immediate friendship.

"Do you remember the problems I told you about with the Braydon Bank?"

"Of course I do," Katherine said, reaching for her laptop.

"Well, dear, I'm still having problems with those folks. I went to see an attorney I know down here to explore a civil suit against the officers of the bank. He thinks I have a case."

"That's interesting," Katherine said.

"A young reporter from *The Braydon Constitution*—that's our weekly newspaper—called me today to request an interview about it, but I've always been skeptical about talking to reporters."

Katherine laughed quietly.

"Oh no, not you, dear. Never you," Alice said. "In all my years with Joe, I learned to be careful when talking to reporters. I don't feel that way about you. I just don't like publicity of any kind, and I want to avoid it if I can. I'm calling to ask if you think I should talk to him."

"Have you hired the attorney? If you did, has the lawyer agreed that it's okay for you to talk to the reporter?"

"Yes, to both. Like I said, he thinks I've got a case. He even called it a good one."

Katherine thought for a moment. "Have you asked him about the hazards of pretrial publicity?"

"I did, and he said pretrial publicity could be helpful or it could be harmful, depending on how it's dealt with. He believes in this instance it will help my position, as it will put pressure on the bank. I wanted to know what you think I should or shouldn't say to the reporter. He's a nice young boy. Real cute, too."

"No time to be playing matchmaker, Alice," Katherine said.

Alice chuckled at that, but Katherine remained serious.

"From the perspective of your community newspaper," she said, "it is certainly a local story of interest, but because it involves bank fraud, it also has broader implications. If your lawyer says publicizing your plight might help your case, I would take his advice. I learned from the bank cases I've worked on that financial institutions do not want to go to court and will do just about anything to avoid it, and the bad press that comes with it. What's your opinion of the reporter who called you, other than he's possibly the man of my dreams?"

"Oh, you're so funny, Katherine. Well, he is young, but aren't they all these days," she said, her voice sounding nostalgic. "Goodness knows you've proven a young reporter can get a story."

"That's right, Alice. It's the quality of the reporting, not the person's age that matters."

"I couldn't agree more. It's just in his case, I don't know how good he is at what he does. He seems in over his head."

"I have a suggestion," Katherine said, still typing on her laptop. "Why don't you tell him you have a friend who's a reporter in New York who has some experience with bank fraud stories? Ask him if he would like to discuss what he's working on off the record, just to get another reporter's opinion."

"Oh I'm so glad you said that. I've already told him about you, and he is fine with your looking at what he's working on. He knew of your reporting on the other bank fraud case, and he acted kind of excited by my offer of your services. I told him how good-looking you are, too."

Katherine grinned. "You're a crafty one, aren't you?"

"I don't know about that," said Alice. "I just know I'd feel better knowing you were looking after me with these reporter types nosing around. Joe was always good at that."

Katherine hurriedly typed some more notes.

"I might have jumped the gun a bit on this, Alice," Katherine said. "Before I can get too involved, I'm going to have to sell my editor on letting me work on the story—our newspaper tends to focus more on local or regional news. He'll probably have a hundred reasons why I shouldn't, but I remember thinking some common denominators existed between both of these bank fraud cases. When the banking patterns are connected, it could give readers a fuller picture of the fraud that has been committed. It's not public knowledge, but I've testified before the U.S. House banking subcommittee on this very subject."

"How impressive. When you have your editor's permission—and I'm sure you'll find a way to get it—tell me what to do next, and I'll take it from there."

Katherine's mind was already abuzz with possibilities. She had no more put down the phone than she was consumed with trying to figure out how best to go about helping her friend—and if that meant tracking down leads on a new story, well, so be it.

CHAPTER 5

O N A GRAY, SNOWY DAY in January, four Russian thieves-in-law gathered in Viktor Goremykin's living room in his ostentatious cottage in the countryside outside Moscow. The members of this quartet were not relatives by marriage, but rather professional criminals with elite positions within Russia's organized crime network.

Goremykin's face, with its lines and scars, resembled a topographical map. He looked considerably older than his sixty years. His proud criminal career had started in Georgia where he earned his first jail term at the age of fifteen for fighting with police. He had acquired thief-in-law status while serving a two-year jail term for currency speculation, cementing his standing among the Soviet criminal elite and post-Soviet underworld.

From there, he had combined cunning and inherent leadership qualities to control various organized criminal groups dealing in illegal gambling, arms, drug trafficking, and the theft of rare and valuable natural resources. In the last decade, he had turned his attention to the international crime opportunities made possible by the Internet. The Russian government, of course, was actively engaged in milking such opportunities itself, using the tools of the digital age to maximize control of the economy, the currency, and the people. The KGB enforced the government's goals while lining the pockets of those in control. The new Federal Security Service of the

Russian Federation, or the FSB, along with the Foreign Intelligence Service, or SVR, and Putin made sure it all worked.

As thick as that blanket of control was, neither the government nor the KGB could bridge the dark gaps in Soviet life that lingered. Goremykin was both an engineer and an artist in navigating such gaps. He and other thieves-in-law had honed their skills while adhering to the sacred code of complete submission to the commandments of criminal life. That meant staying out of political activities, avoiding legitimate employment, and embracing the criminal ideology. Begin with discipline. Never show emotion.

For Goremykin, that also meant pushing back the memories of his father's iron fist, the one that had taught him to obey, to respect, and to question silently. It meant understanding there was no place for love, only for efficiency and energy to move toward the goal. The early goals were simple: survival through power. Prison continued his education; it was where he sharpened his skills and forged his mental and physical being. He learned the art of exploitation, how to strike with lightning speed when presented with the weaknesses of others.

His attention had shifted beyond cyberspace to digital terrorism, cybercrime, and the men who flourished doing both. He was about to meet and assess the men his agents had recommended. They knew a mistake in judgment would be irreparable. He would show them respect and see if they were worthy of it. If they were not, the four men would be reassigned. Permanently. He did not expect that to happen, though. These men were trusted criminals sworn to the code.

Goremykin gave a small nod to Vlad, a muscular man who owed Goremykin his life and was charged with the responsibility of protecting him. The bodyguard stepped outside to get the four men.

Seated near the red marble Rosso Levanto fireplace in his elaborate study, Goremykin knew he had a few minutes before Vlad and his guests returned. To his left, a collection of exquisitely carved and finely painted Russian lacquer boxes were neatly placed on an antique table. To his right, against the wall sat a rolltop desk from

Saint Petersburg that had once been used by Russian czars. He never looked at any of them. Such spoils were irrelevant to Goremykin; they were simply trophies for others to see, like everything and everyone else in his life.

The door opened, and Vlad directed the men to four large leather chairs in front of Goremykin near the fireplace. The first man Vlad introduced was in his thirties, with a full head of black, curly hair and wire-rimmed glasses. He had a clean-shaven face and small, intelligent eyes. The man to his right was about the same age but considerably taller and thinner. They had both graduated from Saint Petersburg State University of Economics and Finance.

The other two men looked as if they had been sculpted from stone. Both had served time in prison, and their sentences were proudly evident by the tattoos on their fingers. Despite their rough looks, these "black hats" also had extensive cyber experience and extraordinary programming and software skills. They were more visible to the FSB, and more importantly, to the SVR. Being on their radar screens would make traveling to America problematic.

Each of the men knew—as did any sophisticated criminal in Russia working on the dark side—of Goremykin's intelligence, his acumen for developing strong relationships with the government, and his success in crime. Their job was to support, without hesitation, Goremykin's orders, no matter how obscure or petty. The purpose of the meeting was to make those orders explicit.

"Our interest is in the New York financial system. We have chosen to start specifically with two banks, J.P. Morgan and Bank North America. The triton has three prongs: obtaining information to sell, transporting money, and showing America why it should not interfere with our motherland," Goremykin said, searching the eyes of each of his guests for the slightest sign of dissent. Each of the four men nodded in accord.

"We love the stupid Americans," Goremykin continued. "They make it easy for us to hack them. They are simple about passwords."

The four men nodded again. Goremykin picked up a notebook from a side table and began reading, "Recruiting bank employees.

Placement of malware. Credit cards. Bank account numbers. Trade secrets. Customer databases. Classified data. E-mails. Texts. Telephone numbers. The navigation accounts and routes for safely moving money . . ."

It did not take long for him to describe the plan; it was simple but effective. The more that went into a plan only meant that much more could go wrong. When he was finished, he slapped the notebook back on the table for emphasis.

Four sets of eyes stared at him, unblinking. They were ready.

"The time has come to act on our plan. I leave the tactics to you, together with the responsibility of perfect execution. America, while not as gifted as we are in this field, nevertheless has its National Security Agency, FBI, Secret Service, and many other agencies, all dedicated to preventing such intrusion. The risks are great, which you understand and accept with pride. If you succeed, you will be honored and compensated."

Goremykin then rose, turning his cold, hard eyes on the men. "If you fail, you will need nothing."

Goremykin walked to a sideboard and poured vodka into five Waterford lowball glasses. The four men stood.

"Do you share my interest in this matter?" Goremykin asked. "Will you raise your glasses and drink to our shared success?"

"*Salyut,*" the thieves shouted in unison. "We will. We will."

With that, all five clinked glasses and drank.

Chapter 6

A S THE NEWLY APPOINTED Special Assistant U.S. Attorney on the Bank North America fraud case, Carol Martin was
headed to her first big meeting with her team. Barely able to suppress her excitement, she flashed her badge at the receptionist and
was directed to a nearby conference room.

Entering the room, Carol immediately recognized Gil Gillespie,
the hotshot Assistant U.S. Attorney assigned to the new case. Seated at the head of the boardroom table, Gillespie looked tanned, as
if he had just flown in from a vacation in the tropics. Carol figured
him to be about forty, and she tried not to be rattled by the fact
that for the first time since they had met, he seemed surprisingly
congenial, though with his stern face, he looked anything but. He
smiled as he stood to greet her. Gillespie's younger associate, in his
Ivy League suit and large Tag Heuer watch, rose as well.

"Welcome, Carol," Gillespie said. "Glad you could join us. This
is Mark Conners, my associate, who'll be assisting."

"I'm happy to join you." Carol gave each a firm handshake. "I
didn't think I'd be working with you on this particular case given
that it's not a high-profile Wall Street scandal."

Gillespie shifted in his chair and frowned.

"We're viewing this as more than a run-of-the-mill, white-collar
crime. Between us, we're getting some heat from the Security and
Exchange Commission on this one. Bad enough to have the SEC

poking around, but we're also getting unwanted attention from Congressman Quinn's House Committee for Financial Services. The implication is that we're not being aggressive enough. Pure political noise, but that's the way this job works."

"I understand, Gil. I'm happy to do what I can to help."

Gillespie's tone picked up noticeably. "You've already testified before one of Quinn's subcommittees, and we're aware of the excellent legal papers you've written on this matter. I also understand you were the one who put the pieces of the puzzle together and showed how the bank's exposure in this investigation extends well beyond the State of New York."

Carol smiled and nodded, unable to conceal her pride. "I have my files with me." She pointed to the wall. "Since we have a whiteboard, it might be best if I diagram everything for you."

Gillespie glanced at Mark. "I told you she was good." Then to Carol, "By all means, do what makes you most comfortable."

With that, Carol picked up a red marker and proceeded to outline the case, first by identifying the main defendants: BNA executives Teddy Thompson and Stacy Bowers, and Russian developer Mikhail Baskhanov. From there, she drew a line and wrote in Wilson Holdings and Austin Disley; with little fanfare, she added another line and another name, this time a woman's, which she underlined for emphasis.

That name belonged to Maria DeSanto, the bank employee who had processed the paperwork for the flawed loans, and after a promise of immunity, had agreed to testify against Bowers, her immediate supervisor and the one who had provided the information she had fabricated.

In meticulous detail, Carol explained what DeSanto had said about creating the trumped-up financial statements and the source of the inflated appraisals, as well as the kickback scheme between Bowers, Thompson, Disley, and Easy Buy Inc., which was the name of the Russian shell company.

"We flipped Maria early, and she wore a wire during her subsequent conversations with Bowers," Carol explained.

The diagram complete, Gil and Mark went to the white board to study it more closely. When all the implications were clear, they sat back down, shaking their heads in disbelief. Carol had been through this already many times at the DA's office. Financial cases were complicated, and when it came to proof, the omissions or comissions that made up the crimes of each litigant had to be crystal clear.

"So who's getting screwed the most in this deal?" Mark asked.

The junior colleague's frankness took Carol aback, and as she began to respond, so did Gil. "Go ahead," Gil said, giving Carol the floor.

She took a deep breath. "The victims of the crimes are the officers, the management, and the shareholders of the bank. The last thing a bank needs in the wake of the 2008 housing debacle is the feds and its shareholders on their backs because of iffy loans and bad balance sheets. Ultimately, the bank's average customers suffer the most because of the higher rates for services that follow, and they're often the ones who can least afford the increases."

Mark ran his hand through his short-cropped red hair as he pushed up his reading glasses until they rested precariously on his forehead. "How does Disley fit into this mess?"

"It seems that the developer, with the bank's knowledge and assistance, was buying lots, building their value, and then flipping them to people known as end buyers, who paid inflated prices for the tracts. Obviously, they needed an incentive to purchase the lots at the higher prices, so the developer threw in a juicy bonus, telling them they could get an ultra-high-end car at wholesale with their purchase. We're talking about a Rolls-Royce or a Bentley at 20 percent off the sticker price."

Gil frowned. "I'm not sure that holds up. The incentive simply isn't big enough. And Bentley Motors, for example, wouldn't want its cars wholesaled. I don't know what wholesale actually is on a super luxury car, but I have to guess a tactic like that would affect other dealers and foul up the whole pricing structure in the States."

"But that's what these guys do," Carol said, in hindsight wishing she had just stuck with the facts.

"I've seen the FBI's reports as well," Gil said. "We need more. Get us the numbers. How much did this *really* cost the bank? What was the dealership's exposure? What was the total amount of the kickbacks? How long did this go on? If all we have are five cars sold at wholesale, even if it's a stupid idea and could cost the dealership its franchise for that make of car, it's not criminal."

"I'll have a talk with the investigators," Carol said, her bravado gone, "and size up the case." She hurriedly scribbled some notes.

"Don't be so hard on yourself," Gil said. "It's a complicated case, and you did a good job with what you were able to provide us." He held up his hand and pointed at the whiteboard. "Forgetting about the dollars involved, and assuming the amount is larger, how does this set up tactically?"

Carol's spirit returned. "We like it because we have a case of a little bank being absorbed by a bigger bank, which is then absorbed by a still larger multi-state bank—and they're all dirty. We like Disley because he's the CFO of a major car conglomerate with stores across the country, and he's tied into Bank North America. My gut tells me we can get a plea from either Disley or Thompson, or both, and maybe go upstairs and get Goldberg, BNA's vice president of commercial finance. Being on the commercial side, even if Goldberg didn't know, perhaps he should have."

Gil gave Carol a knowing smile. "You may want to cool your jets on that one. Remember, this is post-bank bailout. The federal government wants banks to succeed. They'll be fined, of course, for violating regulations, but it's the guys who defraud the banks who do the time. We have to move carefully on this one."

"I've been following the work of a reporter named Katherine Kelly with *Twin Forks Press* in the Hamptons," Carol said. "Kelly brought Maria DeSanto to me in the first place. Her stories have garnered national attention. Word on the hill is that she's been called before Congress to testify."

"You used to work in the Hamptons?" Gil asked.

"Yes, and when BNA became involved, I was moved to the DA's office in Manhattan to be closer to the case."

"Any other defendants?" Gil asked after a long pause to study his notes.

"We've listed twenty-seven unindicted co-conspirators. We're still checking them out. Among them is Preston Wilson, the owner of the car dealerships under the Wilson Holdings umbrella."

"How many are real?" Gil asked. They all laughed.

"In probative terms, we don't know yet, but for prophylactic purposes, they should all be good," Carol said.

"What does that mean?" Mark asked.

"Well, Mark, we use the unindicted co-conspirators to protect us in the case. It is the same mechanism that brought Nixon down in the Watergate scandal."

"Who do you think will cave first?" Gil asked.

"Like I said before, my impression is Thompson or Disley. If we plea bargain one, I'm of the opinion one will turn on the other."

"Tell me what else you know about Preston Wilson," Gil said, busily typing on his laptop.

"As you saw from the file, he and his wife, Marcia, are shareholders in Wilson Holdings."

"I'm still not clear about why Preston Wilson is not in the same boat," Mark said. "His company rents from the bank that's involved. Why isn't he a defendant?"

"The same reason Goldberg hasn't been arrested. We lack the evidence to support his complicity, but it's still early. We still have a lot of people to interview."

"I agree," Gil said. "This will be the first of many meetings, but it's time to wrap up this one. By next Monday, I'd like to see a solid work plan, including who's being interviewed, the timelines for the interviews, and the next steps as this investigation moves along."

Carol nodded, her stomach tight with equal doses of excitement and anxiety.

Just when she assumed Gil was ready to snap his briefcase shut and charge out the door, he leaned back and placed his hand on his chin and said, "I'll also need full details on each of the lead defense attorneys—everything. Depending on the pleas, get me the judges' schedules and find out our chances for a nonjury trial. Then let's meet back here next Monday. Same time, okay?"

Carol nodded again, this time sharply, in hopes of displaying the confidence she presently lacked. What if this case amounts to nothing more than some cars that should not have been wholesaled?

She needed more evidence, and fast. Preston Wilson would be her first stop.

CHAPTER 7

A LEX HERMAN STRUGGLED into Preston's office, lugging a bulging briefcase in one hand and a stack of papers in the other. Preston smiled when he saw who it was. "I can't tell you how good it is to see you, Alex. I know it was a long trip from Phoenix. To tell you the truth, I didn't think you'd come," Preston said.

"Of course I came. I couldn't miss watching your latest train wreck from up close and personal." Alex grinned, placing his pile of papers on the table and his briefcase on one of two chairs in front of Preston's desk; he sat in the other.

In his time, Joe Hart had often called on Alex for help with automotive cases. Alex's efforts had been instrumental in Joe's rec-onciliation of Preston's previous problems with BNA. His past work had made him one of the four shareholders in Wilson Holdings.

"I assume you've read the *Automotive News* article," Preston said, rolling his eyes. "My staff sure has."

"Obviously, fallout from the arrest will be huge, internally and customer wise. How far does it go?" He shifted nervously in his chair. "I have to ask—did you have anything to do with this?"

The question reminded Preston of just how direct Alex had been when he first met him working under Joe's watchful eye. He knew nothing short of a straight answer would satisfy Alex.

"Absolutely nothing." And he returned to his desk. "We're going to get through this," Preston assured Alex. "I'm just not sure how."

"That's why I'm here," Alex said. He abruptly walked out of the room, returning a few minutes later with two cups of coffee.

"If I learned anything from Joe," Alex said, "it is the importance of figuring out where you are before you start. It is what he called the R&A, or Review and Assessment. So I'm gonna ask this question once: As the CEO of this company, what do you know about where Marcia, Casey, you, and I are in the labyrinth at this very minute?"

Preston had no answer for him. Alex pulled a yellow legal pad from his briefcase and drew a series of stick figures, then a circle and a line from each one to a sphere. "The four of us, as officers, have a fiduciary responsibility to Wilson Holdings, as did Disley, even though he wasn't a stockholder. I'm not a lawyer, but that's civil law as I understand it."

"Austin has been arrested for criminal conspiracy to commit bank fraud. My attorney says this doesn't involve us or we'd be charged, too," Preston said.

"Well, you have been named an unindicted co-conspirator."

"From what I've been told by my attorney, that's a leverage thing. It means that if I don't cooperate with the prosecutor, I could be charged with something down the road. Thing is, they need to have something to charge me with, and I haven't committed any crime. I know Austin's been charged, but in truth I still don't know the specific crime he committed and—"

"How could you not know? His arrest has been all over the newspapers."

"It hasn't been established yet that he did anything illegal," Preston said. "It's all allegations."

"We have to find out what the feds have on him. Have you been contacted by anyone?"

Preston glanced at Alex's drawing. "The FBI came to the apartment a few nights ago, right after Marcia and I had sat down for dinner, no less. She *loved* that."

"That would bother anybody, which was obviously their intent," Alex said. "What did they want?"

"I just realized I can't talk about it. My lawyer warned me not to. If I do, I lose any attorney-client privilege."

Alex let out a loud groan. "I understand, I guess." He groaned again. "We need to talk to all of your people in this dealership. You have to know what shape your stores are in financially, particularly this one."

"Relax, Alex. I know I've made some mistakes, but that's over."

Alex arched his eyebrows, clearly unconvinced. "I'm glad to hear that, because this is complicated as hell. Let's take everybody's temperature and see where we are. By the way, why haven't you fired Disley yet?"

"How can I?"

"How the hell can you *not*?" Alex shouted.

"How can I fire a man I don't know is guilty?" Preston hollered back. "A friend, no less?" He softened his voice to add, "I did put him on administrative leave."

"Good grief, man. Just write him a letter and tell him he's fired based on the fact that he has been indicted by a grand jury. If you don't fire him, there will be serious questions as to why you failed to do so, and before you know it, you'll be defending yourself, and it will be too late for your reputation or the company's."

"Point made," Preston said. "I'll check with my lawyer for the wording and fire him today."

"Send me a copy."

"Okay," Preston said. "By the way, here are the reports from when Casey left and Disley became CFO of Wilson Holdings . . . and not just from this store."

He also pulled an employee roster from his desk and handed it to Alex, proceeding to point to the names as he went through them.

"He let go our old general manager—he was about to retire any-how—and brought in Robert Reynolds as GM. Bill Lamb is still our new car sales manager. Sam is handling used cars, Antonio is in parts, Loreen is finance, and Estelle Roberts is still our bookkeeper."

"I need to talk to all of them," Alex said. "They have to know who's in charge."

"You think it should be you?" Preston asked.

"If you don't like me in this position, who do you think it should be? Are you able to step in and deal with the day-to-day rebuilding of this store with everything else you have on your plate? In the past, no one's accused you of being a hands-on boss. So, you tell me, who should be in charge around here?"

Preston needed Alex, and now more than ever. Looking back, he wished he had accepted Alex's offer to expand his role as VP and COO of all the Wilson dealerships. On the other hand, he was also not going to be pushed around by Alex, even in such dire circumstances. Wilson Holdings was still his business. He placed his hand on Alex's shoulder. "I'm in charge of this company, and it's going to stay that way. That said, the staff needs to know you have the authority to go with the responsibility you've undertaken. I'm prepared to let everyone know you have the complete authority to do whatever it is you need to do. Can you live with that?"

"For the time being, and depending on what I learn about this operation. Can you live with that?" Alex let out a chuckle that relaxed Preston, who was a word away from telling his temporary CFO that his tenure was going to be the shortest on record.

Preston measured his next words. "Granted, I have a lot to deal with right now, but I have a good relationship with the men and women in this store, and I still know how to sell a car. How about you're the COO overall and the interim CEO of this store, but I'm the CEO and chairman of the board of Wilson Holdings, and my word is still final?"

Alex shook Preston's hand. "That's fine with me. I don't care about the title. I just don't want any confusion as I try to sort things out. I look at this as a one-time project, and I'll let everybody know what my role is as I get further into this mess." Alex stood and walked around the room, stopping at a window to stare at the car lot outside.

Preston watched Alex closely, knowing what was coming next. "I can't do this just because I'm a shareholder. This is going to take a lot of my time."

"I get that," Preston said. "How much do you want?"

"I don't know how deep the hole is now, or how deep it might become. This store could go down and pull the rest of us with it. I'd like fifty-thousand dollars upfront, with the option of more if it takes longer than a few months to sort through all this."

Without a word, Preston picked up the phone, called Estelle, and ordered the check. Alex smiled. "Thanks. Now, let's call this meeting I've been talking about. I want all your senior people in front and the sales personnel behind them. I'll talk to the rest of the staff in a separate meeting tomorrow morning before their shifts."

Preston nodded and left the room. Half an hour later, the general manager, parts and service manager, finance and insurance manager, and every sales person who was on duty met in the dealership's conference room on the second floor. There was hardly room for Preston, who, when everyone was settled, stood by the door to welcome Alex inside.

"Good morning," Preston said, looking out over his staff. He reminded himself of the importance of projecting an air of confidence. "This is a difficult time, but we're going to make it. We know that Austin Disley has been arrested, and that's been a shock to us all. I don't know what he did or didn't do, but I want each of you to know that this is an honest dealership. When I first heard of Austin's indictment, I placed him on administrative leave."

That brought a murmur from the group and odd looks from some of his key people, giving Preston the impression that they thought his response to be little more than a slap on the wrist or a paid vacation. "That said," he continued, projecting a more powerful voice, "in the interest of our entire company, I'm terminating his employment as of today."

His words changed the smirks to looks of genuine surprise. As the room went dead silent, Preston spotted Robert Reynolds ducking out the back door behind the sales team. He was probably calling his now ex-boss with the news.

"This entire store needs immediate attention, but in addition to my responsibilities with Wilson Holdings, I have a number of personal matters I have to deal with, so I have brought in some help." He turned to Alex, who was standing at his side. "I'd like to introduce Alex Herman. He's been in this business a long time at all levels. He's our chief operating officer at Wilson Holdings, one of the owners of the company, and a CPA. He's going to be reviewing this store—financially and operationally—and I've made him the interim CEO of this dealership. I'm still the CEO of Wilson Holdings and the chairman of the board, but in this store, Alex Herman has the last word. Does everyone understand?"

"Yes, sir!" The affirmations echoed off the walls until the room finally fell silent again, save for the shuffling of Robert Reynolds's shoes as he reentered the room.

Preston smiled at Alex. "It's all yours," he said, with a nod.

Alex looked around the room, taking a moment to make eye contact with each person.

"Good morning, ladies and gentlemen. I'll make this as brief as possible. I have a helicopter view of all our stores throughout the country, but I'm not sure what we're dealing with here, so I need your help. I want each one of you to give me straight answers and a prompt response when I ask for something. First, however, I want a written report from each manager on the status of your department, and I'd like these within the next two hours. Nothing fancy, just tell me what's been going on and what needs to occur to make things right."

Preston watched as a wave of concern swept over the faces of his employees, but Alex did not seem shaken. Instead, he found one attentive face and concentrated on that person as he spoke. "We're taking a PR hit because of the Disley situation. We need to work together to make certain this store can continue to instill a level of confidence with our customers. I will talk to each and every one of you in this room, privately. Thanks for your time, your attention, and your loyalty."

As Alex finished, Preston could see hope, if not confidence, in most of the faces. "Thank you, Alex," he said. A couple of men clapped, and several more in the room gave Alex a thumbs up.

"Excuse me, but which one of you is Estelle?" Alex asked, as the throng was about to depart.

A plump woman in her early fifties, with wire glasses and her hair in a bun, stepped forward.

"I assume Mr. Disley had an office?" Alex said, offering a warm smile and a gentle handshake as she nodded in response. "How about showing me where it's located, and I'll set up my work station in it for the time being."

Estelle led him to Disley's old office, just around the corner from Preston's.

"This used to be Mr. Fitzgerald's office," Estelle said.

"I know Casey well," Alex said. "How's he doing?"

"I've not heard from him since he left—save for a Christmas card." Her eyes got misty. "We all loved Mr. Fitzgerald."

"As well you should," Alex said. "If he were still here, I certainly wouldn't be."

CHAPTER 8

PRESTON WAS ANXIOUS to get an update from Alex. He knew Alex had received the department reports and that material had lent clarity to many issues. The buyers of the exotic cars were concerned the dealership might go out of business and they would have to drive long distances for service. Alex had dealt with this before, and immediately put in a call to a PR firm to start working on a sophisticated ad campaign to dispel such fears—quickly. Thankfully, the standard domestic-line customer would be satisfied with strong incentives and more personal attention by sales and service.

A week later, Preston had Alex and Estelle once again working at Disley's conference table to deliver yet another report for him. Using the latest financials compiled by the CPA firm that serviced Wilson Holdings, they were reviewing the company's current status with the bank, as well as confirming that the operating expenses and taxes were current.

Preston picked up the phone to ask Alex how things were going. Alex explained the bills had been paid, but he was not comfortable with the gross numbers. Preston called them both into his office.

"Where are we precisely?" Preston asked as the two entered. Alex took a seat in a side chair by Preston's desk. Estelle sat at Preston's conference table. Alex didn't pull any punches. "If you're hoping for good news, I'm afraid you're in for disappointment. From what I see so far, profit wise, this store is down 30 percent from a year ago, and heading even further south. In a normal situation we could turn that around in two quarters, but we both know these aren't normal times. Assuming the numbers are correct—and they might well not be—we can tighten up on the expense side, but we can't afford our revenue stream to keep taking a hit."

Preston leaned back in his chair, put his feet on the desk, and tried to absorb what Alex had said. "Tell me more," he said.

"I'm looking over the operating statements Estelle gave me. This store is five-hundred-thousand dollars behind last year's numbers during a five-month stretch ending with this last quarter."

Estelle frowned and nodded sheepishly. "I made that same observation to Mr. Disley on several occasions—that the numbers weren't adding up—but he kept telling me he'd take care of it in a carryover from added sales revenue later on."

"If he did, it doesn't show here," Alex said, breaking off the tip of his pencil. "Is there anything the bank has requested as collateral or support for the cap loan, the property lease, or any other outstanding obligations?"

"Not that I'm aware of," Estelle said. "That's the whole problem, sir. I don't know what I don't know. When Casey was here, he always shared information with me so I knew exactly where we stood. Mr. Disley kept a lot of that to himself and he always carried his laptop, where he stored everything, with him."

Alex spun around sideways in his chair so fast he almost came out of it. "He used our desktops, too, didn't he?"

"No, I'm afraid not. He preferred to keep everything on his own laptop until he had the numbers ready to transfer. He used flash drives, and he handled all his own e-mail. No one else was allowed to read it."

Preston slammed his open hand on the desk. "So we have no paper trail of our communications with the bank?"

Estelle straightened. "We always had the current deposit receipts and the statement balances."

"But no documentation of why what funds went where?"

"No. Mr. Disley handled all of that himself," she said.

He sure did, Preston thought. His face darkened. Slowly, he made a series of interlocking circles on his notepad, and then he got up from his chair to gaze out the window. Without turning, he said, "Tell me, Alex, have you ever worked with a store in this kind of trouble . . . with its CFO being arrested for a . . . a felony?"

Alex appeared to choose his words carefully. "To the first part of your question, it's like 'the butler did it' mystery, but in accounting it's usually the bookkeeper, or at least the bookkeeper always gets blamed. I've also seen some guys at the top, the principals, get into trouble. Ultimately, it doesn't matter who goes down. The customers are going to wonder about staying with the company, and the company is going to lose business. I've started an ad program for the high end, and we'll do some ass-kissing for the basic lines. Obviously, for this store, I can't predict how much will be lost, or for how long."

"So it's too early for me to ask if there's any real light at the end of the tunnel?" Preston realized his voice carried a level of desperation unusual for him even in bad times.

"Right, but it's more than the numbers. We can't underestimate the impact this is having on the entire staff. Right now, with Disley's case so vague but hanging over everything, they're feeling pretty insecure. I have received reports from all the managers except Robert Reynolds. He's had one excuse after another."

"You're not going to get one from him," Preston grumbled. "Ten minutes ago, he handed me his resignation."

Alex raised his eyebrows. "This is beginning to smell worse every minute. You have his files. I think we should take a look."

"I don't have them." Preston looked away, even more aggravated with himself.

Alex punched the speaker button on the phone and called security before Preston could say anything more. "If he's still here, I want Mr. Reynolds stopped from leaving this property. Hold him until I get there, and do not let him out of your—"

"I'm sorry, sir," the guard said. "He's already gone."

Alex shared an irritated look with Preston, who sank back into his chair, his hands over his eyes.

"What did he have with him?" Alex asked Preston, slamming down the phone.

"I think just his hat and coat. Oh, and his laptop computer."

• • •

Alex ran downstairs to find Bill Lamb, the sales manager. He found him at his desk. Winded, Alex asked Lamb, "How long ago did Reynolds leave?"

"I don't know," Lamb replied, turning his attention to a stack of papers on his desk.

Alex stood there, arms crossed, barely able to restrain himself from yanking the guy out of his chair. Apparently sensing that his new boss was not going away, Lamb glanced up from the pile. "I didn't see him leave."

"He just tore out of here," Alex said, curling and uncurling his fist, "and you didn't see him leave?"

"No . . . sir. I did not," Lamb said, his forced pause annoying Alex even more.

"When was the last conversation you had with Reynolds?"

"About three days ago."

"Is that unusual?"

"Yes. We used to—"

"Thought so," Alex said, getting in his face. "That's ridiculous."

"—talk several times every day," Lamb continued as he tried to talk over Alex, "but ever since Disley left, we've been without our normal sales meetings. It's been pretty unsettled around here, to put it mildly."

Alex told himself to settle down. He knew he was tense and probably taking it out on Lamb. He thought for a moment. "I need to see the gross sales sheets for the two months since Disley has been gone, which should bring it up to December."

"They have already been sent to bookkeeping. Estelle has every-thing." Lamb went back to the matter on his desk seemingly either unaware—or oblivious to—the point Alex was trying to make.

Alex had had it with Lamb. What sales manager failed to keep a cheat sheet with a running monthly total that compared numbers from one year to the next? His annual bonus depended on it. Without another word to him, Alex went to Estelle's office and picked up the previous year's gross sheets for September, October, and November.

After studying the sheets in detail and comparing them to the current statements, he locked the door to his office. Then, he collapsed onto the couch, trying to absorb the implications of all he had just learned. The image of a sinking ship came to mind; he stood on its deck frantically waving a flag for help, but no help appeared to keep him from going down with the vessel to the bottom of a very deep ocean.

CHAPTER 9

KATHERINE SAT IN HER cubicle at the newspaper staring at her cell phone. A call to her father was long overdue. He picked up on the second ring.

"I know you must have a lot going on right now," she said. "I was wondering if Marcia could spare you one night this week and I could cook dinner for you. Think you could get away?"

"Would I ever love to get away. How about tonight? Is that too soon?"

Thrilled that her father sounded upbeat and not upset with her, she smiled. "Not at all, I'll run out and get a few things from the store and wrestle us up some manicotti."

"Is everything okay with you?" Preston asked.

"Me? I was more worried if things were all right with you. I imagine you've had a few restless nights lately. I just hope I'm not the reason for any of them. I thought you might like to talk. Nothing to do with the bank matter. I promise."

After agreeing to meet her father at her apartment at seven-thirty that evening and even though it was barely ten o'clock in the morning, she told Chuck she was taking a little comp time and likely would not be back that day. Chuck just grunted, which Katherine took as tacit approval.

She had been driving for less than a minute when the Bluetooth phone in her BMW connected and the sound of her mother's voice began to fill the car. Katherine struggled to understand what Beth was trying to say. Finally, Katherine pulled over on the shoulder of the road, only to hear the words everyone dreads the most: "He was sleeping. His heart just stopped. Apparently it was his time."

Beth sniffled loudly and Katherine could hear her mom blowing her nose. "It was all very fast, sweetheart. God . . . has your grandfather now."

Katherine could only mumble a soft, "I'm so sorry, Mom."

"I'm sorry, too. I know how much you loved him."

Katherine was thankful she'd had the good sense to get off the road—already her hands were shaking and her eyes had welled up with tears so thick she was having trouble seeing. She tried to gather her wits about her, and then she remembered her golden retriever.

"Don't worry, Mom. I'm okay. I'll pick up Hailey and some clothes, and be there as soon as I can. It'll take me about eight hours."

"It'll be good to have you here," her mother said, "but don't rush, dear, and drive safely."

The call went dead, and Katherine quickly turned around and headed back to the newspaper. She went directly to Sol's office, bypassing Chuck. She told Sol her grandfather had just died, and she needed to leave immediately to be with her mother in Marion, in upstate New York. Sol told her to take whatever time she needed and to be careful on the roads. As he walked her out the door, he asked, "You were pretty close?"

Katherine nodded. "When no one else got me, my Grandpa Adrian did. He was my favorite man in the world. For most of my childhood, he was also the only man in my life."

Before the tears could fall again, she gave her boss a quick hug and raced out of the small building. She had many calls to make, and her first was to Preston.

"I know, you want me to bring a nice Chianti tonight," he said before she could say a word.

"I wish that was why I was calling, Dad. I'm afraid I have to cancel tonight. Grandpa Adrian has died. I have to go to Marion."

"Oh Katherine, I'm so sorry. If you want, I can get my travel agent on the line, and you can fly to the closest town, and I'll arrange for a rental car," said Preston, his voice in crisis can-do mode.

"That's so kind of you, but there's nothing close by. Besides, I would probably end up getting there at around the same time anyway. I think I should just drive."

"How's your mom taking this?" Preston asked, so softly Katherine could barely hear him.

"She's strong . . . she'll be fine . . . in the short term."

"I'm sure it's too early to know about the funeral; would you please let me know when you get to Marion? Stop whenever you need to. Your mom would rather have you arrive safely than fast, and so would I."

Katherine heard her father's voice falter, and while an odd thing to think, it pleased her: He cares so much about Mom and me. "I promise to be careful," Katherine said. "I'll call you as soon as I'm there." Her next call was to her boyfriend, but as was too often the case lately, Sean did not pick up. His work for the Secret Service frequently prevented direct contact, so she knew the routine. She would leave a brief message and wait for a call back, which often came a day later, if at all.

Katherine had been dating Sean for eight months, and she was still as attracted to him as the day she first spotted him in an enduro motorcycle race in the Berkshires. He had been a veteran racer and she was just a newbie, but off the trails they had found they shared a love of big dogs, Italian food, and hard work. Sean was as focused on his career as she was on her own, and that was saying something.

Recently, though, his visits had become short and sporadic. She was no longer sure about Sean being the man for her. Yes, he was handsome. Yes, he could be charming. The problem was she did not yet know what kind of a companion he would be in the long run. Still, she found herself longing to be with him, and she believed she was falling in love with him. She did not expect a return call anytime soon, but she speed-dialed him once more, just to let him know it was urgent.

Back at her apartment, Katherine threw a few clothes into a suitcase, packed a couple of diet sodas, some apples, and a banana in a cooler and filled it with ice. Dog food, bottled water, and Hailey's dish went into a canvas bag, and then she loaded everything into the back of her SUV and drove down the street to her friend Becky's apartment to pick up Hailey. Becky loved dogs and took care of Hailey when Katherine was working or away on assignment, no matter how short the notice. After hugs for Becky and Hailey, Katherine thanked her friend, and the big dog jumped in the back seat and they were on their way. With no weather or traffic tie-ups, she should be in Marion by seven.

Once they were on the highway, Katherine's next call was to Susan, her best friend since college. She knew Susan would want to know about her grandpa's passing, as his name had popped up in many of their long talks over the years.

"Hey, stranger, how the hell are ya . . . or maybe I should say, where are ya?"

Was that a slight slur in Susan's voice? Concern for her friend swirled in her head. Still morning. It was obvious she had fallen off the wagon. Why haven't I spent more time with her? Should I ask if she's talked to her sponsor lately? Finally, Katherine could not take another mumbled sentence. "Susan, listen to me. I'm in my car heading north to Marion. I have to go home."

"Well, you love it up there . . . never could figure out why. By the way, how's the ace reporter doing. . . thought I read something about some guy who works for your father's company getting arrested . . . you handling that story?"

"Susan, stop! Grandpa Adrian died."

"What?"

"My grandpa passed away in his sleep this morning. I'm going home to be with my mother and help handle things."

"Oh, I am so sorry, Kat. You and your grandfather were so close."

Katherine went silent for a few seconds. "Yes . . . we . . . were so close."

More silence. "Do you know when the funeral will be?" Susan asked in a voice so clear that the sudden quality of her elocution surprised Katherine.

"I'm not sure, probably in three or four days."

"I'll be there," Susan said.

"I appreciate the thought, but you never met my grandfather, and it's a long way to Marion. Please don't feel you have to come."

"That's bull and you know it. It's what friends do. I'll be there, period."

Katherine was not sure how to respond. The pressure of the situation and Susan's babbling had given her a visual migraine, but after thinking about it for a moment, she said, "Thank you, Susan. It would be great to have a friend at my side."

"That I am, and that I'll be. See you soon. I'm sorry, Katherine, and please tell your mom she's in my thoughts."

"I will, Susan," Katherine said. She hung up before her friend could say anything else, vowing no more phone calls for a while.

After a few hours on the road, Katherine pulled into a rest stop to give Hailey a break and a short walk, and then she was back on the road. She thought about her last trip to Marion, particularly about the time she had spent with Adrian at her grandmother's grave and stopping by the church to light a candle for her.

She could not believe she would never again ride with her grandpa in his old pickup, or shoot skeet with him in Newark. Just thinking about it made her miss the smell of cigar smoke in his old truck. If he were with her, he would be sharing his hard-earned wisdom about how to deal with the passing of a loved one. She would never again see his eyes twinkling through wrinkles forged by countless smiles. No more of his wisdom. No more one-on-one discussions that went to the heart of her soul. She rubbed her eyes before the tears had a chance to fall.

Her thoughts about her grandfather and the Newark Rod and Gun Club triggered memories of one of his favorite shooting buddies, Harry Klaskowski. She and Harry had gotten along so well on their own that when Harry last came to New York City to put on a show with his Oompah Band at the Heidelberg Restaurant in Germantown, he had invited Katherine and encouraged her to bring some friends. She had dragged Susan along and invited Preston to join them, which he had. It had been fun getting to see what Preston looked like after a few drinks. In fact, it was a turning point in their relationship. She needed to call Harry—chances were her mom was in no state to do so herself.

The phone rang and rang. Finally a loud voice answered. "Howdy, Double K," a voice said. "You got the Oompah Man. It must be an honor waiting for me to take your call. Don't be shy, you can tell me how you feel."

As sad as Katherine felt, she could not help but laugh. Bipolar and more than a little over the top, Harry was a dear, and she found him funny. Occasional mood swings be damned, she had come to love the Oompah Man.

"Hey, Katherine, are you gonna talk to me or just give me the silent treatment? Glad it's not my nickel. Take your time."

Pleased that he recognized her laugh, Katherine nonetheless knew she had to get to the point of her call. "I'm calling with some bad news, Harry."

"Whoa. Let's slow the train down. What's going on, little girl?"

"Harry . . . Adrian passed away this morning, in his sleep."

Moments passed. Katherine could feel her pulse pounding against her temples, making the wavy lines of her migraine all the more acute.

"Leave it to Adrian to do it the easy way," Harry said. "God love him."

Katherine could hear Harry coughing and blowing his nose. She would have given anything to be able to throw her arms through the phone line and squeeze him tight.

"Grandpa was everything to me, and I know you were the best of buddies. I'm on my way to Marion now. After I talk to Mom, I'll let you know about the funeral."

"I'm sorry for your loss—for our loss," Harry said. "I know how much you meant to Adrian. I can still see the excitement in his eyes every time he talked about you. You may not know it, but I've talked with Adrian every Sunday for . . . "

Katherine heard another cough and then sobbing.

"I'm so sorry, Harry. I'll see you soon."

Katherine made another rest stop, and then resumed her trip north. When she reached the New York thruway she tried Sean again, not expecting him to answer, but surprised when one of his team did.

"Hello, Johnson."

"This is Katherine Kelly. I'm looking for Sean O'Malley."

After a few minutes, Sean came on the line. "Hi, Kat. You caught me just coming in. It's great to hear your voice."

"I left you a couple of messages earlier today—did you by chance get either of them?"

"Afraid not. Like I said, we've been out in the field. Babe, you sound a little stressed. You okay?"

"I'm fine except . . . actually, I'm terrible. My grandfather died this morning. I'm on my way to Marion now to be with Mom. I just thought you should know in case you tried to get hold of me."

"I'm way sorry, Katherine. I know how close you are—or were—with your grandfather."

"I'm going to remain close to him until I see him again," Katherine said, hurt that Sean had misspoken, even if it was an honest slip of the tongue.

"Of course you are, Katherine. I just wish I were with you right now," Sean said. "We've been apart too long this time . . . is there anything I can do to help?"

"Thanks, but right now, I just want to be with my mom and get her through this," she said, glad he at least seemed sorry about how long it had been since they had been together.

"You should be there within two hours. I know you have a lot on your mind. Drive carefully. If you'd like me to come to the funeral, I'll try my best. Love you."

Before she could answer, the line went silent. As she checked the time, she thought about Sean's "two hour" comment and frowned, puzzled. Did I mention to him where I was? I think I might be losing my mind. He said he loves me. He wants to be by my side at the funeral. That's what matters. Isn't it?

Chapter 10

AUSTIN DISLEY SQUIRMED in his chair in the expansive, spartan office of his attorney, Anthony Spagnello. They had been at it all morning, and they had just returned from lunch. Disley was already covered again in nervous sweat as Spagnello threw yet another hardball question at him.

"So tell me, Mr. Disley, when did you and your confederate, Teddy Thompson, come up with the scheme to defraud the bank? Which of you arranged the kickbacks from the developer?"

"I . . . thought you were representing me," Disley said, his voice rising to a shrill squeal as it often had during Spagnello's brutal examination.

"Welcome to the world of criminal law," the attorney said, adding, with a smug sneer, "If it helps you focus, bank fraud can get you up to thirty years, and Rikers Island will be a whole lot less accommodating than that fancy country club of yours."

"You don't like me, do you, Mr. Spagnello?"

Spagnello, who had been standing in front of Disley, took a seat behind a desk piled so high with files, he had to stretch his neck to look over them. "My opinion of you is irrelevant, Mr. Disley. My job is to keep you out of jail. Your job is to help me do it. You've been living a life of luxury for forty-eight years. If you ever got a speeding ticket, it was fixed. If you were ever caught driving drunk, some lawyer got you out of it. You and your fancy bow tie have probably talked your way in and out of anything else that happened through the years. The good news is, now that you've paid me, I'm committed to representing you."

"I know this is serious," Disley said, shifting his weight again in his chair. "What I fail to see is how it helps me when you're being so difficult, and, if you'll excuse me, so cynical."

Spagnello's tone softened. "If you think I'm tough, wait until you're put on the witness stand and the prosecutor gets a hold of you. One of the most important decisions you and I have to make is whether or not to demand a jury trial. Normally, we'd want a jury trial, but I'm worried that a jury might not like you. Jurors generally are not rich people who have gone to fancy boarding schools and Ivy League colleges. When they have a defendant they can't identify with, who has committed a crime they don't like . . . say, something they think reaches beyond their stations in life . . . they tend to not be objective."

Austin sat as still as a stone. He had no idea how to respond and could not help but notice that his soaked undershirt had started to smell. He did not like his attorney, but Anthony Spagnello had a reputation for being smart under pressure. The attorney was also right, though; he was a child of wealth, born with the proverbial silver spoon in his mouth and with the accoutrements typical of his class: Hotchkiss Prep School, where he had met and roomed with Preston; Princeton University, where he had joined a dining club; memberships at several exclusive country clubs, the yacht club and boat, and more. Indeed, everything had been simply wonderful until five years ago. Yes, he still had money but not like before.

"How can you be so sure a jury won't like me? Do I have to be poor?"

The remark made Spagnello laugh. "No, you don't have to be poor, but take a look at yourself. You're wearing a fancy dress shirt and gold cuff links with your initials engraved on them, and a blue blazer with shiny brass buttons that definitely did not come off the rack. You have a pink handkerchief in your breast pocket. Your belt has embroidered golf clubs on it, your socks are all sorts of colors, your loafers have tassels—and you wear a bow tie. God knows how you dress when you decide to relax."

Austin's face fell. "Do I have any hope of beating this?"

"That depends on what you can tell me that will prove you didn't commit what you're accused of in the complaint. Follow me on this, and you might want to take some notes," Spagnello said, picking up a book off his desk.

He thumbed through a few pages. "Okay, let's look at the statutory language in 1344 again: ' . . . Knowingly executes, or attempts to execute, a scheme or artifice to defraud a financial institution . . . or to obtain any of the moneys . . . or other property owned by, or under the custody or control of a financial institution, by means of false or fraudulent pretenses, representations or promises.' You're charged with conspiring with Thompson and Easy Buy to have your customers buy cars at wholesale as part of a scheme between the bank and the developer, from the latter of which you and Thompson shared kickbacks."

"What we say is confidential?" Austin asked. "Attorney-client privilege, right?"

"Of course," Spagnello said. "While we're on that subject, you must be careful not to waive that privilege by discussing our conversations or writing about them. Be especially careful with e-mails, no matter how private you think they are. Trust me, they are no more private than a billboard and probably easier for the feds to find."

Austin looked at his notes. "I never considered giving a customer a good deal, including selling a car at wholesale, to be criminal. It's done all the time. If it helped my relationship with our bank, I don't see how that's a crime either. As for what they call kickbacks, I looked at it as customers expressing their appreciation to the developer, and he in turn saying 'thank you' to us. I never had any intention of violating any laws. Anyhow, it was Thompson who put everything together. I only found out about this 'supposed' crime after I was arrested."

"You want me to believe that (a) you never had a scheme, (b) you never defrauded the bank, (c) you never got any money from the bank under false or fraudulent pretenses, (d) you never made any misrepresentations or false promises to the bank, and (e) you never intended to violate any law."

"Yes, that's exactly what I'm saying," Austin said, feeling better for the first time since he had sat down with Spagnello. Maybe there was still some hope.

Spagnello opened a file and wrote something in the margin. "Tell me about your conversations with Thompson. Start from the beginning."

"There were none outside of routine discussions about our lease, collateral, appraisals—all the stuff that goes on between a CFO and a bank that holds the financing for our cars and capital loans, and is also our landlord."

"You're telling me you never arranged anything with Thompson that resulted in a kickback?"

"That's right. Wholesaling the high-end cars was my idea to promote business and please the bank at the same time. Everybody won."

Spagnello opened a different folder. "Tell me about these appraisals."

"I don't think the appraisals mentioned in the complaint have anything do with what was going on between Wilson Holdings and what Thompson was doing with Easy Buy, or whatever that Russian's company was called," said Austin.

Spagnello looked doubtful, so Disley tried again, explaining that while the dealership submits appraisals, the bank also does appraisals of its own. "As I was saying, I think the complaint is referring to the bank's appraisals, not the dealer's," Austin said.

Spagnello gave Disley a look of such utter disbelief that an idiot would have caught it. Yet Austin settled in his chair confident he had set his attorney straight. They talked for an hour longer, and when the meeting finally came to a close, the former CFO of Wilson Holdings could be heard mumbling to himself as he left the building, "I think I did pretty well. He acted like he believed me."

CHAPTER 11

L IGHT SNOW FAINTLY FELL on the windows of Beth's two-story frame house. Normally, she would have loved such a day in her cozy home. Instead, she sat in her den, warmed by a fire but with her body numb. She had always known this day would come; still, she was unprepared for the harsh reality of it.

Joan Summers, Beth's most trusted friend from their days in the SUNY nursing program at Plattsburg, had arrived and was in the kitchen preparing food for the throng of neighbors, friends, and relatives who would soon descend to offer their condolences.

Beth looked at her watch: three o'clock. Five hours had passed since she had called Katherine that morning. She figured her daughter would be there by dinner. She both looked forward to and feared seeing her daughter. She could only imagine how devastated Katherine must be. For twenty-three years, her father had been a father to Katherine as well as a grandfather.

The lone crack in their mother-daughter relationship stemmed from her having lied to Katherine about who her father in reality was. Beth was not sure that Katherine had come to grips with why her mother had felt the need to pretend her father was a man more interested in flying airplanes than marrying her. Beth had believed raising her daughter as a single mom had been the best choice, if not the only one, but now that Katherine had met her real father, did she still agree?

Preston had been a one-night stand, albeit a memorable one. Beth had nursed the young patient for just three days when he finally coaxed her to go out for a night on the town. Having met his blue-blooded mother, Beth was fairly certain what would have happened even if Preston had agreed to marry her after she got pregnant—divorce. More shame for her small-town family, and ultimately landing right back where she was: a single mother without a clue about life.

Beth had lived the lie for twenty-four years. If her daughter had grown up to be a baker or a banker instead of an investigative journalist, she might still be living it. It did not take a rocket scientist to know that upon Katherine's completion of graduate school, one of the first investigations her daughter would undertake would be into her own past . . . finding the father she never knew.

Beth had told her the truth but not before calling Preston Wilson for the first time since their long-ago encounter. She had asked for nothing for herself or Katherine; she simply gave Preston her daughter's address and left the rest to him. He had embraced the news and written Katherine, acknowledging how awkward a situation they both found themselves in. The last paragraph of that letter said it all as far as Beth was concerned: "I can't imagine what learning all this now must be like for you, and it breaks my heart to think about it. What I do know is that I want to meet you, get to know you, and love you, if you're willing to let me do that. Since I've not had the chance to be your father before, I'd like to try to make up for it now."

At this point, Preston was a part of both of their lives. Beth assumed Katherine had already called her father to tell him of Adrian's passing. In some ways, her daughter seemed more comfortable with the father she barely knew than with the woman who had been there all of her life. Katherine had eventually accepted the justification for her mother's actions, but no matter what was said between them, Beth knew her daughter struggled with the forgiveness part. Every night, Beth prayed her daughter would one day relent.

She heard a knock at the door. Beth looked out the den window and saw Father Patterson at the front door. The priest, with his wide smile and an even wider girth, was about the same age as her father. He had been friendly with Adrian but had been much closer to Beth's mother, Colina. When Colina had died a decade earlier, it was Father Patterson who had handled the mass and graveside service.

Beth met the priest at the front door, thanked him for coming, and gave him a quick hug. She asked Joan to join them. After Father Patterson had expressed his condolences and said a prayer, he sat quietly for a while before looking at Beth and saying, "I know Adrian was a Presbyterian, but is there anything I can do to help with the service?"

Beth rubbed her raw nose with a hankie. "To be honest, my father would not have asked you to do anything. He wanted to have a simple service at the United Church, but I haven't had time to think about it." Her voice grew strained but she continued. "It all seems too sudden, Father. Dr. Bovet checked him out last year. He had been slowing down a bit, but I thought he was doing fine. Then . . ."

She buried her face in her hands. The old priest rose and reached out to her while Joan looked on sadly.

"I know this is a difficult time," he said gently.

"Father, no disrespect, but I would rather not go through the speech you're about to make. I'm thankful he went so peacefully."

"What about the pain you're feeling?" the priest asked.

She stared up at him. "The pain I'm feeling is one I've lived with for more than two decades. It's not going away today or tomorrow."

"What would be the cause of that pain?"

Beth could not take it anymore. "In a word, guilt. Thank you for coming over, but I think I'd like to be alone now."

The priest nodded once, gave Joan a brief smile as he glanced her way, and left.

Beth went straight to her bedroom, threw herself on the bed, and cried into her pillow. She was exhausted, but sleep would not come. A myriad of thoughts and memories vied for her attention, keeping her awake. She knew she would get through the funeral, surrounded by her friends and others sensitive to her loss, and most of all, with the help of Katherine. Still, she was a nervous wreck. She did not have to look too deeply to know what she was anxious about. His name was Preston Wilson. A sixth sense told her he would be at the funeral—the man she hardly knew, yet who was the father of her only child. The man she had not stopped thinking about for twenty-four years.

CHAPTER 12

HOURS LATER, PRESTON could still not forget the hurt he had heard in his daughter's voice. Katherine had often talked with him about her grandfather—always adoringly, always candidly—and the huge part he had played in her life. Preston wanted to take up where Katherine's grandfather had left off. It was a chance for him to make up for the years he had not been there for her, even if that was not his fault.

He had actually wanted to ride with Katherine to Marion, but had stopped short of asking to do so. He was not sure if she would rebuff him or if he could even free himself from the tentacles of his latest business disaster in order to go. He liked to think of himself as a strong business man, but how powerful was he if he could not even take a couple of days to go with his daughter to a family funeral? The realization stopped him short. Right then and there, Preston vowed to himself that going forward he would be different. He was determined that no matter what, he would henceforth face his problems with focus and fortitude.

A knock on the door brought a rumpled Alex dragging himself into Preston's office. "You know my first cut on where we stand financially," Alex said after falling into a chair. "I think we have a much deeper problem to figure out."

Preston knew Alex well enough to take him at his word, and he steeled himself for what was about to come. "Let's have it," he said.

"I've been studying the gross sheets for this past October. Five cars stood out: four Bentleys and a Rolls. They were sold dead even, no profit whatsoever. The loss of potential margin corresponds to the operating and financial statements." He handed the statements to Preston, who began studying the numbers.

"I never reviewed these sheets. That was Disley's job. Come to think of it, that's around the time when he was arrested, and I put him on leave."

"Interesting timing," Alex said.

"I still don't claim to understand what constitutes bank fraud, but my lawyer says Disley was actually arrested for conspiracy, something to do with the bank and some Russian developer. It doesn't have anything to do with this dealership, at least as far as any of us knows right now."

"But Disley brought in Reynolds as GM, and then Reynolds starts acting squirrelly and resigns in a rush."

Preston looked up from the statements. "And on his watch, Manhattan Mercedes takes a hundred-thousand-dollar hit on five cars sold at wholesale. Why?" Preston tossed the financials on his desk. "Reynolds should be screaming bloody murder at not being given his piece. So would his new car manager . . . unless they were both bonused-over." Preston buzzed Lamb to come up to his office.

"You need to ask him whatever you want—and quickly—because he's likely going to be my first executive personnel decision," Alex said.

"You talked with him already, right?"

"Not about this."

"Talk to him now. I want to see how he reacts."

Alex arched a brow. "I like this new Preston."

A few minutes later, the sales manager joined them, and Preston immediately handed him the gross sheets for October. Alex then pointed to the four Bentleys on one and the Rolls on the other.

"Did you know these went through at wholesale?" Alex asked.

"Yes," Lamb said, without showing the slightest sign of contrition or nerves. "I was told it had something to do with giving five customers of the bank a good deal to help corporate's position with them."

"Where'd you get that information?" Alex asked.

"The general manager."

"Tell us about that."

"That's all I know. The sales all happened in a week. Rob Reynolds told me these cars were going to be handled one-off at wholesale per Disley's orders, and all the financial stuff with the manufacturers was already taken care of."

"Did you ever talk to Disley about it?" Alex asked.

"Of course not—Reynolds was clear about the chain of command."

"How'd you feel about that?" Preston asked before Alex had a chance to do so.

"It's not my place to question. Rob said that my bonus wouldn't be affected, and that's all that concerned me. There was nobody to discuss it with if I wanted to, so what more could I do?"

Preston and Alex thanked Lamb for coming in, and he slipped out the door.

"What's your gut telling you?" Preston asked as he went and closed his office door, just in case Lamb was lingering nearby.

Alex smiled, leaned back in his chair, and propped his feet on the edge of Preston's desk.

"I don't know about Lamb, but he's halfway got me believing he had nothing to do with any of this. Now I may have to keep him around just on principle."

Preston laughed but quickly turned serious again. "I'd like to know why we took a six-figure hit, and I mean the *real* reason those cars were sold that way. The 'help our appearances with the bank' line is total garbage."

Alex removed his feet from the desk. "Why did Robert Reynolds—as your GM—not come to you about it?"

"Maybe he was in on it," Preston said.

Alex walked over to Preston and placed a hand on his shoulder. "You might not like this idea or even want to hear it, but if I were you, I would call the FBI with what we know, let them investigate, and cooperate with them fully."

"I don't get it, Alex. All we have is some guys in my dealership selling cars at wholesale. That may be an offense worth firing some-one over, but it's hardly a crime."

"It's not a crime right now, but you know as well as I that there's a whole lot more to all this—somewhere. If you get the feds involved now, it will demonstrate your lack of knowledge of any wrongdoing. Think of it as preventive maintenance."

Preston smiled and gave Alex a playful tap on the shoulder. "Each day I see more and more why Joe Hart thought so highly of you. I'll call my attorney, tell him what we know, and if he has no objection, and I don't know why he would, my next call will be to the FBI."

CHAPTER 13

A S THE MILEPOSTS clicked by and Katherine drew closer and closer to where she had grown up, her thoughts seemed to spin further and further away. One minute she was back in her office at the newspaper, beginning what was destined to be the longest day of her life; the next minute she was getting a call from her mom with news she had always feared would come. Katherine did what she had always done in the face of trouble or loss: she pushed her feelings down, way down deep inside her.

Even before her mother's call, it didn't take a therapist to see it was getting crowded down there. The bank fraud case was exploding into a major story, and she was on the sidelines watching the parade go by because her father might be involved. It did not escape her that the father she was trying so hard to protect from scandal was the same father she had not even known existed a year ago. When did she start caring about him so much?

Now her mother had lost her own father, and Katherine, her best friend. Life from that moment forward might someday be good again, but it would never be without sadness.

Those thoughts, dire as they were, somehow made the time fly by. Before she knew it, she was off the expressway and driving into Marion. She powered off her GPS as she turned off Mill Road and onto North Main Street. She passed the cemetery on her left. It was dark, and as if someone else were guiding her hands, she made a sharp turn onto the narrow road leading to the graveyard. She came to a stop, both hands still on the wheel, her eyes staring straight ahead. She switched off the ignition, turned off the car lights, and sat in the dark.

She knew this would happen. She was finally losing her mind. Her brooding was interrupted by a wet slobbery lick to the face— Hailey. She could hear her dog's tail hitting the door of her SUV. Katherine laughed and addressed her traveling companion.

"Hailey, you're my savior. You're not depressed. You're excited to be home. You can't wait to see Mom . . . and Grandpa. You don't know he's . . . " The sobs came unannounced and with them came all of Hailey as she climbed up on Katherine, who hugged her tightly. This is absurd. Drive the damn car home, and walk in with the grace your grandfather would expect of you.

· · ·

Beth was waiting for them on the porch with a big smile and watery eyes. Hailey followed Katherine out of the car and immediately bounded past her and up the stairs to Beth. They had to navigate around the dog's lunges, but soon were in each other's arms, mother and daughter, neither wanting to end the embrace. It did not take Hailey long to wedge her way in between them, insisting that Beth give her some attention.

The last time Katherine had seen her mom was eight months earlier, right before she had started at the newspaper and not long after she had learned about her father.

Katherine was overcome with guilt. She'd been so full of anger and resentment against her mother, but the big lie she'd been struggling to forgive did not seem so big at that moment.

"You must be exhausted and starved," Beth said. "Hailey, too. Follow me."

Beth led them to the dining room table, so overloaded with trays of food it appeared it might collapse at the slightest touch. Katherine gave her mom a look of surprise, to which Beth said, "Joan has been here cooking all day, getting us ready for the well-wishers. Georgia, my friend at the library, also stopped by, followed by Barbara, who worked with Adrian at Seneca Foods. What we hadn't planned was everyone else bringing food."

She hesitated a moment. "Father Patterson also made a visit," Beth said.

Katherine rolled her eyes and smiled. "How'd that go?"

"Nowhere. It went nowhere. My dad and that priest have been going at it for longer than twenty years, each trying to prove who's more Irish."

"My money is on Grandpa," Katherine said, with a wink.

Mother and daughter took seats side-by-side at the small kitchen table, devouring the many different foods that they had piled onto their overflowing plates. Hailey stretched out at their feet and waited rather impatiently for the leftovers. With every bite Katherine felt warmer and the light got brighter. She did not ask her mom how she was doing, afraid of the answer. Instead, she took comfort in being with her.

After dinner, Beth placed the plates outside the screen door on the back porch, and Hailey commenced to clean them. Katherine headed for the den where her grandfather's favorite chair still graced its customary spot by the fireplace. She called to her mother, "If Grandpa were here, you know what he'd be doing right now, don't you?"

"Building a fire," Beth replied, walking back into the room.

"How about I make the fire and you make the coffee?"

Katherine took the smile on her mother's face as a yes, placing the kindling on the grate, lighting some pieces of newspaper, and watching the fire start right up. Grandpa Adrian would not have needed paper. She added three logs, and just as the wood was making its first crackles and pops, Beth brought in a tray with two cups of coffee and two slices of German chocolate cake.

"Mom, sit in Grandpa's chair," Katherine said, pulling up another one. "Oh, and let's not forget about Hailey. She's probably frozen, waiting by the door."

She hopped up and found Hailey standing outside, tail wagging and looking as happy as ever. Soon, the golden retriever was stretched out before the fire, too.

"Mom, I've decided Hailey should stay here with you," Katherine said as she watched her mother pet the dog.

Beth pulled her hand back, as if she had been caught doing something untoward. "Really? What's that all about?"

"It's about a lot of things." Katherine had tried to bring up the topic in the past, but her mother had always managed to avoid it whenever asked. Given the circumstances, maybe she would be more forthcoming. "Tell me how your eyes are doing," Katherine probed.

"I don't want to," Beth said and looked away from her daughter.

"I know you don't want to . . . but, please, tell me about your eyes."

"Well, they're beautiful blue eyes, and I've been busy waiting for the right man to discover them."

"How long are you going to do this, Mom? I'm not a child. I want to know . . . I need to know."

Beth heaved a sigh and nodded. "I'm suffering from a form of macular degeneration. It's complicated." She took a long sip of coffee. "My maculae are having difficulty, but it's not age-related MD, and without going into all the chromosome factors that have been explained to me in nauseating detail, the Xs and the Ys don't line up, so it's unlikely to be passed on to you."

"That's the least of my concerns," Katherine said rather sharply. "Please, try and forget you're a nurse for a minute. What I'm trying to find out is how well you're able to see. Is it affecting your work? Are you having trouble driving, getting around, reading?"

"I can still see, still drive, and still read; however, there are spots in my vision that I have to see around, and I need more light all the time to do even simple tasks. It's getting a little worse bit by bit. I've been told I need to learn how to better use my peripheral vision to compensate for losing my forward sight. So I'm working on that. How's that for a report?"

"Good report, and it confirms what I thought. I'm leaving Hailey with you for three reasons: She loves you, she loves it here where she can run free and not have to wait to be walked on a leash when I have the time, and she's also the best company in the world. I figure you could use a little of that right about now."

"Kind of you to leave out the part about the seeing-eye dog," Beth said, laughing.

Katherine glared at her mother. "I knew you'd make it into a joke, but I can also tell that you're concerned. So am I."

"Do you have any other big pronouncements before we go to bed?"

"Actually, I do."

A big smile spread across Beth's face. "That young man you've been dating. The spy or whatever it was you called him. Are you getting serious?"

"Mom, good news doesn't always have to be about a man. But no, I barely see Sean, though we did talk earlier today." She shook her head. "It doesn't matter; it's not about him."

"Is it about that bank investigation that you thought might involve Preston?" Beth came slightly forward in her chair. "Is he going to be implicated in some way?"

"No one knows yet, but he has told me he's 100 percent innocent, and I believe him. We can talk about that later, too. That's not what I want to discuss."

"Okay, I give up. What is it? Wait, if it's this serious, let me get us both some more coffee."

Beth got up and went to the kitchen, returning with a small coffee pot and filling their cups. After taking a nice long drink from hers, she sat back in Adrian's chair and announced, "I'm ready, sweetheart. Now, what's on your mind?"

"It's a request from me to you," Katherine said.

"What do you mean, a request? Is it about your grandfather? I know how close you were to him."

Katherine could see the reflection of the fire's dwindling flames in her mother's glassy eyes. "It's not about Grandpa," she said, walking over to her mother and kneeling down in front of her. She took her mother's hands in hers. "It's about you and me. I want to ask you to forgive me for not forgiving you sooner."

"Stop it," Beth said, shaking her head. "Let's talk honestly about forgiveness. I'm saying that to myself as much as to you."

"I thought we were talking honestly," Katherine replied with genuine surprise.

"You are. I haven't. It's not about forgiveness. It's about guilt. I lied about who your father was because I knew my mother and father couldn't accept—wouldn't accept—any other father than Larry. They adored him. I also was ashamed to have had a one-night stand. I didn't think they would understand. I took the easy way out, thinking it was the best way. I was lying to them, I was lying to myself, and as you found out all too well, I was eventually lying to you."

"Mom, why did you finally call Preston after all those years?" Katherine asked, her heart starting to race in anticipation of the answer with no idea what it might be.

"I wish I could say I came to my senses, but actually I did it out of fear. You were so smart and such a good reporter. You were checking into the details surrounding your birth, and it was obvious to me that you weren't going to give up until you found out the truth. We've talked about this before, so that isn't news to you.

"I also rationalized that telling Preston would be helpful to both of you because you were going to find out anyway." Beth finished her second cup of coffee in one long drink. "Here's the part you don't know: Until I made that call last spring, Preston had no idea I'd had a baby, much less *his* baby. I never even gave him a chance to step up and be a father.

"I don't know if I was scared that his family might take you away from me, or that I might actually love him and end up spurned. He was a rich young man from an even richer family. I felt he was out of my league. I couldn't see a happily ever after there. I had to accept what I was to him—a nurse who had cared for him in his time of need, and an unexpected one-night stand. You deserved so much more. I'm sorry, Katherine." Beth started to cry; Katherine held her tightly.

"Mom, you don't have to apologize. We all make mistakes."

"Oh, but I do. Once I heard how you talked about Preston and what he thought of you, I immediately saw how misguided I had been. What had I cost both of you? All those years the two of you could have had together. I completely misjudged Preston, and I denied you a father.

"All Preston ever wanted is what I now know he would have wanted then: to know everything about you and what he could do for you. I was so selfish to forfeit that for you. I felt like a fool when I realized he would have done the right thing all those years ago. I don't mean he would have married me. I mean he would have stepped up and been a father to you. If you take nothing else away from this conversation, take this—love that man, because he loves you."

Katherine put another log in the hearth, then came back and put her head in her mother's lap. They soon fell asleep, warmed by the fire but more so by their love for each other.

Chapter 14

"HI, CASEY, HOW THE HELL are you?" Alex barked into the phone. It had taken half-a-dozen tries over a three-day period but he finally had the company's old CFO on the line. "Why aren't you answering your phone? I couldn't even leave a message!"

"I'm a man of leisure now and don't want to be bothered by phone calls." Casey laughed loudly. "Seriously, I took the family on a trip and didn't want to be bothered by anything. Voice mail's always full; don't think I even know how to access it. Let me guess what's going on with you. Out of the goodness of your heart, you've left the slopes of Colorado for Manhattan so you can pull Preston's nuts out of the fire yet again."

"Maybe yours, too, my friend."

"Ah, but I didn't put them there."

"Believe me, I know. Your dear friend Disley did the honors."

Casey let out a growl. "I knew I shouldn't have taken this call. I hate to ask, but what is going on with the company that I still hold stock in?"

"Three major problems: One, I can't find your stash of Snickers; two, I need your eyes on the financials; and three, I need your input on Robert Reynolds and how you think he might fit into the shenanigans we've all been reading about."

"Other than the Snickers, I don't particularly want to get into any of this. It's why I left. Washed my hands of the whole mess."

81

Alex knew his window with Casey was small. "Now, don't get upset with me for saying this, Casey, but walking away isn't going to work for any of us. We're all shareholders, and we're all exposed. I can stay on for as long it takes, but this company needs you, and it needs you now. Preston has a lot on his plate, and he's doing better, but he needs the direction only you can provide, both fiscally and professionally as it relates to operations. I'm good, but I'm not you."

"I can read," Casey said, not at all politely. "I feel bad for Preston, I do, but he believed in Disley, no matter how much I tried to convince him the guy was poison."

"I know Disley being kept on is a sore point with you, and rightly so. That said, your staying away from this company could be what puts it under. If that happens, we all leave with nothing. I talked with Preston. He gets it. He's made me interim CEO."

"Well, I'll be, a start in the right direction, at least the part about Preston getting it. I'm also glad you've taken charge. What now?"

"I need to find out if the situation is as bad as I think it is, and I want you to help me figure it out. After I know where we are, I can draft a short-term response to our customers and the public, and then craft a strategic turnaround plan."

"Preston's going along with all of this?" Casey asked, sounding more than a little skeptical.

"Preston may not always pay attention, but he's not flaky and he's certainly not stupid. He knows he has his hands full, and he doesn't want to lose this company."

"So how are you going to maintain control? I couldn't do it."

"I believe you and I together can get things moving in the right direction, and keep it that way. First, I need to know where we are with all this. We may need to restructure. I want Preston, Marcia, you, and me—the stockholders—to get together as soon as possible and have a heart-to-heart talk."

There was a long pause before Casey said, "When I heard that Preston was a potential co-conspirator, I wondered who else might get that tag. You? Me? Marcia? I did call a lawyer, and he told me he doubted I have anything to worry about, but in the next breath he said I'd probably be called as a witness. He also said not to talk to anybody, so I'm already in trouble for talking to you."

Alex could not keep from holding back a laugh; Casey had a way of never letting on whether or not he was serious. "Call him back and ask if you can talk to the three of us if we limit the conversation to how we can restructure the company. If we don't get a handle on things, we're going to lose market share—and our equity—fast."

"Let me talk with my lawyer and I'll call you back. I knew I shouldn't have taken your call."

Both men laughed at that and hung up. Two hours later, Casey called Alex back. "Do you have permission to talk to me?" Alex asked after Casey made a few jokes without getting to the point.

"Only if you buy me a tin of Whammies."

"What the hell is a Whammy?"

"I'll show you when I see you. How do you want to do this?"

"I'd like to meet with you first. If that goes well, then with you and Marcia. Then, the three of us with Preston."

"You're plotting and scheming again, aren't you?"

"Yeah, but in a good way. You'll like it. Is there any way you could meet with me in the next day or two?"

"Let me check with my bride and make sure where my boys are going to be with hockey and whatever at school. If I can make it, where do you want to meet?"

"Everything's here," Alex said. "How about your old office?"

"Unless you hear from me otherwise, I'll be there tomorrow afternoon by three-thirty."

As soon as he heard the click of Casey's phone, Alex let out a loud "Whoop!" Phase I of his plan was in place.

• • •

The next day Alex was at his desk working out the restructuring between bites of a sandwich from a commissary truck that stopped by the dealership every day around noon. He looked up to see Casey standing in the doorway, holding a briefcase in one hand and a red-and-brown tin in the other. After shaking hands and exchanging greetings, Alex said, "I didn't expect you until later today."

Casey put his briefcase on the floor and the tin on the desk and took a seat. "I decided I couldn't wait." He glanced at the mass of papers on the desktop. "This used to be my desk. How's it feel?"

"It still feels like your desk."

"There they are," Casey said, pushing the tin at Alex.

"Are what?"

"What do you think they are? They're the Whammies you bought me." Alex pulled off the lid to find twelve chocolates with an added confection on top of each.

"While you're thinking about whether or not to eat one, give me two. That's sea salt you're looking at. If you were with the program, you'd know that. There's caramel and a pretzel at the bottom of that can, too." Casey had already begun chewing one of the candies before he had spit out the last word.

"What happened to your craving for Snickers bars?"

"These are more upscale. By the way, hope you hate 'em— means more for me."

Alex shook his head as Casey eyed another piece of candy.

"You done?" Alex asked.

"For now, I suppose," Casey said. "What you got for me?"

Alex led him over to a large table and started in on the stack of financials he had lugged in with him. Casey quickly began scanning the documents. Listening to him as he made some preliminary comments, Alex was reminded once again that the amiable-appearing marshmallow had the memory of an elephant and the bite of a tiger.

Without a single break, they worked in earnest throughout the afternoon, designing a *pro forma* for the company's next six months. They also penciled in a best case/worst case revenue forecast, with special attention to the payables based on sliding metrics. Only when they were both satisfied they had done all that could possibly be done did they take a pause and return to the desk.

Convinced he had an accurate picture of the firm's current financial condition, Alex was struggling with just how deeply to go into the rest of the fiasco. Knowing Casey as well as he did, there was a real possibility the man would not stay on if he were told the "other part" of the story; however, in fairness it could not be kept from him any longer.

"There's more to this mess than the financials," Alex said, trepidation dripping from each word.

"Always is," Casey said calmly, surprising Alex.

Taking that as a green light, Alex pulled out the October gross sheets from another stack on the desk, as well as the numbers for the four Bentleys and the Rolls. He handed them over to Casey, who flipped through each sheet, one by one, before saying anything.

"There it is." His eyes narrowed.

Alex gave a single nod.

"You showed this to Preston?" Casey asked, making a note on one page.

"I did. I told him I thought this should be turned over to the FBI."

"He agreed?"

"Yes, but he also said it didn't constitute a crime, just lousy business."

"If this is all there is to it, I'd agree with him. I'll bet he never saw any of this at the time. If he did, he would have raised holy hell. Preston gets preoccupied, but he's not dishonest." Casey reached for another Whammy.

"Preston said he didn't know a thing about any of it, and I believe him," Alex said. He then told Casey about the recent meeting with the entire Manhattan staff, and how Robert Reynolds had ducked out and later resigned.

"Not surprising," Casey said. "Came in with Disley. Runs downhill. So why'd they do it? I'm saying it's those two, by the way. It can't be anyone else."

"They both gave a cock-and-bull story about making the deal to curry favor with the bank," said Alex. He went on to explain what little he knew about BNA's misconduct and who he thought might be involved in the scheme.

"Preston being mentioned as an unindicted co-conspirator in this doesn't necessarily mean that the feds have something else," Alex added.

"So we have at the least a PR question about Preston's connection, and we have BNA to deal with as well," Casey said, trying to chew politely.

"From what I've read—and all any of us are getting is public knowledge, basically what we're seeing in the newspapers—the bank has some serious questions to answer. Disley's buddy, Terry Thompson, got arrested, too." Alex sighed. "My biggest fear is that they'll pull the plug on our inventory financing and our cap loans."

"Neither of which is in default," Casey said.

"Except for the 'deemed financially insecure' covenant," Alex quickly reminded him.

Casey nodded. "You want me to reassure Tom Gallagher at BNA Charlotte, even though things have now been moved to Goldberg here in New York City."

"Right," Alex said, taking Casey's comment as an indication that he had an interest in personally participating in the firm's fight. "That brings me to the next piece. The only way BNA is going to believe in us is if you have skin in the game or—"

"I'm not putting money into this dealership," Casey said flatly.

Alex could see pushing him any harder was out of the question. "Let's stop here," Alex said. "I appreciate your coming in. I couldn't do this without you." He gave Casey a hopeful look. "How late can you stay?"

"A little while longer. My boys are playing hockey, and I want to catch what I can of the game. I know we're in a tight spot, but if we use our heads, we can figure a way out. However, I want to meet with Marcia alone before I do anything else." He smiled at Alex. "We're lucky to have you here."

Alex and Casey shook hands.

Even if it was only a temporary reprieve, a huge weight had been lifted from Alex's shoulders. For the first time since coming back on board, he felt a modicum of relief.

"Keep the rest of the Whammies," Casey said. "They'll help your disposition. Look at what they do for me."

Both men laughed. It was a much-needed momentary lull in the building storm.

CHAPTER 15

THE DAY OF THE FUNERAL dawned in a fine gray mist, as if it, too, were in mourning. Beth walked solemnly with her daughter and Joan to the United Church. Katherine had wanted someone to drive them, but Beth would not have it. She needed to feel the icy air on her skin if only to confirm she was still alive. She had been so numb since losing her father. Her chest swelled when she noticed more cars in the church parking lot than she had seen in one place in Marion in a long time.

As they entered the church, Reverend Wesley greeted them in a small room off the sanctuary. They thanked him and quietly took their seats, waiting for the service to begin. Lost in grief, neither Beth nor Katherine noticed the tall man with dark hair in the finely tailored suit who knocked softly on the church's partially open front door, although the reverend welcomed him like a member of the congregation.

In the middle of a conversation with Joan and two of Adrian's close friends, Beth's breath caught in her throat as she glimpsed Reverend Wesley walking Preston into the room.

"There's someone who would like to speak with you," the minister said.

Beth gave a slight nod. She walked to a table set off to the side and poured herself a cup of coffee, wishing it were something stronger. Suddenly, she could feel the man's presence in the room as if he were already standing right next to her. Then, as if her thoughts had magically materialized him, she felt a gentle squeeze on her shoulder.

"Hello, Beth," Preston said, taking her hand. "I'm so sorry for your loss, and Katherine's. I just wanted to see you . . . here, rather than from a distance. I hope that's okay?"

She indicated it was, realizing she was inexplicably holding his hand as if she would never let go. If Preston noticed, he did not seem to mind; he simply led her back to her chair, where she collapsed, her body shaking and her mouth unable to form words. He was taller than she remembered, and even better looking. How could the years have been so good to him and so cruel to her?

By then, Katherine had also spotted her father, and she stood to embrace him, kissing him lightly on his cheek. "Thank you for coming," she said.

As Beth watched Katherine and Preston talking together, she thought how beautiful her daughter looked. If anything, living in the city had given her more style and independence. Her light brown hair had grown longer since she had left Marion, and her cobalt, knee-length dress and matching jacket were the perfect complement to her blue eyes.

"There is no place else I would be today," Preston said, his heart aching at the sadness in his daughter's eyes.

Katherine invited Preston to join them, and Beth composed herself enough to introduce Preston to Joan. A few of Beth's other close friends had made their way into the room, including three nurses from Rochester General and an elderly woman who had once been Beth's high-school English teacher. Beth guessed the woman had to be at least ninety.

She watched her teacher make her way over, and then in a strong voice that belied the tubes in her nose and the portable oxygen tank strapped to her walker, the woman said, "We never get over it, my dear, but with God's help, we get through it. And God gave you old friends to help you do just that." The tiny old teacher nodded resolutely, and then took a seat.

The group sat quietly after that until it was time for the minister to lead everyone into the sanctuary, with Beth, Katherine, Joan, and Preston taking their places in the front pew.

• • •

Katherine counted more than seventy people in the church, many of whom she did not know. However, there were some familiar faces, one of which belonged to Harry. She spotted him sitting with a group of ten men by themselves in the back pew. When her eyes locked onto his, he gave a quick wave with his right hand. Katherine nodded, doing her best to hold it together.

It was not easy. Each story the reverend shared about her grandfather made her miss him more, and there were so many of them, each told with simple elegance. He talked about the friends Adrian Kelly had made over the years, from the men who had hunted with him, to his farmer friends, to the workers at Seneca Foods, to the youngsters he used to entertain with his stories. He emphasized the level of respect Adrian had earned in the community, and the example he had set for young and old alike. "Adrian Kelly was a man of many interests who appreciated how short our time on this earth is," the preacher said. "Unlike most of us, he worked hard to live each day like it was his last. For Adrian that meant being open to making new friends wherever he found them."

When his words turned to their immediate family, Katherine was touched by the attention paid her grandmother and mother, as he shared stories about what a devoted husband her grandfather had been, as well as a father. Katherine's tears began to fall as the reverend recalled how close Adrian had been to his only grandchild. He made reference to specific conversations he'd had with Adrian to illustrate how proud the grandfather had been of the granddaughter. At one point, Katherine, already short of breath, feared her chest would burst if the minister shared one more memory.

On the drive to Marion from the city, Katherine had told herself that she would remain in control. She realized how naïve that had been. She was so grateful that her mother's friends were there, and Preston, too.

Her thoughts suddenly darkened. What about her friends? Why wasn't Susan there? Or Sean? Feeling as if she did not have a friend in the world, Katherine began to weep. Preston and her mother both immediately reached for the hand of hers closest to them. It was just the comfort their daughter needed.

• • •

At the cemetery, Beth, Katherine, and Preston stood together next to the Kelly family plot, where Adrian would join his wife for eternity. Just where her grandpa had wanted to be. They were lucky to have had him as long as they did.

The graveside service was short, and Katherine found herself feeling grateful for that. The stress of the day had brought on the familiar wavy lines in her vision. Over and over she said under her breath, "This is not about me. This is not about me," but the mantra did no good. She had to stay strong for her mom.

Afterwards, nearly everyone gathered at the house, with most folks moving quickly to the dining room. Joan, having left the service early, was ready for them with a spread of breads, cold cuts, salads, and a crock-pot full of venison stew. The conversation was lively, the stories even more plentiful, and the mood palpably lighter as everyone dug into the food. Hailey made the rounds, becoming best friends with everybody, one person at a time, all the while keeping a keen eye on the dining room table in case a tasty scrap should fall.

Harry, for his part, was in true form, holding court and keeping Joan and others in stitches. Katherine was initially caught off guard at how comfortable her mom and Harry seemed with each other, but then remembered Harry lived in Batavia, only a couple of hours away, and surely through the years Adrian had had cause to invite his old friend back to the house while her mom was there. Maybe what should have surprised her was that Harry had shown up to the funeral with his entire band—who did that?—but as the Oompah

Man and his mates started setting up their instruments in the living room, nothing could have seemed more natural. Grandpa would have loved it. A true Irishman, he had always been more comfortable with the idea of a wake—complete with beer and music—than a funeral service.

As Katherine surveyed more of the crowd, her eyes came to a rest on Harry and Preston, and she pursed her lips. What are they so deep in conversation about over there? They both look so tense. She worried maybe something else dreadful might have happened.

She shook off her concern and scanned the room for her mom. Whatever was going on with those two, it would have to wait. Her first priority was her mother.

• • •

Preston watched Harry weave through the crowd, heading straight for him like a man on a mission. He wanted to talk to Harry, but not necessarily that minute. His mind was still on the service, particularly what the minister had said about Adrian. He wished he could have known him.

"Hey, Big Guy. Thanks for showing up."

Preston shook Harry's extended hand. "Were you close to Katherine's grandfather?"

"Yes, we go way back. We shoot and hunt together . . . *did* shoot and hunt together. In fact, I have something important I need to do for Adrian down at the gun club. Why don't you ride along with me?"

"Now?" Preston asked. His eyes darted to Beth, who was sitting in her father's old chair by the fire silently weeping but surrounded by friends.

"Come on," Harry urged. "I could use your help."

Preston looked about for Katherine, who was sitting across the room, keeping an eye on her mother.

"They'll be fine until we get back," Harry assured him. "They're in good hands."

"Still, I hate to leave them," Preston said, looking uncertain.

"We're only talking about a couple hours. It might make you feel better."

Suddenly Preston remembered he was talking to someone who had just buried a dear old friend; Harry could probably use some company as well. "Okay, as long as we're not gone for too long."

•••

The quarter-mile, dirt road leading to the club was slick with snow and ice. Harry parked out front, and Preston followed him into the small ranch-style building. Harry pointed Preston to some chairs around a long, metallic folding table in the middle of the large open room. Preston sat down and tried to take in the shelves full of trophies, a wall of portraits, and a cabinet containing shot-guns and a few boxes of ammunition.

"So why are we here, Harry?"

"Tradition," Harry said as he pulled a black band out of his pocket. "They help at times like these, and this is one of ours."

Preston watched Harry move toward the wall of hunter por-traits with purpose. Then, he carefully placed the black elastic band across the bottom of one, like a ballplayer might don a black arm-band for a fallen teammate, and then he stood before his friend's picture without saying a word. Preston had never seen the man qui-et for so long.

"He meant a lot to you," Preston said, interrupting the silence.

Harry nodded, then walked back and sat down across from Preston. "I'd offer you some coffee, but we're kind of closed down until the weather gets a little better."

"I'm fine," Preston said.

"You don't look fine," Harry retorted.

He was right. "The funeral. Beth losing her father. Katherine, her grandfather. You, your old friend."

"Yeah. It sucks," Harry said. "Makes you feel all alone in the world." Preston stared at the vinyl floor.

"I will never forget him," Harry said, gesturing to Adrian's picture. "I take comfort knowing he'll always be here on that wall when I visit, looking down on all of us as we toast his memory and remember better times. Nobody can take that away from me. I learned that when we lost Joe. I'm okay, but it's clear to me that you're not. Work? Problems at home? Something else?"

Preston looked up. "Have a lot going on right now."

"Too damn vague," Harry said. "Cut to the chase."

Preston cupped his head in his hands, and then looked up at Harry, the blood draining from his face. "My former CFO was arrested. The company is in trouble again. Marcia . . ."

"Whoa there, one thing at a time," Harry said. "You didn't do anything wrong, did you?"

"No," Preston said, in a barely audible voice and looking down again. "That hasn't kept me from getting caught up in all of it."

Harry's eyes opened wide. "I hear you, man. I know the feeling."

He slapped both knees, stood, and headed across the room to the gun cabinet. He unlocked it and carefully removed a double barrel shotgun.

"This is a Beretta 471 Silver Hawk," he said. He sighted it and pretended to aim at something outside the window. "Can't wait for spring," he said. "Can you?" He placed the gun on the table.

"I'm not thinking of spring, Harry. Got to survive the winter first."

"You're not thinking of offing yourself, are you?"

Preston laughed out loud. "You mean like jumping off a bridge?"

The look on Harry's face grew grim. "There's plenty of ways to do it. I just asked . . . if you had ever considered it."

"No, Harry."

"Ever know someone who thought life had gotten so bad he wanted to?" Harry asked.

Preston thought for a moment and shook his head. "No, can't say that I have."

"Well you're wrong about that," Harry said.

"What are you talking about?"

"You're wrong about not knowing somebody who wanted to kill himself."

"You have?"

"Yes, but that's not who I'm talking about."

"I don't understand what you're getting at, Harry."

"I know you don't, Big Guy."

Preston struggled to come up with the name of another person, but failed. Maybe this was about Harry after all—despite what he said to the contrary. He was bipolar, and probably an emotional wreck right now. Preston thought he had better tread lightly.

"We should get back," Preston said.

"Joe Hart."

"What about Joe Hart?" He paused. "You're telling me Joe contemplated suicide?"

"Yeah, that's exactly what I'm saying."

"How would you know that?" Preston asked.

"He told me."

"Why?"

"Maybe 'cause he's the guy who kept me from killing myself."

Absentmindedly, Preston stared at the shotgun, and with a shaky hand rubbed its wooden stock. Joe Hart? He would have been less surprised if Harry had said, "the Pope."

"Why do you think Joe went to the mountains?" Harry asked. "You don't know, do you?"

"No."

"You never asked him. Even if you had, he probably wouldn't have told you. Talking to you is like talking to a wall, only a wall has more feelings."

Preston pushed away the shotgun and began to circle the room. Harry sat still. Preston came back and sat down. "Anything more you'd like to share to enlighten me?"

"Yeah. After Joe's wife was killed, my take is he put the kid who shot her out of his mind. He knew nothing would bring Ashley back. He thought about talking to a shrink, but he didn't think that would help, either. So instead, he went to the mountains—back to his roots—trying to make some sense out of something senseless."

Preston sat quietly.

"You listening to me? Are you getting any of this?" Harry asked, placing the gun back in the cabinet and carefully locking the door.

Preston's fists clenched so hard he could feel his fingernails digging into his palms. "I'm listening, but I don't know where you're going with all of this. You don't know me. You don't know what I'm dealing with right now, so if you think this is helping, you're wrong. We should get back to the house."

He stood and began walking to the door.

"Preston, why do you think Joe came down from those mountains?"

Preston stopped and slowly turned around.

"Never thought to ask him, did you?"

"I'm well aware of why he came down." Preston said.

"Then tell me why."

"To save my ass," Preston shouted.

"Wrong again," Harry shouted back. "It isn't always about you, Preston."

Taking his seat again, Preston rested his hands on the edge of the table. He was trying his best not to add more tension to the room, but he knew Harry was on a roll—if not out of control—and like a runaway train, there was not much to do until it came to a stop on its own.

"Joe had made it clear to you that night he wasn't going to take your case," Harry said. "Then before he went to sleep, he heard you crying like a baby to Casey about losing your wife. He said it was the first sincere thing he had heard you say all day."

"What . . .?" Preston heard himself say.

He got up and went over to the window, needing no reminder of the words Joe had spoken that day. He remembered every one of them and always would. He turned and looked at Harry, speechless and with a question in his eye.

"In the end, Joe felt no man should lose his wife," Harry continued. "He would never have told you that, and I would never have mentioned it now, except I lost my best friend. Honestly, I've learned the hard way that you can't get anywhere by blaming your problems on anybody else."

Though Preston was shaken all the way to his center, he tried to make sense out of the last thing Harry had said.

"I'll bet that you never once asked him about his wife. Why? You were too busy thinking about yourself. If you're not too pissed off at me, consider what that says about *you*."

Preston slowly shook his head. "I'm not upset with you. You're right. I considered Joe a friend. I should have asked him those questions. I'm surprised—but probably shouldn't be—that you're the one having to teach me this."

It was Harry's turn to get up and check outside. "Snow's stopped. Time we got back to Beth's."

"Before we go, I'd like to ask you for something, Harry. I'm probably the last person you want to help, but if it'd make you feel better, I think in helping me you'd also be helping Beth and Katherine."

"I'm listening," Harry said.

"I'd like to continue this conversation with you," said Preston.

"Now?" Harry asked.

"No. Over time," Preston said. "I need to think about all of this. I have more than a hundred people working for me, not to mention teams of lawyers and advisers. What I need is a friend, one I can trust to talk to me straight, the way you have tonight. You want honesty? I only started out trying to develop a relationship with you as an obligation to Joe. We're so different. I've never been good at letting people in, but you found a way."

"Glad you got to know the Oompah Man, are ya? I write, play, and sing music. My job is to hit the right note."

"Keep singing, Harry. I need it."

CHAPTER 16

THE NEXT MORNING PRESTON could not believe how his talk with Harry had cleared his head. He felt as if he were a bear coming out of hibernation. As he drove to Beth's house, he saw all kinds of birds in the air and the rolling acres of open farmland covered in untouched blankets of snow. To his left, the meandering Ganargua Creek was frozen solid.

The landscape reminded Preston of his first foray into the Adirondacks as a fifteen-year-old with his father and how they had met another fifteen-year-old there named Joe Hart, the nephew of Howard Buckingham, his father's guide. Until that day the only landscape Preston had previously seen involved tall buildings in New York City. He had scoffed at the wilderness back then; a third of a century later, he wondered how he could ever have forgotten how beautiful it was.

When he had called Beth the night before to tell her he wanted to stop by the following day to talk with Katherine, Beth had told him she also wanted to talk to him. He arrived at her house by mid-morning, and she was there to greet him with Hailey at her side.

"Am I too early?" Preston asked as Beth let him in.

"Not at all," she replied. "Kat's at the grave site. She wanted to be alone with her grandpa. This is actually a good time, because I wanted to speak with you alone. Would you like something to eat? Some coffee?"

"Just coffee would be great," Preston said, pleased that Beth wanted to speak with him, even if he did not know what about.

She poured them both a cup. "It's been a long time, Preston. So much has happened. In a way it seems peculiar to meet again . . . especially at a time like this. I wish I could be more—"

"I think you're doing just fine," Preston interrupted.

"I want to thank you for being so accepting of Katherine."

"I want to thank you for the gift of my daughter. She's brought so much joy and light into my life already. I can't explain how much she means to me."

"Tell me about Marcia. Kat was worried at first how Marcia would react to her." Beth set her cup down. "Kat was afraid that by showing up in your life so suddenly, Marcia might have held it against you, and her, too."

"She was shocked at first, but Marcia is a wonderful woman. She's been great with Katherine all the way around. I'm so fortunate she's my wife. I don't deserve her. I've let her down in a lot of ways."

"How could you possibly have let her down, Preston? Seems to me you've given her a fairy tale of a life."

Preston described the circumstances surrounding the birth of their son so late in their marriage, and then the shock of finding out P.J. had been born nearly deaf. "Our pediatrician told us to wait and see if his hearing developed. I was in denial, and wanted to believe P.J. might grow out of it, but Marcia wouldn't have it. She did exhaustive research, and wanted to follow the advice of The Clarke School and have P.J. fitted with hearing aids immediately."

"You resisted?"

"I didn't see my actions as resisting. Besides wanting to wait, I couldn't accept that I'd had anything to do with bringing an impaired child into the world. I can see now why she thought I was thwarting her efforts at every turn. I was an idiot."

"Marcia took your reaction as a personal rebuke?"

"She was furious at me—and then some. How'd you know?"

"As a mother, I can understand where Marcia was coming from, but it's not an abnormal reaction for a person . . ."

For no apparent reason, Beth suddenly stopped mid-sentence. Preston used the moment to finish his coffee, which Beth quickly refilled. He thanked her and said, "Marcia's been everything to me. I've tried to be supportive—and finally got on board with all her plans for P.J., but there have always been times when I got it wrong. I'm just now learning how wrong." He smiled sadly. "I'm a bit down on myself right now, if you can't tell. This is no time to bore you with my problems."

"Nonsense," Beth said. They sat quietly for a few minutes, until Beth broke the silence with a question. "It will be lunchtime soon, and we have tons of food. Everyone has been so kind. Can I make up something for you to take on your way back to the city?"

"I'd love that," Preston said. "Just fix me whatever's easiest. I'm not going back to the city, though. Tomorrow, I'm flying to San Francisco for business."

As Beth was preparing a couple of mammoth ham sandwiches, she said, "I've been following your career for . . . well, since we . . . met."

He followed her into the kitchen. "You have?" The surprise in his voice was real. "I'm flattered. It's probably too early to ask you a lot of questions about you and the past twenty-four years."

Beth smiled in a way that reminded Preston of what had drawn him to her when she had been his nurse all those years ago.

"I don't mind," she said, "It's the least I can do after upending your life. I suppose Katherine has told you about my vision problems. I've been through debilitating diseases with many patients, but you're never prepared when it happens to you. The whole thing has overwhelmed me at times."

"Katherine did say you had some eye issues, but she didn't go into detail. It sounds like it could be serious."

"Yes, but it's more than that, and I want to get this out before she gets back." Beth quickly glanced out the side window to the empty driveway. "Can you forgive me for not telling you about Katherine? She was as much yours as mine. I feel terrible that I never let you know you had a daughter."

Beth wiped a tear from her cheek using the edge of her apron. She shooed Preston away when he stepped closer to comfort her.

"You're a wonderful person, Beth, and a good mother. I am so grateful that you did contact me. What you did was a great blessing for me. You gave me a daughter, one of the most special people I have ever known."

Beth looked at Preston with great pain in her eyes. This time when he drew her close she did not pull back or push him away.

"You're a good man, Preston Wilson."

"More and more I see room for improvement. I'd like to think I would have welcomed your news back then, but honestly, I don't know if I would have, Beth. I've spent a lot of my life being a pretty selfish guy. My wife could tell you how long it took for me to come around. Let's just give each other a break and agree that this all played out just the way fate intended, okay?"

Beth smiled ruefully. "I don't care what you say, Preston, Katherine is lucky to have you as a father."

It was Preston's turn now to be embarrassed, and so he changed the subject. "You know what I would like to see, Beth? Do you have any pictures of Kat while she was growing up?"

Beth's face brightened. "When did you start calling her Kat?"

"I don't know. I guess the closer we became, the more comfortable I felt about using a nickname. She never told me not to. You don't like me calling her that?"

Beth grinned, but Preston could have sworn it was tinged with sadness. "Calling her Kat is just fine; that's what I call her, too. But if you want to prevent an avalanche of tears, just don't call her Kitten. That was her grandfather's name for her."

Preston smiled and took a seat. "I'm curious about something else, Beth. What did Adrian say when he learned I was her father?"

Beth's face became so ashen that she looked as if she might faint. Again, she waved him off, and when she spoke her voice was tight and low.

"That's the other gorilla in the room. I never told my father until after I had to tell Katherine. I was worried that if he learned after all these years that she wasn't the daughter of a pilot who died serving his country, it would break his heart. I waited too long to tell him she was born as the result of . . . well . . . you know."

Preston took both her hands in his. "Beth, stop, it's not your fault. It was a difficult situation. You did the best you could."

"No, I took the easy way out." She shook her head. "At least now you know."

Preston could tell their talk had left Beth exhausted. She needed a diversion.

"Do you have any scrapbooks?" he asked.

Beth nodded as the color returned to her face. She motioned for him to wait, went upstairs, and returned with an armful of colorful scrapbooks.

"Let's go into the den so we can spread these out," she suggested. "I'll go ahead and bring in some of those sandwiches, too."

They poured over scrapbook after scrapbook for more than an hour. Preston studied every picture, asking countless questions about each and every one of them. He stopped for a long time at a picture of Katherine skating on one of the small ponds by their house, something she had told him about in one of their talks about her childhood. He recalled that Katherine always talked excitedly when she described growing up in Marion: Her cheerleading days. The prom. Hanging out with friends. Shooting skeet with her grandfather. Cooking with her mother. Now Preston was finally there in that same tiny village, taking in everything, seeing it the way she did.

Beth and Preston's private time together was eventually interrupted by Katherine bounding up the steps of the front porch and into the house. Hailey gave her a hero's welcome with paws on her shoulders.

"How are you doing, sweetheart?" Beth asked.

"I'm okay . . . after I visited Grandpa, I went to Saint Gregory's and lit two candles, one for Grandpa and one for Grandma. Then I took a slow drive on some back roads in Grandpa's pickup truck. I needed to do that. I needed to smell that musty cigar scent of him. I needed to play some of that old country AM music he always insisted on listening to when we rode together. It helped."

"I'm going to go to Saint Gregory's this afternoon, too," Beth said. "Do you want to join us, Preston?"

Preston hesitated. He had planned to drive back to Rochester and catch a flight to San Francisco that evening so he could check on Wilson's Auto Plaza, but he had also wanted to spend some time with Katherine before he left town. "Gee, I'd love to, but I was hoping do something with Kat before I go."

"I understand," Beth replied. Her mood seemed to have changed for the better.

Katherine got up and gave her father a hug. "How exactly would you like to spend time with me?"

"How far is it to the nearest lock on the Erie Canal?"

"Erie Canal? Didn't know you were into raising and lowering boats."

"Actually, I am. A long time ago I did some research on the connection between Lake Erie, the Erie Canal, the Hudson River, and New York City. I love history."

"You do? Let's go, then. Old Lock 56 in Lyons is the closest. It used to be called the Poorhouse Lock. It's still operating." Katherine gave her parents an odd look before smiling at them. "I see you two have been going through the old scrapbooks. Think I'll leave you alone with that while I take Hailey for a walk."

"Smart girl," Preston said after Katherine had left with the big golden retriever.

"She takes after you."

"Let's hope she got only the best from each of us."

"Preston, thank you for coming and thank you for taking the time to talk," Beth said. "I hope your business troubles work out, but more importantly I hope you, Marcia, and P.J. find some peace. You're so lucky to have a family. Please don't worry about me. My father made sure I would never want for anything. That's how he was, thinking about others to the end." She took a deep breath. "I'm going to be okay. I hope we can stay in touch, if only as parents, because that's what we are. It may well take both of us to see her through life."

"I wouldn't have it any other way, Beth. I'm here for the long haul. Thank you for giving me an extraordinary daughter and a big sister for my son."

● ● ●

Katherine drove, and it took them less than an hour to reach Lock 56. Preston savored every moment with his daughter, as she explained the history of the towns along the way, their origins, how they were developed, where they were today. As she talked, Preston was amazed at her incisive grasp of history, culture, and her insatiable appetite to learn more. After examining Lock 28-A and the canal's dry-dock complex, they visited the locks between Lyons and Newark and Lock 28-B in Newark. Looking out over the canals, Preston could envision rafts coming down the narrow waterways, pulled by mules atop the high banks along the sides.

On their way home, he asked what she was working on at the newspaper. She told him about Alice, and how she was going to try to convince her editor to let her work on a bank fraud case in Braydon, in which Alice and several others like her had lost their life savings. Then, she threw away the holdback.

"It's frustrating watching others write about what's going on with BNA, but my editor won't let me work the story because I'm so close to you. Even though it was the BNA guys I investigated, not your car business, I guess he wants to avoid any perceived conflict of interest."

"That must have been tough on you," Preston said, although he was more than pleased with the decision her boss had made.

Katherine's eyes narrowed. "I hope things work out for you."

"Your mother just said the same thing. It means a lot to have both of you supporting me." He gave Katherine's arm a tender squeeze. "My lawyer told me not to talk to anybody, but that doesn't include you. I want you to know, I haven't committed any crime, though a dark cloud hangs over my head every day. Not to mention what Marcia and my employees are going through."

"Can your lawyer get you out of the unindicted co-conspirator designation?"

"He says it's up to the prosecutor."

"What do you think?"

"I think I've made mistakes. Hiring Disley for starters. He was an old friend, but I should have paid more attention to what he was doing."

"What's your plan now?"

"I've brought in Alex Herman. He knows this business. Remember when I told you about Joe Hart saving my bacon a couple of years ago?"

"Of course I do. We discussed it the first time we had lunch at the 21 Club. How could a girl forget that?" She smiled coyly.

He turned to face his daughter. "Joe brought Alex in as part of that workout. Afterwards, he oversaw the operations of all of our stores for a while. Now he's helping us with Manhattan. I want to get to the bottom of this."

Katherine looked straight at Preston. "I know you're innocent."

"You can't know how glad I am to hear you say that. What I've told you is about all I can say right now."

Preston did not want to admit that his sketchy facts were all he had to go on, and he wanted to change the subject. "I know this has been a difficult and stressful time for you and your mom. She's quite a woman."

"She's awesome. I've been mad at her for not telling me about you sooner, but I'm finally getting over it. She's always been there for me." Katherine paused. "I'm worried about her now without Grandpa."

"I think she'll be fine."

It wasn't long before Katherine was heading up the long driveway to her childhood home. Preston wanted to say good-bye to Beth one more time. Hailey was the first to greet him, complete with a stand-up, two-paws-on-the-chest kiss that almost knocked him over. He was more than mildly surprised, since the dog usually jumped on Katherine. Beth tried to convince him to stay over and leave early in the morning for the airport, but he begged off. His business demanded that he get back to work.

Preston whispered in Beth's ear as they both stood at the door, "If there's anything I can do to help either of you, I want you to let me know. I'll be checking in."

"It was so good of you to come," Beth said tearfully, giving him a warm embrace. "Especially with all you have going on. It meant a lot to both of us."

"I'll see you soon, Kat," Preston said, giving her a prolonged hug. "I love you."

"I love you, too," she answered.

Beth smiled affectionately at them both, making it clear she appreciated hearing the words just as much as they enjoyed saying them.

CHAPTER 17

THAT DAY, AFTER PRESTON LEFT THEM to their new reality, Katherine found herself feeling lonelier than at any time in her life. She could only imagine how her mom must feel. She instinctively knew this was the easy part, and that the rough time for her mother, and probably herself, would be in the months and years down the line. What she did not know was if Hailey's presence would be enough to see her mother through it. As lovable as the big dog was, how could she possibly fill the void of a father? As she packed her bags, she realized saying good-bye to her mother this time would be one of the hardest things she had ever done.

When Katherine had left Marion eight months earlier, it had no longer felt like home to her—and she had thought it never would again. The contrast between her busy, challenging life in the Hamptons and her provincial childhood in Marion was extreme but also desirable. Leaving the town of her youth had been a release of sorts, an escape from a run-of-the-mill life to a promise of something more.

It would be different leaving her mother behind without her grandpa to look after her, and perhaps of greater importance, without anyone for her to take care of in his absence. After all, if her mother could not be a nurse, how else would she feel needed?

Worse yet, what about her eye problems? Katherine's mom acted as if she were in control. But was she? Katherine had researched macular degeneration, but without knowing the particulars, it was impossible to accurately understand Beth's condition. She would have liked to talk to her mom's retina specialist, but she did not want Beth to think she was looking over her shoulder. At times, her mom could be an extremely private woman.

Uncomfortable with feeling so helpless when it came to her mom's condition, Katherine decided to have one more heart-to-heart talk with her mother before leaving.

"Mom, there are so many things I came to say to you that I still haven't said. I hate going back to the Hamptons just now," Katherine confided.

"I know, sweetheart. I hate to see you go, but you have to. You have a job, remember? They need you there." Beth forced a smile. "I know you're worried about me, but I'll be fine. I promise to be a good girl and call you at least once every day or two."

"Well, that's a start," Katherine said cautiously. "I'm serious. I know you have tons of friends here. Took me three days to learn all their names, but I'm still scared for you. I know what it means to feel lonely, and I can only imagine how you must feel. Mom, I'm more worried about what's going to happen over the next few months. I'm not sure you're anticipating what it's going to be like. What's going to happen when the shock wears off?"

"We'll just have to see. I'll be working. I'll be reading. I'll be walking Hailey. Thank you again for leaving her with me. You're going to miss having her around, and I'm already grateful for her company," Beth said.

"Mom, what's the real story about your eyes?"

"I already told you," Beth said, sounding mildly annoyed.

"Can I talk with your specialist?" Katherine blurted out.

"No, and not because I'm in denial." She gave a weak laugh. "You should accept what I've told you. Stop worrying, get in your car, and drive home—to your home."

"This is where I grew up," Katherine said. "It's my home."

"Yes, and it always will be, but your home is where you live. Call me when you get there. Be careful."

• • •

Several hours later, with the music blaring and the second sand-wich gone from the lunch bag Beth had packed for her, Katherine was on her way home when one of the million thoughts in her head centered on Susan. Should she call her? Of course she should. If she did, would it just make Susan feel guilty? Maybe she should wait.

Katherine called Susan. No answer.

After another hour, she tried again. Still no answer. This time she left a message asking Susan to call her back.

Another hour and a half slipped by without a call from Susan. Worried, she tried calling her friend again. No answer. She dialed Susan's mother, who answered on the fifth ring.

"Hello, Mrs. Bernstein. It's Kat."

"It's a cat?"

"No. It *is* Kat."

"You're looking for your cat?"

"Mrs. Bernstein, this is Katherine Kelly. I'm looking for Susan . . . your daughter. My grandfather died, and Susan made a point of saying she was coming to the funeral. She never showed, and she's not answering her phone or returning my calls. I don't want to alarm you, but I want to make sure she's okay. Do you know where she is?"

"I don't want any," Mrs. Bernstein snapped. "Stop bothering me. I've given enough to charity." She hung up.

Katherine pounded the steering wheel in sheer frustration. Through all her time in Marion, Sean had crossed her mind only once. She tried to overlook that he also had not bothered to call to ask when the funeral would be or to send flowers. Yet as irritated as she was about his seeming indifference to the loss of someone he was aware she loved dearly, something else about him was eating at her. She was just too involved with Susan to worry about it now.

As she drove through the Holland Tunnel into the city, Katherine decided to change directions and head to Susan's apartment at Avenue B, between Sixth and Seventh streets.

She found a parking space, walked up the steps of Susan's apartment, and began to bang on the door. No response. She tried Susan's cell number again. No response. Where are you, Susan?

Katherine searched her phone's contact list but couldn't find a number for Susan's father. She racked her brain for where Susan could possibly be, and then cringed when she realized that Hennessey's Bar on the East side, where they used to hang out before she learned Susan was an alcoholic, was the only place left they had in common. It was worth a try.

Twenty minutes later she pulled in front of the bar, double-parked, and ran inside. It was quiet, only a couple of people shooting darts and one man behind the bar. No Susan. Fortunately, the bartender recognized Katherine.

"Hey," the tall twenty-something guy in a white dress shirt with rolled-up sleeves called out. "You're Katherine, right? Whatcha havin'?"

"Maybe later," Katherine said. "Do you remember my friend Susan? Tall. Thin. Pretty. Dark hair. Talks a lot."

"Funny you should ask. Been in here for hours. Had to cut her off. Asked her if she wanted a cab home. She said no. Said she walked here—said she could walk home."

"So you let her go?"

"There's only so much I can do. Can't force 'em to stay."

"How long ago did she leave?"

"I don't know, maybe a half-hour."

Katherine thanked him and headed back to her car. After considering the routes Susan would likely take to get home, she began driving slowly down Second Avenue, searching each side of the street. Then she turned around and went up Third for a few blocks. She pulled over at a couple of Irish bars and ran in to look for her friend. Luckily it was still early; they, too, were relatively empty, filled with just the usual hangers-on, but no Susan.

Katherine had exhausted all her ideas. She could not think of anyone else to call for help. Preston would not be home. He was on his way to the West Coast. It was too personal a matter to bother

Sol. He was out on the island anyway. Should she call Marcia? No, she was home alone with P.J. That would be too much of an imposition. She cursed herself again for not having more friends. If I were not so caught up in work and myself, I might have a few more friends when I needed them.

Katherine tried Susan's cell one more time. Nothing. She decided to retrace her tracks. Miracle upon miracles, she found a parking spot near Hennessey's and went back inside. Susan had not returned. Katherine stepped back outside and thought hard. Where would Susan go? Would she have gone for another drink or gone home?

Once more Katherine plotted the way she thought Susan would have walked back to her apartment. She picked the street heading east. Not seeing any bars or alleys, she crossed over. In an alley, she noticed a figure curled up in a cardboard box. She had learned during her days as a college and graduate student living in Manhattan to be careful not to disturb a sleeping homeless person—who knew how they might react?—but she was desperate to find her friend, so she decided she had to take a closer look. Maybe someone had seen something.

Stepping closer, she noticed a couple of vodka miniatures strewn on the sidewalk, and then a blue knit scarf—a scarf that looked an awful lot like the one she had given Susan last Christmas. Her heart leaped and then fell almost as fast. The passed out figure was Susan, lying face-up, half in the cardboard box, half out, with vomit frozen on the front of her jacket.

Quickly, Katherine checked Susan's pulse. It was weak. When she shook her, there was no response. Katherine gave her a harder shake. Still nothing. She took a deep breath and slapped her friend across the face. Susan's eyes flew open and before they closed again, she slurred, "Leave me alone."

"Not on your life, Susan. It's me, Katherine. Come on. Let's get you up." She put her arms around Susan, dragged her out of the box, and propped her up as best she could. Her friend did not appear injured but smelled as foul as a camp latrine.

Susan's eyes blinked rapidly. "Kat? What? How did you get here?"

"Just happened to be in the neighborhood. You know, freezing night, strolling down Third Avenue, checking the side streets and alleys . . . "

"What? You're lost?"

"Yeah, Susan I'm lost and glad you found me," Katherine said sarcastically. "Never mind the details, just hold on tight. We need to get you out of here."

Katherine searched the box and surrounding area for Susan's handbag. Nothing. After dragging Susan's dead weight a few yards, Katherine had to stop. She was breathing hard. "You know Susan, it would help a lot if you would try to walk with me, and not in the opposite direction."

Katherine struggled to get her friend to the curb in hopes of flagging down a cab. When one failed to appear, she pulled out her cell phone to dial 9-1-1, but before she could enter the number, a black Lincoln Town Car turned the corner and came down the street. Katherine began frantically waving at the car. The driver rolled down the window, took one look at Susan, shook his head, and started to drive away.

"Hold it," Katherine shouted while managing to snag the handle and yank open the rear door. "You guys usually charge twenty dollars, right?"

The driver hit the brakes and nodded.

"I'll give you thirty, just drive us to Twenty-seventh and Third. It's only a few blocks."

After pointing the man in the direction of where Katherine's SUV was parked, Katherine held tightly to her friend for the short ride back to her vehicle. She handed the man a twenty and asked him to please help put her friend in the SUV. Together, they placed the unconscious Susan in the back seat. A grateful Katherine gave the driver another ten.

Katherine adjusted Susan's head to a more comfortable position and checked her pockets, hoping she had not also lost the keys to her apartment. Finding none, she had no alternative but to take her home.

The drive to Katherine's apartment was long and miserable, and she wondered if she would ever get the smell of vomit out of the upholstery. It took every muscle she had, but she managed to get Susan out of the SUV, up the stairs, and inside her apartment, where she cleaned her up in the shower. Afterward, Katherine stuffed Susan into pajamas and propped her on her side on the floor in her bedroom. By doing that, she could prevent her from drowning in her own vomit.

As the smell from Susan's clothes filled the apartment, Katherine decided to gather all the soiled garments up—both hers and Susan's—and leave them to soak until the morning.

It was 3:00 a.m. before she finally fell asleep, only to be awakened an hour later by the ringing of her cell phone. Who could be calling this late? The phone read Blocked.

Katherine would never know. She had no more answered the phone than the person on the other end hung up.

CHAPTER 18

T HE HOT LAVA LICKED at Preston's heels as he ran, unable to escape the shadow of the red building-sized boulders or the heat emanating from the volcano. There was no escaping. His time had finally come. Preston sat bolt upright in bed, covered in sweat, astonished to find himself not running from molten lava, but in a motel with the alarm clock next to him ringing off the night stand. It read 4:00 a.m.

He needed to move hastily, and get on the road to Rochester if he was to catch the American Eagle flight to Chicago departing at 6:30 a.m. If he missed that departure, he could say good-bye to his first-class seat for the second leg of his flight to San Francisco. That was not acceptable.

Behind the wheel of his rental car and with a cup of in-room coffee next to him in the cup holder, Preston heard his cell phone buzz. The screen read Anonymous, but he still picked up. Unless it was a nut, anyone calling at that hour of the morning had to have something important to say.

"Preston, sorry if I *discombobulated* you."

Preston would have recognized Tommy Greco's voice and unique take on the English language at any hour. Tommy was another of Joe Hart's Collectibles, left in Preston's care since Joe's death. Born in the Italian-American community of Niagara Falls, Tommy had survived an abusive father and a whole lot more. The

117

university of the streets had made up for whatever Tommy lacked in formal education.

"Tommy, what's the matter?"

"Nothin'."

"Where are you?"

"Northeastern Nevada Regional Hospital."

"So, it's 2:00 a.m. where you are—and you're in a hospital and you're okay. You sure about that?"

"I'm fine. Are you gonna keep asking questions or clam up so I can talk to you?"

Silence. "Are you there?"

"Just doing what you asked," Preston said, smiling to himself.

"Wiseass. I'm a father."

"Congratulations! That's just wonderful, Tommy." Preston was embarrassed to admit he had had no idea Tommy's ex-showgirl wife was even pregnant. "How's Missy?"

"She's *copacetical*. Want the details?"

"Absolutely."

"Girl."

Preston laughed so hard he swerved the car. "Knowing Missy, she's beautiful."

"She is. And healthy. We wanted you to know right away."

"Thank you. That means a lot. I remember what it was like for us when P.J. was born, so I have a some idea how you two must be feeling right now—top of the world."

"You got that right. When are you going to get out here to *experienciate* the camp?"

Preston thought about how long it had been since he had last seen this Collectible. Obviously, since Tommy and Missy had had enough time to conceive and deliver a daughter, it had been too long. "I'm flying to San Francisco to visit my store out there. Then I'm going back to Charlotte to check on our dealership there. I could make a short layover."

"Spring's better. Camp's under ten feet of snow right now." Preston heard Tommy's sigh.

"I read about that," Preston said.

"Missy told me to tell you our daughter's name. Says you wouldn't think to ask, but your wife will. It's Skylar Ann. Seven pounds, six ounces."

"I would like to see Missy and Skylar Ann, and sit down with you and smoke a damn good cigar."

"Is that a want or do-thing?"

"It's a do-thing," Preston said. "The camp may be buried under snow, but I see no reason not to stop in Elko to see the new parents."

"Today or tomorrow?"

Preston had a few things he had to look into at Wilson Holdings' San Francisco Auto Plaza that could not wait. He needed to square up eye to eye with the managers and personally see the most current bank statements. "I'll check the flights to Elko. If the planes are flying, I'll try to come in tomorrow afternoon."

"Maybe you're not as 'not all in' as I thought," Tommy said and hung up.

● ● ●

Late on the second leg of his journey, Preston called Marcia from the plane and told her all the news from Nevada, including the newborn's name and weight and the name of the hospital, all of which he had jotted down on a note. Marcia gushed at the news. "A baby girl. That's wonderful. I love the name."

"Tomorrow I'm going to try to fly out to Elko to see them."

"That's a great idea. It's been ages since you've seen Missy and Tommy. If you do see them, please tell them how delighted I am to hear about their new daughter. I'll also send Missy some flowers."

She paused, and Preston could sense something else was on her mind, so he waited.

"How did it go at the funeral . . . with Beth and Katherine?" she asked.

Preston breathed a sigh of relief. He had been afraid she was going to bring up the mess at work.

"The funeral was fine, if a funeral can be fine," he said. "I spent some time with Beth and Kat and learned a great deal about both of them. Nothing to worry about, except that Beth's suffering from a bad eye disease that I think may have worse implications than she's letting on. She handled her dad's death as well as can be expected. Kat's given Beth her dog temporarily, and that seemed to help. I'll fill you in on everything as soon as I get back. How's P.J. doing?"

"He's doing fine. Playing on the floor right now with his fire truck."

"Give him a kiss for me," Preston said.

The news of Tommy and Missy's baby had Marcia sounding better to Preston than she had in quite a while.

•••

When he arrived at the dealership in San Francisco, Preston had a secretary check all the airlines for flights to Elko. A seat was found, and she made the reservation for the next afternoon.

Next on Preston's agenda was a meeting with his senior management, in which he asked the right questions and reviewed all the financials in detail, along with the actual bank deposit slips.

Only after he was satisfied that everything was in order did he discuss the future marketing plans for the store and meet the sales team, which he took out to dinner at Scoma's, one of The Wharf's most famous eateries. He did it without the bosses, something Alex had suggested he do to show he was willing to get in the trenches with his team.

After a working dinner, Preston checked in at the Union Square Hilton. He called Alex at midnight Eastern Time to tell him how well the dinner had gone and how much the sales staff seemed to genuinely appreciate his breaking bread with them. Then he filled Alex in as to the state of Auto Plaza's books and the store's future projections.

"By the way, how are things going with the Manhattan store's numbers?"

"Sales are flat. The good news is I talked Casey into coming in for a day."

That caught Preston by surprise. "Well, that is good news. Is he willing to help?"

"I don't know yet. He's thinking about his situation . . . his kids . . . and he wants to talk to Marcia."

"Marcia? If he's going to do that, I'd like to be there for it."

"I'd like to be there, too. He met with me, and wants to meet with Marcia alone. He made it clear. I think he's trying to take this step-by-step. Wouldn't you want to do the same thing in his position?"

Preston thought about it for a moment. "I guess. It's been a long day for me, and here I am calling you after midnight, your time. I'll talk to you tomorrow."

Before he turned in for the night, Preston made one last call to Tommy to give him his flight details. Overall, the day had been a good one. However, at that moment, as he lay in bed, he felt flat-out lousy—and he did not know why.

CHAPTER 19

HAVING SLEPT FITFULLY, Katherine woke exhausted and famished. Her first thought was Susan, so she immediately went to check on her friend, praying that she would be okay. Sound asleep and snoring softly, Susan seemed to be breathing normally. Katherine had to call someone. Susan's sponsor? She didn't know who the sponsor was. Susan's mother? No help there.

Dizzy with frustration, she made a pot of coffee and did what she always did when she did not know what to do. She went on the Internet. She searched "passed-out alcoholics," not finding the slightest humor in the search request. The first link that popped up was for Treatment of Alcoholism—The Treatment Center. The second was for Get Help Now in First-Rate Rehab.

She began to search for rehab centers in New York and Connecticut, finding several that appeared legitimate. She called the first three on her list, one of which was for women only. All three places were receptive to her bringing Susan in for an immediate evaluation, with Susan having the right to leave anytime she desired. Katherine worried she might be crossing a line.

Her warring thoughts were interrupted by a crash. She ran into the bedroom and found Susan sitting in bed, the lamp from the night table in pieces on the floor.

"Are you all right?" Katherine asked, rushing to the bed. "How do you feel?"

"Have I been here all night?" Susan asked, looking around the room like she had never seen it before.

"Yes, you started on the floor so you wouldn't fall out of bed, and I moved you there this morning after I got up. How do you feel?"

"Like my stomach is caught in my throat." Susan said, staring at the broken glass on the floor. "Sorry about the lamp."

"It's the least of our worries."

"How did I get here? I mean, to your apartment."

"I drove you."

"From where?"

"Specifically, Twenty-sixth Street and Third Avenue. I found you passed out in an alley in a cardboard box."

Susan winced at the news.

"You found me where?"

"In an alley—you had been at Hennessey's. Do you remember any of that?"

"No. Nothing."

"Do you want some coffee?"

"I don't know. Maybe."

Katherine stepped into the kitchen to get a cup of coffee, then set it on the night stand next to Susan. Grabbing a broom and dustpan from a closet, she began to clean up the glass.

"Should I call your sponsor?" she asked.

"I don't have a sponsor anymore."

"So what would you like to do? Something's got to give. The next time you end up unconscious in a cardboard box, imagine all the possibilities when the wrong person finds you. What do you want?"

Susan started to say something but opted instead to reach for the coffee; her hand was shaking as she took a sip. Her eyes were bloodshot with bags under them. "Sorry to be such trouble," she said. "What I want to do is . . . is to live."

Katherine did not say a word. She reached over to hug her friend, who had begun to sob. "I don't want to die," Susan said.

"I've been searching online for rehab centers. There are several in Connecticut that look good." Katherine forced herself to put on a happier face. "You can go in and come out whenever you want. Everything is on a voluntary basis. Do you want me to take you down there so you can see if you can find one you'd like?"

"I have no choice. I can't go on like this."

It took two full days of Katherine's time—driving all over Connecticut, faxing insurance forms, and making a ton of calls, but before she left the state, Susan was an in-patient at the We Care Recovery Center of the Northeast.

• • •

The following morning, Katherine was back at her desk at the newspaper reviewing the week's assignments, mindful that Sol had told her to take her time about returning after the funeral but convinced that work was the best tonic for her. It beat sitting in her apartment all alone and worrying about her mom and Susan.

The jingle of her cell phone jarred her thoughts. The screen read Blocked. She hesitated but answered.

"Katherine, I'm calling to apologize. I'm so sorry about the other day."

"Okay, but it would help to know who this is first." Katherine forced a laugh.

"Oh, dear me. It's Rebecca Bernstein, Susan's mother. I thought you would recognize my voice. No matter. The center where Susan is just called me." Her voice cracked. "I want to thank you for what you did for my daughter."

"It's the least I could do, Mrs. Bernstein. Have you spoken with Susan?"

"Not yet. No calls. She wanted them to notify me she was at the facility. Can you tell me why you picked a rehab center in Connecticut, and how long she's supposed to be in there?"

Katherine had chosen Connecticut because it was far away from Susan's alcoholic parents, but she could not say that. "The

Connecticut center has a great reputation, Mrs. Bernstein. I was told it will be at least a month, but it could take longer. It's up to her and her doctors to decide when she's ready to leave."

Mrs. Bernstein hesitated before saying, "Her father and I thank you, Katherine. You've been a great friend to Susan. She adores you. More importantly, she trusts you." Her words sounded hollow.

"Susan's going to need all the support she can get." How in the world was she going to get it when both of her parents were alcoholics? What could she say to this woman that would help Susan? "I'll be going to see Susan when she calls and says it's allowed, and as soon as I hear anything I'll let you know how she's doing. I promise," said Katherine.

"Okay," Mrs. Bernstein said, and hung up.

Katherine sat quietly, staring at her computer but seeing nothing. Thoughts and worries pinged about in her head, like it was a pinball machine. Mom. Grandpa. Preston. Marcia. Susan. And deep down, in some unreachable place, Sean.

CHAPTER 20

KATHERINE REALIZED SHE HAD two choices: let her thoughts consume her, or get over it and move on. Still resentful about being closed out of the BNA bank fraud story, she turned her attention to the bank story she had not yet been cleared to work on in South Carolina. She opened her desk drawer, took out Alice's file, and reviewed her notes. No clear plan of action presented itself. She walked down the hall to her supervising editor's office, knowing before she set foot inside that it was probably going to be a mistake.

"Hi, Chuck."

"Hello, Katherine. I'm sorry to hear about your . . . grandmother, was it?"

"If the *it* refers to the funeral I just came from—*it* was my grandfather—thank you."

"Oh right. You saw the weeklies. What can I do for you?"

"I wondered if you had received a phone call or an e-mail from a reporter in Braydon, South Carolina."

Chuck put his feet on his desk, giving Katherine a perfect view of the soles of his shoes. "He called while you were away, I believe."

"Can I have his number and what information he left, please?"

"I threw it away."

"You threw it away?" Katherine shook her head in disbelief.

"I didn't see any need for it. We sure as hell can't consider a story local if it happens someplace hundreds of miles away."

Katherine often had to bite her tongue around Chuck; this time she was afraid she might have to bite all the way through it. "You seem to have a pretty good memory. You think you might be able to remember what he said?"

"I don't recall. Mumbled something about being disappointed. Said he'd heard a lot of good things about you."

"Did you happen to mention any of this to Sol?" Katherine asked, a little more pointedly.

"We've been through this. You know how I feel about nonlocal stories. I don't know why you insist on pursuing them."

"I'll take that as a no. You didn't mention it."

"Take it any way you like."

As Katherine stood and stared at the poor-excuse-for-a-newspaper-editor, she suddenly realized small minds like his were what was killing community journalism. No imagination. No vision. No ability to connect the dots. No understanding that it was their job to make sure their readers learned about more than who had won the local baby beauty pageant or bowling league.

They had not gotten along from the first day they met. Chuck was all about the new trend of scrapbook journalism—light, fluffy stories that did not ruffle any feathers. She was old school; she believed in following a story where it led her and consequences be damned.

Fortunately, so far Chuck's boss, Sol, had also seen the merit in her reporting. She hoped he would do so again, though she realized Alice's story would take her a long way from Long Island, and one thing the *Twin Forks Press* did not have was a big travel budget. Before approaching Sol, Katherine went back to her desk and called Alice.

"Hello, my dear," Alice said. "I was hoping I would hear from you. That young reporter, Mike McCusker, is determined to talk to you. Apparently you've an overzealous chief in your tribe up there."

Katherine sighed heavily. "You have no idea."

"We're counting on you," Alice said. "I don't see Mike being able to do this without you, either. I'm not a reporter or lawyer, but this seems like a pretty complicated story to me. Please don't give up on us."

"I won't. Any chance you have Mike's number?"

After Alice gave it to her, Katherine hung up feeling a little better, especially when she noticed that Mike had called and left a message while she was on the phone. When she called him back, he had a lot to talk about and wanted to know if she could meet with him in person as soon as possible. It was time to approach Sol.

CHAPTER 21

PRESTON HAD ENDED UP with a short layover in Salt Lake City, so he was relieved when he finally made it to Elko. He could smell the fresh mountain air. Tommy was waiting for him in a large, all-wheel-drive Acadia SUV. The stocky thirty-something looked like he could have lifted the car with his bare hands. With no such need arising, he drove to the hotel so Preston could check in.

"We're delighted to have you as our guest, Mr. Wilson. Your room and all of the restaurant facilities are complimentary," said the receptionist in an exaggerated European accent, flashing a set of brilliant white teeth while handing him his room keys. "Enjoy the Red Lion Hotel and Casino, and don't hesitate to ring me if you need anything at all."

"Thank you," Preston said, turning just in time to see Tommy subtly shaking his head at the receptionist.

Before Preston could ask Tommy anything, a bellman picked up his bag and escorted him to a well-appointed room with a king-sized bed, two comfortable armchairs, and a desk. Through the sliding glass doors and balcony, Preston had a view of the snow-covered valley and the magnificent white-capped mountains in the distance. Tommy was more interested in checking out the box of complimentary chocolates on the coffee table.

"I'm staying here, too," he told Preston. "At least I'll be here until Missy and the baby leave the hospital—hopefully that will be

131

tomorrow afternoon. I'll be in the lounge. Come get me after you've settled in."

Thirty minutes later, Preston found Tommy playing video poker at the bar and sipping a soft drink. They left for the hospital, where Preston quietly followed Tommy into his wife's room. Missy was breastfeeding the baby, so a protective Tommy quickly blocked mother and daughter with his wide body telling Preston, "We'll give her a *privacy* to finish, okay?"

"Sure thing—I know better than to argue with a new dad," Preston joked.

Tommy went back in the room, and soon Preston heard Missy tell him, "We're finished, bring Preston in."

"Hi, Missy," Preston said, standing at the edge of the bed. "You look absolutely beautiful."

"Thank you for going out of your way like this. It's good to see you again. Tommy, show Preston our little angel."

Preston watched Tommy dance over to the sink, wash and dry his large hands, then carefully pick up and cradle the tiny baby in his arms. She looked like an orchid in the middle of an oak tree.

Preston reached out to touch her, but Tommy moved back a step, slowly shaking his head. "Wash first."

Preston complied.

"If you think he's protective now, just wait," Missy said, her voice like gentle rain. "Tell me how you're doing. How's Marcia? P.J.? Your daughter?"

Missy's words washed over Preston.

"May I hold her?"

Missy nodded, and he carefully took the baby from Tommy.

"She's so delicate," Preston whispered. After a few minutes, he handed the baby back to Missy, a warm smile on his face. He also suddenly remembered Missy's questions. "Sorry, lost my head for a minute. Marcia's well. P.J.'s great," he said. "We're all good on the home front. I'm doing fine and just glad to be here. We've all had a few challenges lately, but we're hanging in there. I don't think I told you about Katherine's grandfather dying."

"I'm so sorry for her loss," Missy said. "Now come over here and sit down. Talk to me."

Preston took a seat in a chair by the bed. Tommy kissed Missy on the forehead and pulled up another next to Preston. Missy had always demonstrated the ability to get to the core of any matter quickly, but Preston did not want to surrender the warm aura this precious moment had created.

"Tell me about the camp," Preston said.

Missy looked deeply into Preston's eyes. "It's been doing pretty well. We open again in late spring. I'll have to see how much I'm able to do, with the new baby and all. Tommy's been a huge help. Everybody loves him."

"What have you been doing, Tommy?" Preston asked.

"Overseeing the infrastructure and building of the ranch. It's got a lodge with a great room, fireplace, and a restaurant. Nice rooms for the kids, too. Nothing cheap or shoddy."

"Financing all in place?" Preston asked.

"I think so, and projections look good." He shrugged. "We'll know *how* good after the summer session. Lot of soft costs come into it, but you already know about all that stuff."

"Sounds like real progress. Congratulations."

Tommy was smiling broadly as a nurse came into the room to check vitals on Missy and the baby. She jotted a few things down on Missy's chart and left.

"Are you going to talk to me, Preston?" Missy turned and asked him bluntly.

"I know what's been in the papers. I didn't come here for your help this time. I honestly just wanted to see your daughter and find out how you two are doing with the ranch." Preston gestured to Tommy. "From what he just said, you seem to have everything in pretty darned good shape."

"I appreciate that, and so does Tommy—more than he'd ever want you to know." She winked at her husband.

"Cut it out," Tommy said before Missy could embarrass him anymore.

"Preston, please don't pay attention to him. We want to know how you're doing. We truly want to know." When Missy spoke in a certain way, she was impossible to refuse. This was one of those times.

"Okay," Preston said taking a deep breath. He went on to quickly explain what was happening with Disley, and the impact that was having on him, Marcia, and the business.

Missy's face softened. "With all of that going on, it's even more amazing that you're here."

"It might be hard to believe that while I've never had more going wrong in my life, I've never had more going right, either." He went on to give an update about P.J., Katherine, and how great Alex and all the staff had been in light of the investigation.

"I've never heard you going more right, either. I can't explain it, but I have a strong sense that everything will work out. Sometimes it takes a long, hard storm to appreciate a clear day," she said.

"Then I'm ready for a month of very clear days," Preston said with a chuckle. Missy and Tommy laughed at that.

"When are you flying out?" Missy asked.

"First thing in the morning, I'm afraid. They need me back in the office, but it depends on the weather. I have to visit our Charlotte store first and then get home."

They talked for a few minutes longer, but Preston could tell the new mother was fading, so he said his good-byes to her and the baby. Missy thanked Preston again for coming and for the flowers Marcia had sent.

"Please give our love to Marcia and a hug to P.J. Tell your daughter we can't wait to meet her. In fact, invite her out here next time you come."

On their way to the Red Lion Casino, Tommy said, "You can't bet the ponies, but they have a great craps table."

"Can you smoke cigars there?"

"Absolutely. At the tables and the lounge."

After an hour of shooting craps, getting up, down, and then breaking even, they retired to the lounge and ordered drinks.

Preston pulled out a couple of Graycliff Chateau Grand Cru's, and each of them made a production out of lighting and savoring the aroma. "What a great draw," Preston said after taking a few puffs and blowing out plumes of smoke. "I needed this."

"From the heavy stuff you laid on Missy?"

"She asked."

"What's your real opinion of your *situational?*"

"It's complicated."

"You clean?"

"I've committed no crime. My attorney tells me the prosecutor is using me for leverage so I won't testify on behalf of my ex-CFO."

"He in the soup?"

"I don't know."

Tommy raised his eyebrows.

"I really don't. It's so damn complex."

"Marcia?"

"She's done nothing wrong, and she knows I haven't done anything wrong either."

"Then why's she on your back?"

"Because we're going to take a hit—"

Tommy leaned forward in his chair and whispered to Preston, "Don't talk about that here."

"Not that kind of hit." Preston laid his cigar ash down gently in the ashtray. "I mean financially. She's a stockholder and her name is on all the personal guarantees. She feels insecure and blames me for bringing in my old pal and then not watching things closely."

He went on to tell Tommy about the FBI visit.

"There's a lot of *implicationing* in all of that. What's up with P.J. and you and Marcia?"

"It's like what I told Missy about my response to P.J.'s hearing. I told Marcia I was wrong, and she claims to have accepted that and to be okay with everything now, but I know she's not."

"How can I help?"

"You can't. I'm going to handle this myself or die trying."

"It happens," Tommy said.

"What can I do to help *you*?" Preston asked. "Your wife's in the hospital with the new baby."

Tommy shook his head slightly. "You got your hands full with your wife, the mouth-piece stuff, and the business. I'm glad you're doing so good with your son. Tell me about your daughter."

"You know she's a journalist, right?"

Tommy nodded.

"She knows how to look into things like a real pro, and she's a damn good writer. I feel very close to her already. I also saw her mother, Beth, while I was at Kat's grandfather's funeral."

Preston paused because Tommy had developed an odd look on his face.

"You don't gotta go there now," Tommy said. "Let's shoot some more craps. I feel the juice."

CHAPTER 22

MIKE MCCUSKER HAD gotten the green light to share his research on the South Carolina bank fraud story with Katherine. Now she had to somehow convince Sol to let her work it without getting Chuck so mad that he would try to derail her efforts. Back from lunch, and just as she was about to go see Sol, her cell phone buzzed with another blocked call.

"Hello?"

"Hey, Kat. How are you doing?"

Katherine had been planning how she would respond the next time Sean called after his no-show at the funeral, but his call had caught her off guard. She gritted her teeth. "I'm doing fine, but I want to hear that you've been having a horrible time and that's why you couldn't at least text me that you couldn't make the funeral."

After a brief silence, Sean said, "I'm sorry, Kat. I couldn't make it and I wasn't free to call. I don't determine where I'll go and when. And sometimes we're on virtual lockdown. These past few days have been one of those times. I wanted to be there for you, I did. I know it must seem like my work is always getting between us, and at the worst times."

"I understand," she lied. "Where are you now? Or can't you say?"

"I'm with my parents in Lewisburg."

Sure you are. "Sean, why are you calling me now?"

"I miss you."

"I'd like to believe that," Katherine said.

"Look Kat, I've always been upfront with you about the demands of my job."

Katherine said nothing.

"How did things go at the funeral? I'm sorry your friend couldn't make it, either."

"What did you just say?"

"I said I'm sorry for what happened with Susan."

"We must have a bad connection. Did you say you're sorry Susan couldn't make it?"

"Yeah, and I hope rehab will help her."

Katherine paused. When she finally replied, it was with an air of caution. "I hope so, too."

"Well, duty calls. I have to leave early tomorrow morning, or I'd come see you. I'll set up something at the first chance. Love you."

"Right," Katherine said, a little confused by his declaration of love and not caring what he thought about her curt reply as she hit the End Call button.

She had finally pinpointed what had been bothering her. There was no way that Sean should have known about Susan's no-show at her grandfather's funeral, and he certainly had no way of knowing that her friend was in rehab. Unless . . . unless he was having her phone calls monitored.

Katherine decided to put her visit to Sol on hold and hunkered down at her computer.

Opening her screen, she wrote an e-mail to Angelo Bertolini, the retired New York City gold-shield detective now working as a private investigator that she had met before joining the newspaper. He had proved a great help on her first bank fraud story, and had since become her go-to P.I., someone she could trust to help her with her investigative stories.

After a couple of e-mails back and forth, she and Angelo agreed to meet later that afternoon, once again at NYC's Flatiron Building, the site of their first encounter. She put away her notes and files and dropped by Chuck's to let him know she was headed into the city to follow up a lead and would not be back until the next morning. He just grunted a reply.

• • •

"Hi, Angelo. Thanks for coming on such short notice. Sorry I'm late," Katherine said, a bit out of breath as she sat down. "Couldn't find any parking nearby."

"No problem. Been watchin' the people. Never gets old."

She pointed to a second cup of tea on the table. "Is this for me?" she asked, already reaching for the handle.

"Yes," he said, smiling. "It sounded like you had something pretty good to tell me."

"Or bad," Katherine said, leaving her coat buttoned. It was nippy outside, and she still felt chilly.

"Let's have it."

She took a hearty swig of the tea. Lukewarm at best, it still felt good going down. "I met a guy in April of last year named Sean O'Malley. He was in the final stages of training with the Secret Service. We started dating and have been close ever since. At least I thought we were."

"I don't mean to be indelicate, but how close is *close*?"

"You got it. We've been exclusive for awhile."

"So now you're gettin' married?"

She pretended to throw her tea in his face. "No, we're backtracking if anything. As you know, I've been heavily involved in investigating bank fraud cases in New York for the past year."

"Hey, I'm the guy who investigated your father and who told you that other investigations were going on at a federal level . . . Wait a minute. Secret Service. Is that where this is going?"

"I don't know. What I do know, or at least suspect, is that he may have bugged my cell phone."

"What makes you think that?"

Katherine sighed. "Angelo, I'm not imagining things. My best friend, Susan, is an alcoholic. My grandfather died recently and she insisted she would be at the funeral. Long story short, she never made it. When I got home, she went into rehab. This morning, I get a call from Sean—who didn't come to the funeral either—and he's sorry about Susan not being there and hoping rehab will work for her. There's no way he could know any of that."

When Angelo finished scribbling he sat quietly for a few minutes looking at his notes while Katherine drank her tea. "There are other possible explanations," he said, "but they would be highly coincidental. Have your cell phone with you?"

Katherine handed it to him. She watched him take a small cord and attach one end to her phone and the other to his phone. A minute later, she saw him nodding. "So, my phone is bugged?"

"Yep."

"How did he do it? More importantly, why would he do it?"

"All he needed was five minutes at the most. In a weekend, how many opportunities would a boyfriend have? All he had to do was wait until you took a shower. You may want to have your apartment swept. Get your car checked, too. He probably has access to everything you're doing on your computer, so I'd also get your laptop checked. All your e-mails, documents—it might all be compromised. Be glad you didn't say much about our meeting when you e-mailed me."

"I guess I caught a break," Katherine said. She could hear her stomach making gurgling noises. "Angelo, could you please get me another tea? Take your time. I don't want you to see me having my first official meltdown."

Angelo nodded sympathetically and went to the counter. Katherine was left to talk herself off the cliff, but the one-sided conversation quickly turned on her. When she got serious with a guy, she screwed it up. Every time. Still she hadn't been the one who screwed this up. How did she deserve this? She wanted to scream but didn't. Maybe later, but not now. Angelo returned with two more steaming cups of tea.

"Is there any chance you can get the bug off my iPhone without Sean knowing it's gone?"

"You can do it yourself. Go back to your computer, plug it into your iTunes, and then hit Restore. Back up everything first. You'll probably lose some stuff but the bug will be gone." Angelo winked. "In the old days this surveillance stuff was all done with micro-devices, then it went to chips, and now it's all software. After you restore your phone, go to the Internet and download SpyTrap. Once you have that installed, it will tell you if anyone has put or tries to put another bug on your phone."

Kathleen wrote "SpyTrap" in her own notepad. "Assuming Sean did this, what would you say were the reasons?"

"He's in the Secret Service. That agency is about a lot more than taking a bullet for the president. They're part of Homeland Security and work with the FBI. A big part of that is dealing with financial crimes—including banks."

"Like bank fraud?"

"That, and hacking, credit cards, identity theft. It's a broad reach."

"I'm not my father, and I don't work for his company. Why would they spy on me?"

"Why? Because you may know something they don't. I'll say this: If they can do it, they will. The agency isn't nearly as clean as the public is led to believe."

"I thought I was cynical . . ."

"By the way, he wouldn't need to put a tracker on your car to know where you are. All he'd need to do is triangulate your phone. Police do it all the time for missing persons. Men are the biggest two-legged frauds on earth."

"Except for women."

CHAPTER 23

A S HE WAS BEING JOSTLED AROUND in the backseat of a taxi on the way in from LaGuardia in heavy traffic, Preston was fast learning what it meant to slide down the corporate ladder. Before the Disley fiasco, he would have made the trip from the airport in a comfortable, smooth-riding limousine, reading the paper and catching up on his phone calls. Instead, he was in a smelly cab with bad shocks, a window that would not crank down, no legroom, and a driver from hell.

The clank of the windshield wipers provided an annoying rhythm as a pelting rain turned to snow. In the last four days, he had experienced sun in San Francisco, snow in Elko, sun in Charlotte, and now rain and snow again. He was tired, but to his surprise he also felt strangely buoyant, even upbeat. An encouraging review of his store and staff in San Francisco; seeing Missy, Tommy, and Skylar; good morale and numbers coming in from Atlanta; and stability and growth in Charlotte had made the whirlwind trip worth the time and expense.

According to his calendar, his first meeting upon returning to the city would be with Alex back at the office. He would be there shortly if the weather did not cause a traffic snarl.

Less than an hour later, Alex was briefing him on the status of the Manhattan dealership; he had a lot of questions about the stores Preston had visited on his trip. Alex also told Preston another FBI

143

agent had called while he was gone. The man had wanted to know if Preston would agree to another meeting. Preston quickly rang his attorney about the call and whether or not it was time to tell the FBI about Terry Thompson and his former general manager's actions. Snyder said yes, and they set the meeting for three o'clock that afternoon in the conference room at his office, pending on whether or not the FBI agents could make it.

"Can Alex be a part of it?" Preston asked.

"If he wants to be," Snyder said, adding quickly, "but I only represent you."

Alex, who had heard the attorney's caveat, nodded.

"Should I bring Wilson Holdings' attorney into this?" Preston asked.

"I'd rather you didn't—but that's up to you," Snyder said.

"I'll have Alex call the FBI agent back, and then I'll touch base with you."

Hanging up, Preston turned to Alex and asked, "Are you good with coming along today, even though Barry isn't representing you?"

"Sure. Even if I have to fend for myself in this pool of sharks."

Preston's tone became more serious. "My gut tells me to call our corporate attorney and see what he has to say."

"Can't hurt," Alex agreed.

Later that morning, the meeting with the FBI confirmed, Preston called Whitcock, Brookfield & Stevenson, Wilson Holdings' corporate counsel. He told Andy Brookfield about the upcoming meeting with Barry Snyder and the FBI that afternoon and that he would feel better if Andy were there to look after the holding company's interest.

"We don't do criminal work, of course, but I'll be glad to sit in," Andy said. "I'm under the impression that Wilson Holdings is not a defendant."

"Not at this time," Preston said. "I want to keep it that way. The FBI requested this meeting, and I want to cooperate. As you know, I fired our CFO, and he's a defendant. The GM is also gone, and he's probably involved, too, in some way."

"I can be there," Andy said. "Just let me call Barry to make sure I'm welcome. Sometimes attorneys can get tetchy."

"Fair enough," Preston said.

By noon, all was set for the meeting. Preston and Alex arrived at the Met Life building a little before three, as did Andy Brookfield.

They rode the elevator up together to Snyder's office, checked in with the receptionist, and took seats in the elegant waiting area. Preston immediately recognized, sitting across the room on a lone couch, the agents who had ambushed Marcia and him at their apartment. Bonetti was wearing a white shirt, blue suit, and solid-gray tie, while Sullivan, also in a blue suit and white shirt, was wearing a purple tie. Bonetti's and Sullivan's were two faces he would never forget.

A secretary Preston had not seen before greeted everyone and showed the men to a large, well-appointed conference room, where Barry Snyder soon joined them.

Barry sat in the solitary chair at the end of a long, boat-shaped cherry table. The two agents watched as Preston took a chair on Barry's left side. Next to him sat Alex and Andrew Brookfield, a tall man in his mid-sixties with intelligent eyes and a presence that screamed Harvard. After everyone else was seated, the agents went to the other side of the table and picked two chairs in the middle.

After a few stuffy greetings, an exchange of business cards, and the usual offer of refreshments—the latter refused by all—they got down to business. Barry Snyder steered the meeting from the start.

Looking to his right and directly at the FBI agents, he said, "You, gentlemen, have asked to speak with Mr. Wilson, who has indicated his willingness to cooperate with you. I ask that no recording devices be used in this meeting by anyone. However, you're free to take notes. You both okay with that?"

Both agents nodded. "Please proceed then," invited Snyder.

"Would you describe your relationship with Alex Herman?" Sullivan asked. "What is his role with Wilson Holdings?"

Preston answered both questions and the others that followed, most of which dealt with current employees, such as the sales managers and finance and insurance personnel.

"We understand Robert Reynolds was the general manager of your Manhattan Mercedes dealership. What can you tell us about him?" Sullivan asked.

On the table in front of him, Preston pushed around a pair of reading glasses that he had just removed from his coat pocket. Sensing that such fiddling would make him appear nervous, he placed them on the bridge of his nose.

"I don't know a lot about him," Preston said. "Disley hired him last year in late September."

"Did you approve the hiring?" Bonetti asked.

"No. He didn't consult me," Preston said.

Sullivan jumped in. "He had that much authority?"

"Yes, he was the CFO of the Manhattan store and of Wilson Holdings."

"What exactly were Reynolds's responsibilities?" Sullivan asked.

"I don't know what Austin told him when he brought him in, but the GM is head of store operations. He heads the new and used car sales team, including the managers, who all report to him, along with the service department and the fixed side of the store, as well."

"Fixed?" Bonetti asked.

"Body shop, warranty, and finance and insurance," Preston said.

"Did he have an employment contract?" Sullivan asked.

"No. He was 'at-will.'"

"How did you feel about that?" Sullivan pressed.

"Knowing what I know now, I would have fired him just as I fired Disley," Preston said.

"Why did you fire Disley?" Sullivan asked.

Preston sat upright in his chair, taking care not to answer too quickly. "He was arrested and never told me."

"What caused you to decide to fire Robert Reynolds?" Bonetti asked.

"After Disley was arrested, Reynolds acted weird in our first informational meeting with the staff. Then he left that meeting in a hurry. That's why I reached out to you, but you called before I got back to town," Preston said, feeling more comfortable.

"Go ahead and talk to us now," Bonetti urged, a hint of sarcasm in his tone. Preston sat back in his chair and pointed to Alex.

"Alex came in to help us after Disley left. In looking into the financial side, Alex talked with Bill Lamb, our new car sales manager, and they discussed what we call the 'gross sheet' that lists all our sales numbers so we can do reviews and track metrics." Preston proceeded to explain the low sales prices for the four Bentleys and the Rolls, and how that had cost the store six figures.

"So you believe Disley and Reynolds were part of a scheme to benefit themselves at the expense of your dealership?" Bonetti said.

"I'm not sure how it went down or how Disley or Reynolds benefited. What I do know is it hurt us. Alex can tell you more about it."

The agents turned to Alex, who said, "While we'd still get our manufacturers' rebates, any general manager would pick up on five upscale cars going through the system at wholesale. A GM's livelihood depends on profit. Our financial team would know about this, too. It would create immediate red flags. The only way this could go undiscovered would be for the GM to go to accounting, upfront, with an explanation. He'd have to have the approval from either the CFO or CEO, and a damn good explanation on top of that."

"Was there an explanation?" Sullivan asked.

"According to Lamb, Reynolds told him that Wilson Holdings wanted to do a favor for the bank, and these five cars were being passed through as a courtesy to them."

Sullivan asked Preston, "Did you want to provide the bank with that courtesy?"

"No. Never. The first I heard about this was from Alex. There was absolutely no accommodation to the bank. It doesn't work that way. On the contrary, we need to show the bank the strongest profit picture we can. The whole concept was ludicrous."

"Mr. Lamb appears to have the most direct knowledge of what went on with these cars. We're going to need to talk with him," Bonetti said in a tone full of authority.

"Bill's an honest guy. Been with us a long time." Preston glanced at Alex, aware of how wary Bill Lamb had acted around his interim

CEO. "He's been under an enormous amount of pressure; I imagine he's worried about his job. I'll talk to him. I don't know why he wouldn't cooperate."

Sullivan got up, walked the long way around the conference table, and stopped between Preston and Snyder.

He glared at Preston. "Mr. Wilson, do you expect us to believe that you knew nothing about these five cars and had no knowledge that Disley—a friend of yours for more than thirty years—and the general manager of your dealership were scheming together?"

Preston slowly rose, swung his six-foot-two frame around, and directly faced the agent; their noses, inches apart. "I don't expect you to believe anything. You came into this room with a fixed point of view and a long fishing pole. I've told you exactly what I know."

The two men remained at a standstill. Barry seemed cemented in his chair, clearly sensitive to what was happening—as indicated by his darting eyes—yet appearing uncertain about what to do to ameliorate tensions. Bonetti was on his feet and walking around the table. Alex stood and stepped away from his chair to block his path.

Andy rose, slowly walked over to a credenza at the far end of the room, and poured himself a cup of coffee. Then he turned, faced the other men, and said in a confident, measured tone, "These matters might be better discussed sitting down."

"I agree," Barry added, as if shaken from his fog by Andy's sage comments. "Please, gentlemen, take your seats."

The agents and Alex sat while Preston remained on his feet. "I'm happy just as I am," he said.

Andy, still standing at the end of the conference table, looked at the agents. "I've known and represented Mr. Wilson for more than twenty-five years. I've watched him build a highly successful automobile business that survived the downturn. He is a man of impeccable character, one who has the respect of his peers and the community. I doubt if he's ever even had a parking ticket. If indeed you are on a fishing expedition, I suggest you look elsewhere."

Andy then sat down, causing Preston to follow suit.

"I think we've accomplished our purpose here this afternoon,"

Snyder said. "Mr. Wilson and Mr. Herman wanted to convey what they had learned from Mr. Lamb and to make themselves available to answer further questions. I believe they've done exactly that. Do you have any more questions?" Snyder glanced from one agent to the other.

"No, we're good for now," Sullivan said, without even a look at his partner.

As the two agents got up to leave, Preston stopped them. "If you don't mind, I have a question. So far as I know, the handling of the five cars at wholesale—if that is a crime—amounts to somewhere around a hundred-thousand dollars. Why, in this day and age, would the FBI be concerned about such a small amount of money in what is essentially a private matter? Is it because a bank's involved? The men in this room are excellent attorneys, and I have to say not one of them has the slightest clue as to why we are here."

Bonetti looked at Sullivan and said, "We aren't at liberty to discuss the case until it goes to the grand jury. In the meantime, we'll let you know if we want anything else."

"Are you going to want to talk to Lamb?" Preston asked.

"We'll let you know." Bonetti led his partner out of the room without so much as a "thank you" to anyone.

Preston shook Andy's hand before he left and said, "I appreciate your comments, Andy. It has been a lot of years."

"Thank you for not decking him," Andy said, chuckling as he put on his overcoat.

Barry caught Preston by the arm. "Can I talk with you privately for a minute?"

Alex nodded, saying he would wait for Preston in the lobby. After Andy and Alex had left and the door was shut, Barry said, "That was quite a meeting. I won't keep you long. I just want to go over a couple of things. My guess is that Reynolds will soon be arrested, and Lamb will be subpoenaed to testify against him. I would like you to bring Lamb here so that I can take his statement. We don't want to get blindsided if we can help it. We don't know what Lamb might say."

Preston's thoughts went to Snyder's one-thousand-dollar-per-hour fee; however, he knew the attorney had his best interest at heart. "That's a good idea. Alex told me that Lamb has been difficult to communicate with. I've never found this to be the case, and as I said, he's probably feeling a lot of pressure. I'll smooth things over with him."

"Remember, our focus is to keep you from being indicted. Right now, we're walking through a minefield. At some point, I'm fairly certain the government is going to want you to testify. We'll ask for immunity, and unless the prosecutor consents, which I doubt will happen, it'll be up to the judge. Without immunity, you'd have to take the Fifth. I don't want to alarm you, but you need to know what might happen as this case moves along."

"I know this is complicated," Preston said, throwing his reading glasses, which he had accidentally just broken, into a trash can. "I may have shot myself in the foot trying to cooperate with those FBI guys. I don't trust them for a minute."

"If I didn't think you were doing the right thing, I would've advised against it. Let's just see what happens next."

As Preston rode down in the elevator, Snyder's last words reverberated in his head. Yeah, let's see what happens next.

CHAPTER 24

KATHERINE AND CHUCK WERE in Sol's office finishing up their weekly review when Katherine decided the time was right. "One other item, Sol, if I may."

"Yes?"

"Senior officers in a Braydon, South Carolina, bank were recently found guilty of criminal fraud. Braydon is a small town, like ours, and a local law firm was hired to sue the bank and its officers in hopes of making restitution to the private investors whose monies were misappropriated. A local reporter is covering the story focusing on Alice Hawkins, an elderly woman who's well known in the community and who lost her entire retirement savings in the debacle. The reporter has asked me to join him in fleshing out the story into a series on how such fraud can hurt a community."

"Why did he call *you?*" Chuck snarled.

Watching Chuck squirming in his seat, obviously scared she would tell Sol he had unilaterally vetoed the story, she just smiled and continued. "I know the lady. She and an attorney she worked for as a legal secretary are legends in Braydon. The reporter is in over his head, and she suggested he call me since I have experience covering bank fraud."

Sol looked at Chuck.

"Ah, I already turned it down," Chuck said, glaring at Katherine for broaching the subject. "This is just another Katherine Kelly

151

love fest. The story is not local or even regional, and therefore it is not for us. Period."

Sol shifted his gaze to Katherine, who gestured at Chuck. "How soon we forget," she said. "A few months ago we saw real growth in circulation and readership thanks to our bank stories. Local banks committing fraud with national implications. Leads poured in. Congressman Quinn testified in Washington before the House banking committee, calling for the elimination of fraud and curbing wrongdoing in our banking system. They cited my articles. The supporting articles since, from big-name reporters, haven't stopped."

Chuck snorted. "Yours have." He smoothed out the wrinkles on his slacks.

"I can always count on you for a low blow, Chuck," Katherine said, finally having had enough of him. "I could have chosen not to disclose that Preston Wilson was my father and carried on, as you well know, but I decided to be upfront and transparent. I felt I owed the newspaper and our readers that."

"Settle down, guys," Sol interjected. "You made the right call, kiddo, and you did it for all the right reasons."

Sol turned to Chuck. "We are a local paper serving our community. The response to Katherine's bank stories was phenomenal. I have a reputation that I've worked damn hard to earn and maintain, and that Pulitzer certificate hanging in my office says that our little paper means something. I'm getting old enough that I probably won't have too many shots at another one. South Carolina isn't South Africa, and since Braydon is a small town and we're a small town, the people in this community will likely see parallels. So, if Katherine can help our readers see how such abuses in our financial system hurt not just Wall Street but Main Street, I'm going to let her go for it."

The look on Chuck's face, already grim, turned sour.

"I have a green light?" Katherine asked, ignoring Chuck.

"For now, but don't forget that lights can change."

Katherine decided to quit while she was ahead. "I understand. Thank you." She gathered her files and started for her desk, only to spin around and return to Sol's office just as Chuck was leaving. "I think there's a little more we need to discuss, if it's okay?"

"Go ahead," Sol said, taking a seat behind his desk as Katherine stood in front of him.

"To do this right, I need to go to Braydon, talk with Alice, meet with the reporter face to face, see what he's uncovered—and just as important—what he hasn't. I want to talk to the lawyer handling her case. It takes a day to drive down—it means at least a week on the road. That's if I don't get side-tracked with other things there."

Katherine could feel the heat of Sol's best see-through stare.

"You could have told me this during our meeting. So what else have you held back?"

"Nothing. Nothing at all."

"So this is all about how long you're going to be out of the office on my nickel?"

"Yes."

"I've been doing this too long. There's something else and you need to spill it."

"Not on this, but there's something going on I don't understand that might be related. I don't know. Before I finished my bank fraud article last year, I tried to talk to my boyfriend, who happens to be a Secret Service agent. He shut me down. Now I find that he's tapped my phone, and I'm worried my apartment may be bugged, too."

"What?"

"I'm dead serious. A private investigator I know just found a bug in my iPhone, and he wants to check my apartment."

"You lead an interesting life, kiddo. I'll order a sweep of the phones in the office while we're at it. Thanks for telling me. In the future, I'd rather hear about such things sooner rather than later, okay? Is that it?"

"Yes, and yes." Katherine was humbled by what Sol hadn't said.

"Knowing you, you're going to dig deep in Braydon. That will certainly take some time. If it weren't you, I'd make you take an unpaid leave of absence, but I'm not going to do that. Take the time you need, go to Braydon, and follow your nose to the story. Just document every dime you spend if you expect to be reimbursed," Sol said.

"Are you doing this because you pulled me off BNA?"

"I don't know. I do know you're too damned good to be sitting in this office when there's a story to write. So, get going before I change my mind."

Katherine felt her face flush with pride. "Thank you, Sol," she said. "You're the best."

"I'm just thinking . . . this boyfriend of yours bugging your phones," said Sol, giving a low whistle.

"What? Now you've got me nervous."

"I don't want to scare you, but there might be a lot more to this than a paranoid agent with sophisticated surveillance at his disposal who wants to keep track of his girlfriend."

"What other reason could he have?"

"I don't know, but you can bet we're going to try to find out. Be extra careful and keep in touch. You've got my private cell number. Call it if something is going on you're not comfortable with. That means anytime, day or night."

Katherine left her boss's office unsettled at best, but knowing there was little she could do at the moment. She could not make any decisions about Sean until she received Angelo's report. Damn it, Sean. What's your game?

• • •

After six hours in heavy traffic, Katherine finally pulled off the highway and got a room for the night in a motel on Interstate 95 just short of Richmond. She woke early and refreshed, pleased to be returning to Braydon. When she was introduced to the charming historic South Carolina town last May while visiting Alice, it had felt like she had stepped back a hundred years—and she could not wait to do it again.

The next day required another six hours of steady driving to reach Braydon. As she drove down Main Street, the first sight that she recognized was the huge live oak growing through a space in the roof of the old, white wooden building with "The Live Oak Inn—Since 1946" sign out front. On her last visit she had found the people of Braydon charming, warm, and sincere. One of her favorites was Bobby McKenzie, the youngest scion of the clan who owned The Live Oak Inn.

Katherine and Bobby had been on a few dates, and while she was not ready to jump into a new relationship—with things between her and Sean still unresolved—she would be lying if she said that Bobby's presence had not influenced her desire to revisit Braydon.

With each passing landmark, she remembered more from her first visit. That trip had been partly about understanding her newly discovered father; she had also wanted to know more about Joe Hart. This time, she looked forward to getting to know Alice Hawkins, Joe's long-time secretary, better. Her journalistic instincts still told her there was far more to learn about Joe Hart and the impact he had had on people, including her own father.

The last time Katherine was here, she had yet to start work at *Twin Forks Press*. Now, with a bevy of articles under her belt that had garnered national attention, her career as a journalist was on solid footing, and she welcomed the invitation to join another reporter on a big investigative story. Her journalism professor and mentor had encouraged her to always get to the emotional core or heart of a story, and that was exactly what she intended to do.

Katherine parked in back of the inn, in an open lot bordered by tall pine trees. She relished the sound of walking on finely crushed oyster shells on the path leading to the entrance. As she climbed the steps to the front porch and entered the reception area, she was awestruck again, just as she had been on her first visit, at the massive trunk of the magnificent oak tree that was the lobby's centerpiece. She was also tickled to see April, an energetic young woman in her twenties whom she had met on her earlier stay, staffing the finely finished oak front desk.

"It's so nice to have you back, Ms. Kelly," April said. "Where is Hailey?"

"Wow, great memory," Katherine said. "All inns should be so lucky to have someone like you on the front line."

"Oh my memory's not all that good, but I'd never forget your beautiful dog. Whoops, no offense. Not that I would forget you, either."

Katherine smiled at April's fast recovery. "Hailey is taking care of my mother. Long story, but they're both happy to be together."

Katherine signed in and accepted the old-fashioned brass key engraved with the number of her room, where she was heading when April called her back and handed her a plain envelope with her name on it: "I'm sorry, you got away before I had a chance to give you this."

"Thank you," Katherine said, putting the envelope in her handbag as she ascended the wide, carpet-covered stairs with the dark, wooden railings. She was delighted to see April had her staying in the same room as before, with an escritoire, a Queen Anne bed, and a window overlooking a park. Katherine climbed up on the bed. But before taking a quick nap prior to a much-needed meal, she opened the envelope. Handwritten, it read:

Welcome back. Kindly accept an offer of hospitality
in the form of a properly drawn Guinness over the thick
oak bar you so admired during your last visit. Bobby.

Katherine carefully folded the note, placed it back in the envelope, and put it on her nightstand.

After a brief nap and a soak in the old-fashioned, claw-foot tub, she dressed for dinner, paying a little extra attention to how she looked. Standing before the full-length mirror hung on the bathroom door, she tried to gauge what might be different from the last time Bobby had seen her. Her figure appeared about the same, her hair was longer, and her face looked, well, a lot happier. Not a bad report card all in all.

As she went downstairs, Katherine headed for the dining room with the red velvet drapes and matching swag, but so early on a

Friday evening in January, it was empty. She moved along to the taproom, which with its lighting turned down had taken on a mysterious air. She sat at the bar, her fingers slowly running over the highly finished wood and its perfect joints. Katherine was so busy admiring the craftsmanship of the wood that she failed to notice a handsome man with a swimmer's build, some ten years older than Katherine, enter from a small door behind the bar.

"Katherine Kelly," Bobby said, reaching over the bar to take her hand in his. "A moment ago this room was empty, and now it's full."

Katherine sat still, neither saying a word nor moving her hand.

It was Bobby who broke the spell. "Guinness?"

"Please."

Going to the middle of the bar, Bobby carefully drew a Guinness from the tap, then another, allowing them to settle before presenting one to Katherine.

"It's been seven, eight months since I last saw you," Bobby said. "You were easy on the eyes then, and I must say you look even better now."

"Thank you," Katherine said, feeling the flush in her cheeks and thankful for the bar's dim light.

After a little small talk and another draft, Bobby said, "I've been following your career by reading your articles online. What brings you back to Braydon?"

"I'm here to see Alice and talk . . . confidentially . . . with some people."

"I understand," Bobby said. "Your secrets are safe with me."

"Okay, here's one: I haven't had any dinner, and I don't want to chance getting sick from drinking a lot of beer without any food in my system. Here's a bonus: It's so good to see you."

He laughed loudly. "If you're hungry, you can eat right here at the bar."

"You haven't eaten dinner yet?"

"Nope—I was hoping we could eat together."

Ignoring her own advice, she took a big swig of beer, her eyes already getting glassy. "What do you recommend?"

"I have some fresh duck, and I can promise it will be delicious," Bobby said.

"How do you get fresh duck?"

"With my Remington 1100."

"Where?"

"On our land, not far from here. In fact, I was hunting there just this morning."

"Then duck it is." She laughed and touched her glass to his.

Bobby left to place their orders. When he returned, he observed, "You're back in town to work on that Braydon bank fraud case, aren't you?"

"That I am, but let's talk about you," she said, starting to feel the heavy beer on her empty stomach. "Your father and mother and their ancestors go back a lot of years here. I fondly remember our discussion about your great-great-great-great-grandfather Hugh McKenzie coming to this country in the mid-1700s. I'm fascinated with that era—all the more so because somewhere way back there are my great-great-great-grandparents on my mother's side. I checked out the genealogy and the good news is we're not related."

"Well, that's a relief. Now you can have another Guinness," Bobby said, seeing her glass was almost empty.

"And children," Katherine said, "Or is it a little too soon for you, Bobby?"

"Before dinner, yeah," Bobby quipped.

Their dinner arrived, and at Bobby's direction, the young waitress set up a table in front of the fireplace. There were only a couple of other patrons that quiet night, so he and Katherine were free to eat and talk as the fire blazed under Bobby's careful watch. Katherine realized at one point that she had consumed more pints of beer than she had in a long time. She knew she would pay for it in the morning, but tonight she just did not care, as she found Bobby's company delightful.

Talk turned to his interests. He told her about his hunting and fishing, how much he loved Braydon, and his part in running the inn. Bobby's passion for boating and fishing reminded Katherine of

Preston's love of racing, which her father had talked about with her at length. She told Bobby about Preston, her grandfather's passing, and how much she loved her work. She never violated her personal code of ethics, carefully steering clear of Preston's current trials and tribulations.

When the evening came to a close, Bobby escorted Katherine to her room. "How long will you be staying in Braydon?" he asked.

"I have to guess you already checked my reservation, didn't you?"

"I admit, I did take a peek, but I had hoped maybe it was an open-ended stay."

"I'm not too certain about how long I'll be here. Perhaps a day or two more. Depends on how work goes," Katherine said, as she braced herself against the door to her room while she fumbled in her purse for the key.

"It was good to see you again," Bobby said, gently taking the key from her and opening the door. He carefully guided her inside, and then wedged the heavy door open with his foot as she collapsed on the bed. He stood quietly, their eyes locked on each other's, until he finally smiled. "You must be exhausted after such a long trip. I've kept you up way too late."

Katherine felt certain emotions tugging at her that far out-weighed the hour of the night or her fatigue, but she decided to err on the side of caution, knowing she would curse herself someday for doing so. "I had a great time," she said, closing her eyes but opening them immediately for fear she might fall right to sleep. "It's been so good to see you again, Bobby."

He gave a little nod, a half-salute, and started out the door.

"Where are you going?" Katherine asked softly, and then could not believe the words that had come out of her mouth. Her heart was pounding against her chest as he walked over to her.

"Sleep well," he said.

She felt a kiss on her forehead and heard the door lock as Bobby pulled it closed behind him. Not bothering to take off her clothes, she shut her eyes and immediately fell asleep.

Chapter 25

T HE SUNLIGHT SHINING THROUGH the window woke Katherine after nine hours of the soundest sleep she could remember enjoying in a long time. Even better, she had only a slight hangover instead of the monster she had anticipated, and her breakfast coffee took care of the remaining aftereffects of the prior night. She almost skipped, with heavy briefcase in hand, the three and a half blocks to *The Braydon Constitution*, easily making her 10:00 a.m. meeting with Alice and Mike.

The three-story colonial redbrick building had a similar look to her own newspaper office, and as she walked in, she loved the smell. Reporter Mike McCusker greeted her. With his toothy smile and big, rawboned good looks, it was as if he had just stepped off a high school football field. He was quick to share that he had earned a degree from the College of Charleston, a school with a fine journalism department. It was not two minutes before Alice joined them, giving Katherine a big hug and sparing her any more details from Mike's résumé.

"It's good to see you, my dear; you look wonderful," Alice said.

"You do, too," Katherine replied, hugging her again for good measure.

The trio moved to a small conference room. Mike opened the discussion with a recount of his recent conversations with Marshall Livingston, the litigator half of the local law firm of Livingston &

Wright, whom Alice had retained to represent her. "Livingston is bringing a civil suit on behalf of the shareholders, led by Alice, against the officers of the bank for breach of fiduciary duty. He believes their criminal conviction proves they acted outside the scope of their authority, and therefore are personally liable."

Katherine reached into her expansive briefcase and took out two books, a small bound one and a three-ring notebook. Crimson pen in hand, she began taking notes, pausing only to ask, "Can you tell me more about why Mr. Livingston believes Alice and the others like her have a case?"

"Mr. Livingston says the officers are personally liable because it was their decisions that caused the bank collapse. My idea is to follow the civil suit as it progresses throughout the trial, but I would also like to talk to the people who were harmed, which would put a face on the crime. I think it would be powerful to show how innocent, trusting locals, like Ms. Alice, were bilked out of their life savings and what that means to them going forward."

Katherine was impressed. He was already twice the reporter he'd been when they'd first talked. He was obviously a quick learner, and now it was her turn to provide some background for what they were trying to do.

"Assuming the officers and directors are liable, there are going to be two issues. One, how much could the shareholders possibly expect to be awarded if the bank officers were found guilty, and two, how much would be collectable in the end?"

"I hadn't thought about that," Mike said, a little uncertain again. "How would we determine that? Can't imagine the bankers would want to tell us."

Katherine gave Mike an understanding smile. "I'm not a lawyer. Still, perhaps with the right kind of support from the media, the case could be settled for an acceptable sum for those who were harmed. There might not even be a need for a trial, though I kind of hope there will be one. Being paraded through the public square is sometimes the only way to stop bad people from playing fast and loose with the money of those who trusted them."

Both Alice and Mike nodded at that. "I am upset about the money I lost," Alice said, "but it is also the principle. I would hope if we make these officers and directors pay, it will make other bankers think twice before trying to do something similar in the future."

"You are so right, Alice, and I hope we do just that," Katherine said. "First let's get your money back. As my journalism professor always said, 'follow the money.'"

Mike grinned. "I volunteer to find out which bankers have the deep pockets."

"If there's money to be had, I might have enough clout from my last banking fraud series to perhaps get the big media players to come take a look. If CNN or the network news teams sent a crew, and this was followed up on the morning talk shows, locally—and hopefully nationally—you'd be amazed at how quickly people could come around."

Katherine could not help noticing that McCusker once again had a deer-in-headlights look. It made her realize the weight she would be carrying on this story. She shot a sympathetic look at her potential partner.

"If I decide to work with you, Mike, are you planning to have us share the byline in the stories? Or do you view me more as a behind-the-scenes consultant?"

"Gosh, no, Katherine. I mean, I've already received approval from my editor for dual bylines. We're in this together, and I think your name should go on top."

She laughed. "That's more than generous, but let's slow down. I came here to get an understanding of the nature of the story before I decided what I could contribute, if anything. Basically, I'm here to help Alice get her money back, and if my national contacts can help make that possible, then so much the better."

"I know you'll make a valuable contribution," Mike said.

"Mike, perhaps you're missing my point. What I'm trying to say is that if I'm going to be a part of this story I want the end result to be consistent with the quality of my prior stories. I don't want to be at odds with you or what you're doing. To me, this isn't about a trial.

It's about what got this to the trial stage. It's about the people like Alice who were harmed."

Mike looked shattered. "Do you think I'm a liability?"

"I don't know," Katherine said, aware as she said them that the words would hurt him, but if they were to move forward together he deserved to have a partner that would be straight with him. "What I mean is, I just don't know anywhere near enough yet. That's why I'm here. My approach is to dig, dig, dig, and then dig some more. It's not about reporting on the way the trial proceeds. Any intern can do that, and most do it pretty well. If I'm going to get involved with you as a co-reporter, I'll want us to drill down and ask the right questions and do the legwork and research necessary to get the answers no one wants to hand over."

"Such as?" Mike asked, making it clear he was still miffed.

"What is the specific conviction potential? What about the economic impact on each person and the community if the civil case doesn't go anywhere? The part the fed played? Will the depositions be made public? How long until a trial if the case isn't settled? Was the FDIC involved or aware of what was going on? As a company that sold stock to private investors, was there any SEC exposure?

"I've learned that a company does not have to trade publicly to draw SEC attention. There just has to be enough money and people involved. I doubt this bank's total capitalization is enough for SEC interest, but we'll need to confirm that. As difficult as getting the story will be and knowing what questions to ask can be, writing such a story in a way average readers can understand may be even harder."

"I can see how it could be a challenge," Mike said, and his voice carried a newfound respect for Katherine.

"The bottom line is that we have to have the facts to be able to show what happens when people like Alice lose their nest eggs because of greedy, dishonest bank officers."

"I'm with you 100 percent," Mike said. "Just tell me what you need me to do. You should definitely be the lead reporter, and I promise to do my best to keep up."

Katherine smiled and nodded. She knew how difficult it was for a reporter to be as candid as Mike had just been, especially in front of a source. She looked at Alice.

"How do you feel about the most personal aspects of your finances being made public knowledge? Everybody reading about your life savings, how you arrived at that money, the gifts you received from Mr. Hart, and whatever else your bank accounts might reveal?"

Alice reached into her handbag and took out a tissue. "I'll have some of that iced tea you offered earlier, Mike, if I may?"

Mike slumped back in his chair, clearly displeased to be asked to leave the room, but before Katherine could say anything, he thought better of it and jumped up from his seat and left.

Alice smiled as he closed the door and said, "I have nothing to hide, my dear. You do what you need to do for the story. Just know I will always be proud of you, no matter how this turns out. I only wish Joe were here right now to listen to the way you handled that young man. Don't worry about me. I'm sure the path you create will be one I want to walk."

Katherine basked for a moment in Alice's approval. "Thanks, Alice, and please know I appreciate you suggesting to Mike that he bring me in on this. I'm also glad you didn't mind sitting in on our come-to-Jesus meeting. It's important that Mike has a clear understanding of the purpose behind these stories. Call it vanity, but in the end, I have to be proud of what my name goes on. He and I both need to know we did the best possible job; otherwise we're doomed before we start."

Before Alice could respond, Mike returned with a tray of iced teas. After serving everyone, he sat down and addressed Katherine.

"After thinking about what you said, I realize how shallow my approach must sound to you. I can see I haven't researched this as thoroughly as I should have. I'm happy to dig deeper. I hope you'll stay and work with me on this. I have a lot to learn."

Katherine fixed her eyes on his. "You're not patronizing me, are you?"

"I'm not, I promise." His response came much more quickly and enthusiastically than Katherine had expected, and she gave him a big smile.

"I appreciate your attitude, Mike. Let's take it step-by-step. Either one of us can stop at any time we want. Fair enough?"

"Absolutely," Mike said.

"I knew you young folks would figure it out," Alice said. "I've been keeping a notebook of my own, and I can tell you what I have found out so far about the criminal sentences for such cases."

"Thank you, Ms. Alice," Mike said, holding to the southern tradition of addressing an elder by the first name, "but I have those, too. Raymond Smith, vice-president and chief credit officer of the Braydon Community Bank and Trust, was convicted of federal bank fraud, conspiracy, and violation of various FDIC and other regulatory statutes. He was sentenced to ten years in federal prison. I have the same kind of details on the other officers."

"Do you have the part about Ray Smith's sentencing being delayed because he tried to kill himself?" Alice asked.

"That was reported," Mike replied.

"But did he actually try to kill himself, or was it just a sham to get a psychiatric evaluation to avoid the penitentiary?" Alice asked.

Katherine grinned. Alice would have made a good reporter. "How would you like to move to New York and work in our office, Alice? I'm sure my editor could use your sharp mind and legal experience."

"Well, thank you, my dear, but I don't believe I'll be moving to New York anytime soon. It's awfully chilly up there, and I'd miss the flowers, the weather, the ocean, and the people here. That's not to imply anything is wrong with New Yorkers, bless their hearts."

"Probably most important of all, where would you get pastries like those at the Home Dairy?" Katherine asked, and both women chortled at that. Alice's soft spot for Home Dairy pastries was one of their private jokes.

"You've been to the Home Dairy?" Mike asked, as Katherine stood and shoved her notebooks into her briefcase.

"I have, and I suggest we take a break and go there for lunch." She did not have to ask twice.

As they finished their meal, Katherine thought about how quiet and hassle-free life seemed to be in Braydon. "Is Johnny still working here?" Katherine asked Alice.

"He is—no one else can keep up with the dishwashing demands. He may be mentally challenged but he is a hard worker. You know about Ashley, Joe's wife, developing educational programs, and Joe did more with the programs after she was killed in the drive-by shooting."

Katherine nodded. "My father took it a step further, providing Johnny with specific help on speech therapy. I loved that."

"Would you like to say hello?" Alice asked Katherine, who nodded with enthusiasm.

"We'll be back in a minute," Alice said to Mike.

Katherine followed Alice to the back of the restaurant where food trays filled with dirty dishes were passed through a large opening. On the other side, Katherine could see a short, stocky manchild in his mid-thirties clearing the trays, spraying cutlery clean, and moving dishes into stacks with the artistry of a juggler.

When Johnny looked up and saw Alice, he broke into a big smile. "Ms. Alice. How is Ms. Alice? Johnny is good. Johnny is very good."

Alice led Katherine by the hand around the cash register, through the swinging doors and into the large kitchen. Johnny hurried over to them. A soiled white apron covered his ample front. Sweat poured off of his round, smiling face.

"Johnny, you remember Katherine Kelly."

Johnny nodded. "Katherine Kelly. Nice lady."

"Thank you, Johnny," Katherine said, offering her hand. "You're a nice man." Johnny smiled.

"You remember Preston?" Alice asked Johnny.

"Mr. Preston, tall man. Helps Johnny."

"Katherine is Preston's daughter."

Johnny shook Katherine's hand so hard it pained her, but she would not let go until he tired.

"I glad to see you, Ms. Katherine. You pretty lady," said Johnny, grinning broadly at Katherine.

Alice softly put a hand on his arm. "We have to get back to our table, Johnny. We just wanted to say hello."

"You go. Johnny has work to do. You tell Preston, I'm good. You tell him for me, I'm good?"

"Of course," Katherine said.

They retrieved Mike, and on their way out of the restaurant, Katherine asked Alice if she wanted to go with them back to the newspaper. She was surprised—but then realized she shouldn't have been—when Alice said, "Absolutely."

At the newspaper, Katherine prepared the first draft of a work plan and a list of people to interview. She wanted to meet with Mr. Livingston while she was in town, if the lawyer would consent to see her, and asked Mike to see if that could be arranged as soon as possible.

Katherine and Mike agreed to meet again the following morning. "Above all, as we agreed, we have to go right to the emotional core of the story," Katherine said.

Mike nodded and grinned, obviously relieved that they were on the same page.

Katherine and Alice headed out the door, but not before Alice tossed a final sally over her shoulder: "You'll do fine, young man, just follow the hurricane."

CHAPTER 26

IT HAD BEEN NEARLY a month since Austin Disley had met face to face with his lawyer. He'd had little to do in the interim but worry, which probably explained why he had welcomed the call from Spagnello's office, summoning him that morning. He had barely unbuttoned his overcoat when his attorney began shooting questions at him. "Who's Robert Reynolds?" Spagnello demanded.

"The former GM at Manhattan Mercedes," Austin answered, hanging his coat up and taking a seat, neither via invitation.

"Yeah. *Former*. He quit. Why would he do that?"

"I'm not sure. Maybe it was because business was down. Maybe because I quit."

"Fired, right? Tell me about Reynolds. The truth. All of it."

"I will. I promise. Before I do, I owe you an apology. I've been defensive and stupid the way I've handled things with you." Austin poured himself a glass of water from the pitcher on the table.

"Apology accepted," Spagnello said. "I understand why you're being defensive. It's not uncommon for defendants in a criminal case. As for the 'stupid' part, you must tell me everything in order for me to be able to help you. I know you're scared. You don't have to try to hide it. Remember, whatever you say stays between us. Now tell me about Reynolds."

"I hired him from Ruby Exotic Imports, an upscale Bentley/ Rolls-Royce dealership in downtown Chicago. I thought maybe he could add some pizzazz to the store—a little European flavor," Disley said.

"How did you hear about Reynolds?"

"*Automotive News*—one of our main trade papers."

"How long have you known him?"

"Feels like forever, but only about six months."

"Trust him?"

"Absolutely."

"Interesting. I received a call from the prosecutor's office today," Spagnello said, pulling a thin folder, the only one with a blue tag on it, from a stack he had in front of him. "They believe Reynolds conspired with you to defraud the car dealership in a scheme to supply luxury cars to an outfit called Weaver Construction. They're questioning the numbers behind the deal. Selling at wholesale makes no sense to them. They think there's more to it."

"Why would they think that?" Austin asked, straightening his bow tie, which had no need of it.

"They're experienced federal prosecutors with strong investigative noses. They look for the logic in the criminal mind. Your explanation is that you were simply selling cars at wholesale to help the bank's customers. What's a discount like that come to? It can't be that much. Twenty thousand per car? Fifty? A couple hundred grand total? I doubt it. They tell me they have evidence that the bank lost millions. Five cars and the numbers they generated in losses seem insignificant, even if you had given the bank the vehicles."

"Maybe they don't understand the automobile business," Austin said.

Spagnello folded his hands and rested them on the top of his head. He leaned back in his desk chair. "Giving you the benefit of the doubt, you're suggesting the deal with the cars was doing the bank some kind of favor. As your criminal lawyer, I can't afford to give you the benefit of the doubt. And if you try to play me you only screw yourself."

Austin considered his attorney's words, including the warning at the end. How could he possibly know what he seemed to know?

Had Teddy Thompson talked to the prosecutor? Surely he was smarter than that, but if Teddy had talked, what could he have said? "I'm not playing you. I'd just like to know where the prosecutor got the erroneous information he's spreading around."

Spagnello pushed his glasses up on his face and glared at his client. With a quick jerk of his head he put his glasses right back where they had started. "I can only assume at this point that their investigators have information that puts your story in the shredder. No one is buying your claim that selling the cars at wholesale was just a way for Wilson Holdings to better its relationship with its bank."

"Have you tried interviewing Reynolds?" Austin asked. "He won't return my phone calls. Maybe you could subpoena him or something?"

"It doesn't work like that, but if he'll come in, I'll interview him. Regardless, I can't force him to answer my questions. We've played this record before. Why don't you tell me everything you know about Reynolds? Or maybe I should ask why you won't tell me everything you know about him."

"I told you what I know about him," said Austin, fussing with his colorful suspenders and brushing an imaginary hair off the front of his suit jacket.

Spagnello stood up and put his hands on his hips. "Talking to you is like pushing a heavy boulder up a hill. You're not stupid, but you're hiding things. You either tell me everything, or enjoy your freedom while it lasts."

Disley flinched, worried that a crack had appeared in his self-made fortress. He hated traps, and he resented his lawyer for putting him in one. Lawyers always said to tell them everything, but Disley was convinced that Spagnello had to believe he was innocent or the jury would sense it, and he would end up in prison.

Austin knew he had to word his next response with care. "Reynolds was our GM. I talked with him about my desire to help the bank. I explained to him that Wilson Holdings needed a good relationship with BNA, especially since traffic had been off for a couple of quarters in a row. I explained our long history with BNA, and

that the bank was also our landlord in New York. Reynolds said he
got it and would support me."

"It's not just Reynolds," Spagnello said, referring to the file
opened before him. "The U.S. Attorney told me about the Russian
developer and his corporate entities. Baskhanov had two bank officers on the take in a land development scheme, and the prosecutor
believes you sold these cars at wholesale to his customers, who became bank customers. He thinks you were part of the global conspiracy. He says he can prove that you and Reynolds participated in
all the kickbacks that were ultimately paid out."

"I'll tell you again, I'm innocent." Austin said, trying not to
sound desperate, even though he could feel his brow begin to per-
spire. "Where are you going with all this?"

"It's where they're going. They want you to plead to a lesser
charge and cooperate with them so they can put the bankers and the
Russian away, and they want to know whether Preston Wilson knew
about this or was involved in any way. Was he?"

Spagnello's last words tightened the screws on Disley. There it
was, the plea bargain. He knew it, but he couldn't implicate Preston.
They went back way too far, and even if he had wanted to, Preston
had nothing to do with this. Still, he did not want to go to jail either.

It occurred to Austin that if his attorney was trying to get him
to turn on Preston, then somewhere someone else was trying to do
the opposite and turn Preston on him. That made him think of how
his old prep school buddy had fired him, which still rankled. How
could Preston turn on him, especially at a time like this? Hadn't he
worked tirelessly for Preston? Covering for him when he was out of
the store? Doing his job, as well as the job of CFO? Bringing donuts
to the staff and the hot-looking receptionist in the front with those
super-long legs? Preston never did appreciate all he'd contributed
to the company.

He blinked his eyes, realizing he had been a long time getting
himself in this current mess. Austin gave his lawyer his most trust-
worthy look. "Preston is my best friend and the most honest man I
know. He wasn't involved in any wrongdoing. If you believe nothing

else I've said to you, believe that Preston Wilson would never do anything to compromise his business. Reynolds and I were trying to make points with the bank."

Spagnello shut the folder he had been holding so loosely. "Okay, let's leave the holier-than-thou Preston Wilson aside for a moment. What about you, the bank, Teddy Thompson, and Baskhanov? You haven't explained anything about how they are all connected."

Austin stood and glared at his attorney. "Frankly, I don't intend to. If you don't believe me, just say so. I need a lawyer who's got my back."

"Sit down and listen," Spagnello said in a cool, determined voice. "Bank fraud and conspiracy—if proven—will mean an ugly life change for you. I need the straight story from you, and so far my gut tells me I have not gotten it. There are too many pieces missing."

Disley sat down, feeling a little faint. "I don't know how much more I can tell you," he said.

"Can or will?" Spagnello asked with ice in his voice. "Why don't you get out of here and think about everything you haven't said while I decide if I still want to represent you?"

Austin stormed out of the room, not even bothering to put on his overcoat until he was on the street in the frigid cold.

• • •

Back at home, Austin rehashed the conversation with his lawyer over two neat twenty-five-year-old Glenlivets on ice. Spagnello had been so direct. Abrasive even. And so damned expensive. Austin didn't like him, and he sure didn't trust him—but he needed him.

Then Austin's thoughts returned to Preston. The more he thought about it, the more worked up he became. Didn't Preston realize the burden this arrest would place on him? Not just the time and energy, but also putting up with the interviews and inquiries. Then there was the money. That damn Italian lawyer was charging him a fortune—and knocking him around in the bargain. Austin had always thought that he and Preston, being both men of station, were united against the rest of the world. They went so far back, all the way to Hotchkiss. In their day, you did not go to Hotchkiss without real money. Old money. "Children of wealth" was how Austin's father had always referred to them.

Some might think parents sent their children to prep school to ensure a good education. Austin knew better. The school was actually the first step on the way to a life of corner offices, board memberships, Hampton golf games, and charity balls. He knew he needed to develop a good relationship with his roommate, keenly aware that his time at Hotchkiss and in the future could depend on it. So he had watched Preston carefully. It was not long before he could see through the politeness and facade—realizing, for example, that Preston had a problem with his father.

As letters came from their mothers, their talk often turned to their families. Preston loved his mother dearly and wanted to feel the same way about his father. He had told Austin about being forced to go to the mountains on summer hunting and fishing trips with his father and a guide. It was supposed to be their time to bond as father and son. Otherwise, he rarely saw his father—the elder Wilson was always away on some so-called business trip.

It was also soon clear that Preston was a leader, a quality that had always eluded Austin. In their studies, however, they were more evenly matched. Austin maintained a slight edge over his roommate in math and science. Preston did better in English, history, government, and the arts.

Socially, Austin tried harder but with less success than Preston. Both on the tall side compared to the other boys, Preston's body tended to muscle, while Austin's to water. Perhaps that's why Preston was more outgoing, better at sports, and more attractive to girls, all traits Austin aspired to but could never seem to attain. One thing Austin undeniably had over Preston was a substantially wealthier father. He took great pride in reminding Preston of his dad's monetary wherewithal whenever the opportunity arose.

Through all of that, Preston was a good roommate and friend, always looking out for Austin, and including him in circles in which the boy would not otherwise be accepted. That inclusion was crucial to Austin. He instinctively needed assurance, even insurance, that it would never stop. He was all too aware that he was riding Preston's coattails.

As their differences became more apparent through the years, Disley looked for some way he could achieve parity. He saw his opportunity when Preston returned from spring break one semester, quite upset. Preston confided in Austin that his father had entered a private venture with Lehman Brothers; his commitment: $4 million. He had paid the half-million down, but because Preston's mother had cut him off from her trust fund, he had no way to meet the overdue $3.5 million call. If his situation became public, he would not only lose what money he had already invested, he would also be ruined in the eyes of his cronies.

Austin offered to talk to his father about the matter, and as it turned out, his father called one of his colleagues at Lehman Brothers and told him, off the record, that he knew Peter Wilson was coming up short on a deal, and if the deal made sense, he would like to take Wilson's position.

In just a matter of days, Preston's father called his son with the news that, by a stroke of luck, he had been able to get out of the deal, and he was sorry if he had worried his son. No mention was made of Mr. Disley's intervention; however, Preston knew what had happened, and he told Austin he would never forget the help, no matter how long they lived.

After Hotchkiss, Preston went to Princeton; Austin, to Colgate. They promised to keep in touch but did not end up seeing each other again until Austin attended Preston and Marcia's wedding several years later. By then, Preston was operating a highly successful car dealership in Manhattan, was in the midst of starting another, and was clearly on his way to building an automobile empire.

Austin had not fared as well. Wall Street had not been kind to him: eight jobs, each lasting no more than a couple of years and paying less than the job before. How could such a talented and bright financial genius have such bad luck? Austin, never short on

vainglory, finally called Preston to tell him he was available if he
needed help in his business. Preston hired him on the spot.

Austin poured himself another Scotch. He had backed up his
buddy in there today, but he deserved better treatment from him.
Preston never should have fired him.

Austin grabbed the highly confidential CFO files that he had
taken with him when he left Wilson Holdings, went to his computer, and methodically entered the company's bank account numbers
and passwords for the operating account for the five stores. Without
the slightest hesitation, he arranged to have eighty-thousand dollars
from each dealership wired to an account he had set up for himself
in Nevis, a little-known island paradise in the Caribbean, southeast
of Puerto Rico. He convinced himself that two years of his annual
two-hundred-thousand-dollar salary was only fair, since with attorney fees he certainly needed the money.

CHAPTER 27

A GREAT DEAL HAD HAPPENED in the short time that Katherine was in Braydon. After an extensive interview with Marshall Livingston, she was more convinced than ever that he was the right attorney for Alice and the class action lawsuit. He seemed to have a good grasp on the bank's exposure, and he was definitely interested in seeing that the community of local investors was made whole, or as close to it as possible.

To that end, Mike had gotten some early financials together, and from the looks of them, unless the bank officers who were charged had done some fast work to protect or hide their assets, there would be plenty of money to spread around even after Livingston's firm took its third of the proceeds.

It was not just progress on the story front that had Katherine feeling better. She had found she loved spending time with Alice—and with Buck, the elderly woman's black German shepherd with the know-all brown eyes, which had been a gift from Joe Hart. Then there was the time she was able to spend with Bobby, always the perfect gentleman. No regrets there. Okay, maybe one or two, but all things considered it had made for a good trip.

After a second short meeting with Livingston the next morning in the attorney's office—a conference in which she was careful to include Mike—and a quick, early lunch with Bobby, Katherine began her journey home. She stopped near Washington for the night, and arrived at her apartment on Thursday. She had planned to go to the office the following morning, but she wanted to see Susan first, if she could. She called the rehab center and asked to speak to her friend. It required the patience of Job, but Susan finally came on the line.

"I hope I'm not imposing," Katherine said. "I've been out of town, and just wanted to hear your voice and see if I could visit you, but after talking to a half-dozen people just to get you on the phone, it sounds like it might not be all right. Susan, should I even be calling you?"

Susan let go a silly laugh. "You're fine. I spoke with my counselor. I told her you're my best friend. She asked me if you would be supportive. I told her, 'more than anybody I know.'"

The uncertainty Katherine had been feeling about calling Susan was replaced by optimism. "Then I'd like to come up to see you. Tomorrow, if possible."

"Let me ask my counselor. Can you hold on for a minute?"

"Sure." What was another minute after a half-hour?

It ended up being neither a minute nor a half hour, but nearly fifteen minutes.

"Sorry, it took longer than I thought," Susan said, sounding out of breath. "I asked my counselor, and she said tomorrow morning between ten-thirty and eleven. She also said to tell you we won't exactly be by ourselves."

"Would you still like me to come?"

"Are you kidding? I'd love to see you. There are a lot of people here but I always feel alone. It's hard to explain."

"It makes perfect sense to me. I'll be there at ten-thirty."

• • •

Katherine arrived at the center a half-hour early, anticipating a gauntlet of security. She was not disappointed. After Susan's counselor verified her visit, a photo of Katherine was taken. She was then given a badge with her picture on it and directed to a stately four-story brick building covered in ivy. A male staff member built like a weight lifter, escorted her down a long hallway to a large room containing several tables with chairs, with small couches arranged in clusters. The pleasant room, with its soft colors and rich appointments, could have been a sitting room in a resort.

A dozen or so people were already milling about the room—adults and teenagers of various ages and ethnicities. As soon as Susan spotted Katherine, she rushed to greet her friend with a warm hug. Katherine was pleased to see Susan in what appeared to be a brand-new white blouse and blue skirt, a far cry from what she had been wearing when she checked in.

"Let's sit over in the corner," Susan said, pointing to an empty couch with no one close to it.

"You look wonderful," Katherine said after they sat down and took each other's hands. "How are you?"

"A lot better. In fact, I think I'm ready to leave here, but they don't agree with me just yet."

"You feel like talking about it?" Katherine asked, smiling.

"That's all I've been doing since I got here. I've never revealed so much about my personal life to so many people—people that I don't know. It's just like the movies. You sit in a big circle and spill your guts. But you have no choice. Believe me, I *need* to talk with you." Her eyes dropped. "First, I want to tell you how sorry I am about your grandfather, and how crappy I feel about not being there. I won't give you any excuse. I hope you'll forgive me."

Katherine squeezed Susan's hands. "Of course I forgive you, Susan. You don't need an excuse. I understand."

"What's going on with you?"

Katherine had not come prepared to talk about herself, but it seemed that she had no choice. "I'm back from Braydon. Remember Alice from my trip down there last year?"

Susan nodded.

"I've been invited to co-author a series of stories about a bank that failed because of malfeasance by its officers. The shareholders lost everything—Alice was among them. It's an interesting case about the people who suffered, and what's happened to them," Katherine said.

"I remember you took Hailey with you last time. Alice has a big German shepherd, right?" It was now Katherine's turn to nod. "What was the name of that restaurant you loved? You went gaga over the pastries."

"Oh, you're talking about the Home Dairy." Katherine smiled. "I might have eaten there a time or two while I was in town. Those éclairs, the lemon-meringue pie . . . they call to a person. Bobby and I went there for dinner one evening, too."

"Wait a minute," Susan said. "Bobby? Who's Bobby? What happened to Sean?" Her voice had grown steadily louder.

"Quiet down, or they will kick me out," Katherine said. The last thing her friend needed to hear about was Sean and his machinations.

"Come on, let's have it."

Katherine, her brows furrowed, rested her cheek in her hand. "It's on hold with Sean, and, yes, I like Bobby. It's early, but I like him a lot and I think something could develop. I just don't want another long-distance romance."

"So what happened with Sean? Was it just the long-distance thing?"

"Susan, we only have a few more minutes, and I want to make the most of them. Let me just say that Sean let me down. Badly."

Susan stared at Katherine like a sad puppy wanting more.

"Oh all right, he put a bug on my cell phone, and then he used the phone to track me."

"What? That's like something out of a stalker movie," Susan said, her small face and big eyes contorting in confusion. "Why would he do that?"

"I don't know why he did it, but I intend to find out."

"How did you figure out your phone was bugged, and that Sean was the one who had done it?"

Katherine let out a big sigh. She was not going to avoid telling Susan more, so she explained how she knew her car was tracked and her phone bugged, and how she deduced, with the help of Angelo, that it was her boyfriend behind it all along. "What I don't know is why he did it," Katherine said.

Susan sat quietly for a minute, chewing on her bottom lip. When she finally spoke, she seemed puzzled.

"Sean isn't stupid, is he?" she asked.

"What's that supposed to mean?" Katherine asked.

"You said he slipped with the mileage, and then he made another mistake talking about me—not once, but twice."

"So?"

"I don't know. Maybe he's trying to tell you something. He's no dummy and he sure knows you're not."

Katherine scowled. She wasn't ready to believe there was a good reason or a deeper meaning behind Sean's behavior.

"Forget it," Susan said. "Maybe I have it all wrong. I just know you cared about him a lot, and he sure seemed to like you. From what you've told me in the past, I have always picked up a good vibe from him."

"How can you care about someone you can't trust?"

"So then to hell with Sean. Tell me about Bobby."

The mere mention of Bobby's name picked up Katherine's spirits. "His name is Robert McKenzie. His family is old South, and they own a beautiful historic inn he oversees. He's gorgeous, too. Smart. Funny. Hunts. Fishes. I'll say it again, he's gorgeous."

"How is he in bed?"

"Susan!"

Both women laughed.

"Well . . .?"

"I'm not ready to get into that—at least not right now," Katherine said. She noticed an attendant motioning to the other people in the room that it was time to go. "If you're able to, call me anytime. Do you want me to tell your parents about my visit and how you're doing?"

"Please don't. I'm working with my doctor and sponsor on all of that."

"Then I won't say a word." She hugged Susan, gave her a kiss on the cheek, and walked with the other visitors to the door, where they were shepherded from the building.

Back in her car, Katherine was thankful that she had gone to see Susan. She felt she had done right by her friend in doing so, and felt better for having made the effort. Their discussion about Sean, however brief, had brought a number of questions to the surface for which she was going to need answers. One way or another.

CHAPTER 28

WHILE THE REST OF THE country was guzzling beer at their favorite sports bars or finding other ways to celebrate President's Day, Carol Martin was stuck in her office on a calculator, attempting to assess the damages from the bank fraud conspiracy. So far she had run the numbers four times, mainly because she could not believe the staggering tally—more than $50 million.

The specific damages were not as easy to delineate, but she kept trying. She knew asking Gil and Mark for help would only draw attention to her inexperience.

She pushed on into the night, and finally at about one in the morning, she could go no further. She would see in the morning if there were any holes in their case that might stop everything before it got to trial.

• • •

The next day Gil began the meeting with a request for investigation updates. "Carol, do you have anything for us?" he asked.

Carol scanned her reports again and nodded.

"We have the architecture and the bank officers. The loans to Baskhanov's companies were to buy twenty-five lots valued at $75 million. Fairy-tale financial statements and bogus bank appraisals supported the loans. To reinforce the developer, BNA provided the sub-developers of Easy Buy—which became Weaver Construction—with its own financing."

"What's the link to Disley? Can we tie it to Wilson?" Gil asked.

"Baskhanov apparently felt he needed a hook with his buyers. Thompson came up with the idea of having his buddy, Disley, throw an upscale car at wholesale into the first five sales. When Baskhanov did the math he wanted more. He squeezed Thompson for additional money from the bank, and he talked Disley into buying five of his company's used Cadillac Escalades at three times their value, an approximate $1.2 million hit to Wilson Holdings—in addition to the new car discounts."

Gil pressed her. "Again, what about Wilson?"

"Preston Wilson and Alex Herman, a car finance expert who also happens to be a shareholder of Wilson Holdings, and their attorneys, recently met with the FBI to tell them about the resignation of Robert Reynolds. He was a relatively new GM who they believe helped Disley with the car deals as a way to garner favor with BNA."

"For the third time, was Wilson in on the cover story?" Gil asked.

"From what he told the FBI, no," Carol said.

"So Wilson's unlikely to testify on Disley's behalf?" Gil asked.

"That's my take," Carol said.

"Walk us through the way this entire thing shakes out so we all understand the money trail," Mark requested.

Carol flipped though her files and pulled out a particular page, which she then put on the viewer. She took out a laser pointer and began to set the stage.

"Developer applied to the bank for financing to buy fifty lots in the Hamptons, each appraised at $3 million. These were three-quarter acre, high-end residential building lots. The appraisals were artificially inflated—the fair market value of each lot was only $1 million not three, so the total actual value was $50 million not $150 million. Yet the bank agreed to loan the developer 85 percent of the bogus market price, or a little more than $127 million, leaving the developer to come up with the remaining 15 percent, or $22.5 million."

Gil, typing furiously on his iPad, looked up and said, "So, to meet the bank's down-payment requirement, the developer simply takes the 15 percent he's supposed to put in." Gil paused while he did some calculations and then continued, "That amounts to $22.5 million out of the $102.5 million, and he's left with $80 million—before the first lot is even sold. Damn, that's quite a payday."

"Right," Carol said, "except to complicate matters, two of the lots did each sell for $3 million. That's the irony. If there weren't any kickbacks, we'd have a weaker case because two of the lots were sold for the inflated appraisal amount."

"What's the big picture in terms of damages to the bank?" Mark asked.

Carol put up a different page on the screen. "It's too early to tell, but the bank lost the money it loaned the developer, its lending department was tainted by the fraud, customers lost trust in the bank and the hit to its reputation cost it new business. Its stock value took a nosedive as a result, and hasn't shown any sign of recovering. There will be severe SEC fines for the bank's negligence."

"Outline the bank's misconduct," Gil said.

Carol put a bullet point chart on the screen.

"Here's the first page," she said. "It's pretty straightforward."

BNA Misconduct

- Failure to follow bank protocols for loans
- Breach of commercial loan commitments and related agreements
- Bad faith in commercial transactions
- Fraudulent and negligent representation of credit information
- Failure to disclose improper conduct of bank officers
- Breach of covenant of Good Faith and Fair Dealing
- Engaged in fraudulent inducements
- Engaged in conduct that constitutes a violation of the Racketeer Influenced and Corrupt Organization Act, or RICO
- Breach of duty to disclose information
- Fraudulent misrepresentation of information to third parties
- Breach of duty to loan participants

- Breach of duty to construction borrowers
- Conspiracy to commit fraud with borrower and sub-borrowers

"That'll do it for now," Gil said.

Carol removed the bullet-point sheet and replaced it with an outline of the damage calculations.

"The numbers I've given you aren't hard costs, but, as the projections indicate," she pointed to a set of numbers at the bottom of the screen, "the bank could conceivably, if its stock stays down, show a billion dollar loss this year—most all of it attributable to this off-the-books deal."

"Have you been able to determine how the money from this scheme was supposed to break down?" Gil asked.

She put up yet another page in the viewer, complete with pictures of the alleged perpetrators, and aimed her red laser light at one person. "Stacy Bowers, a vice president and principal at CCB, is who I believe originated the scheme. She's been talking to the FBI, trying to cut a deal."

She flipped to another page. "When BNA acquired the bank CCB, it took some doing by Teddy Thompson, the VP of Real Estate, to keep the mess from being discovered during the acquisition. He also brought in Disley to help them close the deal with Baskhanov. Their plan was for the developer to get 45 percent, or $36 million; Thompson and Bowers were to get 45 percent or $36 million; and Disley would get what was left. Not bad work, if you can get it."

With a smug look of satisfaction on his face, Gil got up from his chair, "You've done a great job, Carol."

He spun around to Mark.

"Let's arrest Reynolds and see if he'll help us get Disley. We'll pressure Baskhanov to cooperate in nailing Bowers and Thompson. Then we'll negotiate the pleas and see if we still have a trial." Gil rubbed his hands together. "Either way, this will give us a lot of good press for putting a bunch of white-collar money-grubbers in a federal prison—for a long time."

Gil called the meeting to a close but asked Carol to stay behind for a word. He motioned her into his office and closed the door.

"This is sensitive and strictly between us. Understood?"

"Understood."

"I routinely get interagency alerts and inquiries from the NYPD Intelligence-Counter Terrorism Bureau. One came by this morning about a possible Russian intrusion into BNA and J.P. Morgan— money laundering, credit cards, bank account numbers. They believe entire customer databases have been compromised. It also mentioned something about the whereabouts of Goremykin. That's what caught my eye, the inquiry about a possible association between Baskhanov and Goremykin. Those are common Russian names and may have nothing to do with our case, but do you know anything about a Russian named Goremykin, or any connection between him and Baskhanov?"

"I've never heard the name Goremykin before, and my FBI investigators have never mentioned any ties between Baskhanov and others in Russia. Do you want me to ask them?"

"No," he said, taking a file from the safe behind his desk and removing a sheet of paper from it. "I would like you to take a look at something. It's supposedly an English translation of a Russian e-mail communication. Does it mean anything to you?" He handed the paper to her.

End Web COM. Set Up site. Execution RUB BK
Cargo:G arrives Platform 33 NY Off Shore 19/2 22:15

"Is that all there is?" Carol asked.

"It's all we have."

Carol studied the page for several minutes. Finally, she looked at Gil. "I'm no analyst, nor am I qualified to interpret this sort of thing. I imagine there are more pieces, but if I had to speculate, I would say that it looks to be a transmission indicating notice of termination of prior communications between parties, and an instruction to proceed with a plan to set up something. With regard to Goremykin and where he or she might be, I would look for a connection between cargo arriving off shore and *G.*"

Gil nodded.

"But then again, it could mean none of those things," Carol said.

"I agree," Gil said. "I don't know what it means, either. You never saw the paper, and we never had this discussion."

"Got it."

Carol left Gil's office pleased to finally be running with the big dogs on a major case. Gil might be only interested in the possible publicity it could bring, but that did not dull her excitement about putting some sleazy bankers away and helping recover some of the money they had cost a lot of ordinary people. As Carol sat in traffic on the way home, she recalled her husband's response when she had first told him about the magnitude of the case, and what it might mean for her career: "Be careful what you wish for, honey."

The memory made her turn up the radio a little louder so she wouldn't have to hear the doubts circling in her head.

CHAPTER 29

CASEY FITZGERALD SAT IN his well-worn leather chair in his favorite corner of his wood-paneled den, replaying in his mind what it had been like to sit in the bleachers with his first- and third-born sons, watching every move his middle son had made in that afternoon's preseason Little League game. Filled with pride and hope for his trio of boys—comparisons inevitable, introspection unavoidable—he divided his life by three: where he had been, where he was now, and where he was going.

As a chubby teenager with thick glasses, he had nonetheless dreamed of playing professional baseball. Once he accepted that that would never come to pass, he had compensated by getting straight As in high school. By the time he was twenty-two, he had an accounting degree from the University of Pennsylvania, and a year later he was a CPA. He followed this with a short jaunt to another part of the campus for a Wharton MBA, which he earned two years later. He married Amy, his high school sweetheart and the love of his life, and they were blessed with three healthy children.

Most recently, he had enjoyed the challenges of being the CFO of an interstate mega-automobile dealer. That is, until last June when he had resigned in something of a huff from Wilson Holdings, mainly because his friend, Preston, had chosen to back an old prep school buddy over him. All of this passed through his mind in a blur as he stared out the picture window in his den. Freedom now? Absolutely.

He had a lot more time with his wife and kids—and tons less stress. Security? Not nearly what he had enjoyed after twenty years as an in-house financial counselor, with a dependable salary and benefits, not to mention a car for himself and one for his wife.

His current finances were indeed weaker, and building an accounting practice took time; however, he was also still a 15 percent shareholder in Wilson Holdings, and until recently, his stock had carried a seven-figure value. That brought him to where he was going—maybe. With Disley gone, how could he not try to turn the company around and protect his financial interest? Yes, it was time for him to take a deep breath and see if he could step back into the fray, but not before he spoke with Marcia.

He reached Preston's wife on her cell, and they arranged to meet for lunch the next day at P.J. Clarke's on the corner of Third Avenue and Fifty-fifth Street in Manhattan.

• • •

"Casey, you've lost weight," Marcia said, unable to contain her happiness at seeing the man she held in such high regard.

He laughed. "Eight pounds. We'll see how long it lasts."

"How are Amy and the boys?"

"Amy's great. My guys are growing. All three are dynamite athletes and smart as whips." He clasped her hand. "You look wonderful. How are you doing?"

"You need stronger glasses. I'm a wreck. Preston, well, you know Preston. There is also this business with Disley and the store. . . ." Marcia's eyes went moist and cloudy. Casey could see her famous composure was about to break.

"How about a beer and a hamburger," Casey offered.

Marcia smiled her agreement. He motioned for the waiter, who came and took their orders, and then he turned to Marcia. "Talk to me," he said.

"My lawyer tells me—and I can't believe I need a lawyer—not to talk to anybody. I know talking to you will be between us."

He nodded and gave her hand a reassuring pat. "Alex asked me to come in and help straighten matters out. He says Preston is facing all this squarely. I need to get with Preston, but I wanted to talk to you before that happens."

"What do you think we can do?" Marcia asked.

"Alex is assessing the fallout from Disley's arrest, particularly the damage to the Manhattan store. That's a good starting point, but what we need is an accurate analysis of the financial condition of all of the stores."

"Preston tells me the GM walked out, and he believes—whatever his name is, was working with Disley." She gave Casey a disgusted look. "Preston has screwed up all of this. You have to come back. We have too much to lose."

Their beers came as Marcia was about to come apart, and they both drank heartily. As Casey watched, Marcia guzzled hers as if the answers she sought could be found at the bottom of the glass, and he could not help but feel concerned. He had never thought of her as a big beer drinker, and had almost stopped himself from ordering her one. Truth be told, he had only ever known her to drink wine. Things were changing in the Wilson household, no doubt about it.

Lunch arrived, and after a few bites Casey said, "It's true that we've seen this picture before. I thought we had this all behind us. Then comes Disley and Thompson. He was at the bank during the merger. Don't know how Disley's involved in this, but he's up to his eyeballs in it somehow. Now with Preston being named an unindicted co-conspirator, well, that's both vague and scary."

"My lawyer says that all of us who are shareholders might join him, too, before this is all over," Marcia said. She twisted around uncomfortably in her chair. "I don't think I can take any more."

"Let me see what I can do. I'm not making any promises." Casey chomped down on his burger.

Marcia finished her beer and ordered another for both of them. "I get that you'd be walking into a hornet's nest if you come back, Casey, but you could also save the day."

"I don't know about that, Marcia," Casey said, fiddling with his napkin.

"You have to at least try."

"You think, Mrs. Wilson?"

"You have conditions?"

"No, I just want an understanding. I've been on the bench, having to watch the plays go haywire. If I come back, I want a level of authority to match my responsibility."

"Understood," Marcia said as the beers arrived. "Can you meet with all of us later this afternoon?"

"Sure, if everyone else can." Casey had never seen Marcia this assertive about the business, and he was duly impressed.

With a wink, she picked up her cell phone and called Preston. She said she was with Casey, and he wanted to meet with everyone. She listened patiently and then nodded before hanging up. "We need to be at the Manhattan store at four," she told Casey.

"I'm there."

• • •

Everyone was early for the meeting, and Preston immediately ran up to embrace Casey. "It's great to see you."

"I wish it were under different circumstances," Casey said.

Alex joined the group before Preston could respond.

"Want me to fetch you a Whammy or two?" he asked Casey with a grin. "I think I still have some in my office, and you know what they say: 'sugar helps the medicine go down.'"

Casey waved him off with a roll of his eyes and a quick "maybe later," as they moved into the conference room and got down to business.

Before he took a seat, Preston went to Marcia, put his hand lightly on her back, leaned over, gave her a polite but warm kiss on the lips, and then led her to the head of the table. He smiled and said, while pulling out the chair for her, "You called this meeting—and I'm glad you did. It's all yours."

"Casey's the real mover here," Marcia said addressing the group. "He called me to talk, and we have already done that over lunch. We believe the four of us need to discuss our situation, company-wise. A shareholder meeting, if you will—but off the record so my lawyer won't fire me and Preston's won't fire him."

Everyone laughed, although it was clear Marcia was not to be trifled with. "Casey?" Marcia asked, indicating that she wanted him to proceed.

Casey addressed Preston directly. "As you know, I have met with Alex and now Marcia. Before this mess started, this company had a legitimate market value of somewhere in the neighborhood of $200 million. I don't need to tell you that the exposure posed by Disley and Reynolds has diminished this.

"I just learned from Marcia at lunch that she and I could also be classified as unindicted co-conspirators before this is all over. I'll worry about that later, as I sure as hell haven't done anything wrong. As for the present, I need to know how deep the hole is and if we need to restructure Wilson Holdings in some way."

"This store is holding its own," Preston said, "and I have just returned from San Francisco and Charlotte. Auto Plaza was down last year but is trending up this quarter. Charlotte was up slightly last year, with that trend continuing so far this quarter. Until recent events, I am told morale in these two stores was pretty good. I do not believe any of our managers are exaggerating that. I made it clear to each of them that if the smallest ink smudge is found on a piece of paper with numbers on it, the responsible person is out. They know I am not the kind of person to normally make that kind of statement, so I think it shocked them enough to understand we have some serious times ahead—and the bookkeeping has to be squeaky clean."

"Have you actually reviewed the operating statements and balance sheets in detail for each store?" Casey asked. "Or are you relying on the financials as reported?"

"I don't blame you for asking me that." Preston said, glancing at both his wife and Alex. "I did personally review each of them, and yes, even though you haven't said it, that was the first time in a long while that I sat down and spent a couple of afternoons with the numbers." Preston, who was sitting next to Casey, put his hand on his old CFO's shoulder. "I could spend a year with the statements and not be able to come close to doing the kind of analysis you're capable of in a day. Heck, I'm the first to admit that Alex can run circles around me with the financials as well."

"Give yourself a break," Alex said. "Casey and I are both trained accountants. What the firm needs is Casey full-time, not me part-time." Looking at Casey, Alex asked, "Which way are you leaning?"

Casey put his hands together. "Honestly, I'm torn. I have put a lot of my heart and soul into this company, not to mention twenty years of my life. I certainly don't want a repeat of what happened a couple of years ago. I also don't want to see the value of my stock in Wilson Holdings go down the drain, or yours either. Still, I just don't know if I want to jump into the fire again."

Preston got up and walked around the room, ending at the head of the long conference table behind his wife. He put a hand on her shoulder, as Marcia seemed to shrink at Casey's last remark.

"This is a good company. We've been through one crisis and survived, and we can do it again. It starts with understanding the problem. The problem is here. In this store. And in large measure you're all looking at the source, but I am fully vested in this turn-around, and if we stick together, I think we can get through this in a manner that will benefit us all."

Preston walked to the whiteboard in front of the room, picked up a marker, drew five circles, and demonstrated the cross-benefit and interdependency of the stores from a financial, operational, and sales perspective.

"In all respects, the business has always been stronger together than as solo stores, and for that reason, I don't want to see Wilson Holdings broken up. The New York store is the anchor and usual-ly carries the others, which we've seen repeatedly in the past. The reason we're in trouble is because I failed to exercise critical over-sight of Disley. He deserved to be fired sooner rather than later, and unfortunately by the time I did, it was much too late. Now there's evidence of more wrongdoing on his part. As you and Marcia know, Alex and I have reported this to the FBI."

Preston sat down next to Casey again and said, "I owe you a huge apology. You had Austin's number from day one. My lifelong friendship with him blinded me to his true character, but that is no excuse. I'm sorry. I hope you will come back."

"My conflict is—"

"Stop there. I know what your conflict is. I've caused it. You don't want to have to watch me not do my job."

Casey looked down and nodded.

"I propose to transfer twenty-five of my thirty-five shares to you, and I'm going to now ask Alex and Marcia to transfer six of their shares to you as well. That will give you a majority. Alex is acting as temporary CEO, but he will have to withdraw eventually to get back to his own business.

"I can step in to help handle sales, new and used, if you'll handle the financials along with operations in this store and the other four. If he can spare the time, I'm also going to ask Alex to remain here for as long as he can, or until you get everything running the way you want it to."

"What's the price of the transfer of the shares?" Casey asked.

"You've already earned it, Casey. Zero."

"Alex?" Casey asked.

"I'm in," Alex said.

"Marcia?" Casey asked.

"Me, too," she said, her features drawn but her voice strong.

Casey sat for a minute, staring stoically at the whiteboard and Preston's analysis, then he turned to Preston. "It sounds like a plan, but I accept your offers on one condition. If we ever get out of this mess, and I wouldn't be doing this if I didn't think we could, I reserve the right to return the stock to each of you for the same price."

Preston shook his hand, and then pulled him into an embrace. "It's great to have you back," he said. "Your being away has . . . well, you know." They hugged again.

Casey leaned in closely and said, "If you had run the business in the past with the same degree of know-how you demonstrated in this meeting, you wouldn't need me."

•••

That night, when Preston opened the door to his apartment, he could smell a roast cooking. He gave a warm hello to Marcia, joyfully helped P.J. stack blocks, and then gave his son a bath, read him a book, and put him to bed.

When he returned to the dining room, he was surprised to find Marcia waiting for him at a candle-lit table. She handed him a glass of wine, followed by a kiss.

"I take it I can stay for dinner," he said, his face beaming.

Marcia kissed him again and her eyes welled up. "Today, I saw the man I fell in love with."

CHAPTER 30

PRESTON WAS AT HIS OFFICE EARLY the next morning, fully committed to doing whatever he could to help matters on any level, including car sales and improving staff morale. He had no way of knowing his newfound resolve would be tested within the first half hour.

He had barely settled behind his desk when the receptionist poked her head into his office to tell him a Mr. Barnes was asking for him personally. "Barnes? What does he look like?"

"Lean, middle-aged, red hair. Drove up in a metallic blue Porsche Panamera Turbo."

"I'll be right down."

Moments later, Preston was shaking the hand of Red Barnes. The last time he had seen the man was at Joe Hart's funeral. If he remembered correctly, Mr. Barnes had been dressed in formal Navy dress blues and had spoken at the service.

"Preston. Red Barnes. It's good to see you again."

"You as well, Mr. Barnes. Welcome to our store," Preston said with a smile.

"Please, call me Red. It has been a while. I'm sorry we didn't have a chance to talk more at Joe's funeral. Pretty tough time for all of us."

"The service was beautiful," Preston said. "I was quite impressed. So many people knew and obviously loved Joe. We should all be so lucky to leave that kind of legacy. What brings you to the dealership?"

"I've been reading a bit about you, and wanted us to talk. I also hope to buy an Audi."

"That sounds great on both counts. On the car side, do you have a specific Audi in mind?"

"I do. A 2014 R8 V10 Coupe Quattro manual."

"Actually, we happen to have that car in stock," Preston said. "I've known the Audi people for years, and we were pleased that they allowed us to have a hot car a few months before the official release."

"May I see it?"

"Certainly," Preston said. "Before we go downstairs, however, would you like some coffee? Or water?"

"No, sir. I'm fine."

Preston led Red out of the corporate suite, across an expanse of highly polished marble, and into a large, well-lit room filled with new Audis. Red strode right past him and over to the Garnet Red Audi R8 with the silver-pearl, vertical broad stripe behind the doors and black leather interior with beige stitching.

Red took several minutes, studying the list of standard equipment and options listed on the sticker, periodically checking the notes in his leather notepad.

"You've done your research," Preston said.

"Yes, sir," Red said, opening the door and getting in. He sat with his hands on the hand-stitched, leather steering wheel, looking at the dash, taking in the distinctive smell, and admiring the fit and finish of the vehicle.

After several minutes, Red got out and carefully closed the door. "I'm interested in buying this car. How much will it cost me?"

"Will you be trading in the Porsche?"

"If the deal works. It's a 2011."

"Do you mind if I have one of our managers look your Porsche over and take it for a quick drive while I work up the numbers? He'll need your registration as well."

Red complied, removing the registration document from his wallet and handing it to Preston.

"Let's go upstairs," Preston said while motioning for a manager to take the registration.

Red nodded and followed Preston up the elaborate wrought iron staircase. As Preston entered numbers on his computer, he noticed Red taking stock of his office, particularly some photographs of Preston in a Porsche GT3 race car.

"Those were taken at Daytona and Le Mans," Preston said. His intercom buzzed. "Excuse me." It was his used car sales manager. He listened, crunched a few more numbers, and ran off some papers. "Is this moving too fast? I don't want to get ahead of you."

"Fast is good," Red said.

Preston smiled and handed him the papers. "This offer includes the trade-in allowance for your Porsche and assumes that you're happy with all of the equipment and options on the R8 Quattro as it stands."

"The options I wanted are there," Red said as he studied the numbers. "It all looks good. Let's do it."

"You're making this awfully easy for me," Preston said.

"That's what I had in mind, but it's also a fair deal," Red said. He looked back at the pictures. "So you've raced Porsches?"

"Back in the day," Preston said. "How about you? What do you plan to do with this car?"

"Go fast and have fun," Red said. "I haven't raced. Always wanted to."

"I hope you have a good lawyer," Preston said. "This car spawns speeding tickets."

Both men laughed.

"Tell me about yourself, Red."

"Navy man, retired. I have a house in Edgewater, Maryland, on the water near Annapolis."

"Married? Children?" Preston asked.

"Neither. Came close a few times, but no woman could compare . . ." Red cut himself off and quickly changed the subject. "I don't mean to rush things on your end either, Preston, but when can we complete this transaction?"

"Today, if you like," Preston said. "To be honest, things are a little slow here at the moment."

"I thought that might be the case, and it's part of the reason I'm here. Is the negative publicity responsible for the slowdown?"

"Yes, along with the weather and such, but that's a big part of it."

"How are you handling all of it?" Red asked.

Preston looked at Red and then softly said, "I'm back into day-to-day operations and all other aspects of our store. I've brought in one of our owners and an excellent car finance guy. I've also been spending a lot of time with my lawyer." Preston turned and looked out the window. "I just wish my real lawyer were here."

"Your lawyer's not real?"

"Oh, he's real all right and good at his job, but I was thinking about Joe. He was always more than a lawyer; he saw the big picture. Once again, I'm in a box. And I was thinking of something Joe once said: It's not the trap that kills the bear, it's the thrashing around trying to get out of it."

"He had a way with words—and I couldn't agree more, he was no ordinary man," Red said, sounding nostalgic. "Tell me more about your racing."

"After having the Porsche point—or franchise—for a while, I was able to get Porsche to sponsor me in GT racing. I saw it as an opportunity to expand our business and have fun in the process. I raced for ten years and did pretty well."

"What's it feel like to drive a car around the track?" Red asked.

"Exhilarating. Stressful, but in a good way. Requires focus, concentration, and most of all, discipline. It gives your mind a break from everything else."

Red nodded. "So why'd you stop?"

"We kept buying stores. That took a lot of time and money."

"Understood."

"Speaking of money, how would you like to pay for this?" Preston asked. "Do you want us to arrange financing?"

"I'd like to give you a check, or a wire transfer if you prefer," Red said.

"A wire transfer would be best for us," Preston said, handing Red a wire instructions card. He then made some phone calls to arrange the details for delivery. "The make-ready will take a few hours. Would you like to have lunch?"

Red looked at his watch. "Sounds good. Give me a minute to arrange the wire transfer."

• • •

Preston took Red to a nearby Irish pub where they ordered beers and steaks. After some light conversation, the talk turned again to Joe's funeral.

"It was emotional," Preston said. "I gather you were close to him."

"Yes," Red said. "We went all the way back to rooming together at Annapolis. I was his executive officer on the *SS BN Trader*, a nuclear submarine employed in naval intelligence. Our crew completed several tours, each six months at a time. When you live in close quarters with one hundred and sixty-five men at depth and in danger, you get to know each other pretty well."

"I can only imagine," Preston said, ordering another round of beers. "Have you enjoyed your Panamera?"

"Yes, it's a great car—particularly with the advanced steering option and turbo. Perfect for long trips, a little like a four-door 911."

"If you'd like to see what your new car can really do," Preston said, "how about coming with me sometime to the Monticello Motor Club? Have you heard of it?"

"No. When I think Monticello, I think of gambling and horse racing."

"Oh, then you're in for a real treat. We're talking about 4.1 miles of billiard-smooth, twisting asphalt with manicured green lawns in a beautiful resort setting about ninety miles from here. I'm a member, so we could drive the track in your car, and I could show you how the car is built to go, and then you could drive the same track," Preston said, with a smile.

They finished their lunch, and Preston was answering with enthusiasm Red's countless questions about racing when his phone rang. After the call ended, he told Red, "Your new car is ready."

They returned to the dealership where Red signed the necessary papers, turned in his Porsche, and then climbed into his new car. "Did you mean what you said about showing me how to drive this?" Red asked.

"Absolutely."

"Set it up," Red said, "as soon as you can."

• • •

The next day Preston and Red were in Monticello. Preston could see Red was anxious, understandably worried about how he would handle his new Audi on America's premier private racetrack.

"Don't worry," Preston told him. "Your car is made for this."

The temperature of the crisp March morning was perfectly suited to hot rubber tires spinning on asphalt. Preston, driving a new 911 GT3, followed by Red in his Audi, rolled past the metal sculpture gracing the Monticello Motor Club gateway. Through the gate, they stayed in the right lane. Preston entered the member's private code, and led his guest to the center aisle of the gatehouse to sign in. After a tour of the facilities and a review of the track rules, Preston parked his car in one of the designated temperature-controlled garages for a check-up by the track's top mechanics, then with Red in the passenger seat of his R8 V10, Preston took the wheel of the Audi.

After reviewing the four track options with Preston, Red chose the 3.6-mile full course with eighteen turns and four hundred and fifty feet of elevation changes. Preston wondered how many times Red had been exposed to danger and welcomed the tension.

"I'd like to start with the basics," Preston said. "The seating position in the cockpit, different hand-steering techniques and foot pedals."

Preston demonstrated all three as they sat in the car, and to the extent practical before they started, talked about cornering techniques.

"The idea is to find the correct line and the right pressure on the throttle as you drive your car through the corner," Preston said.

Preston started the Audi and drove it onto the course and to the straightaway before curve one. As they approached the first curve, Preston explained the gear he was in and why he had chosen that gear. As he drove, he calmly explained his view of the minimum speed required for each corner.

Within minutes, Preston smoothly piloted through curves three, four, and five while defending his choice of gear, acceleration, and the curve-specific methodology for braking to find the precise distance from the apex, or innermost point of the line taken through the curve.

Red's 525 horsepower Audi seemed to welcome, without strain on its 5.2-liter ten-cylinder FSi direct-inject engine or body, the next eight curves, and Preston was anxious to demonstrate its full capabilities in the next straight stretch.

"Wow, 156," Preston heard Red say. Preston made no reply, his full focus on completing the straightaway and the forthcoming curves.

When they finished, Preston drove back to the clubhouse, where he and Red had lunch. Red peppered Preston with more questions about how to interpret the behavior of his car and the nuances of driving it. By the time their meal was over, no understanding or detail about the car remained undiscovered.

"When you were going down the longest straight," Red asked, "What were you thinking when you hit 156?"

"Not about the speed. I was concentrating on steering down the apex of the kink."

"What is the kink?"

"The straights are not always exactly straight. Where they're not, it's called a kink. It's not that you have to reduce your speed, but you do adjust by steering down."

"When I drive," Red asked, "should I try to be in the same gear that you were in?"

"Let's say I was in third gear in a corner. I'd suggest you be in second gear at that point until you build your confidence and see where you are in the corners. On the other hand, you don't want to stretch the gear."

Over the next hour and a half, Red expressed more than once that he had not expected the experience to be so exciting. He knew he would love it, but he was surprised by what his car was capable of doing, just as Preston had told him he would be. Preston had him do a "cool lap" to give Red a feel for his car and the track. Preston then discreetly commented on the position of Red's car going into, through, and out of each turn, with a measured commentary on what gear Red was in and for how long.

Soon they were nearing the completion of the lap. "Your speed is fine, and you're handling the car through the curves and on the straights well. You're way ahead of the game," Preston said.

The next time around they tried a "hot lap." Red negotiated the turns and the straightaways—his confidence building with each—although still not at the speeds Preston had taken the car earlier. Red managed to reach maximum comfort speeds on the straights.

When the driving was over, they headed to a nearby resort for the night. It just happened to have a casino, a lot of cold beer, and a good selection of cigars.

"I can see how a guy could get addicted to racing," Red said. "Have you ever felt that way?"

"For me, it's an exhilarating escape."

"An escape from what?"

"Changing diapers."

They both laughed.

"No, seriously," Red pushed.

"The automobile business is tedious, and right now I'm also exposed to a lot of bad stuff—stuff that I can't control. I'm in legal limbo. Racing is dangerous, especially if you push hard, but it's a different kind of danger, and I get to steer it. In a car on a track, I'm not at my office, my lawyer's office, or at home. I find it clears my head and gives me perspective."

Red nodded.

"There's something I'd like to ask you," Preston said. "I hope you don't take offense."

"Proceed," Red said.

"You know my dealership is in a tough spot. You like cars. I think you want to help me, but is there more to your being here?"

"More? Like what?"

Thoughts swirled around Preston's head with the speed of a fan set on high.

"You knew I was one of his Collectibles?"

"That was always Ashley's term, not his," Red said, but with a beat of hesitation. "Look, I knew you were one of his friends— someone he cared a lot about."

"You decided to come and see me . . . and buy a car . . . and what? See how I'm doing?"

"That's right."

"Tell me about the 'see how I'm doing' part. You probably know I also made a bargain with Joe."

"I do."

"Did he ask you to check on whether I've been keeping my end of the deal?"

Red tilted his forehead slightly forward. "You do Joe a disservice with that question," he said softly. "Joe did not ask me to check on you in the sense I believe you mean it. The fact is he never asked you to be accountable to him—although he could have."

"Then are you making me accountable? I don't get it," Preston asked with a clear edge to his voice.

"I agree. You don't get it. Settle down and think about it," Red commanded. "Joe made a bargain with you to help his friends. He didn't do that so you could be accountable to him. Knowing Joe, he felt that it was up to you as to if and how you performed. He knew that helping some people he cared deeply about would hopefully help you, too. Facing death, he then asked me to do what he could not—stand by you and his other friends, in case you ever needed a hand."

"And you agreed to do that?"

"It didn't take any agreement. It wasn't an order. It was a request. That's all I ever needed."

"And Joe's request was driven simply by his caring about me."

"That and more. Leave out the *simply*. Joe wasn't like most men. He saw their cracks, but he treated them as whole—he saw what they could be. He brought out their best side. He saw potential in you and he acted on it."

"So it comes down to whether I completed my end of the bargain?"

"It starts with whether you had an expectation for yourself to complete your end of the bargain. Then, whether you held *yourself* accountable for meeting that expectation."

Red's last comment rendered Preston speechless. The more he thought about what Red had said, the more what Joe had asked of him seemed to take on new meaning, additional weight. Preston thought about Marcia and all he had put her through over the last several years—how he had failed to act clearly and decisively on so many fronts, business-wise and at home. He tried to grasp the true context of this before it could slip away. He somehow knew these thoughts were evolved thoughts: newer, deeper, and more nuanced than he had been capable of before. He felt like his brain was shedding a skin and emerging stronger.

"I owe you an apology, Red. I owe one to Joe, too. You're right. My question was a disservice not only to Joe but also to myself. That's your point, isn't it?"

Red picked up his beer bottle and clinked it against Preston's.

"Understood," he said. "Let's have another beer."

CHAPTER 31

WHEN THE NEWARK ELECTRONIC Crimes Task Force merged with its New York counterpart, space was made on the third floor of the New York field office for the fifteen New Jersey Secret Service agents transferred there.

With his buff, six-foot frame crammed into the small swivel chair behind his metal desk, Sean stared at all the pictures he had pinned on the cubicle's fabric wall in front of him. He hated the boxed-in feeling that these cubicles created.

That particular morning, Sean had come in to write his report on the sweeping bank fraud case jointly being investigated by the FBI and the U.S. Secret Service. He pursed his lips at the sight of Russian mobster Mikhail Baskhanov's name alongside that of Wilson Holdings and its CFO. He knew it created two major complications: one personal, one professional. Baskhanov's involvement, while low-level, was with one of the banks his team was investigating as part of its efforts to block the organized crime move by the team's heavyweight Russian target. To make matters worse, they had learned from the FBI that a reporter named Katherine Kelly was helping the U.S. Attorney in setting up its case against BNA.

Things became even more complicated when Sean's team leader asked him to increase surveillance of Katherine, including tracking who she visited, in the hopes of finding out what she might know about the relationship between Disley and Baskhanov. Sean had thought it a long shot. Katherine practically reeked of respectability, but he also knew agents did not get promoted by contradicting their boss. Their romance had given him plenty of opportunity to bug her cell phone and stick a GPS tracker on her BMW, but so far all he had learned from the tap was that Katherine's father was working hard to keep his company going, and that Katherine was dealing with a lot of personal tragedy.

Sean could see all kinds of risks in the assignment, but he told himself he could stay two steps ahead of the game.

It had been weeks since he had last talked with Katherine, personally or professionally. He knew his usual "it's all part of the job" excuse was wearing thin. There was no denying how cold she had been to him last time they talked, and he thought he knew why.

• • •

Katherine slept late on Sunday morning, and when she awoke her hand instinctively reached around for Hailey. She had missed her the past few weeks, especially on the weekends, a time when she always looked forward to their long runs on the beach. Running on the beach put Sean in her head, but before his face could materialize she quickly pushed the fond memory of him from her mind.

After coffee and cereal, Katherine settled on the couch and into her Sunday newspaper routine, starting with *The New York Times*, *The Wall Street Journal*, and *The Washington Post*.

Before she could get through Section A, her reading was interrupted by a knock at the door. She threw a bathrobe over her pajamas and went to see who was there. She froze in place when she saw Sean's face through the window of the storm door. She had half expected he would show up sometime, just not so soon—and not this Sunday morning.

"May I come in?" he asked through the steamed-over pane.

Katherine hesitated. She had thought she never wanted to see him again except on her own terms, but she had yet to figure out what those terms should be. She thought she was done with him—

the fracture of trust was severe and she could not imagine it being mended. Susan's words, however, had resonated with her. He looked so vulnerable, and it had to mean something that her heart was now in her throat just at the sight of him.

"Of course you can come in," she said, slowly reaching for the door. "I didn't mean to leave you out there, but I have to admit I'm shocked to see you."

She flipped the latch on the outer door. He burst inside. It had been snowing lightly and he brushed the snow off his jacket. Before Katherine could ask to take his coat, he stepped forward to embrace her; she stepped back out of reach, bringing him to a halt.

"I'm sorry," he said, taking off his coat. "I forgot I just came in from the cold."

How prophetic. "I don't know why you didn't call first. If you had, I could have saved you a trip. I'm about to get dressed and head out to a meeting."

"Do you have time for a cup of coffee?"

"Just about. You like it black with one sugar if I recall." Katherine went to the kitchen and poured a cup for Sean.

"You're not having one?" Sean said, taking a seat at the table.

"No. My stomach's a little unsettled. Did you just happen to be in the neighborhood?"

"No, Kat. I've wanted to come see you for weeks. It's been way too long and I miss you. I know you've been through a lot, and I know I haven't been here to help you through it. Again, I'm sorry."

Katherine's shoulder muscles tightened as she struggled not to react to Sean's casual use of her nickname. She took a deep breath and let it out slowly, forcing herself to smile all the while. "It's been a rough time, but under the circumstances, I'm feeling pretty good about things. I have my family and friends and my work, and that's what matters."

Sean reached over and tried to take her hand in his. Katherine eluded him by suddenly getting up to check something on her computer. When she returned to the table, she decided to address the obvious. "Work must be keeping you busy. How are things going?

Getting the bad guys? Doing a little eavesdropping on the American heartland?"

Sean's head snapped up. "We've had a lot going on. I was hoping I could get a break so we could get away together for a weekend real soon. How does that sound?"

"I'm always for getting away for the weekend. Sadly, I'm so tied up with my work right now and being there for my family and friends, I don't see me having a free weekend for a long, long time."

Sean looked confused. "Is it just me, or am I missing something? I didn't expect you to act quite this way."

"I hear that all the time. Join the crowd."

"Are you all right?"

"Never better, Sean. Thanks for asking. Now I do have to go. You'd better put your coat back on. It looks chilly out there."

"It seems colder in here. Have I done something, Kat?"

"Sean, you haven't done a thing," Katherine deadpanned. And that was the honest truth: not a thing to help her through her grandpa's death, or Susan's falling off the wagon—or anything else for that matter.

"Well, you know, it would only be natural to be out of sorts with all you've gone through. Losing your grandfather. Susan's problems."

Katherine almost laughed. Too little, too late, Sean. "None of those are your problems, though," she said. "So why in the world would I be mad at you?"

Sean got up and put his coat on. "That's good to hear. I should have called first. I'm sorry."

Katherine walked Sean to the door but she kept her distance. "I have to run."

He took a step toward her. She took a step back and he was gone.

• • •

On the return drive, which he had not planned to take until Sunday evening, Sean had to use every trick in the book to stay awake, including opening both front windows. By the time he reached the rental car return, he had convinced himself that he was not surprised by Katherine's reaction to him showing up unannounced.

He thought about the bug he had placed on her phone. He assumed it remained undetected. He knew what he was doing to Kat, and he knew if she ever found out, she would probably never forgive him—but it was necessary. He believed in the purpose and goals of the mission. The mission, for his employer, was all that mattered.

He had thought he could thread the needle. Instead, he could feel it.

CHAPTER 32

EVER SINCE HE HAD returned to Wilson Holdings, Casey Fitzgerald had been practically living at the office. He was having his meals brought in—sometimes even his dry cleaning. He found it telling that he had developed a first-name relationship with most of the night cleaning crew as well as the fellow who opened the building at six o'clock each morning.

It was all in the name of saving Wilson Holdings. He was in the final phase of completing a financial review of the beleaguered company from the top down. Always extra careful—to the point of being downright cynical—regarding the numbers, he was pleased to spot some light peeking through the clouds. That was, until Estelle delivered a solar eclipse.

"You asked me to earmark anything unusual," she said, her voice sounding as if she were delivering hemlock. "Well, it's worse than unusual. Late last week, eighty-thousand dollars was withdrawn and wired to an account in the Caribbean. I don't understand it. If Preston had wanted to do this, he would have told me."

Casey studied the withdrawal Estelle had highlighted in yellow. "Do you know anything about this offshore account in Nevis? Has Preston ever used it before?"

"No, and no," Estelle said.

Casey had Preston and Alex on the phone in seconds and both men in his office within minutes.

"I've just completed a preliminary review of the consolidated operating statements, balance sheets, and cash flow for all five stores, but as I told you on the phone, Estelle got a nasty surprise this morning on the monthly bank statement. What I didn't tell you was that a withdrawal of eighty-thousand dollars was transferred to a bank in the Caribbean Islands. Do either of you know anything about it?" Casey asked.

Casey had watched Preston and Alex enter the room ready for bad news—a possible expense overrun or a cash flow issue. He could tell Preston had not expected anything like this.

"A withdrawal of eighty-thousand dollars. You have got to be kidding." Preston stood up so abruptly that papers went flying. "No, I don't know anything about it."

The men were interrupted by a knock at the door quickly followed by ashen-faced Estelle. "I just got a call from Atlanta. The bookkeeper wanted to know if I knew anything about an eighty-thousand-dollar withdrawal from the store's operating account. No one at the dealership authorized it."

"This is the same withdrawal we're talking about, right?" Preston asked.

Casey's face hardened. "I'm afraid not, and I have a feeling it may not be the last."

"What can I do to help?" Estelle asked.

Casey stood and began giving orders. "Estelle, call the other stores and see if they've been hit. We need to know if this is a one-off or a pattern. Preston, since you have the passwords in your safe, you need to get them immediately so we can change them. Let's do that now."

Preston nodded. He and Casey headed to the safe. Alex followed on their heels.

"Who has access to the usernames and passwords to pull this off?" Alex asked as they covered the short distance to Preston's office. "Could this be the work of hackers?"

"In all the years I've been here, the username and password for each dealership have been provided to each store's controller, and as far as I know, no one else, not even the GM at each location. The only file with all five sets should be in the safe in Preston's office," Casey said.

"And I'm the only one with the code to the safe," Preston said, as he led the men into his office. "Except for Marcia."

After retrieving the information from the safe, the three men sat down at Preston's desk, and Preston changed all of the usernames and passwords. With that done, they returned to the hard work of following the money trail to figure out who was behind it.

Casey asked Estelle to pull up last week's bank transaction reports for the other three stores. "Let me know as soon as you're done," he said. "Then have Atlanta send a copy of the wire-transfer documentation as quickly as possible."

It seemed like forever before a somber Estelle returned with the bank reports from the remaining stores. "It's not good," she said, handing them to Casey. "It looks like it's happened at all of them."

Casey quickly flipped through the statements, confirming that each store indicated a wire transfer of eighty-thousand dollars from its operating account, all going to the same Caribbean Blue Water Trust, account #38276404412, Bank of Nevis.

"That's exactly what it looks like," Casey said.

"Let's look at this. Aside from myself and Marcia, the controllers were the only other ones with access—and that's only to their store's accounts—unless they acted in concert."

"How could that be?" Alex asked, looking dumbfounded. "I'm the CEO, and I can't transfer money from the individual accounts. I'd have to get the username and password from either you or the controller at each store. That couldn't be done without a lot of red flags going up before those codes would be released to me."

"I don't believe it." Casey said. "I know these people, Preston. Worked with them for years."

"It's either inside or outside," Alex said. "Hackers. I just read about Russians hacking a bank in New York."

Preston looked at Estelle. "We've been together forever, Estelle. What does your gut tell you?"

"I hate to say this, but I remember Disley wanting to gather together all the financial files for his review. I'm just wondering—"

"Whether . . . actually he *did* tell me he wanted to clean up and organize the financial reporting systems for all the stores, and he asked for their pertinent books and records," Preston said in a deliberate voice. "I didn't think about it at the time, but I opened the safe and gave him those files. I guess it's possible that he could have picked up the password files as well."

"There it is," Casey said, groaning as loudly as Preston had earlier yelled. "He came in like a cool breeze and went out like a twisting tornado."

"Can we get the details on this Caribbean bank?" Alex asked no one in particular. "I thought Homeland Security tracked everything nowadays."

"Offshore accounts can still be set up to hide money," Casey replied. "I'm going to call Andy. In the meantime, I think we should immediately turn this over to the FBI and see where they take it."

"This is four-hundred-thousand dollars that we didn't count on going missing," Alex said, shaking his head.

"Best-case scenario, if Preston is right and it is Disley, then changing the passwords should stop it," said Casey. "If it doesn't, I don't know what will. We also need to bring in a cyber-security expert."

Alex and Preston both nodded.

"Worst-case scenario, where does this leave us?" Preston asked.

"In deep doo-doo," Casey replied, shrugging his shoulders. "Isn't it just great to be part of a growing organization?"

CHAPTER 33

MARCIA HAD TIMED P.J.'s nap so he would be alert when Preston got home from the office. She had also prepared her husband's favorite dish, lobster tails in a white wine sauce, with a side of asparagus tips as a surprise. The dining room table was dressed in a French tablecloth and the candles stood ready to be lit.

It was not lost on Marcia that despite all his problems at work Preston had been making the effort to spend more time with P.J., feeding their two-year-old dinner, watching cartoons with him, taking him to the Central Park, giving him his bath, and reading to him before bedtime.

Marcia had replayed their recent meeting with Casey and Alex over and over. She remained impressed with the way Preston had handled everything, but did not need her doctorate in psychology to tell her that the mood swings she had been having were bumping against what was regarded as acceptable limits.

For the past few weeks, she had oscillated between wanting to divorce Preston and start a new life on her own with their son, and wanting to renew their vows as a couple and recommit themselves as parents. She had always loved Preston—since those first shared beignets in the French Quarter. With all the pressures of the last few months weighing more heavily on her than ever, there had been times when she felt at her wit's end. Once or twice she had even found herself hating him, a feeling that terrified her, as it was not in her makeup to harbor such negative emotion for anyone, let alone her husband.

She believed his first responsibility was to protect her, make her feel safe, and provide a warm, stable, secure home for her and P.J. She had not been able to overlook his past inattention to his business and his overall indecision about almost everything. Once their life together had been a beautiful tapestry, too beautiful to ever consider unraveling. With increasing frequency, there had come gaping holes and tears, rendering the once beautiful image a shredded, grotesque rag. But not this night.

Tonight Marcia would put the past aside and welcome Preston for the man he had shown he could be, an insightful man sensitive to others, doing the right thing, taking the longer view; in short, a man in total control.

The sound of Preston's key in the door interrupted Marcia's thoughts. She smiled as her husband walked in. Tall. Confident. She not only saw him, she felt him. She pushed the negative thoughts as far back in her mind as she could and went to give him a hug.

"P.J., Daddy's here," she chirped.

"Daddy, Daddy, Daddy," P.J. shouted, running into Preston's open arms.

The evening proved to be as close to perfect as Marcia could recall. If only the tug-of-war in her head would stop. It seemed no matter what she did—or even worse, what Preston did—the insidious thoughts would not stop. She had to go in a different direction.

• • •

Midmorning, after attending to P.J. and sending Preston off to work, Marcia made a long-distance call to Ann, her roommate from her undergraduate days at Smith. Marcia missed seeing her best friend, who lived in Phoenix—two or three time zones away—and came to New York only a couple of times a year in connection with her editorial work for *The Arizona Times Magazine*. Marcia had tried forever to get Ann to move to New York, and so had Mary, the third leg of their tight friendship trio from college. So far their pleas had not worked. After Marcia apologized for calling Ann so early, her friend asked, "How's P.J.?"

"He's into everything now. Did you see the pictures of him I posted on Facebook?"

"I did—so adorable. I also liked the new ones of P.J. with Preston. Seemed to be a lot more of those than in the past, am I right?"

"You are—Preston's been all over P.J. lately. They're so good together. I tell you, Ann, at times it seems like the old days with Preston."

"You're not going to get all mushy and tell me the story of how you two met again, are you?"

"Not now," Marcia said, laughing. "It's just that given all he's facing right now at work, it's pretty amazing. He has been handling it all quite well. The store. Disley's arrest. Not knowing when the other shoe's going to drop."

"The other shoe being the unindicted something-or-other."

"Right," Marcia said.

"I thought you said Preston hasn't done anything wrong."

"He hasn't," Marcia said, "but, according to our lawyers, he's still at risk, and Casey and I are, too. That's one reason why Casey is back in the fold. We're so lucky to have him. No one knows the numbers like Casey."

"You have a lot of confidence in Casey, don't you?"

"I do. He's always been the Rock of Gibraltar. Preston's pretty much given him the reins to ride out this situation along with Alex, another fellow who used to work with Joe Hart. Preston's been unbelievably strong in all of this, too. I know I already said that, but I need to hear it, even if it comes from me." Marcia laughed softly.

"Considering everything, you sound damn good," Ann said.

"I've just got to sort it all out. I may need help doing that, though."

"What do you mean?"

Marcia said nothing for several seconds. "It's . . . I keep going back and forth. I'm up one minute and horribly depressed the next.

Being a psychologist, I tend to over-analyze myself. I've thought I might be borderline manic depressive—"

"Never. Not you. You're under huge stress and reacting like anyone would in such a situation."

"I'm not so sure, Ann. I'm thinking about talking to someone; much better to catch these things early. I just wanted you to know."

They said their good-byes, with Ann promising to visit New York as soon as possible. When Marcia thought later about the call, she wondered why she had even made it. It hadn't accomplished anything except to let her friend know she feared she was having mental problems. That must have come as a shock. Marcia would call Ann back later. The difficult phone call would be the one to her mother.

Marcia played with P.J. until he was ready for his nap. After putting him down, she delayed the call to her parents as long as she could. The apartment had been quiet for more than an hour when, with shaking fingers, she punched in the numbers on the phone.

"Hi, Mom."

"Hello, dear."

"I know you're upset about what's going on here," Marcia said.

Her mother had been worried about her for weeks, and she hated not being able to ease her concern. As for the news about her possibly being indicted right along with Preston, well, that had only made matters worse. Yet instead of her mother starting right in with her opinions as usual, there was stark silence. Finally, her mother said, "Preston has put you in an awful spot. No man should do that to his wife. The way I see it—"

"Stop it, Mom. I'm proud of the way Preston is handling everything. He's under enormous pressure, but I've never seen him so in control. He's been loving and more attentive to P.J. and me than ever before."

Marcia winced as her mother slipped into the routine Marcia knew only too well.

"That's good to hear, my dear. I have to leave for the library now. Give my little guy a big kiss and hug, and please don't forget to call your father later. He wants to talk to you about Preston. He has some clear ideas; you'll—"

"I will," she said, and hung up. She hated cutting her mother off, but found herself doing it more and more as of late.

It was much too early to be drinking, but with thoughts whirling through her head like an overloaded washing machine, Marcia retrieved a bottle of merlot and a glass. She had never felt better and she had never felt worse. Much was clearer; more was in conflict.

She thought about what she would tell her students if a situation like this were posed in class. The answer was easy.

Marcia called the office of Dr. Kristine Mourer-LaVerdiere, a psychiatrist she'd come to know and admire during her years teaching at Columbia. It took most of the afternoon before she could get the therapist on the line, but after a brief discussion, and pleased that Kristine remembered her from their time together, Marcia was given an appointment in two weeks. She wrote down the time and address on her desk calendar, hoping the step she was taking would not take her over the cliff.

CHAPTER 34

PRESTON COULD NOT sleep, kept awake by the thought of Austin stealing from him. He thought about the day when Austin had first come to him for help. The elder Disley was dead, and between mismanagement and the downturn of 2008, the family fortune was gone.

When he hired Austin, he knew it might be problematic, but not in his wildest dreams could Preston have imagined the conflict hiring his old friend would create. He had only thought that bringing him in to assist Casey would be a way to provide his friend with an income as well as some much-needed self-esteem. He had never thought that Austin's presence would ultimately result in Casey leaving as CFO. In the wake of losing him, promoting Austin to replace him had been more about necessity than desire.

Yet even as Preston was realizing the full impact of his decision to bring his friend into the business, he could not forget what Austin had done for his father all those years ago.

That memory stirred up other regrets. Preston still struggled with why he and his father were never close. As a young boy, he had overheard his mother kick his father out for being a financial failure, and he had vowed then and there that he would not follow in his footsteps. Preston could still feel the wedge that had come between his father and him, driven by that vow. Helping Austin had been part character, part gratefulness, and part his way of overcoming

223

the hurt and guilt he had always carried for having a fractured relationship with his father until the day he died.

Neither his wife nor Casey nor Alex knew it yet, but in his mind he had already gone so far as to forgive Austin for the hundred thousand dollars he had essentially given the Russian developer. Preston planned to pay back the Manhattan store out of his own pocket. The real question was if Austin had been involved in anything else, anything illegal. If he had, well, even if Preston wanted to, there was nothing he could do about that.

Only too aware of the dim prospects available to him when it came to protecting Austin, Preston could not get the commitment to his friend out of his mind and resigned himself to another sleepless night.

CHAPTER 35

BOTH MIKE AND ALICE HAD been calling Katherine with more frequency, and she found it was time to make another visit to Braydon. Sol liked the preliminary material she had been providing and approved the trip, once again to Chuck's utter disdain.

She checked in at the Live Oak, as the citizenry of Braydon referred to the local historic inn, on Sunday afternoon. By happenstance, Bobby was there, and with a little cajoling he talked her into a light picnic in the park. He packed a basket full of snacks, and they enjoyed dinner before heading back early so she could call it a night.

Katherine could not explain why she was not yet ready for her relationship with Bobby to extend beyond a friendship. Early on, she had thought it might someday be more, but that might have had more to do with her feelings about Sean than Bobby. All she knew for now was she had no desire to have Bobby as a bedmate, and thankfully he had been nothing so far but a gentleman.

The next morning at breakfast with Alice and Mike at the Home Dairy, Katherine found herself disappointed at how little had been accomplished by her colleague since her last visit. While Mike had managed to interview a number of the people on their list—and those leads had led to some others—much was still missing. He was just not digging deeply enough.

She refrained from saying anything, but vowed to give him more direct to-dos in the future. As soon as they parted, she took up where he left off, starting with the investors who had lost the most money. As she asked the questions, each one had a different story—but the responses ultimately led to the same place.

Katherine reviewed her notes:

The owner of a family-held hardware store: "I've lived in Braydon all my life. The local leaders called a meeting to tell us about the new bank. They said the special entry-price-per-share was five dollars, and they wanted to see investments of at least $25,000, which meant everybody would own at least 5,000 shares of stock in the bank. It was predicted the bank would grow steadily, and over a five-year period, we'd see our stock worth many times more. They made it sound like a sure thing."

The widow of the owner of the canning factory: "My husband, Henry, loved this community and always talked about the need to give back and support it. And it would be *our* bank. I was a little nervous, but I knew I couldn't let my money—well, Henry's money—just sit there. Lord knows the interest was as low as I could ever remember."

The owner of Braydon's corner drugstore: "I knew these folks. Mr. Nicholson, who was the bank's president, sat next to me at Rotary. He had a perfect attendance pin for four years. And Mr. Smith, the vice president . . . well, he was in the Lion's Club. I thought he was a good man. Who would have thought these gentlemen would do such things? It amounted to stealing our money."

The president of Braydon Oaks Country Club: "This is where the leaders of the bank came to play golf, relax, have a drink, a nice dinner. Naturally, you get to know them. I thought they were good people. When they asked for investors to support and be the cornerstones of a local bank, I was all in, but I did it as a businessman first. I saw an opportunity for a return on my investment. What I did not expect was that the bank would go upside down financially, and I would be a victim of fraud."

After a long week of interviews with townsfolk, and a little time spent getting Mike back on track, Katherine was happy when Friday finally came. Her thoughts centered on Bobby, who had invited her home to meet his parents. Katherine had been introduced to the McKenzies at the inn on her first visit to Braydon, but only briefly, and she looked forward to getting to know them better. She only hoped neither Bobby nor his parents would misconstrue the evening.

Bobby was to stop by at seven, and Katherine had left Mike's office early to give herself plenty of time to get ready, something that usually never took her long. However, time had gone by too fast. She had showered, washed and dried her hair, styled it the way she wanted, and carefully applied her makeup.

The problem was the choices that followed. None of the shoes she had packed seemed right, and when she looked in the mirror, neither dress she had brought with her seemed appropriate. She could not remember ever having this problem with Sean, and reminded herself that Bobby had said not to spend a lot of time worrying about what to wear. Her thoughts were interrupted by his distinctive knock: one hard followed by two soft—low-key and casual, just like him.

The McKenzie home was like everything else in Braydon, a short walk away on clean sidewalks, shaded by moss-covered oaks and maples. She and Bobby strolled hand-in-hand to the stately, three-story, wood-frame house with a front porch on each level. Katherine noticed Mr. McKenzie sitting in a rocker on the main porch, iced tea in hand. A large, round sun with streaks of gold through hues of blue was showing off its beauty just before its slip over the horizon.

"Hey," Bobby said, nodding to his father. "I'd like you to meet Katherine."

Katherine looked up to find a tall Scotsman with a trim gray beard and the ruddy complexion of someone who enjoyed a nip now and then. Mr. McKenzie shook her hand warmly.

"Welcome to our home," he said, with a trace of a brogue. "Mary's fussin' in the kitchen. May I get you an iced tea? Or something stronger, maybe?"

Katherine thanked him for inviting her and said that tea would be nice. Mrs. McKenzie soon joined them on the porch, greeting Katherine and announcing that dinner was ready. The dining room was filled with antiques; the table set for four with Danish linens, exquisite silver, and cut crystal. Katherine loved the combined aroma of fresh ham trimmed with pineapple mixing with the scent of corn, peas, and freshly baked biscuits.

Mrs. McKenzie said, "Bobby tells us this is your third trip to Braydon. Are you finding enough time to enjoy our little community?"

"I love Braydon, Mrs. McKenzie. I do wish I had more time, but there are deadlines to meet. It's a work trip after all."

"Please call me Mary. I'm told you're working on some scandalous articles with Mike."

Bobby's and his father's heads simultaneously jerked up, and they shot each other a glance.

"Mike asked me to assist him with *The Braydon Constitution*'s coverage of BCB&T's failure and the impact upon local investors. Actually, it was Alice Hawkins who first got in touch with me after Mike approached her with his plans to do an investigative series on the collapse." Katherine noticed all passing of dishes had come to a halt at the table.

"That's what I understand," Mrs. McKenzie said, finally handing off a basket of rolls.

"If I may be direct, I see the conduct of the officers as scandalous, not the articles. A lot of people were hurt, including Alice Hawkins."

"I know I'm being nosy, but how is it that you know Alice?"

"It's a long story. Alice was Joe Hart's legal secretary." Katherine smiled. Mary reciprocated with a little forced one. "He helped my . . . a friend out of some serious problems a couple of years ago."

"We, of course, knew Mr. Hart," Mary said. "A fine man, indeed, and a credit to Braydon."

"Joe Hart helped a lot of people," Bobby said. "He and I used to fish together."

"I wish I'd known him," Katherine said. "I find his philosophy of life fascinating. Always looking out for others. His reach was enormous."

"That's one thing no one will ever argue," Mary said, smiling with sincerity. "Would you pass the peas, dear?"

The meal was superb, and after Mary cleared the plates with Bobby's help, she returned from the kitchen with a blueberry pie, a pound cake, and an ice cream and éclair mixture topped with chocolate and nuts.

"Tell us about your parents," Mary said, once everyone had selected a dessert.

Katherine forced a smile. "My father is Preston Wilson. He was born and raised in Manhattan. He's a businessman, who started with one auto dealership there and built it into a series of stores around the country."

Katherine turned from Mrs. McKenzie to her quiet husband. "I can't help but ask, were you raised in Scotland?"

"Early on. Came here in the sixties. Family had been here a long time, but my brother, who ran this inn, died unexpectedly and—"

"And your mother?" Mary interrupted, making Katherine certain that the woman must believe there was a lot more to her and Bobby's friendship than she did.

"My mother was born and raised in a tiny village in Marion, New York, as was I."

"Aye, it's cold up there in Upstate New York, isn't it? Reminds me of the Scottish highlands," Mr. McKenzie said, obviously trying to redirect the conversation again.

"It certainly is," Katherine said. "There's plenty of snow on the ground right now in Marion."

"Goodness gracious, snow in March," Mary said. "Have you been up there recently?"

"Yes," Katherine said. "I went up last—"

"Mother, I think Katherine's had enough questions for one night," Bobby said, finally putting a stop to what was fast becoming an inquisition. "She has a master's degree in journalism, and she graduated at the top of her class. She works for a newspaper on Long Island whose editor once won a Pulitzer Prize. Anything else you want to know will require another dinner."

Everyone laughed, albeit a bit uncomfortably, but Katherine's mind was racing. She had no idea how Bobby knew her class rank or who her boss was, much less that Sol had won a Pulitzer back in the 1980s while a beat reporter for the *Times*. Regardless, unlike with Sean, Bobby's effort to learn more about her left her feeling good. As for the rest of her time with the McKenzies, the night ended on an amicable note, and Mary refrained from asking for Katherine's dental records.

When the evening broke, Katherine thanked Mr. and Mrs. McKenzie for dinner and their hospitality, but she left knowing she did not want a repeat visit anytime soon. Of course the first thing Bobby did once they were alone was apologize for his mother's enthusiasm about Katherine. He seemed to know his mother's inquisitiveness had cast a pall on the evening. Instead of a goodnight kiss, he simply said, "Thank you for a lovely evening."

Katherine stayed three more days in Braydon. The attorney, Marshall Livingston, had told her she was welcome back anytime, and she took him up on his offer for a couple of brief meetings before she had to leave.

• • •

The morning of her departure Katherine stopped by the Home Dairy. Marshall Livingston had agreed to meet her for breakfast and then she would head to New York. She also had something she thought the class-action attorney would want to hear.

"Mike is going to interview the remaining investors, but there's one family I would like to find out more about myself," Katherine said.

Their booth was away from everyone else, but she still glanced around to make certain no one was listening. "You might want to have your private investigator look for a relationship between Mary or Bruce McKenzie with any of the bank officers who were indicted in connection with the bank case. If either had—or now has—a relationship with any of them, what was or is the nature of that relationship? Also, if you would, please keep my name out of this."

An odd cockeyed grin came to Livingston's face, which did not suit him at all.

"I know how this must look," she said. "This is a small town, and I'm positive anyone who cares knows that Bobby and I have been on a few dates. I had dinner with him and his parents a few nights ago, and his mother made some comments that got me thinking."

Livingston said, "Mrs. McKenzie is a powerful force in this town. I'm not particularly worried about her, mind you, but she knows a lot of people in high places—and not just here."

Katherine smiled to take the edge off what she was going to say next. "I don't mean this the way it sounds, but I get the impression you don't want to look into what she might have had to do, if anything, with the bank."

He sighed. "It's not that. It's that a lot of business people around here could get hurt."

"What about the regular working people who lost their life savings, like Alice? I don't mean to be indelicate, but didn't she hire you to seek damages to repay the losses she and other elderly retirees like her suffered when the bank collapsed?"

Pushing back his coffee cup, Marshall said, "I assure you that I will do what I set out to do for these people. I had just hoped to get the money returned without having to turn the town upside down in the process."

"With all that Mike has discovered about everyone on the list, isn't everything going to come out, anyway?"

"Young Mr. McCusker isn't you. I think what you've stumbled onto might force the hand of those who control the money, and the end result will be that the folks in this community, including Alice Hawkins, will be made whole."

"I didn't know bringing up the McKenzie family was stumbling onto anything. Even so, isn't that a good thing?"

Livingston smiled. "Sometimes mentioning the right name is all it takes." He softly whistled a few notes. "Like I said, Ms. Kelly, I'll do what has to be done. It's probably time for the dirty laundry to get hung. Just know that it's not going to be pretty. Mr. McCusker and you will have a pretty good story when this is all done, and I'll be practicing law in Charleston with my brother."

No matter what his private investigator found, Katherine was not confident that Livingston would tell her much about the "real" McKenzie family story in Braydon. She made a mental note to ask Angelo to look into it for her as well.

As Katherine went to pay the check, the attorney gently grasped her hand. "This one's on me," he said.

• • •

With the Braydon city limits sign disappearing in her rearview mirror, Katherine gave the BMW a little more gas, realizing for the first time in a long time that she felt good about her life. The story about the bank fraud's impact on the good people of Braydon was exactly what Sol had wanted. The narrative would be a strong one, with all sorts of documentation and human interest. She did not know how she knew, but she was convinced there would be enough money from the settlement to return most, if not all, of the money to the local investors.

CHAPTER 36

THE CALL CAME EARLY in the evening on Katherine's first day back in New York. Exhausted from a long day of driving, she had just fallen asleep for the night. The ringing of her phone, however, was insistent. She fumbled for the phone.

"This is Rebecca Bernstein," the voice said.

This was a first. Susan's mother sounding sober two calls in a row. "Yes, Mrs. Bernstein, what is it?"

"I tried to call you earlier but you didn't answer."

"I was driving and probably in a dead zone. What can I do for you?" Katherine asked.

"Susan's in the hospital."

"Yes, I know. She's in the recovery center."

"No, she's in a hospital back here in New York City. Beth Israel."

Katherine sat up in her bed. "What happened?"

"She'd been doing well. She decided to visit us, even though they told her she wasn't ready for that. She got into the vodka, took my car, and had an accident."

"When?"

"Late this afternoon."

Katherine was wide-awake. "How bad is it?"

"The doctor said she was fortunate. A broken arm and some cuts and bruises, nothing life-threatening. Could have been a lot worse. She's been asking for you. The doctor says you can see her."

"Call Susan and tell her I'll be right there," Katherine said. She hung up the phone and quickly said a little prayer for her troubled friend.

• • •

With little traffic on the highways, Katherine made good time, and by eleven she was in Susan's hospital room. Her best friend was awake, with an I.V. in her wrist and bruises on her face and neck. Her right arm was in a cast.

"Some people will do anything to get attention," Katherine said, gently touching Susan's left hand.

"Don't make me laugh. It hurts too much," Susan said.

"I'd like to know what happened."

"To me or the other guy?"

Katherine began to worry. "Please, Susan, tell me there was not another guy."

"The other guy was a fire hydrant, and I left him gushing. At least that's what they told me." Her face crumpled. "I'm sorry I let you down again."

"I'm sorry you let yourself down. As for me, I'm glad you're alive and no one else was hurt."

"I don't know, maybe I shouldn't be alive. I thought I had this thing licked. I never should have gone to my parents'."

"Were they drinking in front of you?"

"No. Believe it or not, my mother's been on the wagon and my father's been keeping his drinking away from her. I just knew where to find the liquor."

Susan stared at Katherine for a long while and shook her head. "I'm so weak. So out of control. They talk about that in rehab, that it has to be self-realized, but I do not have the strength to do it on my own."

Susan's words struck Katherine in a profound way. She was left with nothing to say in return. She only hoped if she could get some professional advice from Marcia, maybe she could raise her game on how to be of some help to her friend. In the meantime, the best she could do was keep the conversation going.

"What did the doctors say?" Katherine asked, taking a seat in the lone chair in the room.

"It's funny, they keep telling me how lucky I am."

"What did your new sponsor say?"

"He's pissed. Favors a tough love approach."

Katherine smiled at Susan, hoping to pick up her spirits. "What are your plans?"

"I'm going back to the center as soon as I get out of here."

Katherine nodded. Time for a little chitchat. She told Susan about her trip to Braydon, her research and interviews, meeting Bobby's parents, and her suspicions.

"You think about Sean anymore?"

"Ha! Do you want the other arm broken?"

"Seriously."

"I haven't taken the bug off the cell phone, if that is what you are asking. I still use it, but I bought another one. I'm letting Sean hear only what I want him to hear. Other than that, well, the verdict is still out."

"Somehow, that doesn't sound like you."

It was probably the most astute comment Susan had ever made. Katherine set her purse on the floor.

"No, it's not like me. I agonize about this every night before I go to sleep. If I allow myself to compromise my beliefs, everything I stand for in my own mind is a lie, but I have an idea Sean's eavesdropping has something to do with my father and what's going on with his car dealerships. And I believe in my father, and I hate Sean using such means to go after him."

"You think you can learn what Sean has on your dad—if he has anything."

Katherine frowned. "If he has anything?"

"Right, if he has anything."

"I just don't know. Probably not, but I am not going to let him listen in on what I say to people I care about. I'm having all sorts of second thoughts, but I'm not ready to let him get away with this. Can we talk about something else?"

"How about Bobby?"

Katherine smiled. "Good subject choice. Entirely different guy. Strong, but gentle. Great sense of humor."

"Maybe this is the guy."

"Maybe you assume too much."

"That never stopped you. I'm glad the reporting is going well."

"Thanks. Sol's been so great about all of it. Chuck, of course, is practically seething with resentment."

"What else is bothering you?" Susan asked.

"Don't think you're enough?" ·

"Something else is on your mind," Susan said.

"My mother's on my mind. Her eyes are getting worse."

"Life sucks," Susan said. "Then we die."

"And since you're not going to die, I think our visit is over now. It's been uplifting. I'm going to get some sleep. I'll check in with you tomorrow. To make sure you don't slip up and mention anything you shouldn't on my old phone, I'm writing down the number for the new one." Katherine ripped a page out of her notepad and jotted down the number before leaving it on the small table by the bed.

She got up and headed to the door. The last thing she heard as she walked down the hall was Susan saying, "Thanks for coming, Katherine, and for caring."

• • •

Katherine went into the office late the next morning; she spent the first hour or so returning e-mails and phone calls. After a good meeting with Sol about the bank story, she returned to her desk to find a new e-mail from Mike with a draft of his first major article on the bank collapse attached. He wanted her input before it went to his paper's editor. As agreed, she and Mike shared the byline. She spent the rest of the day working on the draft, calling him twice for clarifications before returning her version of the finished piece.

Exhausted from so little sleep the night before and her recent trip, she later dragged herself up her apartment steps, reheated a simple stew concoction she liked in the microwave, and then called her mother while she ate.

"Hi, sweetheart," Beth said, sounding strangely upbeat. "Now don't go into a tizzy, Katherine, but my eyesight has gotten worse, and I've decided I shouldn't work anymore. It's not fair to my patients or the hospital."

Katherine went to the kitchen and poured herself a glass of wine. "Tell me about it."

"More dark spots. Less peripheral vision. I need much more light to see."

"Mom, what does your specialist say?"

"He started me on a regimen of shots to decrease the fluid that's leaking in and around my maculae."

"Damn, shots right in the eye?"

"It's not as bad as it sounds."

"I don't know, Mom, it sounds pretty bad." Katherine rubbed her eyes, knowing that doing so still wouldn't make the wavy lines of her own tension headache disappear. "I'm so sorry you're having to go through this. I hate that you're all alone."

"I'm not all alone. One of the nurses on my shift took me to my eye doctor and then drove me home. She stayed with me last night. Joan is coming tonight. I am going to be fine. Of course Hailey's here, too."

"Why didn't you call me sooner? I feel so helpless. I should be there with you."

"No, you should be right where you are. You can't live your life and mine, too. I don't have to work, and I'm not going to. I just wanted you to know."

They said their good-byes, and Katherine finished her glass of wine and poured another. She knew that her mom's euphoria over not having to work would soon disappear, only to be replaced with the harsh reality of the empty hours she would now have to fill. Beth had to be helping others to stay alive. Taking care of Adrian these past few years, especially since Katherine had left, had been a second full-time job for Beth. Katherine had never realized that until Joan happened to mention how often she had been called to go over and tend to Adrian when Beth was at work.

She fumbled around for her old phone, pulled up Harry's number, typed it into her new phone, and pressed Call.

"Hi, little lady," Harry's booming voice came on the line. "How ya doing? Got a Pulitzer yet?"

"Working on it, Harry. How's the band?"

"We have a gig in downtown Buffalo. We're singing to the Polish choir on this one. They're gonna love it."

"And how are you doing?" Katherine asked with a bit of trepidation.

"I'm fine. I miss my friend. You know I ride it up and I ride it down, but the music and the guys keep me going. I haven't seen your mom since the . . . since we said good-bye to your granddaddy. How's she holdin' up?"

"That's why I'm calling you, Harry. I just talked to her. You know she has macular degeneration."

"She told me she had some problems seeing, but she always seemed to get around pretty well."

"It's gotten worse. She feels she can't work as a nurse anymore. I'm worried sick about her. Nursing means everything to her. After a month at home, she'll go crazy. Hailey can't help with this one."

"Who, on the human side, is lookin' after her?"

"Her friend Joan drops by often, I think."

"She lives a fair distance from Beth, if I remember, and she has a job of her own."

"She's forty-five minutes from the house, and you're absolutely right, she works."

"I tell you what. You're too good-looking to be worrying. Too good a dancer, too. I'm going to go see your mother."

"That would be so great," Katherine shouted, as if she had never in a thousand years had the first inkling this might happen. "I would appreciate it, Harry."

"So would I, little lady. That's what the Oompah Man does. And Beth could use a little oompah right now, I suspect."

"Bless your li'l' ol' heart."

"Don't go all southern on me," Harry said.

She laughed. "I won't if you won't. And thank you, Harry."

"I'll give you a ring later on. Let you know how it's going."

Katherine had called Harry on her new phone, and when she ended the call the phone buzzed almost immediately. Anonymous flashed on the screen, and she assumed it was Harry calling her back for some reason.

"Hi, Harry," she said.

There was no reply, only the sound of a car horn before the line went dead. She looked at the phone funny, and then recalled another hang up she had received a few weeks earlier. That time, the call had come on her old phone.

CHAPTER 37

CAROL MARTIN MET Anthony Spagnello, along with his client, Austin Disley, in one of the conference rooms at the courthouse. Their meeting followed a phone call in which she had told Spagnello a short window existed for a plea deal. Spagnello had requested a meeting to discuss the possibility, and he had asked permission to bring Austin with him in the hope that the harsh reality of his situation would finally dawn on his client. Martin had agreed to both requests.

"This is Assistant District Attorney and Acting U.S. Attorney Carol Martin," Spagnello said to Disley as they gathered around a small, worn table in the conference room.

"It's nice to meet you," Disley said with a smile.

Martin returned the smile, saying, "You as well, Mr. Disley."

Spagnello raised his hand, as if to indicate "enough of this." "Ms. Martin is going to review the proposed plea-bargain with us. This would normally be done without your being present, but I thought it might be helpful for you to hear it firsthand. I would ask you not to talk during this discussion."

Disley nodded.

"This case is quite straightforward," Carol said. "I would like to outline the procedure of a plea, should you be interested in making one. Of course your attorney will advise you as to what you should or should not do."

Disley nodded again, accompanying it with yet another smile. As Carol Martin outlined the basic facts of the bank fraud case, Disley's face went white and emotionless. He looked as if he might be sick when she mentioned that one of the other defendants, whom she declined to name, was also discussing a plea arrangement.

"Let's talk about what you have in mind for Mr. Disley," Spagnello said.

"We have Mr. Disley on one count of conspiracy to commit bank fraud in violation of Title 18, Section 1349, and three counts in violation of Section 1344, in addition to felony larceny charges. Based upon Mr. Disley's plea to the other charges, we'll drop the 1349 charge. That way he may have a shot of serving less than the full twenty years."

Spagnello tried to keep his face neutral—he did not want to show his shock at the paltry bargain the government was offering. Disley also stayed quiet, which bothered the attorney almost as much as what he had heard from Carol Martin. Something was off with his client—way off.

Assessing Carol Martin's body language, Spagnello said, "Let me see if I understand this. Conspiracy and bank fraud charges go away, and what we're left with is a plea to a felony relating to the money disbursement from the five cars sold at wholesale that no judge would ever find to be a crime."

"No, we'll drop that, too," she said almost offhandedly. "It's the other larceny count we're not vacating."

Spagnello's instincts were confirmed. The other larceny? He couldn't ask her about it in front of Disley. If he did, Disley and he would both look like asses. "Let me talk with my client," Spagnello said. "I'll get back to you."

"Before you do, I suggest you and I chat for a minute alone." She put the papers outlining the plea bargain in her briefcase.

"Of course," Spagnello said, escorting Disley from the room. "Wait for me in the lobby."

As they watched Disley leave and Spagnello took his seat at the table, Carol turned to the lawyer, "You don't know about it, do you?"

"Why don't you just tell me what you think I should know?" Spagnello said.

"Mr. Wilson has been cooperating with us. He called the FBI to report that your client lifted eighty-thousand dollars electronically from Wilson Holdings' operating accounts in each of its five dealerships. That's four-hundred-thousand dollars. We can have him arrested for grand larceny right now—I have an officer standing by—or we can have him arrested someplace else."

"I'd rather not have him arrested here, but I will make sure he fully cooperates with you. I need to talk to him."

"That's fine. Just know the clock's ticking." Carol nodded and walked out the door.

Anthony Spagnello liked to be in control and, like every attorney, hated being blindsided. He sat at the table trying to compose himself, unaware that he had twisted a legal pad into a grotesque figure. He found his client in the lobby, sitting on a bench as though he did not have a care to his name.

"We need to talk," he said, gesturing for Disley to follow him back upstairs to the conference room.

"Where's Ms. Martin?" Disley asked as he took the same seat as before.

"She left, Austin, but not before dropping a grenade. Enlighten me about the eighty-thousand dollars you removed from each of the Wilson Holdings stores."

Disley gave Spagnello the stupid grin the attorney had come to expect whenever a client was about to try to play him. "Sure, no problem. It was my severance pay. Two years' worth. I had it coming, and when I didn't get it, I figured Preston was either preoccupied or had forgotten. So I arranged for the transfers."

"Do you have a contract with Wilson Holdings that provides for a two-year severance?"

"That was our understanding."

"Do you have that in writing?"

"Not on paper, exactly, but it was definitely what we agreed on," Disley said.

"Can I assume you didn't tell Preston that you were taking your severance pay?"

"You told me not to talk to him, remember?"

"You're clear then that you were entitled to take this money—that it belonged to you—and that Preston would see it the same way?"

"Absolutely."

"Then you're going to be *really* surprised when I tell you that the U.S. Attorney plans to have you arrested for grand larceny for stealing that money. It is my responsibility as your attorney to ask if you would like to cooperate and present yourself for arrest, or would you like to have the U.S. Marshal Service find you and take you in?"

"That's absurd. It's just another trumped-up charge. I'd like you to do the job I'm paying you the big bucks for and make sure I don't get arrested."

Spagnello rose from his chair and leaned over Disley. "I'm going to ignore that comment. Chalk it up to being defensive, nervous, or just plain crazy. If I withdraw as your counsel, you'll have to go through all this again, and at the same expense or more. Is that what you want?"

Disley fiddled with the lapel on his coat, since it was one time he had taken his attorney's advice and not worn a bow tie. He mumbled, "No, I guess I don't want that."

"Then tell me how you'd like to be arrested."

"There's no way I'd *like* to be arrested," Disley said, getting up as he paced around the room. "If I have to be arrested, I'd like it to be in the least intrusive way possible. Will I have to post bail for this as well?"

"You should *hope* you will be able to post bail for this as well."

Disley took his seat, thought for a minute, and then slammed his fist against the table. "Go ahead and do whatever it is you have to do."

Spagnello glared at Disley, bit his tongue, and said, "Sit tight, and whatever you do, do not leave. If you are not here when I get back, you are on your own—and do not even think about calling me. Ms. Martin will have a marshal come in and arrest you. I will stay with you, and I will try to find a judge and have an arraignment while we are here. With a little luck, you will not spend the night in jail."

Spagnello went to find the marshal, half hoping that when they returned Austin Disley would be gone.

CHAPTER 38

PRESTON, ALEX, AND Casey had started meeting daily at eight a.m. at the dealership in what had become known as the War Room. It was Casey's idea—to enhance communication and ensure execution, as he put it. The men had come to welcome beginning each workday at that time together. They were, however, still reeling from the revelation that Disley had appropriated almost half a million dollars from the company.

The discussion this particular morning centered on a letter from Arthur Goldberg, vice president of commercial finance at BNA. Two paragraphs in Goldberg's communication had not escaped anyone:

> *BNA, in good faith, believes it is unsecured based upon Wilson Holdings' current financial condition. Specifically, it is in a Negative Covenant Breach of Continuity of Operations by making a $400,000.00 unauthorized distribution and its failure to maintain a required Debt Service Coverage Ratio of 1.10 to 1.00 for the prior 12 months.*
>
> *You are hereby notified that Wilson Holdings is considered to be in material default of its obligations under its Business Loan Agreement, Capital Loans, and Manhattan Mercedes' Flooring Line Agreements. Accordingly, all*

indebtedness, under all notes and agreements, shall imme-
diately become due and payable to BNA.

"Are we that off on the ratios?" Alex asked Casey.

"No, and certainly not as grounds for cutting us off across the board."

"What about the financial insecurity argument?" Preston asked.

Casey went to the whiteboard and posted the numbers from the company's current balance sheet, a copy of which he had begun carrying with him at all times. The amounts reflecting Disley's theft were displayed in brackets.

"There are legal questions, to be sure," Casey said, "but in my experience, any entity considering itself insecure rests on the ability of the debtor to pay, and we aren't in default of a single payment obligation."

"The only thing they cite is the unauthorized distribution of the four-hundred-thousand dollars Disley took," noted Alex.

"That clearly hurt us. It was unauthorized, and it does appear it was taken by us since BNA does not know the money was stolen. The bank needs to know that. All BNA sees is the hit on our consolidated statement," Casey said.

Preston poured himself a cup of coffee. "Whatever the explanation, our profit is down, and we'll be out of business without a way to finance our cars. We need access to our capital lines to operate, and they're calling both." He let out a sour laugh. "As far as deeming themselves financially unsecured, I can feel their pain."

Casey chuckled and attacked the donut tray on the credenza. Alex failed to see the humor in the situation. "How are we going to deal with this? The bank has to give us notice, right? How much time do we have?"

"The bank does have to provide notice, even if the boilerplate says otherwise," Preston said. "To your last question, we need all the time we can get."

"We get that time, how?" Alex asked.

"I will talk with Andy Brookfield on the legal side," Preston said.

"What makes this even more complicated is that one of BNA's vice presidents, Teddy Thompson, is a named defendant in the bank fraud case. I don't know what he's supposed to have done, but Goldberg must know him and the particulars of what the feds have on him."

"We still need to answer this letter," Alex said.

Preston fixed his eyes on the numbers on the whiteboard. "Andy will answer the letter. If you take the four-hundred-thousand dollars out of it—which is on Disley—I'll be surprised if BNA would push for a default and full payback. Too many other lender-liability concerns."

Casey noted that Preston was talking like a CEO again. "You have something in mind?" Casey asked him.

"I do. You and I need to take a trip to Charlotte and talk with our buddy, Tom Gallagher."

. . .

Preston had no more walked through the door that evening than P.J. came running. The boy wrapped his little arms around his neck, and it was as if a valve somewhere in Preston's head popped open, releasing the tension of the day. He embraced his son tightly and kissed him on each cheek. As Preston hung his coat in the hall closet, P.J. entertained himself by donning Preston's dress hat.

When the two Wilson men settled themselves on the floor with a pile of blocks and P.J.'s favorite truck, Preston looked up to see Marcia taking it all in. A few minutes later, he heard her laughter coming from the kitchen, a sound he had not heard enough of lately.

Eventually P.J. moved on to another toy, and Preston strolled into the kitchen where he found Marcia at the sink rinsing some pots and pans. He put his arms around her and gave her a soft kiss on the back of her neck.

She did not pull away but did not move toward him, either. "Dinner is just about ready," she said.

After they had finished eating, instead of clearing away the plates, Marcia poured herself a glass of wine and asked how his day had gone. Preston decided this time not to spare her any of the gory details.

"The bank has declared us in default and is calling our notes and dropping our financing on everything."

Preston's voice had been calm as he relayed the bad news, but Marcia's reaction was anything but. "How . . . how can they do that?"

"The bank is concerned about our financial condition." He took a sip of the Scotch whiskey he had poured for himself and added, "with good reason."

"Things have been going well . . . *improved* . . . right?" Marcia said, finishing her glass of after dinner wine in one gulp.

"We're organized, in control, and have clearly made improvements. Casey and Alex are working hard to fix everything, and so am I."

"Then how can they question our financial condition?" Marcia asked, picking up her wine glass as if she might throw it at the wall.

Preston gently took the glass from her and set it on the table. "Because our profit is down and our reserves are off."

"Why is that?" Marcia asked.

"We took a four-hundred-thousand-dollar hit."

"What?"

"Seems on his way out the door—or sometime right after-wards—my old friend, Austin, helped himself to some extra compensation, like four-hundred-thousand dollars worth."

"That son of a bitch," Marcia shouted. "Wait . . . how could he? He was fired."

"Somehow, Austin had the passwords to the bank accounts for each store. I have turned everything over to the FBI. Casey and I are going to talk with Tom Gallagher in Charlotte and explain what happened. We plan to meet with him as soon as possible."

"Tom likes you both," Marcia said, her tone dialed down to almost normal.

"He's a fair man," Preston said, "and his bank is also a defen-dant in the fraud case, so he has skin in the game in a different way.

What I'm afraid of is that Disley's stuff may play into that. Nothing will surprise me about any of this."

"Would you like another Scotch?"

Preston shook his head while his wife poured herself another glass of wine. He took her hand.

"I know this has been awful for you, sweetheart. I want you to know we're making progress at the dealership, even though at times it may not feel like it."

She squeezed his hand and pulled away in the same motion. "I know you've been working hard on all of this, but I can't help hating Disley. I hate what the bank's doing to you . . . to us."

"I've put you under a lot of stress these past months. And if anything, it's gotten worse of late. Honey, I'm terribly sorry."

"I'll be fine and so will P.J. I know I've been running hot and cold myself lately." She stared at her wine glass, and then looked up at her husband through her eyelashes. "I think you should know that I've been in touch with a psychiatrist. I have an appointment with her tomorrow afternoon. I tried to work this all out on my own, but I realize now I could probably use some help."

Preston leaned back in surprise. Marcia had hinted before that she might seek help, but he had never thought she would actually follow through on it. "I take it you know this person pretty well?"

"I trained under her in college. I think she can help me."

"Would you like me to go with you?"

"No, actually, I want to go by myself, at least this first time. Okay?"

Marcia sounded resolute, so he simply nodded and let it go. "You have my support 100 percent," Preston said.

Preston realized that the best-case scenario would be for his wife to get the help and perspective she needed so their marriage could get back on sure footing. He would never have said anything to Marcia because trying to anticipate what mood she would be in each time he returned from work had become grueling.

Later in his den, Preston considered his options. It was too late to call the bank. He had Tom's personal cell phone number but had never used it before. He decided to break protocol. Tom answered on the second ring and told him that he was on his way back to Charlotte and would be in his office in the morning. Tom would work Preston in.

CHAPTER 39

CASEY AND PRESTON were booked on a 6:30 a.m. flight, but the flight was canceled, and their departure was moved to 8:45 a.m. Not knowing how long their meeting at the bank would take, they scheduled their return flight for 8:20 p.m. A salesman from the Charlotte dealership picked them up at the airport at eleven and drove them to BNA headquarters.

They were ushered right into Tom Gallagher's office. After greetings all around, Tom said, "Since you boys got up so early to make your flight, I would imagine you could both eat a horse. How about we get a table in the executive dining room upstairs and eat and talk at the same time . . ."

Preston was amused when Casey said yes before Tom could finish his offer.

The private dining room on the fortieth floor of the bank offered a panoramic view of Charlotte and the special sort of quiet dignity only old money could provide. Tom led them to an area with an elegant silver "Reserved" sign in front and then to a table in the corner.

"A lot has happened since we last talked," Preston said after they were seated and a waiter had taken their drink orders. "I'm sure you know why Casey and I flew down here. We wanted to tell you face-to-face some pertinent information about the four-hundred-thousand-dollar withdrawal."

The waiter returned to pour the coffee and iced tea, and Tom waited until the man left before saying, "The two of you making this trip is the way Joe Hart would do things. I'm sorry he's no longer with us. That man was something else."

"Amen," Preston said as Casey nodded. The men looked over their menus, and soon the waiter returned for their orders. Once they were placed and the waiter was nowhere to be seen, Tom asked without the slightest sarcasm in his voice, "Why don't you go ahead and share this pertinent information you were talking about."

Preston nodded and said, "I'm sure you know that Austin Disley is a defendant—"

"I'm sorry, I need to interrupt you for a moment," Tom said. "I'm going to listen to you, but please understand if I don't comment—given the circumstances."

"Of course," Preston said, "my lawyer has advised me to not even have this conversation."

"Yet you're here having it anyway," Tom said.

"Yes, sir, I am. Neither Casey nor I know anything whatsoever about what the government has that supports the allegations against Mr. Disley. At first we thought his involvement was limited to his orchestrating the sale of five cars at wholesale to customers of a developer with a connection to your bank. We still do not know what that tie-in involved, or if it ever existed. What we do know is that we lost about a hundred-thousand dollars in potential profit because of the way these cars were let go, and that it is inconsistent with the protocols of our Rolls and Bentley franchises."

Tom listened and, as promised, offered no comment, though Preston observed one of the banker's eyebrows rise slightly in what he thought was surprise. Preston continued. "Recently, Alex Herman—you've met him before—"

"I remember Mr. Herman. Finance. He supported you on the workout," Tom interrupted.

"He has come in to help us. Casey, as you can see, has returned to right the ship. I probably should note that Casey is now the majority owner—"

"Let me interrupt again. I want to congratulate Casey." Tom reached over to shake Casey's hand. "No matter what happens, I'm glad to see you're back."

"Thank you," Casey said as the first course was served.

The conversation turned to sports and other pleasantries as everyone tackled their salads and soups, and then their entrées soon thereafter. When the meal was finished, plates cleared, and the drinks refilled, Preston said, "What I wanted to say earlier was that we were shocked to find out that Mr. Disley—after he was fired by me—used our passwords to wire eighty-thousand dollars from the operating account of each of our five stores to an offshore account."

Preston watched a frown form on Tom's face and plowed on, "When we found out about Disley's stealing the four-hundred-thousand dollars, I called the FBI, but we have kept all that in-house. In hindsight, we should've notified you, too. I apologize."

"What do you think about all of this, Casey?" Tom asked.

"I know Preston's done nothing wrong. He's been put in an awkward spot and is handling it quite well, considering. Maybe Arthur Goldberg could shed some light on some of the areas that right now are more than a little muddled. You're aware of the letter he drafted, pulling our lines?"

Tom nodded. "Now that I know what's happened, I'll see that everything is put on hold until we can do a full analysis."

"We're current all the way around," Preston said, breathing a huge internal sigh of relief.

"It won't be easy," Tom said. "There's more at play here, and it's going to take me a while to get to the bottom of it. If you keep your accounts with us current, I'll see that your capital loans and flooring lines stay intact." He tossed the spoon he had been using to stir his coffee on the table and it clattered against his saucer. "Now, what about Disley?"

"I never liked Disley," Casey said. "He's always been a liability and a jerk in my eyes, and now he's a crook in everybody's."

Tom could not contain his laughter. "Y'all ought to come down here and visit us more often, Mr. Fitzgerald. If you ever get tired of Mr. Wilson, and when the dust settles with this mess, you might want to consider working for us."

"I'll pretend I didn't hear that," Preston said with a smile.

A dessert cart was wheeled to the table, and with everyone in better spirits than when they had started lunch, they all decided on something fattening. Casey appeared to show the most restraint, ordering fresh raspberries in light cream. Yet his dessert arrived with a second plate, covered by a silver lid, which when removed revealed a giant Snickers candy bar. Tom Gallagher winked at the waiter, who nodded and quickly turned way.

Preston and Casey thanked Tom for lunch and for taking the time to meet with them. "It has been quite informative," Tom said before looking at Casey. "I'll have that little chat with Mr. Goldberg as soon as I get back to the office."

"We appreciate it," Casey said. "Always a pleasure to do business with you."

As they shook hands and said their good-byes, Preston and Casey headed downstairs to meet their ride to the airport. When they arrived at the terminal, they immediately went to the U.S. Airways ticket counter to see about getting an earlier flight back to New York City; both were anxious to get home. The reservationist looked at their tickets, checked the computer, and said, "The 5:25 is booked, and the 6:25's sold out, too. I'm sorry but there's no earlier flight to LaGuardia or Kennedy than the one you're on at 8:20 p.m."

With about three hours to kill, they headed to the U.S. Air lounge at the intersection of concourses C and D. They checked in, and Casey ordered a couple of beers for both of them from the bar. Preston realized he had been so excited about not losing his financing that he had forgotten to turn on his phone after leaving BNA's headquarters. All the quiet areas and phone booths were occupied, so he told Casey he was going to step outside for a minute. On the side of the D Concourse, he found a quiet spot halfway to the gates and called home to check in with Marcia.

"Hi, Nadine, this is Preston. Could you please get Marcia? I need to speak with her."

"Oh, Mr. Wilson, it's you! I'm so glad you called." Nadine said in a shaky voice. "I've been trying to call you all day but couldn't get through. I'm worried sick."

"What happened? Is P.J. okay? Where's Marcia?"

"I don't know," she cried.

"What do you mean, you don't know?"

"Well, P.J. is fine, but I don't know where Marcia is. She went to her appointment this morning but never returned. Have you seen the news?"

"No. I've been at a meeting all day, and I'm at the airport now. What are you talking about?"

"There's been an explosion. Gas. Upper West side. Maybe I'm . . . I don't know. I'm just worried. It's not like Marcia to be late or not to call. I get no answer on her cell."

"Nadine?"

"Yes?"

"Marcia had a doctor's appointment this morning."

"Yes, I know. I saw that on my Cozi."

"On what?"

"It's an app for Marcia's calendar that she put on my phone so we would know each other's schedule. Hang on while I check it."

Preston waited for what seemed like forever, and with each passing moment his instincts told him something was wrong.

"Her appointment was with . . . do you want the doctor's name?"

"Of course," he replied, trying not to sound too terse.

Nadine gave Preston the name and the address: 550 West 114th Street. Then Preston could have sworn that she dropped the phone.

"Nadine? Nadine? Are you there?"

After a few seconds: "I'm here. I'm here. The news says the explosion was on 114th Street. That doesn't mean—"

"Nadine, I have another call coming in. Can you hold? It might be Marcia."

"Oh, yes, of course. Please hurry."

"Don't hang up," Preston heard himself yell to Nadine. He punched the hold button and accepted the other call. It was Casey.

"Preston? I'm looking at a gas explosion in Manhattan on TV. Where are you?"

"In hell. Can I call you back? I'm on the line with Nadine. Marcia's gone missing. I'll be back shortly." Preston ended his call with Casey and switched back to Nadine. "Are you there?"

"Yes, Mr. Wilson, I'm holding."

"That was Casey. He saw a TV report on the explosion," Preston said. "Nadine, I need you to stay put and take care of P.J. until I can get home and find out what's going on. Can you do that?"

"Certainly. Don't you worry, Mr. Preston. I'll be here and P.J. will be fine. I promise."

Preston hung up the phone and ran back to the lounge. A group of subdued men and women were gathered around the large television screens, Casey among them. "What do you know?" Preston asked Casey, staring at the newscast.

Casey replied, "The reporter was interviewing a first responder."

Behind the firemen, a five-story building was engulfed in black smoke with bright flames belching from its top and sides. Preston stared at the disaster. It was as if he were trapped in the fire himself. He felt Casey squeezing his arm, and then he heard him ask, "Preston, tell me about the call."

"I called Marcia. Our nanny answered, and she's a nervous wreck. She saw news about the explosion on TV. She hasn't heard from Marcia and hasn't been able to reach her on her cell phone. My wife had a doctor's appointment this morning on the upper west side. Nadine thinks Marcia may be in there," Preston said.

"Oh, my God," Casey said as more images of the blown-out windows, rubble, and chaos flashed across the screen. "It looks like a war zone."

"I've got to get home, Casey."

CHAPTER 40

FOR THE NEXT HOUR, Preston made one phone call after another, in between trying Marcia's cell phone every ten minutes. He called Katherine, told her what he knew, and asked her if she could use her press connections to find out if Marcia was one of the victims. He told her that, according to CNN, the injured were being taken to Saint Luke's-Roosevelt Hospital on Amsterdam Avenue. He also gave her the office address of Marcia's doctor.

"I'm on my way to the scene," Katherine said. "I'll look for you at the hospital."

Frazzled and distraught, Preston found himself consuming pretzels one right after the other and washing them down with black coffee so strong it could have revived a corpse. Casey had arranged for Alex to pick them up at LaGuardia on the upper departure deck to save time, only to find out that Preston's plan was to take a cab directly to Saint Luke's in hopes of finding Marcia—unless Katherine found information to the contrary beforehand. It was 11:15 p.m. when their plane touched down and almost midnight before Preston's cab pulled up at the hospital. Casey and Alex had wanted to come along, but instead Preston had asked Casey to let Alex drive him home so he could get some sleep, figuring he might need to be on call the next day.

Preston found Katherine waiting for him in the hospital lobby. "I checked with 3-1-1, and Marcia's not showing up as a victim, but

259

I was cautioned that there are victims whose identities are unknown at this point. They won't talk to me here," she said, explaining that her status as Marcia's stepdaughter had not been enough to glean any more information from the emergency room admission staff, nor had any of her contacts been able to do better. The laws involving patient privacy were too strict to be sidestepped or ignored.

"I'm sorry, Dad, but I can't even get them to confirm that a Marcia Wilson has been admitted," Katherine said.

"I appreciate your trying. Maybe they'll talk to me," Preston said.

Preston approached an admissions nurse, identified himself, and established that he was Marcia's husband. He showed the nurse a picture of his wife, only to be informed that no Marcia Wilson had been admitted that night. Preston was about to walk away in despair, when the nurse spoke again.

"Sir, I don't want to give you false hope, but I can tell you we have an unidentified female patient who might fit the description of your wife."

"Could I see her?" he asked. "At least I could maybe help you determine who she isn't."

"That might be possible. I know this is stressful for you, but if you could please take a seat in the waiting room, I'll see what I can do. I promise to come get you as soon as I know anything." The nurse pointed Preston and Katherine to a room where they could wait.

As he took a seat, part of Preston wanted the unknown woman to be Marcia; another part wanted anything but that. The best he could hope for was that somehow she was not involved in this tragedy. Maybe her cell phone battery went dead. Maybe that was why he couldn't reach her.

The thought briefly buoyed his spirits, and he checked in with Nadine, praying she would say Marcia had returned and all was well. Instead, he was told nothing had changed. Nadine had still not heard from Marcia and her calls to his wife had continued to go unanswered. The only good news was that P.J. was sleeping peacefully.

As he put his phone down, Preston turned to his daughter, who had been busily working her phone since he had arrived. He watched her hang up and give a sad little shake of her head. Still no news. After what seemed like hours, but in fact was more like twenty minutes, the admissions nurse approached them with another woman in her fifties wearing a hospital photo ID badge. Preston and Katherine rose.

"Mr. Wilson, my name is Beatrice Jones. I'm with the hospital's Health Coordinator's Office. Here's the situation: we have a woman who generally matches your wife's description but who, at this time, is an unidentified patient. She has suffered severe head trauma and internal injuries, and required brain surgery. She's in ICU now. We will allow you to see her to assist in identification; however, that will have to wait until we have the neurosurgeon's permission."

Preston fell back on the couch. Katherine stood in silence. For a moment, no one spoke.

"When will that be?" Preston finally managed to ask.

"We don't know," Ms. Jones said. "Generally, in a situation like this, the doctor will insist on waiting until the patient has stabilized."

Preston tried to protest, but it was quickly made clear he would not be allowed in the ICU anytime soon. He had no choice but to go home until the condition of the unknown female patient was deemed stable. Katherine went with him. She had had the foresight to pack a bag, and as soon as they arrived back at the apartment, Preston showed her to a guest bedroom after explaining what they knew to Nadine.

"As if you haven't done enough today, Nadine, could you possibly stay over until I get a handle on what's going on?"

"Of course, Mr. Wilson, I already made plans to do so."

Preston recalled that she had a young son, about five years old. "Do you have someone to take care of your boy?"

"My son is with my mother tonight. My sister will watch him tomorrow. We all look after each other."

Nadine's comment about her mother reminded Preston he should call his in-laws at some point. When the facts were clearer, but certainly not before. There was no reason to worry them unnecessarily. That decided, he went to check on Katherine to make certain she had clean towels and everything else she needed, but as he caught a glimpse of Nadine scurrying around the apartment, he chastised himself for harboring such a silly worry. He should be half as organized as P.J.'s nanny.

It was 3:00 a.m. by the time Preston had undressed and put on his pajamas. He had been up since four the preceding morning, yet still found himself too wound up to sleep. He put on a robe and padded into the kitchen for a soft drink. Nadine was sitting at the kitchen table, looking at one of Marcia's magazines.

"Aren't you going to bed?" Preston asked her.

"I need to be awake if someone calls from the hospital."

"Don't worry about that. You need to get some sleep. I'll answer the phone. You take one of the other guest bedrooms," Preston said.

Nadine nodded and turned to go.

"Nadine, before you turn in, do you have a minute?" Preston asked.

Nadine turned and faced her boss with a puzzled look on her face. "Of course, Mr. Wilson."

Preston took a seat at the kitchen island and opened his cola. "I've been thinking about something you said earlier about your family. If I recall, you said, 'We all look after each other.' Who did you mean by 'we'?"

He watched as a look of deep pride settled on Nadine's face. "My family. We're Jamaican. We support each other."

"Tell me about your son," Preston said, watching Nadine take a small step back as his words registered.

"His name is Delonn," she said, smiling.

Preston listened attentively as Nadine described her son, when and how he had come with her to the United States from Ocho Rios, Jamaica, and how much better their lives were since they immigrated. She talked about her son until Preston had finished his soda, and not once in the course of her story did she refer to herself beyond her opening remarks about bringing Delonn to the States with her when he was barely a year old. Her eyes twinkled as she told Preston that her son not only knew his ABCs, but he could also count to one hundred and already print his name.

"He sounds like a great little guy. Thanks for telling me about him," Preston said.

Nadine smiled and Preston's heart swelled. With a quizzical look, Nadine said, "It's funny, Mr. Wilson. In all this time I've been working here as P.J.'s nanny, you've never asked me about my son or my family."

"I know." Preston swallowed. "It's not funny. I'm sorry."

"Sorry?"

"Yeah, I'm sorry."

She gave him the same puzzled look as before.

"Don't concern yourself with what I'm saying, Nadine. Just know that I'm finding out I've been wrong about a lot of things lately, and I learned of another instance of it just now. You go on to bed. I'll turn off everything."

CHAPTER 41

S EAN DIDN'T KNOW what to make of Katherine's phone calls from the night before. He had heard about the natural gas explosion on the Upper West Side, and Katherine had called a great many people not listed in the file he was keeping on her. Was she onto him? More likely she had simply never called any of these people before on her office cell, and that was why he had no record of them until now.

He was particularly interested in her call to Angelo Bertolini, an ex-cop with a solid reputation as a top-notch surveillance expert. Katherine must not know that her phone was bugged, or Bertolini would have made short work of finding it. As it stood, since she was operating in remote mode, he would have to keep tabs on her via her cell phone. In the past weeks, he had compiled quite a dossier on her father, but so far it was all supposition.

The pressure to make a case against Preston had been growing because the powers that be thought it could be the key to bringing down an international Russian cartel involved in everything from hacking and cyberterrorism to sex trafficking. His job was to follow the money and learn how it was laundered so they could trace it back to the bad guys. Their best hope, if any, to pressure Wilson Holdings would come from Katherine's phone calls, or at least that was how his boss saw it. Right now, however, he was focused on a puzzling call Bertolini had left yesterday on her phone:

Katherine: Anything more on our friend of the family?

Angelo: Quiet. But it's early. Alice still okay?

Katherine: She's nervous, but I believe she'll hold up.
Nothing at all on the folks?

Angelo: There was some serious money there. Not as
much now. Could explain some things, but I've
got more work to do.

Katherine: You know I can't pay you for this.

Angelo: Didn't ask you to. But like the guy in *The
Godfather* said, I might need a favor someday.

Katherine: [Laughs and hangs up].

All sorts of ideas ran through Sean's mind as he played that loop over and over. Something was about to happen, and he was positioned to be right on top of it when it did. This was the kind of break that made a career.

CHAPTER 42

HARRY, THE OOMPAH MAN, sat back in his blue leather chair, the same one he had been sitting in two years earlier as he positioned the muzzle of a fine Italian single-barrel shotgun between his eyes, ready to blow his head off. This time his outlook was decidedly different. Yes, the gun was once again in his hand but only so he could clean it. He had everything to live for now, and intended to enjoy every bit of what the rest of his life offered him.

Yet he would never sever his ties to the Fishtown section of Philadelphia where he was born or Dunkirk, New York, where his family eventually moved. It was not just about location but also the warmth and tightness that had come with such poor but proud Polish communities in each place. On Lake Erie, he had become a boater and learned to fish. In the Pocono Mountains, a few hours' drive south, he had learned to shoot and hunt. And then there was his high school, where the forever-popular Harry had made good grades, lettered in three sports, sang in the choir, and starred in his junior-senior play. Those were some okay days, he thought.

Neither his grades nor his athletic skills had been quite scholarship level, so with no family money for college, Uncle Sam had beckoned. It was in the U.S. Army, while stationed in Germany, that Harry had taken up photography by day, and by night, he had regaled the locals with his clear baritone and prowess on the accordion.

After the Army, he had become a professional photographer and taught music in Chautauqua, New York, where he met the love of his life. Soon thereafter he was dancing, drinking, and singing at his own Polish wedding. Life could not have been more promising until suddenly it was touched by betrayal. His young wife broke her promise, ran off with one of his close friends, and never returned. For Harry, losing his wife was not just a tremor—it was an earthquake that registered off the Richter scale.

It took years for him to regain any semblance of his signature wide smile and the twinkle in his bright blue eyes. He sought solace and security in a few talented buddies with whom he formed an oompah band, fashioned after the ones he had played with in Germany and had come to love. He found comfort in playing the rousing old tunes and watching people in the audience sing along and dance. He loved the laughter and joy of a crowded dance hall. He just wished he didn't always have to watch it through a window—with him always on the outside looking in.

Eventually, he moved to Batavia, New York, not far from his beloved Lake Erie and Chautauqua, and closer to his friends at the local gun club and, of course, Adrian. The guys you shoot and hunt with become family. The unexpected loss of Adrian and something he had not been able to put his finger on had brought him down as of late. After some reflection, he had finally zeroed in on the problem: He was lonely and needed love. The good news was he could clearly see the means to eliminate one and secure the other.

• • •

Harry had spent the last few weeks getting his ducks in line, including purchasing a brand-new 2014 Chevy Suburban LTZ 1500. It was time to put his plan into action. He was off to visit Beth Kelly in style.

On the drive from his home in Batavia to Beth's, he had reviewed what he would say to her. It had all seemed to be going as planned until he had pulled into Marion that bright, clear spring morning. Suddenly he was worried his rehearsal would fail him. He scratched his jaw. The hell with it. He would just let it roll.

Harry had long admired Beth. He had tried sending out some signals to that effect, but she had never picked up on them—or maybe she had but wasn't interested. Perhaps he was too subtle, although he had never before been accused of that. He took comfort in knowing he had always managed to make her laugh, yet he could not pinpoint why. Was she laughing because of him? Or was she laughing at him? Or was she just humoring him, thinking of Old Harry as she would a dotty patient?

He pushed the negative thoughts aside and contemplated whether or not his current medications were working. Convinced he was on about as even a keel as he ever would be, he eased the SUV forward—realizing there would be no turning back once he pulled into Adrian's driveway. He reminded himself it was Beth's driveway, too, now more so than ever. He parked the Suburban in front of the house, got out of his new chariot, brushed what remained of his thin, once-blond hair across his head, and slowly walked up to the side door, the one he had always used when visiting Adrian.

As he reached up to knock, he found Beth and Hailey already opening the screen door. Beth threw her arms around his neck and planted a big kiss on his cheek. "Hello, stranger, it's about time you . . . wait a minute . . . what's that big, beautiful vehicle in my driveway, Harry? It looks brand-spanking new."

"I wouldn't be visiting you in anything but the best. You know that. Besides, a man's gotta have room for his instruments—and maybe a passenger or two."

"Would that include Hailey and me?"

"You know it does."

"Then why don't you quit jibber-jabberin'—let's go for a ride."

"Come on, Hailey," Harry shouted as he led them to the Suburban and opened the rear door for the dog and the front passenger door for Beth.

"Are you going to be this polite your whole visit?" Beth asked, pretending to be shocked.

"If you can stand it, I am," Harry replied.

No differently than if he had had the prom queen sitting next to him, Harry cruised Main Street, past the S&L Café, and then into the country. Between raving about all the fancy features on Harry's SUV, Beth pointed out the local changes and improvements since the last time he had visited before finally suggesting they go back to the café for lunch. It was too early for the noon crowd, so they practically had the diner to themselves. They ordered and took a seat by one of the curtained windows.

"We're going to be the talk of the town, you know?" Beth said, with a knowing smile.

"I hope so," Harry retorted.

They both laughed at that before Harry's voice turned serious. "Tell me how you're doing, Beth. I know you miss Adrian. Hell, we all do. More importantly, I want to know how you're getting along. I want to know the truth."

"I'm okay. I'm not at the hospital anymore. My eyes have gotten worse, so I'll have to find something else, if I want to work."

"I'm sorry to hear that. May have an upside, though."

"Meaning?"

"You can't see that I haven't trimmed this beautiful beard . . . and that I'm getting a little heavier."

"I would never have noticed either even with twenty-twenty vision. You always look great to me, regardless." She touched his arm. "Harry, I appreciate your driving down here. So why don't you tell me why you're *really* here? Did Katherine send you down here to check on me?"

Harry frowned then laughed. "You are one suspicious fussbudget of a woman, pretty lady. Straighten up. You're talkin' to a hungry Oompah Man."

"If the Oompah Man is hungry, why doesn't he go over to the counter and get our lunch?" Beth asked, as she gave a little wave to the gal at the counter.

"Bossy, too, but your wish is my command," Harry said with a gallant bow as he exited the booth and headed to the counter to retrieve their order of white hotdogs, chili con carne, and two black coffees.

They took their time with the meal, including two coffee refills each. Beth seemed content to just sit and listen to Harry as he caught her up on what was going on with each member of the band and then proudly shared every detail of a recent gig in New York City that both Katherine and Preston had attended. He went on and on about what a wonderful girl Katherine was, and he even managed to make a nice comment or two about Preston, though it pained him. Finally, having oiled the pump, he tried to turn the conversation back to Beth and her future. To his disappointment, his questions only brought a few, noncommittal responses from Beth. Harry decided to try another approach.

He swallowed a big gulp of coffee and then put his mug down a little firmer than was necessary. "I don't know if you're aware of it, Beth, but in addition to being one of the world's finest musicians, an expert shooter, a skilled photographer, and a great dancer, I'm also bipolar."

"From that résumé alone, I wouldn't expect anything else," Beth said, laughing. "You wear it well as far as I'm concerned."

"That's what I want the world to think, and a lot of days, I am. Still, some days are dark. You're a nurse. Probably know all about depression."

Beth stared deeply into Harry's eyes before saying, "I am familiar with clinical depression. It can be difficult if not impossible for some people to control. However, when I said it doesn't concern me, what I said is the way I feel." She placed her hand on his. "You're coping with it extremely well from what I can see. Harry, we all have bad days. You think I never get lonely or down? Katherine's been gone to the city, and Dad's . . . " She wiped her eyes with a table napkin.

Harry handed her his handkerchief but she politely refused it. He stuffed it back in his pocket and said, "I'm not telling you what I'm about to say because I know more about loneliness than you or anybody else. I have just had this idea running around in my brain for some time now—ever since Adrian passed away and you now bein' here alone. It's a little like writing music, and it's all my idea. I have a tune in my head that could make both of us sing the same song." He took her hand back. "You get where I'm going with this?"

"I'm going blind, Harry, not deaf. Of course I know. You're as subtle as a dump truck hauling a bulldozer."

Harry noticed she was smiling from ear to ear as she teased him. "Settle down, pretty lady, you need to know the good, the bad, and the ugly. I was married once, but my wife left me. I thought at the time that she just didn't understand me or maybe the guy she ran off with was richer or better looking. I'd be lying if I said it didn't do a number on me. I had my music, my guns, and my pickup truck, and when the ladies heard me play and sing, I had my share of company, too. I recovered."

"I'm sure of that, Harry. That gleam in your eyes is a magnet that can't escape even my lousy eyesight."

"What I didn't ever find again was someone special who I wanted to stick around for the long haul. What I'm trying to say, Beth, is there's still a lot of life in me and in you, and time left to enjoy it. Why should you live alone in this little town when I have a good house in Batavia and no one to share it with? The way I figure it, we can live together, save money, and help each other. Who knows? Maybe in time you'll catch some real fondness for me."

Beth stared out the window for several minutes, leaving Harry with his own thoughts. When she turned back to him, her eyes were full of tears.

"How about you, Harry? You think you'll catch some of that fondness you're talking about for me?"

His voice was shaking as he said, "Oh, I've caught it. I've known for quite a while you were someone I wanted to stick around. I'm here, but it ain't because of Katherine. Sure, she called me because she loves you and she's worried about you, but she's not alone in feeling that way."

Harry held his handkerchief out to her again, and this time she accepted.

"Are you sure this chili's not too spicy for you, Harry? You're pretty far out on that limb."

"I just wanted to be straight with you . . . about everything. The bipolar thing isn't something I can control all the time. I can get real low and I get real high, but I'm getting better at being around the middle more often than not."

"Like now?"

"Yeah, like now."

She leaned forward and kissed him on the cheek.

"You told me everything, Harry, so I'll tell you the truth, which is that I've always found you appealing and believed that underneath all your bluster is a kind and considerate man." She took his hand in hers. "I want you to stick around. I'm just not sure I'm ready to live with anyone yet."

Harry gently pulled his hand away from hers and sat back in his chair with a little smile playing on his face. "This is only my first pass, pretty lady. My plan calls for completing the song and writing the lyrics and then performing it in front of a live audience. That may take some time, but that's something we both got plenty of right now. I'm just asking you not to shut the door. Give me a chance to give us a chance."

"Fair enough," Beth said, reaching for the hand he had just pulled away and giving it a tender kiss. "Who's buying lunch?"

He headed to the counter to pay the cashier. She returned his change along with what he considered to be a much-too-knowing smile.

"You've been listening to us?" he asked, giving her a version of the evil eye.

"Not a word," the woman said, solemnly crossing her heart.

Yet as Harry turned to walk back to Beth, he could have sworn he heard the woman whisper behind him, "You're doing great. Just keep trying."

CHAPTER 43

PRESTON AND KATHERINE followed the red line through what seemed like endless twists and turns and a mile of hallways. As they approached the ICU, the smells became less pungent, but the constant alerts from the overhead speakers intensified. It all added to Preston's anxiety, pounding his head like a fist.

Dr. Li, the neurosurgeon, met them with a little nod. He punched a code into a keypad and a pair of automatic doors swung open, revealing a large room with a dozen beds separated by drawn curtains along each side. The middle of the room was dominated by what looked to Preston to be a command post with six nurses, each monitoring a different screen. Dr. Li paused to whisper something to one of the nurses, and Preston could feel the beat of his heart quicken in fear. Before he could say anything, the doctor motioned for them to follow him.

He led them to one of the partitioned beds, pausing in front of the curtains with a solemn look on his face. "I want to prepare you both for what you are about to see and hear. The patient is attached to many life-support devices and is on a respirator. The respirator is loud, and some people find the sound it makes disconcerting."

Preston and Katherine looked at one another.

Preston said, "We understand, don't we, Kat?" Katherine squeezed her father's hand and nodded. The doctor explained a little more about what they could expect to see, but his words did not register with Preston; he was too focused on seeing his wife. He started as he heard Dr. Li ask, "Are you ready to go in?"

Preston nodded to the doctor and gave Katherine a look he hoped appeared reassuring. He had never seen his daughter look so scared. Dr. Li pulled aside the curtain, and Preston heard the *shhhhh . . . shhhhh . . . shhhhh* of breathing amplified by a respirator. He stared at a head as large as a pumpkin, wrapped in gauze. There were tubes everywhere and dried blood around the nose and the left ear, which was also encircled in stitches. Both eyes of the patient were swollen shut and the bones above the right socket appeared broken. What little skin could be seen was black and blue. The upper-left arm and shoulder were in a cast, as well as the left leg. The right arm had an IV in it and a number of other lines in different colors running to it.

Dr. Li stood quietly as Preston, taking in all that he saw, asked himself if that could possibly be Marcia. If only he could look into her eyes, see her hair, touch her, or hear her voice. Preston turned to the doctor. "This isn't my wife," he said in a flat tone.

Dr. Li did not flinch, but he leaned in a little closer so he could make eye contact with Preston. "I know how hard this is, Mr. Wilson. Please take a closer look."

Something primal and deep within Preston made him want to scream no. He forced himself to do as the doctor had asked. He studied the swollen and discolored face, then turned away—convinced the woman before him could not be his wife.

Katherine whispered to her father, "Do you mind if I ask the doctor a question?"

Preston nodded.

"Doctor, is there a way to find out if this woman was wearing a wedding ring when she was brought in?"

The doctor signaled for a nurse, who quickly joined them, and relayed Katherine's question, and the nurse nodded. She motioned for Preston and Katherine to follow her, and she led them to a cabinet. The nurse removed a light-blue plastic container with a bed number on it. A note inside read: "Fourth finger—left hand."

Preston stepped forward and his legs started to give way. "My wife's engagement and wedding rings," he said as the doctor and the nurse took him by the arms. Preston screamed, "God, help us."

Someone grabbed a chair, and the doctor and nurse guided Preston into it. Katherine hugged her father. "God did help us. Now we know Marcia is alive."

The truth of her words sank in as Preston regained enough composure to stand. "That is my wife in that bed, doctor. Please tell me the truth, will she make it?"

"Your wife has suffered a subdural hematoma, which is post-traumatic bleeding between her skull and her brain. Her brain has continued to enlarge, causing subsequent clinical deterioration. We performed a craniotomy and drainage."

Preston closed his eyes as tightly as he could, to try to alleviate some of what was going on in his head. "I'm sorry, Dr. Li, but I'm not sure I understand any of what you just said."

"Your wife has a traumatic brain injury and dangerous pressure has built up in her skull. We took steps to reduce that pressure by surgery."

"Did it work?" Preston asked.

"Time will tell. We're in a critical phase. We need to take it minute by minute."

"What does that mean?" Preston asked faintly.

"At this point, it means she could go at any time."

Blood drained from Preston's face. He collapsed into the chair again, his head dropping into his hands.

Dr. Li put a hand on Preston's shoulder. "Don't give up hope," he said. "I hate to leave you now, but I have other patients I need to see. I'll be back to talk with you again as soon as I can get free."

"Can I stay here with her?" Preston managed to ask.

"For now, yes, but visits and visitors will continue to be limited and dependent on her condition at any given time. The nurses will explain the protocols to you, and I'm sure they will need to obtain other information. They will also have some forms for you to fill out. Now, I have to go."

Preston thanked Dr. Li as he tried to comprehend what he had just heard.

"Are you okay?" Katherine asked.

"I'm not sure what I am. At least I know at this moment Marcia's alive and in good, competent hands. I do thank God for that."

Preston staggered to his feet and moved to the right side of Marcia's bed; he held the bed rails to steady his trembling hands and gazed at his wife. The look on his face was that of a devastated but grateful man, and it would have broken Marcia's heart had she been able to see it.

"Marcia, it's me. I don't know if you can hear me, but I want you to know I'm here. And I'll be here as long the doctors allow. I love you."

Signs of Preston's weariness and anxiety were beginning to show. He was functioning on only a few hours' sleep and pure adrenaline, and it was catching up with him. Nurses soon came in to attend to Marcia, and Preston and Katherine were told they would need to return to the waiting room. Preston felt Katherine take his hand and suggest that they go to the cafeteria for a cup of coffee. Back in the lounge, Preston fell asleep in his chair before he could take a sip. He woke to Katherine pulling on his arm and saying his name.

"Dad, we need to go home and let you get some rest."

He nodded, and followed her out of the hospital and to the street where they hailed a cab. The ride to the apartment was done in complete silence.

Once upstairs and inside, Preston crumpled onto a couch in the den. When Katherine came back from the kitchen with a cup of tea Nadine had made for him, Preston looked up at her and said, "What if she doesn't make it?"

"What?"

"What if she doesn't make it? How would we go on? I can't even begin to think about P.J. growing up without his mom. She's too young to die."

Chapter 44

EVEN AFTER SHE WOKE THE NEXT day, Katherine felt exhausted, but she forced herself to take care of what needed to be done. Calls to be made. Updates to be imparted. Preston had mentioned the need to contact Marcia's parents right away but that did not seem like an appropriate call for her to make. That could wait until her father had time to call.

She would start with her mom. She punched in the numbers and waited. She was surprised at how relieved she felt when her mother answered.

"Oh, I'm so glad you're there," Katherine told her mother. "I need someone to talk to."

"What in heaven's name has happened?" she asked.

Katherine told her about the explosion and about Marcia being one of the victims, as well as the doctor's diagnosis that Marcia had suffered a traumatic brain injury, along with some deep abrasions and broken bones. "Mom, it was awful. Her head is swathed in bandages. Dad didn't even recognize her. He identified her from her wedding ring."

Beth asked some clinical questions about Marcia's condition that Katherine could not answer before asking about Preston. "Preston must be in shock. How's he holding up?"

"He's doing as well as anyone could under such circumstances and with everything else he's got going on in his life. He fell sound asleep on the way home from the hospital. Mom, honestly, what's your professional opinion of Marcia's chances?"

After a considerable pause on the line, Beth said, "Kat, all I can tell you for sure is that the next few days will be critical." She paused again, much shorter this time. "I'm glad you're with Preston. You'll be a big help and a comfort, I'm sure."

"I hope so, Mom. Right now I feel pretty helpless. Are you doing okay?"

"I am. Guess who's here visiting?"

"Let's see, could the guy's name begin with an H, by any chance?"

"I always knew you were a smart girl. I'm indeed being visited by Harry. He surprised me this morning, and we just came back from lunch—in his spanking-new SUV. It's a real eye-catcher. Chevy, I think, and top of the line."

Katherine grinned. Good ol' Harry. Never missed a beat. "Say hello to the Oompah Man for me."

"It's funny, considering all those backhanded references to the Oompah Man, but under all that bluster he is a good guy. Your grandfather once told me Harry was a like a big maple tree damaged to the core by a lightning strike. The tree refuses to die despite the trauma it has been through, each year growing new branches with leaves greener than ever."

As she absorbed her mother's words, Katherine's grin turned into a huge smile. "I called you with bad news, and I end up feeling better—thanks, Mom!" Katherine was so glad her mom understood Harry. This was good.

"You better go ahead, dear. Knowing you, you have more to do. Thanks for looking out for Preston. He's . . . well . . . he'll always be . . . Preston."

They said their good-byes, and Katherine put her phone down so she could check on her father, who was still asleep on a couch in the den, much to Nadine's chagrin. She knew she should wake him so he could call Marcia's parents, but she couldn't bring herself to do it. He looked so weary and vulnerable in his sleep. She decided she would call some of Marcia's friends instead.

Katherine found an address book next to the phone, and she opened it to the first page to find only two listings that were not alphabetized with the rest. They looked like the ones used the most because of all the smudges. The first was Ann, whom Marcia had often referred to as her best friend from her days at Smith. She called that number first. Ann burst into tears at the news. All Katherine could do was hold onto the phone and listen.

At twenty-four-years of age, Katherine knew as she listened to Ann cry that she had not one person with whom she was anywhere near as tight as Marcia was to Ann. Her closest friends were a dysfunctional drunk still recovering after an accident she had caused and the man who paid her salary, someone old enough to be her father. Where were her friends from school now?

She tried to remember if it had always been like that. She recalled finding the boys she dated in high school boring. College had not proved a fertile ground, either. She had never particularly connected with the various guys she had gone out with there. After graduating, while she had been intimate with a few men, Sean was the first person who made her feel like a woman. That, as much as anything, was why it had killed her to find out about his deceit.

After hanging up, Katherine turned her attention back to the address book. She noticed the other prominent entry was for a Bill and Mary. She called the phone number.

When Mary answered, Katherine gave her the news. Mary expressed shock and dismay, and said she would tell her husband. She asked Katherine to please keep them advised and made her promise to call if they could be of any help taking care of P.J. or cooking meals.

After getting a glass of juice from the refrigerator, Katherine began slogging through the rest of the names in the address book, ones Nadine had described as Christmas card friends. Katherine debated whether she should even be calling those people. She also thought of doing a Facebook post to alert the remaining people in Marcia's life, but she did not want to overstep. That decision could wait until she talked with her father.

She remained ambivalent about waking Preston, but P.J. made the decision for her when he jumped on top of his father, pushing his teddy bear in his face. P.J. squirmed as Nadine quickly intervened. Katherine watched as the two left the room, and then used the time alone with her father to bring him up to speed on everyone she had called and their expressions of sympathy and support.

"I didn't feel it was my place to call Marcia's parents without talking to you first."

"I need to be the one to tell them what we know. I probably should've done that when I first got home. I was just so tired I was afraid I couldn't even get the words out." Preston rubbed his eyes. "You've done so much, and I can't begin to thank you enough . . ."

"We're family."

• • •

Preston shaved, showered, dressed, and called Marcia's parents. Her mother, Ida, answered his call. He explained that their daughter was a victim of an explosion, and described her condition as clearly and as gently as he could. He was not surprised by her response.

"We're coming to New York. I'll have Harold check the airlines as soon as we hang up," said Mrs. Campbell.

"I'll arrange a car to pick you up," Preston said.

"That would be nice," Ida replied.

"I'm going to give you a phone number. When you get the flight booked, just call it and tell the person the name of the airline and the flight number. You don't even need to bother with arrival time. Everything will be taken care of on this end."

The call finished with Preston disappointed that the long-standing tension with his in-laws had not abated; he knew they had never been fond of him. Guilty about having been away from Marcia for so long, Preston hurriedly set out for the hospital.

He had no more stepped inside Saint Luke's than he found himself running down the corridor to the ICU. One thought kept whipping him forward: Would she be alive when he got there?

He immediately spotted Dr. Li, who greeted him calmly. "While her right eye remains closed as a result of the swelling from the bone fracture, her left eye is now opening without much stimulation. That's a good sign because she's showing signs of consciousness."

The nurses were attending to Marcia, so Dr. Li showed Preston to the ICU's shared workstation, where he introduced Gertrude Quick, a no-nonsense charge nurse with short, gray hair. Nurse Quick went over several consent forms that Preston had yet to sign. When he handed them back to her, she asked, "Do you know whether Mrs. Wilson has a living will?"

Her question brought back memories of a two-hour discussion Marcia had made him sit through the year before with Andy Brookfield, during which they both reviewed their wills and signed living wills. It had seemed a prudent thing to do at the time, but something that he did not think they would ever need. Not even a year later, he faced a situation in which the clear language in Marcia's living will mattered greatly.

"Yes, she has a living will," Preston finally said in response to Gertrude's question. "I guess you need it?"

The nurse nodded, and Preston made a note on his cell phone to make a trip to the safe deposit box. He looked up to find Dr. Li motioning him back inside.

At the sight of his wife, his heart ached with an almost unbearable pain and his chest tightened as if in a vise. *Shhhhh, shhhhh, shhhhh.* The sound from her breathing device was the only noise in the room. He flinched at the sight of her poor distorted and bandaged face, and the awful spike protruding from her head that monitored the pressure on her brain. He pulled up a chair, buried his head in the bed sheets, and hoped no one could hear his sobs.

When he could cry no longer, he sat up, took out his handkerchief, wiped his eyes dry, and then put a hand lightly on Marcia's. Both of her eyes were closed. He could see no movement. He tried to speak but choked on the words.

Finally, he whispered, "Marcia, it's me. I'm here. I don't know if you can hear me. I pray that you can. I love you so much. You're the strongest woman I know. You can't give up." He paused, searching for the slightest sign that his words had been heard. A twitch. A moan. Anything. He saw nothing, and the silence that followed was broken only by the incessant *shhhhh* of the ventilator and intermittent beeps from the other medical devices surrounding his wife. Each new sound brought a new worry about what it might mean. Yet when a sound stopped, his heart seemed to stop with it.

He sat quietly for what felt like hours, staring at his wife. Then, from somewhere deep inside him came a voice that was soft and steady: "Marcia, I've made so many mistakes, all of which I regret and none of which I can take back and fix, though you have to know that if I could, I would."

Hearing his voice crack yet again, Preston reached for the water pitcher on the table, poured himself a glass of water, and took several swallows.

He turned back to Marcia, determined to say what needed to be said before it was too late. "I know now that I've let you down in many ways, and myself, too. Please, please don't leave me. I love you so much, and I need you desperately."

While he waited for the response he knew might never come, he felt compelled to tell Marcia what he had harbored inside for so long, hoping that somehow she would hear him. He pushed on. "I will be with you, stay with you at your side, look after you, and protect you, no matter what. I'll do everything possible to be the best father to P.J. that I can be. Just don't leave us."

A gentle tap on his shoulder made him jump.

"I'm sorry, Mr. Wilson, but we need you to step out again so we can attend to your wife. You can check back in about an hour," the nurse said.

"Did something happen? Is she getting worse?"

"It's not better or worse. Our job right now is to get her stabilized. If something changes, Dr. Li will let you know. Please, we need to get started."

Preston leaned over, took his wife's hand, and carefully kissed it, whispering to her that he would be back as soon as he could.

Then he willed himself to get up and leave her behind. Turning to the nurse on the way out, he said, "Thank you for all you're doing."

Preston went to the lounge and found it empty, so he figured it was a good time to call Casey. When Casey picked up, Preston explained that Marcia had indeed been critically injured in the explosion and that the next few days would tell whether she would survive. When Preston quit talking, all he could hear was Casey's heavy breathing, some sniffling in the background, and then some low chatter.

"Are you still there?" Preston asked.

"Alex and Estelle were in the office when you called. I hope you're not upset; I put you on speaker. We're all in a state of shock. I didn't want to call you, so I'm glad you called. All we want to know is what we can do to help."

"Just say a prayer," Preston said softly.

CHAPTER 45

KATHERINE DID NOT WANT to leave Preston or Marcia, but she had to get back to her office or she was fairly certain she would soon be out of a job. In the fading evening light, she drove to her apartment in the Hamptons and was back at her desk bright and early Monday morning. Chuck, of course, could not resist making a couple of snide comments about her having been gone so much, but as always she considered the source and ignored them.

Sol came in at 9:30 a.m., and she followed him into his office.

"I want to apologize, but I have to go back to the city to be with my father at the hospital," Katherine said. She went on to explain that her stepmother had been a victim of the explosion in Manhattan and was hanging onto her life by a thread.

Sol tossed down the pen he was holding, spun around, and retrieved two cups of coffee from the machine he always had turned on behind his desk. "Like I said before, Katherine, nobody can say you don't have a lot going on in your life." He stared into his coffee cup before taking a drink. "I know you're not making up this stuff. I am so sorry about your stepmother. Take whatever time you need."

"I hated telling you, but—"

"Don't worry about it. We all have to be with our family in times like these."

"Did you have all the office landlines checked for bugs yet?" Katherine asked.

"Funny you should ask. I was thinking of going to the phone book and finding somebody to do just that."

Katherine reached into her wallet in her purse and pulled out Angelo Bertolini's business card.

"This is the P.I. that found the bug Sean placed on my cell phone. He knows what he's doing, and he's been extremely good about helping me."

"Great, I'll talk to him."

She handed Sol her new cell, he punched in the number from the card, and Angelo picked up on the third buzz.

"What you got, Katherine?" a loud voice asked on speaker-phone.

"This isn't Katherine; it's Sol Kaplowitz. Katherine works with me, and she's sitting here with me now. We have an issue I would like to talk to you about. Do you think you could make it over to the Hamptons in the next few days?"

"I can make it tomorrow, if that's not too soon. Katherine's told me where you're located. I could be there sometime after lunch, if that will work for you. And if you don't mind, I need to talk to Katherine for a minute."

After agreeing to Angelo's fee, Sol gave Katherine her phone and stepped outside.

"I need to talk with you as soon as possible," Angelo said. "In private." The emphasis on "private" left her speechless. "Will you be in your office?"

"I take it you have more bad news?"

"It ain't good."

"I wasn't planning to be here much longer. My father's wife—it's a long story—was in the explosion Friday in Manhattan. I need to get back to the city and be there for everybody."

"Katherine, you need to make time for this. We can meet before I check out your paper's office, then you can be on your way."

She tapped her fingernails on Sol's desk.

"Okay, what time?"

"I'll be there by eleven."

Since neither Angelo nor Katherine trusted talking on the new phone, they both said a quick good-bye, and she left to tell Sol he could have his office back. She assumed the P.I. wanted to discuss Bobby's family with her, and from the sound of his voice, she feared what his report might say.

• • •

Carol Martin pulled her overcoat tight and leaned into the strong, cold wind coming off the river as she walked as fast as her high heels allowed to her early morning breakfast meeting. She met Gil Gillespie at the front door, with Mark Conners joining them at a table a few minutes later. The Blue Spoon, with its ample open space and good coffee and pastries, had become a favorite spot for their informal status meetings.

While Carol sipped a white chocolate mocha and Mark munched on a banana-nut muffin, Gil asked Carol for the latest news.

"Robert Reynolds was the easy piece of the pie," Carol said. "He'll take the misdemeanor plea, he'll testify against Disley, and he'll help us against Thompson. Baskhanov, however, is another story. He has retained a lawyer that I've never heard of before. I've offered a plea in exchange for his testimony against the bank, but his lawyer shut me down."

"So where does that leave us with the bank?" Gil asked.

"With Maria DeSanto. She's our foundation witness. She reported to Stacy Bowers, the bank's real estate supervisor. She saw the bogus appraisals—not only the bank's but the ones from Baskhanov—and she wore a wire to nail Bowers."

"What about Disley?" Gil asked.

"I don't think he'll plead, and I doubt his lawyer can budge him on that," Carol said, adding, "Wouldn't surprise me if Spagnello dumped him."

Gil ordered some more coffee.

"I like it," he said. "We try the case against Thompson and Disley. If Disley's attorney is getting cold feet, see if he'll agree to a nonjury trial. We try the case against Disley first and then go after Thompson."

• • •

From what Preston had been told by Dr. Li, every minute was critical in Marcia's fight for survival. It was day three. She was out of the coma and, according to the neurosurgeon, there was hope for a meaningful recovery. When he had pressed the doctor for what *meaningful* meant, Dr. Li had taken Preston through the stages of brain injury. "We have eye opening and finger movement," the doctor said. "Both are clear signs that your wife is moving out of a vegetative state."

Preston had yet to see any of these movements himself, which may have been why the words "vegetative state" stuck in his brain like poison, making him feel dizzy and unable to think clearly.

"I don't want her to be in a vegetative state," he heard himself shout at the doctor.

Dr. Li crossed his arms. "Yes, you do. It is a phase she must go through to recover full consciousness. These are the first signs of that."

"I'm sorry, doctor, I didn't mean to raise my voice. I didn't even realize I had said that out loud. I guess the pressure is getting to me," Preston said. "Can you tell me what her chances are for a normal life?"

In the usual measured tone that Preston had become accustomed to, the doctor said, "Statistics in these kinds of cases can be elusive. She remains in critical condition; what I can tell you is that I see hope. Intracranial pressure has decreased dramatically, and her response to pain and stimulated eye movement is encouraging. We just have to see how she progresses. It's all one small, slow step at a time. You need to conserve your energy. It's going to be a long haul, and what your wife needs from you is for you to remain positive."

Preston nodded and thanked the doctor as he left. He turned back to Marcia and commenced doing just what the doctor had asked. "Stay with me, sweetheart." He put his hand on her arm, gently squeezing it. "Can you hear me? Can you feel my hand? I see more than hope, Marcia. You're going to get well. I know you are."

Preston searched Marcia's wounded face, praying for a flicker of movement. Something. Anything. There was nothing save for the awful sound of the breathing machine. A nurse came in, checked all of Marcia's vital signs, and told Preston she needed some time alone to attend to his wife. He knew the drill.

"I'll either be in the lounge or the chapel if you need me," he said as he gently kissed Marcia on the forehead and left the unit.

Preston had almost reached the elevator at the far end of the hall when he heard someone running behind him. He turned and saw the nurse he had just left, panting to catch her breath as she jogged up behind him.

"Mr. Wilson, you may want to come back. There was some fluttering in Mrs. Wilson's right eye; I thought you'd want to see it. I think she's doing it on her own."

Unfortunately, when he returned to Marcia's bedside, whatever had been happening was over and she was the same as before, but later that afternoon when he came back, something was markedly different in the room, though he could not put his finger on it. After a minute or two of concentration, he became convinced the whooshing sound of Marcia's breathing was less frequent. His mind went into overdrive: Keep breathing, sweetheart. This cannot be the end. Stay with me.

He turned to call a nurse and was surprised to find one standing at the end of the bed.

"Is she all right?" Preston asked. "Please, tell me the truth."

"We've slowed the ventilator down to see if she can tolerate the reduction and start to breathe on her own," the nurse replied.

"What if she can't?"

"We can increase the rate again if necessary, but so far she's doing fine on her own."

Preston took a deep breath and told himself that if he did not calm down, they would need to be treating *him*. After fifteen long minutes and with less than a few hours of sleep in three days, he fell asleep in the chair by his wife's bed. When he woke, he did not know if he had been out a few minutes or several hours. All he knew was that he had heard a noise and suddenly saw a jerking motion in Marcia's left thigh.

Preston pushed the buzzer for the nurse and tried to shake the sleep out of his head. The nurse almost sprinted into the room, and shortly thereafter came Dr. Li. All three saw her leg jerk again, and then Marcia's left eye opened and fluttered before closing again.

"I'm here, Marcia. Sweetheart, I'm here," Preston said.

Marcia's left eye sprang open and then shut just as quickly. Could she have heard him? Preston was so busy trying to absorb what was going on with his wife that he failed to notice Dr. Li turning off her ventilator. The physician then examined each of Marcia's eyes through an ophthalmoscope before whispering something to the nurse that Preston could not hear.

Preston was just about to ask what was going on, when the doctor patted him on the shoulder and smiled.

"At this moment, your wife is breathing on her own. Her limb and eye movements are good signs, too."

Preston gave the doctor a great big smile of thanks. Dr. Li excused himself while Preston stood vigil by his wife until the nurses needed him to step outside.

He called Nadine to check on P.J., and then called Katherine and Marcia's parents with the good news before worrying about whether both calls were premature. Katherine told him she was thrilled with Marcia's progress, and she would be back in the city the following evening.

His calls completed, he made a quick trip to the hospital cafeteria for a sandwich and ginger ale. Preston had not taken two bites of his food when his phone buzzed. It was Marcia's parents. They would be at the hospital in less than an hour—they had finally found two open seats on a regional flight from Dayton to New York.

Preston ran his hands across his face and then through his hair. How shocking it would be for them to see their daughter in her current state, and how he wished he could make it easier on them. He decided he would ask Dr. Li to arrange a brief conference with Marcia's parents as soon as the physician had a free moment.

CHAPTER 46

A NGELO MET KATHERINE just before eleven o'clock at a café a few minutes from her office. She was expecting to hear that Bobby and his family were involved in some turn-of-the-century land grab and that the townspeople of Braydon were all indebted to the McKenzies in one way or another. She forgot that she had offhandedly mentioned to Angelo the spate of recent hang-ups on her new phone.

"I ran down that new cell phone number you have and found out who has been calling you at all hours," he said.

"How is that possible? My caller ID always said Anonymous, and, of course, I could never get a callback number."

Their coffees came, and Angelo paid for them, saying, "Least I can do for you getting me a job today at your paper. Thanks, by the way."

"No thanks needed—this is a two-way street, remember. I'm just hoping the office phones aren't bugged. Were you able to put a name with the numbers for whoever is calling?"

"You're not gonna want to hear it, but it's your old boyfriend."

"Sean?" she said, louder than she intended. Angelo nodded.

"How could he possibly know I got another phone?" She took a swig of her coffee and wished she had ordered a beer.

"The Secret Service can do pretty much whatever it wants as long as it's in the name of national security."

"Come on, Angelo," Katherine said. "My phone calls are a threat to America?"

"There could be an interest in somebody who knows you. As for your phone, my guess is you've made one of the government's watch lists—so that when you buy a phone, for example, it's triggered. You had to give the store where you bought the phone your Social Security number, right?"

Katherine nodded and her face turned somber. "Sean would often press me for information on my father. It was always low-key, but I sensed he wanted me to say something about Preston and the business. I never did and never would. As I think about it now, I don't remember one time that I went out with him that he didn't bring up Preston and the car dealerships in one way or another."

"You said you never told him anything. You sure about that?" Angelo wiped a puddle of coffee from the table.

"I never knew anything I could tell him, even if I wanted to."

"It may be time to start using a throwaway phone, or I could get you a phone with a number he couldn't trace because he wouldn't know you had it."

"Forget it, Ang. I have nothing to hide and I'm not going to let him disrupt my life, though I'd sure like to know why he keeps playing this childish game of anonymous hang-ups."

"I'll tell you why. As long as the phone is on, your location can be verified. Since he knows you have two phones, you could leave the first one at your apartment and go anywhere and he wouldn't know you were gone unless he heard your voice. He or anyone else working your file could simply be making sure you're where your phone says you are."

Katherine frowned. "That means he's aware that I know my phone is bugged."

"Not necessarily. A lot of people have more than one phone. Again, I can get you a phone he can't trace, and I can add it as a buddy line so your calls and texts won't cost me a dime."

"That's an incredibly nice offer," Katherine said, pulling both phones from her purse and setting them on the table, "but for now

I'm going to leave everything just like it is. As for a third phone, as long as the lines in my office are clean, I can make any sensitive calls from the newspaper." She put the phones back in her bag. "I'd just like to know what Sean is expecting to learn from all this."

"I imagine a lot of people are asking that same question."

Angelo tucked a tip under his cup, and then left for the newspaper. Katherine grabbed her keys for another trip to the hospital.

• • •

Ida Campbell was a frail, neatly dressed woman in her late sixties, with short, curly black hair and round, wire-rimmed glasses, yet she walked into the lounge with the purpose of a woman half her age. Harold, a pharmacist by trade, casually dressed and a bit rumpled, followed at her heels.

Preston embraced his in-laws warmly, although Ida caught him off guard when instead of pulling immediately away she lingered in the embrace as a tear fell below her glasses. Harold remained as stone-faced as a mannequin in a department store window, his body just as rigid.

"I'm so glad you're both here," Preston said, tearing up himself. "I'm sure you'll want to see Marcia right away."

"That's all we've thought about since you first called," Ida said.

"Are you . . . ready to see her?" Preston asked.

"This has all been such a shock," Ida said as she reached into her handbag for a tissue.

"We're ready," Harold said, seemingly oblivious to his wife's need for a moment to compose herself.

"Let's give Ida a minute," Preston said.

He waited for Ida to indicate she was ready to proceed, and then led them into the ICU and to Marcia. Harold held his arm around his wife as they approached their daughter. Preston moved quietly to the chair. Once again the only sounds were the various beeps from the medical equipment. Marcia's mother gently touched her daughter's arm, and then leaned over to look into her eyes. The swelling of Marcia's head had subsided, and Preston was relieved to see it was now almost normal in size and minus that awful spike. As Preston thought about it, maybe it was just as well that Ida had not been able to see her daughter as she had looked those first two days after the explosion.

"Hello, sweetheart. I'm here. I love you. You're going to be fine." As she spoke her words of encouragement, Ida continued to stare at her daughter, desperate for a reaction. Preston prayed for a response, any response at all. He could scarcely believe it when Marcia blinked her eyes several times and moved her left arm in a short, jerking motion. Her mother patted her lightly. "I know you can hear me. I get what you're telling me, I . . ."

Ida fainted in mid-sentence, and came just shy of the floor before Harold swooped in and caught her. Preston helped his father-in-law place Ida into a chair.

"I'm all right," she said a short while later after Preston had given her some water. "Just a little dizzy, I guess."

With Preston comforting Ida, Harold Campbell stepped to his daughter's bedside, saying nothing but taking in the bandaged body and all the tubes and monitors helping to keep her alive. "I wish I could give you the right pill for this one, Sweetie Pie," was all he said through his tears as he finally turned away.

Preston asked Harold. "Would you like me to see about getting another chair?"

Harold looked over at his wife. "No, I'm worried about Ida. It's been a long trip. I think we should go now. We can come back tomorrow."

Preston nodded. Harold took Ida's arm, and together the two men walked her out of the ICU and across the hall to the lounge.

"Ida, can I get you some water or coffee, or maybe tea?" Preston asked.

"Some more water, please," Ida said weakly. "I knew she would look bad, and I tried to prepare myself, but I guess I didn't do a good enough job. I just did not expect her to be like this. I'm ashamed of myself for not holding up better."

"You did just fine," Preston said. "No one can be prepared for something like this. I just want you to know she is doing better; Marcia is moving parts of her body, and the doctor says that's an important step in her recovery. It might be hard to believe, but she's a lot better than she was yesterday."

Preston thought it best to stop there. He did not need to describe what he and Katherine had witnessed when they first came to Marcia's bedside—the sight of her motionless figure, bandaged like a mummy, with only the telltale *shhhh* of the breathing machine to indicate life.

At that moment, Dr. Li came into the lounge. He nodded to Preston, who introduced the doctor to the Campbells.

"I must apologize for how brief my time is today," Dr. Li said. "I am the doctor attending to your daughter. She has suffered brain trauma and trauma to her body. The brain, of course, is the most important organ to stabilize first. We were able to eliminate excess fluids in her cranium, and she is now breathing on her own. Mrs. Wilson is conscious and responsive in some ways, which is encouraging." He paused. "She does remain in critical condition."

Preston said, "Dr. Li, we all saw her move her arm and her eye. Do you think she can hear us, too?"

"There is no way to be certain. She is responsive to stimuli and at times makes eye contact. She also moves her arm as well as her legs. Some of that may be voluntary, but some might not be. Her brain has been assaulted by the trauma. Sometimes, we're not entirely sure how, the brain mends itself. Other times, the damage is permanent. It's far too early to determine how this will turn out. It would, however, be good for you to talk to her. Just don't expect a response yet."

"Is she in pain?" Ida asked.

"Yes, it is being modulated with medication."

"How long can it go on like this?" Ida said, her voice rising. "When will we know if she will live—or be herself again?"

Preston went over to Ida and put his arms around her. "Dr. Li has been with her every step of the way. He will do all he can. I know this is devastating to see. How about getting some rest, and we'll all see how she's doing tomorrow."

"You're right, Preston. This isn't just our daughter, she's your wife, too." Harold turned to Ida. "I think it's time we do just what Preston said." Then Harold stepped forward to shake Dr. Li's hand. "Doctor, we appreciate what you've done and what you're doing, and we thank you for taking the time to talk with us today."

Dr. Li bowed his head slightly and left the room. Ida gave Preston a hug, while Harold gave him an understanding pat on the back.

"I know this has been hard for you, too," Ida said. "It's all in God's hands now."

Preston watched his in-laws leave the lounge, hand in hand with their heads down. In the past fifteen minutes, Harold, who had made it clear for years that he believed Marcia had married beneath her station, had spoken to him as an equal, and Ida had treated him like a beloved son-in-law. It was cruelly ironic that it had required such a horrific tragedy to produce the first signs of affection they had ever shown him.

Preston returned to his chair by Marcia until the nurses once again told him he needed to leave. After getting something to eat in the cafeteria, he set about calling each of the Collectibles. Tommy was the first of the group he could get on the line.

"Preston," Tommy said in an upbeat voice.

"I have some bad news." Preston said, and he quickly recounted all that had happened over the last two days, updated to the minute.

Tommy asked for the name and address of the hospital. "You're with her?"

"Yes. How are Missy and Skylar?"

"Good."

"And you?"

"I'll be right there."

The declaration choked him up. "You don't have to come, Tommy," Preston said.

"See you soon." The line went dead. Before Preston could dial the next person on his list, his phone buzzed.

"Preston, it's Alice. Katherine called and told me what happened. Is this a bad time to talk?"

"No. It's fine, Alice. It's great to hear from you. I should have been in touch sooner."

"Nonsense, and I won't keep you long now. I know you have much to do. Just know that you're in my prayers. Also, be prepared for a call from Johnny. He's been asking about you ever since he learned Katherine is your daughter. You may also get one from Barbara, Corey's daughter. Maybe even from Corey, himself."

That last name made Preston smile—Corey Corrigan was the patriarch of Corrigan Yachts, which were as famous for Corey's woodwork as their boats were among yacht owners throughout the South. Corey's family had been building boats for several generations, and Preston had always found Corey to be as humble as he was accomplished. He hated that he had Alzheimer's.

"Thanks for calling, Alice, and thanks for the heads up, too."

Her warning had not come too soon. Johnny's voice was heard next on the line.

"This is me, Johnny."

Preston did not know how much Johnny knew, or understood, so he simply asked how he was doing.

"Johnny not good because Preston not good. Alice talked to Johnny. Was she all blowed up?" Johnny asked between sniffles.

"She's hurt bad, Johnny, but she's not blown up. She's all in one piece and she will take a while to heal."

"You tell wife, Johnny come and put her back together again if she is blowed up."

"Johnny, how about this—someday we'll have a big party, and Marcia will be the one to invite you herself."

"I'd like that. Johnny do all the dishes. Johnny good at that."

"I know you are, Johnny, I know you are."

The call from Johnny lifted Preston's spirits immensely. No matter what happened with what he was facing, he vowed to do something for Johnny that would be life changing for a young man who gave so much to everyone and asked so little in return.

For the next couple of hours, Preston stayed by Marcia's side, a small island of calm in the sea of ICU activity that never seemed to die down. When he stepped outside to the lounge to check his phone calls, he found a message from Barbara leaving her telephone number and telling him how sorry she and Corey were to hear about Marcia. Preston quickly returned the call, and was surprised when Corey answered the phone; he sounded remote and disconnected. Preston wondered whether to try to continue their conversation or simply ask for Barbara right away.

"Remember. You have to feel the wood," Corey said.

Preston's face lit up remembering the wooden box Corey had sent him after Joe Hart's funeral. Maybe the old yacht maker was having one of his increasingly rare lucid moments. "I do remember, Corey. I love that box. Are you with your daughter, Barbara?"

"She's a good woman. Looks after me."

"May I speak with her?" he asked finally.

"She's a good cook."

"Is she there?"

"Why don't you talk to her?"

Preston was left holding for a minute or two until he heard Barbara's voice.

"Hi, Preston."

Preston explained to Barbara what had happened to Marcia. She thanked him for the call and told him that she would try to explain it to Corey. Some commotion followed, and she said, "Corey wants to speak with you again. May I put him on?"

"Of course," Preston said.

"Use cherry. It's the best wood there is."

"Thank you, Corey. Please put Barbara back on."

"I was listening," Barbara said. "My sweet father was trying to say that he wants to make a rocking chair for your wife."

Preston felt a lump in his throat. "Please let him know how much I appreciate that thought."

"You and your wife will be in our prayers, Preston. Let me know how it goes."

When the call ended, Preston could only shake his head and wonder what had made Corey suddenly know who he was. His conversations with Johnny and Corey had improved Preston's disposition. A call to Katherine confirmed that she had spoken with her mother, and he assumed Beth would tell Harry. Still Preston knew Harry would appreciate a call from him.

"Hey Big Guy, I was just about to call you. You got it stuck to ya. How you doing?"

"I'm . . . "

Harry interrupted him. "I know. It's terrible. I'm with Beth now. How about I drive there?"

Preston struggled for the right words but could not find them.

"What hospital is your wife in?"

"Saint Luke's Roosevelt. There are two of them. She's at the one on 114th Street. But Harry, you don't have to come."

"The Oompah Man will be there."

Preston thought for a second. "When? I have a guest room in my apartment you can use."

"Beth's kicking me out tomorrow. I'll arrive as soon as my truck can get me there."

Preston could only smile.

"I'll cook for everyone. Bet you didn't know that was another of my many talents?"

"No, but why am I not surprised."

Each ensuing call to a Collectible did more for Preston than the one that preceded it, until he had replenished his emotional reservoirs, like a lake after a much-needed rain. His conversations with Tommy and Missy were always so personal, and now his conversations with Harry were becoming the same way.

CHAPTER 47

KATHERINE HAD FELT A PANG OF guilt after leaving Angelo, so she changed her plans and essentially followed him to the newspaper. She arrived about five minutes behind him, and caught him talking to Sol. Both men raised their eyebrows at seeing her walk in. She gave them a faint smile. "I had to find out if my *boyfriend* had somehow managed to get the lines in this office tapped, and I needed to know right away. I have plenty of work to do until that's finished. I'm hoping this won't take Angelo more than a day."

Angelo replied, "I should be able to do it in one afternoon, so let me get started."

It ended up taking him three hours. He had to install and then run some sophisticated software before he could test the phones, all the incoming and outgoing lines, and any place in the building— from the bottom floor up to the roof—where a listening device might have been placed. When he was done, he proclaimed the building free from any form of eavesdropping device. Sol had the paper's bookkeeper cut Angelo a check on the spot. The P.I. doffed an imaginary hat, tucked the check into his coat pocket, and was off.

Convinced Sean's reach had not extended to her office, Katherine felt a wave of relief wash over her. He was only interested in her personal business—and to whom she was talking. Since Angelo was in the area, he stopped by her apartment on his way back to

Manhattan and did a quick scan; he found no eavesdropping devices of any kind.

•••

Katherine's drive into the city that evening was miserable. She still didn't know what to make of Sean. All she knew for sure was that she was starved and wanted to be by herself. At that moment, even the company of her father, half-brother, and Nadine would be too much.

She parked and walked the short block to Eighteenth Street and crossed it to reach Pete's Tavern. It was one of her favorites and reputedly the oldest restaurant in the city. She walked in, passed the bar, and asked for a booth in the back. One was open, and with it came privacy and room to spread out. She folded her coat and hat, placed them beside her, and ordered a Guinness.

The beer had never tasted better. She drank the first one fast and ordered a second, along with the Easter special. While she waited for her food, she called her mother, and was glad to hear that Harry would be coming to stay with Preston tomorrow at his apartment. Katherine had just ended the call when she noticed two men in suits surveying the back half of the bar. They screamed Eastern European, which certainly was not unusual for New York City, but the duo also had all the trappings of mobsters in an old time gangster movie. Everything about them was big, their bodies, the overcoats slung over their arms, their thick scarves, and the hats pulled low over their dark hair and bushy eyebrows. Katherine could not help wondering who they were.

Nonetheless, no one was more surprised than Katherine when the men walked briskly to her booth. One of them, the one with a thick neck covered in tattoos, sat down next to her, pushing her hard against her coat and hat. The other man slid in across from her, taking up the entire bench. Before she could ask who they were or even object, the man beside her pulled back his suit jacket just enough to show the handle of a pistol. Warning bells went off in

Katherine's head. It was clear the two giants were not cops and they meant business. She thought about screaming for help, but worried it would only make matters worse.

"What do you want?" Katherine demanded, keeping her voice low and calm.

"We don't want to hurt you, Katherine Kelly," the man across from her said. He had a thick accent—she guessed Slovakian, maybe Russian. He placed his hands palms down on the table, revealing tattoos on the knuckles of his thumbs. "We just want to talk."

Katherine could not take her eyes off of the tattoos. She struggled to control her voice. "Why would you hurt me? I don't even know who you are."

"Who we are is not important," said Big Hands. "What we want to talk with you about is."

Katherine grabbed her beer in an attempt to keep calm but the man beside her just as quickly pried her fingers from it, shook his head, and set the glass out of her reach.

Big Hands said, "You are, how you say, an *aggressive* journalist. You go after bad banks. We know all about you. We read papers, too."

"That's my job."

"You know many people. One such people is Maria DeSanto. You remember Maria DeSanto?"

"I don't have to answer any of your questions. I could scream right now."

The man with the thick, tattooed neck turned and put his face right next to hers. His breath reeked of liquor and tobacco, and he smelled of sweat. "You could do lot of things, but we don't think you're stupid. So shut up and listen."

Cramped between the wall and the big man pressing against her, Katherine's legs began to tremble. Thick Neck gave her a sick, twisted smile.

"Go ahead," Katherine said, trying to steady her voice.

"You're a smart girl," Big Hands said. "We want you to be especially smart. Talk to your girlfriend, DeSanto. Tell her that you're okay that she testifies against the bad bank. But tell her that she has trouble remembering about Baskhanov. She doesn't recognize him or his companies—you know, she sees so many names of developers."

Developers. Baskhanov. These two words kept replaying in Katherine's head. As if he could read Katherine's mind, the man at her left squeezed her harder against the wall and said, "This DeSanto lady gets confused, and she needs to stay that way—but just about the developer in the case."

Katherine looked from one man to the other. Her journalistic instincts screamed for her to ask more questions, but her survival instincts gave her a case of lockjaw.

"What we ask is very reasonable. It will be better for you if DeSanto has this confusion. Better for your father. Better also for your career," the man sitting next to her said.

Without another word, the two men got up and left the restaurant as quickly as they had come in. A few minutes later, Katherine's meal was served to a booth that was empty save for a few wrinkled bills left on the table.

Katherine drove to Preston's apartment, squeezing the steering wheel and reliving the encounter every minute along the way. She had tried her best not to let the two gangsters know how scared she was, but suspected her shaky leg had probably given her away. In fact, her legs were still shaking. How did those guys know where she was? How long had they been tracking her? How did they know Preston was her father?

She thought about calling the police but figured that might just get her killed. Instead, she called Angelo. The P.I. did not pick up. She would try again later. Could someone have put a tracking device on her car? That was the one thing Angelo had not checked yet, and it was the only way Katherine figured the men could have known her movements.

She pulled up to Trump Tower, and the valet rushed over to park her car. Such Trump perks had once been off-putting to her—overdone and elitist—but she could not help welcoming them with open arms today. Inside, she made a point of telling the doorman that before he rang anybody else up to the apartment that evening, she wanted to personally talk with them.

"Of course," the man said.

As Katherine rode the elevator up to her father's apartment, she realized she could not tell him about what had just happened in the bar. The last thing he needed was something more to worry about. The one thing she knew for certain was she would not be doing what the men had asked of her.

That was out of the question.

Nadine greeted her at the door, and after a quick hello and a status update on P.J., Katherine grabbed a notepad and pen, went into the bathroom off the bedroom she had been occupying, and locked the door. Sitting at the vanity, she wrote down every detail she could recall from the encounter in the tavern. She even went so far as to do a rough sketch of the faces of the men and of their tattoos—both the one man's neck art and the knuckle tattoos on Big Hands.

Being strong-armed to influence the testimony of a witness in a federal case was a felony. Katherine considered her options, knowing that inside she was a wreck. She remained at the dressing table long after she had finished the descriptions of the two men. It would have been great if she were able to talk to Sean. Instead, she went to the kitchen and grabbed a couple of cold beers. She took them into the bathroom, filled the tub with hot water, undressed, and climbed in.

She hoped the huge sigh that escaped as the water enveloped her was not too loud.

• • •

Preston spent the night in the hospital, and the next morning dressed in the clothes Nadine had rolled up in his gym bag—slacks, a sport jacket, a dress shirt, and a tie. Somewhere along the way Nadine had learned how to pack for someone who traveled, as Preston found not one piece of clothing wrinkled. He was certainly pleased when he spotted the fresh underwear and the shaving kit.

When he stepped into the lounge, he marveled at all of the flowers. He took a look at the notes on each, from his mother-in-law and father-in-law, Casey, Alex, even Estelle, bless her, Tommy and Missy, Harry and Beth, P.J., and Nadine. There was a bouquet of roses from Corey, not exactly the normal get-well flower, which made him smile. Additional plants and bouquets from Marcia's other friends had been delivered. On his way to the ICU, Preston felt a bounce to his step that had been missing in recent weeks.

Back in the ICU again, he was reassured to see his wife was continuing to breathe on her own. Both of her eyes were open, and the swelling in her right eye had gone down. For the first time since the accident, she was clearly recognizable.

"Good morning, sweetheart," he said, kissing her softly on her forehead. "You're doing a lot better every day. I know you are going to make it. I have some surprises for you this morning."

No response, but still filled with hope, he returned to the lounge. He called the store and thanked Estelle first, and then Casey and Alex for the lovely flowers. They assured him all was well with the business.

Then Casey said something that Preston knew he would never forget: "Everybody in this store gathered this morning first thing for an update on how Marcia was doing. They are all so worried about her. There were even some nice things said about you. Your people love you, Preston. They'll be doing whatever it takes to make this store recover. The news about Marcia has reached the other stores, and this place is covered with cards. Some people even sent fancy candy. I guess I should take care of that, right?"

"Thank you, Casey." Preston had too much respect for Casey to respond to his self-deprecating humor. Besides, all the wonderful words were a blur after, "Your people love you."

Preston went back to the restroom in the visitors lounge and pulled himself together. In the span of an hour, he had experienced two of the most touching moments of his life.

When Preston stepped back into the lounge, Marcia's father and mother were there, with P.J. in Ida's arms. Preston had never been so happy to see his son. He took the boy from Ida, and P.J. immediately wrapped his arms around his father's neck and gave him an airtight hug. As far as Preston was concerned, it could have lasted forever.

They could not all be in the ICU at once, so Preston signaled Ida to go with him. Preston handed P.J. to Harold, and Ida took Preston's hand.

"I'm ready to see her again," Ida said. "I'll be okay."

Preston gave her hand a reassuring squeeze, and the two of them entered Marcia's room. Ida headed immediately to her daughter's side. Bending over to cup Marcia's still swollen cheek, Ida looked back at Preston and said, with a little smile, "She is looking so much better. Harold needs to see this."

Preston agreed and stepped out to get his father-in-law. Preston remained with P.J. in the lounge, and that was where Katherine found him, looking out a window at what appeared to be the start of a nice, early spring day.

"Hi," Katherine whispered, as she moved quietly to his side.

Preston jumped and a sheepish look crossed his face. "Oh, hi, Kat. Gosh, my mind was so far away."

Katherine took P.J. from Preston. "I can only stay a few minutes this morning. I'll be back later today. I just don't know when."

"You have a big story you're working on in the city?"

She worded her answer carefully. "Ah, yeah, it's kind of big. Anyhow, I'm on my way to a meeting with a P.I. We're going to have a late breakfast. How's Marcia today?"

"She looks more like Marcia. There's still no consistent movement, but both her eyes are open, and the swelling is way down. I've been wondering if it's maybe time for P.J. to see his mother. Or do you think the bandages and machines will scare him?" Preston looked at his son. "What if he tries to reach for her face?"

"I don't know," Katherine said as she stopped her little brother from pulling her hair, just the sort of spontaneous mischief Preston was worried about. "I suppose you could ask the doctor or a nurse, but you might get a no. I'd let him see Marcia. You'll be right there if he needs to be taken out."

Preston smiled; it was the answer he had wanted. He put P.J. down, knelt beside him, and looked in his son's eyes. "Mommy's sleeping. She fell down and hurt herself. She's got some booboos on her face, but she'd like to see you."

"See Mommy, see Mommy," P.J. said too loudly.

Preston held his finger up to his lips, and P.J. nodded.

Katherine waited until Ida and Harold returned to the lounge, and then she left. With a quick hopeful smile to his in-laws, Preston picked up his son and carried him to the ICU.

"Ready to see Mommy?" he asked as they stood outside the curtain surrounding Marcia's bed. "Remember we have to be gentle."

"Mommy, Mommy," P.J. squealed.

Preston inched into the space, watching as P.J. got his first look at his heavily bandaged mother. When his son did not react, Preston gave a sigh of relief and took the precaution of untying P.J.'s shoes and setting them on one of the chairs. He gently positioned the child on Marcia's left side, with the little boy's head under her shoulder. Preston held his breath while his world stood still.

The silence was broken by a shout. "Mommy's sleeping! Mommy's sleeping!"

Preston put his finger to his lips. "Quiet," he said softly.

P.J. would not be shushed. "Mommy's sleeping," P.J. shouted again.

The joyful words of his son made Preston's heart swell, yet he worried the noise would inadvertently summon the nurses. He leaned over about to whisk P.J. away when he heard soft words coming from Marcia—the words he never thought he would hear his wife say again: "I love you."

"Mommy's awake," P.J. announced, adding some of his own cooing noises.

"Yes, Mommy's awake!" Preston hollered louder than any of P.J.'s earlier screams.

Preston watched Marcia fall back to sleep. He hoisted P.J. into his arms and grabbed the boy's shoes from the chair, not bothering to put them on. "Mommy needs to rest now. I'm going to take you back to Grandma and Grandpa."

Then, with his son in tow, Preston speed-walked to the nurses' station, where he told everyone that Marcia had spoken to them. Two of the nurses immediately dashed to her side.

Back in the lounge, Preston gave Ida and Howard the good news, dropped off P.J., and returned to his wife. He was well aware of the routine by now. He knew he had only a few minutes before the doctor came, followed by the nurses, and he wanted to spend whatever little private time he could have alone with Marcia.

Preston stepped into Marcia's little curtained area just as one of the nurses was leaving. She gave him a warning look that told him she would be back soon. He rushed over to Marcia and placed a hand on her cheek.

"If you can hear me, sweetheart, I want you to know I love you so much. I've been by your side from the beginning, and I'll be with you forever. Keep fighting. You're going to get better. Your son is counting on it. Your mother's counting on it. Your father's counting on it. Katherine is counting on it. So many others who love you are, too. I'm going to take care of you no matter what. I love you so much."

"I love you more," Marcia said.

CHAPTER 48

KATHERINE MET ANGELO AT the Flame Restaurant on Fifty-eighth and Ninth. It was noisy and busy, but she was able to get a table in a quieter section. They ordered immediately. Katherine told the waitress she could bring their coffees with the order. Angelo raised an eyebrow but nodded. "This must be serious if you don't want your coffee first," he said with concern in his voice.

Katherine knew better than to try to fool the former detective.

"Two guys accosted me last night at Pete's Tavern. I was in a booth in the back and they both just muscled into it—one beside me so I couldn't leave even if I had tried. He also made a point of showing me he had a gun."

"Were you hurt?"

"Only my pride. I'd be lying if I said I wasn't scared. They were big men with tattoos. Heavy accents, I'm guessing Eastern European or Russian. The guy who did most of the talking had tattoos on the back of his hands and knuckles like these."

She reached into her briefcase and handed Angelo the sketch she had made the night before, pointing as she spoke. "The other guy, the one who penned me in, had a tattoo on his neck that looked like this. I'm no artist, but I think what I drew is close."

Angelo only glanced at the sketch before sliding the paper right back to Katherine. "Let's eat something before I get into what you have here."

"That bad?" Katherine's face grew dark with concern. "You're scaring me, Angelo."

"Like I said, let's get something in our stomachs first."

The food came, and they both ate as if they hadn't eaten in a week—even the waitress could not help commenting on it. Angelo assumed she was also hinting about the need to turn the table so he slid her a ten and asked if they could have more coffee. The woman smiled and said she would be right back with a fresh pot.

"So, you going to tell me what's going on?" Katherine asked.

"These guys are Russian mafia."

"Russian . . . mafia . . ."

"You need to let me finish. This group is the most dangerous crime organization in the world. Worse than anything you have ever read about that goes on with the Mexican drug cartels or in the Arab countries. Those crews just behead people. The Russians don't just kill; they maim and torture people who get in their way. Then they kill them and often their entire families for good measure. If you think I'm trying to scare you, I am."

"The first thing one guy said was that they didn't want to hurt me," Katherine said, her hand shaking as she raised the cup of coffee to her lips.

"It's because they must need you for something. What did they tell you they wanted?"

"I'm to tell the DeSanto woman—remember her?" At Angelo's nod, Katherine continued, "She's supposed to have a selective memory when it comes to Baskhanov's involvement with the real estate appraisals."

"The feds must have the woman well hidden, and the Russians must think you're their best shot at getting to her."

"I don't have access to her anymore."

"They must think you do."

Angelo took a spoon and stirred his black coffee as if he had put something in it. He appeared to be thinking while doing it. Finally, he spoke. "Somehow they have the idea they can influence you to get to the DeSanto woman. Before you ask, all any run-of-the-mill

P.I. would need is a couple of hours and a laptop with Wi-Fi to know everything about you. It's what we do. Trust me, this group has a lot more resources than a P.I."

Both of Katherine's hands had begun to shake. Her voice did as well. "I called you because I thought the Russians must have placed a transmitter of some sort in my car. It's the only way I could think of that they could have known I was back in the city last night. Do you have your equipment with you so you could check it out?"

Angelo frowned deeply. "I was going to get to that next. If I find a device, you need to leave and go somewhere far from the city, and you're going to need to do it immediately."

"I've got—"

"You don't got nothin' if you're dead. This isn't anything to screw around with. Nobody messes with the Russians, and I mean nobody. The old Mafioso wouldn't go near them, and for the most part, neither will the feds."

"Our government is afraid of them?"

"When's the last time you read about a Russian mobster going to jail in this country?"

Katherine could only think of one—Vyacheslav Ivankov—who served ten years.

Angelo paid the check. "Let's take a look at your car."

They made it to her car, which she had parked a few blocks away, in a matter of minutes. Sure enough, Angelo quickly located a tracking device held inside a fender well by a magnet. He crawled out from under the car and disabled it, taking care to show Katherine the on/off switch.

"Keep this with you and turned off as you go about your business today. Then go to your apartment, get together whatever you want to take with you, and go someplace far from Long Island."

Katherine's stomach was churning, and she strained to speak. "I don't know where to go. I can't go to my mother's. That would be the first place they'd look."

"I'm sorry I can't help you with that part. I can tell you that because it's the Russians, if you go to the police, you'll be signin' your own death warrant. Just leave and let this blow over. It's supposed to come to trial soon, right?"

She nodded.

"You leave and it's apparent you didn't go to the police, that will be your best chance."

"What about the tracking device?"

"Go to the Hamptons, find a parked delivery vehicle, turn the device on, and stick it under a fender. That'll make anyone interested in your whereabouts think you're in the area and moving around. Once you do that, leave by car right away—and I mean right away. From now until this is over, pay for everything with cash."

She nodded and gave Angelo a hug. As he walked away, once again, she felt a pang of loneliness.

• • •

Katherine went to the hospital—scared, hurt, and confused that she could find herself in such a position just for doing her job. She had always assumed being an investigative reporter came with risks, but certainly nothing like this.

When she had called Preston to say she was coming to visit Marcia, he had asked her to meet him in the visitor's lounge and that he had good news. She had no more walked into the lounge than the look on her father's face said it all. Her stepmother had turned a corner. She ran up and gave him a hug, and he told her Marcia was speaking and moving a little on her own. Katherine went through the motions of trying to express her excitement, but she could not shake off her sadness. She tried to distract her father by asking to see Marcia.

"Of course, Kat, you go right in," he said.

She gave him another little hug and headed for the ICU. When she pulled back the curtains to see Marcia, she found the lights dimmed and Marcia asleep. Katherine thought how helpless Marcia looked lying there; it was almost more than she could bear. When she returned to the lounge, she caught her father looking at her kind of funny. "Kat, is something wrong?" Preston asked.

"No, why?" Katherine asked.

"Because you're so quiet, and your face has a sadness to it. Sweetheart, what's going on?"

"I found out . . . I'm going to have to go out of town to work on a story. I'll be gone for a while. I'm upset about not being able to be here for you and Marcia."

"Kiddo, we'll be fine. You go do what you need to do." Preston hugged her. "Marcia's in good hands. You've had one family crisis after another. It's probably best if you got back to work. Maybe it'll help take your mind off things."

She started crying at that, and Preston held her steady.

He asked if she wanted to stay the night at the apartment, but she begged off, saying she had to go pack and would be leaving the next day.

• • •

On her drive home, Katherine felt guilty about lying to her father. Luckily, he had been so caught up with Marcia's recovery he had seemed to believe her cover story. As frightened as she was right now, she could still see clearly enough to know that it was time to go see Sol, although now the meeting would be for an altogether different reason.

She had kept the truth from her father so she could protect him. Sol, on the other hand, was different. He did not have a wife who was fighting for her life or a company on the verge of failing because of someone else's malfeasance. Sol was a seasoned journalist. He would know what to do. It was late when Katherine reached her boss on his cell phone and asked to meet him as soon as possible. Sol did not even bother to ask why, he simply suggested an early breakfast at a café near the office.

Katherine slept little that night. She woke to one of those clear Hampton mornings that made the place so popular with tourists and locals alike. On her way to meet Sol, she spotted a parked U.S.

postal truck and stopped long enough to stick the tracking device under its front fender.

The café was jammed with people, most of them in town for a local art show. She found Sol already in a booth, and he was pouring her a cup of coffee from the pot on the table by the time she sat down.

"Are you quitting me?" he asked as he set the coffeepot down.

"Gosh, no, and I hope you won't fire me, but—"

"Then what's the emergency? Has Chuck been on your back again?"

"I wish it were that simple. I can deal with Chuck, but something else has come up that I can't handle, and I need to leave town for a while until the trial with the BNA bank exposé finishes up. It should come to trial in a couple of weeks, and as—"

"Damn it, somebody has threatened you. Who?" His raised voice caused some people at nearby tables to glance their way.

Katherine did not make eye contact with Sol. She concentrated on a child sitting in a high chair at the table to their right. "That boy is remarkably well-behaved. They must eat out a lot for him to be so quiet in public."

"If you're going to try and manage me, I'm going to get up and eat someplace else. Now what the hell is going on? I can't help you without the facts."

She managed to fix her nervous eyes on Sol. "I met with Angelo yesterday. I called him because two guys in the Russian mafia followed me to a restaurant the night before last and told me to tell Maria DeSanto to lie about Baskhanov's role in the bank scam."

"You know they're in the Russian mafia, how?"

She reached in her briefcase for her drawings. "Here are some rough sketches I made of the tattoos. Angelo took one look at the pictures and told me to leave town."

Sol did not spend any more time with her drawing than Angelo. "Have they been tailing you?"

"Yes. They planted a tracking device on my car, and I've handled that. Don't ask."

Sol's face, naturally pale, became as white as Calacatta marble. "Let's eat our breakfast and get to the office."

The newspaper was not open on Saturdays, so Sol had to turn off all the alarms before opening the front door. It took a minute, and once inside he guided Katherine to his office, where he added water and coffee to his coffee maker, turned the switch, and pointed to the chair in front of his desk.

"Now, get comfortable," he said as he washed out two cups in the small office sink, "because we're going to be here awhile. I want to know how one of my reporters could get involved in something like this without me knowing about it. I want to know every damn thing that's gone on with this bank case that involves Baskhanov."

He paused for effect. "This means starting with your very first interview with the very first person."

Katherine started to open her laptop but stopped when Sol raised his hand.

"You have one of the best memories of anyone I've ever met. Put that thing away and tell me what you know. If I need something more detailed, I'll have you print it out later."

Katherine slowly began to explain how she had gotten the first leads on the bank fraud story and who had led her to what sources. Sol had taken out a stack of typing paper, as was his style, and was taking detailed notes. Whenever she stopped, as if there were nothing more to say, he motioned for her to keep going, which she did.

They drank the coffee pot dry, and Sol made another. The only breaks they took were to the bathroom. When Katherine's stomach finally tightened in hunger she glanced at her watch and saw it was almost three o'clock. She talked for another half hour, finishing with, "The prosecutor convinced Maria DeSanto to testify under the threat of otherwise being a named defendant."

Sol, who never placed his feet on his desk, at least that Katherine had ever seen, pulled out his desk's double drawer and propped his feet on it. "Take off your shoes if you want. We're far from done. I'm going to order a pizza. I want pepperoni on my half. What do you want?"

Katherine picked a vegetable combination that made him shudder as he flipped through his contacts for the number of a nearby pizza parlor. He placed the order and then turned back to Katherine.

"Guy said it'll be here within forty-five minutes. Now, why don't you go to your desk. I'm sure you have some personal calls you need to make. Feel free to use our phones to call whomever necessary while I see what I have in this ream of notes I've taken."

Katherine went to her cubicle and called Beth on one of the newspaper's landlines; she told her mom Marcia had begun breathing on her own and was able to talk and move somewhat. She then hinted she might have an assignment that could prevent her from calling for a while. Their call ended with Katherine thinking her mom had sounded better than she had in a long time. Good job, Oompah Man.

Katherine's next call was to Susan at the hospital, only her friend was unavailable. She did, however, learn that Susan remained in stable condition, which was good news in and of itself. It did not escape her that she had no one else to call. Thank goodness for Preston and his family, and then she thought about Marcia and how awful it would be if Preston lost his wife and P.J. lost his mom.

She headed back to her boss's office and found the pizza had arrived. They ate it all—down to the cheese stuck on the wax paper inside the cardboard delivery box. After they both freshened up, they resumed their spots as before.

"You are in a hell of a spot, Katherine. You could ask to be placed in protective custody, but you do that and your life might as well end as you know it. I don't think you want that. Am I right?"

Katherine sat as still as a statue as Sol spoke.

"I'm going to take your silence to mean that I'm right," he said. "So here are a couple of ideas for you to kick around. You say you've kept the cell phone that kid bugged?" She nodded. "You don't think Sean knows you're onto him?"

"No, something tells me he does know."

"Okay, let's assume you're right. Place that in the corner of your mind with a big check mark next to it, because somewhere in this whole mess, that might come back to save your pretty face. Look at this circle I drew with all the players." Sol handed her a chart that mirrored the one she had drawn a year earlier. "Maria DeSanto rats out Stacy Bowers, who is in cahoots with Baskhanov. Now somewhere in this scrum is Teddy Thompson, who likely has a tie-in with someone else at your father's Mercedes dealership in Manhattan. It's probably this Disley character, whom you've mentioned several times—seven to be exact if I've counted correctly. I figure him for being up to his eyeballs in this cesspool."

Sol shuffled through several pages of his notes. "This Robert Reynolds is also a good candidate for being in this confederacy of crooks. One of the people I've just listed has been flipped like Maria DeSanto, although she remains the one person who can add credibility and tie it all together."

"I hate to think this way, but why wouldn't the Russians go after her directly?" Katherine asked.

Sol propped his feet back on his desk drawer. "There's no telling. Maybe they can't get to her. Maybe Baskhanov thinks that if she were killed, it would put even more pressure on him. The government obviously has a good case, and this Russian has to be a very big fish.

"If Maria DeSanto doesn't corroborate what the person who was flipped says, the government's case will be severely weakened, perhaps to the point of having no case at all. This Baskhanov case fails, and it ruins the careers of some prosecutors on the fast track. How many of these hotshots are then going to want to come after the Russian? From everything you've told me, you're involved in one big cat and mouse game, with all sorts of moving parts. I want you to stay alive, so why don't you head down to Braydon for an extended stay?"

"You won't believe this, but that was my first choice," Katherine said. "I think I could blend in there, though I'm thinking I might have to give Mike McCusker the entire byline—"

"A small price to pay to save your skin in the process. I'll know what you contributed, and you can write a bigger story later."

Katherine blinked a few times and scooted forward in her chair. "You think this can just go away, and I'll be okay."

"That's impossible to know. Maybe a false story could be planted that a key witness in the BNA bank fraud case, referred to only as MX, is being kept undercover and protected until the trial. Of course the Russians will never believe that, but that would make it more plausible that you don't have access to her. Anything to soften or distract."

"That may work. I know you're trying to protect me—it just doesn't feel right."

"It won't feel right if you get hurt because of this, either. I'm just saying, it's an option." Sol thumbed through several other pages of his notes. "We're close to finishing up. I just need you to give me a few minutes. Go to your desk, and I'll call for you when I'm ready."

Katherine did as she was told. On the way to her cubicle, she could not resist looking around the newsroom and wondering if it would be the last time she ever saw the place. She organized a few files and cleared out a few e-mails. Before she knew it she heard Sol calling her. She walked back to his office and sat down. Her eyes widened as he handed her an envelope with a string tied around it.

"Open it and don't say anything."

Inside was a *Twin Forks Press* credit card in the name of "M.K. Hunt, Principal" along with a stack of hundred dollar bills an inch thick. Katherine could not help but gape at the pile of money.

"That credit card should not be traceable to you under any circumstances. You can use it for gas, and you won't be asked for an ID for most other stuff as long as the purchases are less than twenty-five smackers. Use credit, not debit so you just have to sign the name. The zip code is for here."

"The money . . . ?"

"The money is your salary for the next two months. If you need more for some reason, call me, but whatever you do, don't use your personal credit cards—and don't so much as get a library card or anything else that requires your Social Security number. The smartest thing you can do right now is let me hold onto all of your credit cards. I'll get your mail and make the minimum payments, and I'll take care of the rent at your apartment until you come back."

"I can't believe you'd do all this for me."

He chuckled. "Neither can I, but in a way I got you into this by not giving you better direction when you were investigating the bank. Maybe I'm getting old and not thinking as clearly as I once did." He sighed. "One thing you must do is get rid of that second phone you picked up. So I'm going to trade you for it so you don't accidentally use it."

Sol handed her a phone from his drawer. "Now you have a phone with a number no one knows but me and you. It has a number block, so no one can pick up the number or do an automatic callback. Downside is some people won't take a call from a number they can't identify. You'll just have to work around that. Now give me your credit cards and your phone."

Katherine handed Sol everything. "You've been with me from the beginning, Sol. You're a true friend." She stood on tiptoe to give him a kiss on the cheek. The old newspaperman blushed. "Thank you for believing in me, Sol. I promise to write one heck of a story when it's all over.

"I know you will, kiddo. Now get out of here."

CHAPTER 49

INSIDE THE HOSPITAL IT had become impossible for Preston to tell time, let alone if it were morning or night. After a while, it didn't even matter to him. He was too absorbed in his wife's slow but steady recovery. He had learned to wait until Dr. Li was making his rounds before asking the questions only the doctor could answer. In between, he tried not to go crazy with worry. When he saw the doctor, he got right to what he needed so desperately to know. "Can you tell me, doctor, am I going to get my wife back?"

Dr. Li responded with a technical explanation that only a trained medical professional could have understood, and Preston was just about to give up hope when the doctor, for a moment, slipped into layman's terms. "Mrs. Wilson is doing much better. She is not out of the woods, but if she continues, the outcome should be good. No promises, but she's getting stronger every day. Soon she may be upgraded to serious condition and put in a regular hospital bed."

"Serious condition?"

"Serious is much better than critical."

Preston stepped to Marcia's bedside and took her hand in his. "The doctor said you're getting much better. Keep fighting. Everyone's asking about you. A lot of people out there love you, but nobody as much as I do." He squeezed her hand. "Can you feel that, Marcia? Can you hear me? If you can hear me, sweetheart, please squeeze my hand."

327

He waited for a minute, and then another, but nothing happened. He was about to give up and head back to his chair, when he felt the soft squeeze of her fingers.

That slight pressure went all the way to his heart.

• • •

Preston was in the lounge waiting for the nurses to finish attending to Marcia when Tommy appeared at the door. He couldn't remember when a face had been so welcome. He strode over to Tommy and gave him a firm handshake, followed by a hug.

"Thanks for coming," Preston said.

"How is she?"

"Let's go in so you can see for yourself."

Preston watched Tommy as he pulled back the curtain and saw Marcia for the first time. The frown that followed, in spite of how quickly he made it disappear, made it clear he understood she was incredibly lucky to be alive. As Tommy bowed his head and whispered a few words, Preston felt his throat tighten.

Back in the lounge, Tommy seemed determined to cheer Preston up. "She's gonna have to fight a fifteen rounder to win this one, but I'm bettin' on her." Tommy looked over all the flowers. "Did you get ours?"

"How could you miss them? It's the biggest arrangement there."

"That's what Missy wanted. Me, too. Is your daughter here?"

Preston hesitated. "She's on an out-of-town assignment for her newspaper. It just came up . . ."

"And?" Tommy asked.

"I can't help feeling she is keeping something from me."

"The way she acted?" Tommy asked.

"That's right."

"That's wrong. Want me to check it out?"

Preston knew from experience how well Tommy could check something out. He'd seen him in action when Tommy made Missy's abusive ex-husband go away long before she became his wife. As he thought about it, he realized there were few men he trusted as much as Tommy.

"Yes, Tommy. I do."

"What's the name of her newspaper?"

"It's in the Hamptons, the *Twin Forks Press*. It's probably nothing. I've been up here and away from home so long I'm going a little stir crazy. Probably read more into what she said, or didn't say. I'm sure it's nothing to worry about."

"If it was nothing, you wouldn't have said it. Missy has family with her and the baby. I have some friends on the island. I'll make some calls. Maybe make a visit."

Preston knew not to ask for any more details; nonetheless, he was grateful for Tommy's help. Before Preston could say thank you, he heard a knock and Harry walked through the partially opened door. "Hey guys. You know it's the Oompah Man."

Tommy rolled his eyes. The three men sat down to catch up, and then Harry asked if he could see Marcia. Preston hesitated, concerned about Harry's unfettered enthusiasm. He sometimes was a little too happy. Still, Preston did not want to insult Harry or disappoint him. He was right to worry, however. Harry was a mess after seeing Marcia and barely managed to hold it together before ducking out of the ICU. Preston worried he might be off his meds.

Harry calmed down later in the lounge, and Preston was glad he had refrained from saying anything. The conversation eventually turned away from Marcia and to what was going on outside the hospital. Tommy talked about Missy, Skylar, and the camp. Harry talked about Beth, and how things were going with his band. Both men made a point to ask Preston how P.J. was doing.

Eventually, Tommy checked his cell phone and abruptly stood. "I've got to go. Got a *situational*." He gave a wave and left.

Preston stiffened. He had no doubt the call had been about Katherine's situation. He told himself Tommy had it under control, so he turned and tried to focus his attention on Harry. It was his chance to tell the Oompah Man about taking P.J. to his first sports-themed birthday party.

"You should have seen us in the double-sided bounce house. I came down the slide at the same time P.J. did, and when we got to the bottom he gave me a high five."

"You know what, Preston?"

"What?"

"Right now, you remind me of Joe Hart."

Preston was so touched that he didn't know what to say. Before things could turn maudlin, Harry slapped Preston on his shoulder with a broad smile and said, "Okay then," and walked out of the visitors area.

• • •

Tommy was sitting in the back of a black limousine when his cell phone buzzed. He recognized the number, smiled, and answered the call. "Harry?"

"Tommy, I should tell you that I overheard some of your conversation about Preston's daughter. I just want you to know I'm here to help if you need me."

"Good to know," Tommy said. "It could get complicated, and sometimes these things don't go as expected. I have to be careful who's involved and how things are handled."

"This is Preston's daughter we're talking about," Harry said in an unusually low and intense voice. "On top of that, I'm in love with Katherine's mother. Please let me help."

"I get the association. It's just the risks. I can't be looking after you as well."

"I accept the risks, Tommy. There's a lot wrong with me, but I'm no newbie to such things, and I'm not afraid."

"Okay, I get that you want to help. Let's take it a step at a time. See how it goes. All I ask is you gotta agree to do what I say when I say it—no matter what. Can you do that?"

"Absolutely."

"I'll be in touch."

CHAPTER 50

ALTHOUGH KATHERINE'S DRIVE to Braydon had proved uneventful, it was still difficult for her to keep her eyes off her rearview mirror, and she felt, given recent discoveries, that her paranoia was more than warranted. At the least it explained why she had decided to drive straight through to Braydon without stopping overnight—the better to throw anyone trying to track her moves off-guard. Per Sol's advice, since leaving the city, she had also limited her contact with the outside world to one brief phone call to Alice asking if she could stay a couple of days with her. She was beyond pleased that Alice had not pressed her for details.

She arrived at Alice's at 1:00 a.m. and found the key Alice had left her under the flowerpot. Buck barked a couple of times as Katherine slipped inside, quickly calming down as he recognized the late-night visitor. Alice never even woke up.

Katherine found a light on in the dining room, along with a note from Alice and some chocolate-chip cookies on the dining room table. She gratefully carried the cookies and her bags to her room only to fall asleep atop the covers before she could enjoy her snack or unpack. The next thing she realized, she was being wakened by a knock on the bedroom door. Her heart raced as she tried to get her bearings in the unfamiliar room. It all came into focus with one question from the other side of the door: "Katherine, you going to sleep all day?"

331

Katherine looked at her watch and groaned. It was past noon. "I'm so sorry, Alice. I had no idea it was so late. Be out in a minute."

After a quick shower, she went downstairs to see Alice. The house, as always, was warm and inviting, and the sound and smell of the coffeepot perking away was a relaxing change from everything she had had to deal with over the last forty-eight hours. She found Alice in the kitchen frying eggs and putting out a plate of biscuits and jam on the kitchen table.

Alice paused long enough in her cooking to give Katherine a tight hug and a quick word of advice, "Don't turn your back on those biscuits." She shook her finger at the big German shepherd sitting innocently under the table, leaving no doubt why she had issued the warning.

Katherine smiled and felt herself relax for the first time in days. She felt a bond with Alice that went back to the first time they had met. Since having met each of the Collectibles, she now attributed some of their connection to Joe Hart's magic, a spell that seemed to linger comfortably over everyone he had ever touched. For Katherine, Alice was like a soft sweater that felt good no matter the temperature.

"Don't you worry," Katherine said, "Buck's not getting any of my biscuits. They're too good. By the way, this peach jam is wonderful."

"Picked the peaches and made it myself. You hang around long enough, I'll show you how to make peach cobbler, too—that is, if you want to learn."

"I can barely boil water, so it's about time I learned something about food that doesn't involve a can opener."

Alice laughed, and Katherine smiled as she slathered more jam on her biscuit. She asked Alice what had been going on in Braydon, and whether Mike had been around to discuss his story.

"He's not been by lately, but you might find this of interest." Alice removed the front section of the morning's *Braydon Constitution* and motioned for Katherine to follow her. "Let's go into the living room, the lighting's better."

She directed Katherine to one of a twin pair of cushy antique reading chairs, and then handed her the newspaper. The front page shouted in caps:

"BRAYDON BANK FAILURE: BROKEN DREAMS FOR INVESTORS. OFFICERS AND BOARD FEAR LAWSUIT."

The byline read: "Michael McCusker and Katherine Kelly." So much for keeping a low profile, Katherine thought. Still, Katherine could not ignore the goose bumps. Eighty percent of the words she was reading were hers. Her first impression of the article was that it was perfectly crafted in every way. She paused midway through and asked Alice if she could have a glass of water. Alice told her to keep her seat and that they could do better than that. She returned shortly with a pitcher of sweet tea and glasses for them both. Katherine took a sip of the Southern favorite, caught her breath, and then read every word of the lead article again. Same impression.

"You look pleased," Alice said. "Think I'll leave you to it. I need to clean up in the kitchen."

"Do you need any help?" Katherine offered.

"You just stay right where you are, dear. You're coming off a long night on the road. Buck and I have it all under control."

Alice and the German shepherd headed to the kitchen, and Katherine immediately rang Mike, using the phone from Sol.

"Did you get it?" he asked, sounding a bit apprehensive.

"Got it and read it. Twice."

"Well?"

"I think it's going to drive a stake right through their hearts."

"We're already getting calls at the paper. It's a ten. I'm ecstatic. The bosses are thrilled."

"They should be, Mike. You did a great job."

"We both know where the real reporting came from." He chuckled. "The writing, too."

"It took both of us to do this story justice, and I think together we may also get some justice for Alice and her friends. Mike, could you have your circulation department save me some tear sheets? I want to send one to my mom and my journalism professor. Have you thought about sending out a news alert e-mail to your sub-scribers?"

"I've already set some aside for you," Mike said, "and our man-aging editor had circulation send out an e-blast today to all our subscribers and half the town telling them where they can buy extra copies."

"How about sending a couple copies to my editor up in New York. You've got the address. Just put them to the attention of Sol Kaplowitz." She spelled out Sol's last name.

"Wouldn't it be just as easy to send them to you at the paper," Mike said.

"Between you and me, I'm here in Braydon. Might be down here for a while. Please don't tell anyone I'm here though, and that includes your editor. I'll call you tomorrow, and we can meet some-place and I'll fill you in. By the way, did you get anything from the attorney on whether or not the McKenzie clan is connected to any of the bank officers who were arrested? I didn't see anything about that in the article."

"Mr. Livingston told me he was still working on it. He doesn't like me as much as he likes you, so I'm glad you're in town—you're probably going to have to be the one to drag it out of him. So far, it doesn't look like the McKenzies had anything to do with the bank's officers directly, though they might be silent investors in the bank."

"Silent?"

"Their family has lots of relatives who could have done the ac-tual investing for them. If the McKenzies were known to want a major position in the bank, many other people would have backed off. The McKenzies are popular, but they're not that popular. It's difficult to explain. Let's just say when it comes to the McKenzies, the McKenzies always come first."

"I get it," Katherine said.

"Hey Katherine, thanks again for everything. I realize now I didn't even know what I didn't know. Thanks for keeping me from embarrassing myself. I'm a better reporter for having worked with you on this story," Mike said.

"Aw, you're making me blush," Katherine said. "I do have one question for you. Last I heard Mr. Livingston was working off the list of people you and I interviewed for his depositions. Do you know whether he's planning to depose anyone else?"

"Honestly, I didn't think to ask that."

"Let's explore the relationship between the FDIC and the shareholders in the class action more in the next installment. What did Livingston say about the percentages the investors might recover?"

"Unfortunately, I do know the answer to that," Mike said. "He said there are no guarantees."

"Typical attorney talk," Katherine said.

"I'll speak with Livingston some more, and see if I can get a better answer."

"While you're at it, please see if you can get us an appointment with him—the sooner the better."

"He'll be my first call when I get to the office tomorrow morning," Mike said.

"Thanks, and congratulations on that headline—above the fold and all caps, that's 'Jimmy Hoffa's Body Found' kind of placement. Oh, and please tell your editor I appreciate being included in the byline."

"He was glad to do it."

"See you soon. Again, other than Livingston, please don't tell a soul I'm down here."

"I won't. I promise."

Katherine's next call was to her mother; she told her about the newspaper article coming out and promised to send her a copy. Beth made a big fuss over her news, which made Katherine smile. Her mother couldn't care less about the article, but she knew how much it meant to Katherine—and that she would like seeing her daughter's name on it.

What Katherine didn't tell Beth was that she was in Braydon. Things were still too unclear to worry her mom unnecessarily.

"How's my favorite dog doing?" Katherine asked. "Taking good care of my mother, I hope."

"Hailey's fine. Misses you. Big help to me though. You're not getting her back unless you come back here to live."

"What's the latest with Harry?" Katherine asked, skirting that last subject as fast as possible.

"He's been over twice. Calls every day."

"Mom, how do you feel about Harry?"

Katherine heard Beth heave a big sigh. "Honestly, Kat, I don't know. I like Harry." Another beat. "You know he has problems?"

"If you mean that he's bipolar, yeah, I know that. He's able to control it if he's on his meds."

"I think that's true, and frankly, his condition doesn't bother me. I've worked with a lot of manic depressive and bipolar person-alities. Heck, I'm in the first category half the time myself." She laughed. "Seriously, sweetheart, he does seem to have his life under control. The problem is that he wants me to move to Batavia and live with him."

"Wow, Mom, that's great. So what's the problem?"

"That's a big step—I mean a *big* step. I don't know if I'm ready for that kind of commitment."

"Why wouldn't you be?" Katherine asked, unable to suppress a meddlesome tone. "He'd be great company. He sure seems taken with you."

"I'm pretty much out of the nursing business."

"Come on, Mom."

"I'm kidding, of course, except it does come down to whether I want to ride his roller coaster."

"You just said you thought he was fine as long as he's taking his medication."

"To some extent. It's just when he's in his manic phase, it can be a little exhausting."

"Now you're just making excuses."

"Well, at least they are my excuses. Give me some time with Harry. This is all happening too fast."

Katherine could tell there was no use pushing the subject of the Oompah Man any further. "Please give Harry my best," was her final salvo.

"You going to tell me where you are?" her mother asked.

"You're relentless, aren't you? I'm sorry; all I can say is that I'm working on an out-of-state story. I will, however, send you a tear sheet of today's article."

"My daughter, the investigative journalist," Beth said, sighing so loudly it sounded like she was sitting next to Katherine. "Are you having fun?"

The last sentence stopped Katherine cold. "I'm having . . . the time of my life."

"You sure don't sound like it."

Katherine forced a laugh and promised to call her toward the middle of the week, if not sooner. They said their good-byes, and next she called Susan. Her friend sounded better. She had had some complications with her recovery from the accident, so her stay in the hospital was taking longer than initially planned. She hoped to be released soon. Some of the counselors and sponsors from the rehabilitation center had already called to see when they could visit her and when she would be back. Katherine could tell their concern meant a lot to Susan.

Her last call was to her father. She wanted to see how Marcia was doing, and she knew her father would be worried about her. To her surprise, Preston sounded upbeat.

"Dr. Li and the nurses are encouraged," he said. "Every time Marcia wakes up, it seems that something better happens. This morning she was moving all of her fingers, and she can now move her toes. She tires easily, after talking more than a few seconds, but she's asking about P.J. She asked about you, too, Kat."

Katherine felt a lump in her throat. "That's so good to hear, Dad. Give her my love, and tell her I'm terribly sorry I can't be right at her side with you."

"Believe me, she knows. I swear she smiled when I said your name," Preston said.

Katherine beamed with pleasure. "Thank you for telling me that, Dad."

"I hope wherever you are, things are going well," Preston said.

"So far, so good. I will keep in touch, and I hope to get back there soon."

• • •

Preston was sitting tranquilly by his wife's bedside, just like he had done so often since the explosion, when suddenly he blinked in surprise. If he was not mistaken, Marcia's head had moved slightly. He told himself not to read too much into it, although it could be a watershed moment in her recovery. If Marcia had moved her head, it meant she had control of her neck muscles. He leaned over so he could whisper in her ear.

"There's so much that's happened, Marcia. So much I want to tell you. I don't want to live without you. I know how foolish I've been, the mistakes I've made."

He buried his head in the sheet and raised his voice. "The way I dealt with P.J.'s hearing was horrible. Thankfully, you ignored me. You did the right thing. You're the best mother a child could ever have. I promise I will never second-guess you again when it comes to our son. And I—"

"Stop . . . beating . . . yourself . . . up," Marcia whispered, touching her fingers to his forehead. "You're not . . . alone. I'm a big part of . . . the problem."

Preston wiped his eyes and took Marcia's hand. They sat together in silence. Preston could feel his heart beat. He looked into his wife's eyes. "I love you so much. I'll do whatever it takes to make sure you and P.J. are safe and secure—for the rest of our lives."

Marcia began to blink slowly. Preston could see she was getting tired. There was so much more he wanted to say to her, but she needed her rest. He stayed for another few minutes and then it was time to let the nurses do their thing. Preston kissed his wife on the arm and the cheek, and told her he would be back soon. He left the

ICU and walked faster than he thought he was capable of through the halls, down the stairs—no elevator to wait on this time—and to the chapel.

When he returned to the ICU a little later, he found Ida sitting by the bed, reading to a sleeping Marcia. He greeted Ida and told her about his earlier conversation with Marcia and what he had witnessed.

"Yes, son, she has been talking to me, too, and I saw her move her arm."

Ida had never addressed Preston as "son" before. Preston stepped closer and put his arms around her, saying, "Things between us are going to be different."

She smiled and her eyes came alive. "You're right, a lot of things are going to change—for the better and for all of us."

CHAPTER 51

ETH WAS STILL THINKING ABOUT what her daughter had said when the main subject of their conversation called later that afternoon.

"You missing the Oompah Man yet?" Harry asked.

"Just waiting for your call," Beth said, though in truth she had been agonizing over what Katherine had said, too distracted to miss anyone.

"My band has a gig in Wheatfield, a little town not too far from Niagara Falls. How about coming with us?"

"Oh, I don't know, Harry."

"I'd like you to come. What else have you got to do? It'll be a lot of fun."

Beth looked to Hailey for the answer. The dog's eyes gave nothing away. "When is it?"

"Saturday, the twentieth. Almost two full weeks away."

"I'm not sure, Harry. I don't mean to be an old fuddy-duddy, I just don't know what would I do with Hailey."

"You can bring Hailey. She can ride in my truck, and she can sleep in it, too, or if you prefer, she can stay with us in the motel."

"The motel?"

"Don't get the wrong idea. Wheatfield's a nice little town. A lot goin' on. A speedway, plenty of social events . . . the Berthold Band plays there all the time."

"The Berthold Band?" Beth repeated. "What in the world is that?"

"It's another oompah band. Not as good as ours, of course, but still terrific. Got them a gig someplace else, so that's how we got this one."

"Does the motel you are talking about happen to have more than one room?"

"You have to understand something, pretty lady, I care about you. I'm not trying to push you where you don't want to be."

"You think I'm too guarded and cynical, don't you?" Beth said, handing Hailey a dog biscuit.

"I don't look at it that way. I just think you're trying to play a song from the wrong music sheet."

"Honestly, Harry, I'm not sure I know what that means."

"I think you know exactly what it means. You're not fighting me, you're fighting yourself."

"I guess I've been living alone for too long," Beth said.

"We both have."

Beth again turned quiet.

"Let me ask you a question, pretty lady. Are you being totally honest with me?"

"Probably not," Beth replied so fast it surprised her.

"If you were, what would you say to me? I'm asking you to tell me the truth."

He was right. She was not being completely honest. How could she be? What should she tell him? When Harry hit bottom, which they both knew he would again, she did not want to live through his depression.

Beth had seen too many cases like Harry's over the years. She also had not been kidding when she had told her daughter that morning that she had plenty of her own psychological issues to contend with—but were those issues best addressed alone, or with someone by her side?

"Harry, you are a good man. You deserve the truth. You're right. I haven't been completely honest. I've told myself it's because I care about you. The truth is, I have my own problems. The biggest one? I don't like myself very much. On top of that, I'm scared."

"We're all scared. We all also have to go on, and staying in the fight is what matters most. There's still a lot of song left in both of us."

"I have an idea," Beth said as Hailey devoured another dog biscuit in a single bite. "How about you come over this Friday night, and I'll cook you dinner. After dinner we'll sit down in the den and talk over everything."

This time it was Harry who paused. "Afraid I've got somethin' to do that might take me away for a while, and I might not be back by Friday. If I am, does the offer still stand?"

"Of course it does," Beth assured him.

CHAPTER 52

KATHERINE HAD BEEN TYPING away on her laptop for some time when Alice walked in with a cup of lemon tea. "Drink some of this. It will settle your stomach."

Katherine pushed the cover to her laptop shut and looked up at Alice. "How did you know my stomach was bothering me?"

"Just a guess. It was either your stomach or your head, and I imagine both have been giving you trouble lately."

"So you overheard me on the phone? I'm sorry. I should've gone outside."

"Nonsense, but I would like to know the real reason you're here. You're not in Braydon solely for our case. Of that, I'm certain."

Katherine warmed her hands on the hot teacup but she did not take a sip.

"Please don't be mad at me, Alice; I can't discuss it."

"I also can't help you if I don't know what's going on."

"I don't need any help," Katherine blurted, though she regretted it the moment she had said it.

Alice came over to Katherine, took her by the hand, and pulled the younger woman to her feet. She then gave Katherine a hug that was amazingly powerful for such a tiny woman of her age—and she did not let go until Katherine gradually began to wilt in her grasp. Before she knew what was happening, Katherine felt her tears dampen the shoulder of Alice's sweater.

"Now you sit down and drink your tea and tell me what's going on," Alice said.

Katherine had expected to find it difficult to confide in Alice. Instead, she found telling Alice her most private matters to be one of the easiest things she had ever done. While she did not go into as much detail as she had provided Sol, she also did not leave much out. Alice listened stoically, showing emotion only when it came to the Russians, which caused her to cringe. Katherine was amazed at how calmly she took in everything else, including Sean's antics. By the time Katherine finished, it was time for dinner.

Alice finally spoke. "I'm going to reheat some stew and make some cornbread. I have a suspicion not much has stuck to your ribs lately. You're going to stay with me until all this settles down."

"You don't know how much I appreciate the offer. It's just not safe, and it could put you in danger. I won't have that. I was planning to see if I could get a weekly or monthly rate at the Live Oak. I figured if Bobby thought I was on a confidential assignment he would let me check in under an alias."

"Don't be ridiculous. You're staying here with me, and I won't have any more discussion about it. Buck won't let anything happen to either of us. This might be a sleepy little town, but we have our share of crime like every community has to deal with at one time or another. Trust me, this old gal is not going to let anything happen to you in this house."

"I'm going to have to do something, though. I can't sit in the house all day."

"Why not? You can read, call the people you have to, and go for walks with Buck and me."

"I know. You're right. I'm just restless. Nervous, actually."

"The Home Dairy is looking for a waitress. You could help out there once in a while if you feel like it. The owner, Dave Niemeyer, is a friend of mine, and he'd be glad to have your help. Johnny will be there."

Katherine called Buck over to her and gave the big dog a hug. "Alice, I don't know what to say. I don't know how long I'll be here, and I'll pay you for room and board, just as if I were staying some-where else."

"That's quite unnecessary. I won't hear of it. I consider you family. Do you want me to call Dave?"

"Sure, I love the Home Dairy. Thank you, again."

• • •

Katherine had left New York fast and had to pack without a lot of thought. A quick trip the next morning to Charleston, less than a half-hour from Braydon, fixed that. She returned with a couple of pairs of jeans, new Nikes, and several shirts with patch pockets, the better to blend into her new surroundings.

Alice remarked, "You look like you've lived here all your life. I talked to Dave, and he's excited to have you. He said you could come in when you like, pick up an apron, and work at your leisure."

"You're amazing," Katherine said with a smile.

• • •

Having waited tables off and on while in college, Katherine had no trouble at the Home Dairy, whose clientele was substantially less demanding than busy type-A New Yorkers who were always in a rush and then some. Mr. Niemeyer had agreed to let her work part-time for tips with the understanding that her tenure at the Home Dairy would most likely be short. One of the perks of the job was getting to work alongside Johnny, whom Katherine had found to be the most joyful co-worker she had ever had. Johnny insisted on telling her how much the customers liked her, though how he could have known, since he worked in the back with the cooks, she never figured out. Still, the praise made her feel good just the same.

"You nice lady. Preston's daughter. Preston nice man. He was Joe's friend, too. Johnny loved Joe."

"I know you did. I've learned that a lot of people loved Joe. I'm among them, and I never even met the man. Johnny, there are some

bad men after me because of a true story I wrote in the newspaper.
No one can know but Alice and you that I'm in Braydon."

"Tell Johnny where you are."

She smiled. "I didn't mean it like that. I'm here, but no one can
know that I'm staying in Braydon."

"You staying with Ms. Alice?"

"Yes."

"Johnny not tell anybody where you are."

She kissed him on the cheek—and he turned beet red.

• • •

When she had first started work at the diner, Katherine had
been nervous about who might walk through the doorway and possibly recognize her, but by the second week she calmed down and
fell into a routine that she wore like an old pair of shoes. She avoid-
ed the Live Oak even though she was pining for Bobby's company.
She had toyed with what she would do were he to come into the
dairy, yet so far it hadn't happened.

She called Preston every day to check on Marcia. Her stepmother had been moved to a regular hospital room, and something called
a therapy regimen was in place. In a best-case scenario, it would be
months before Marcia would walk again on her own. Yet her dad
seemed to find hope in knowing that Marcia could move limbs not
in a cast, and she had started eating solid food. She appeared to
have suffered no memory loss and was doing so well that Ida and
Harold were flying home. They had been staying with Preston and
not in a hotel, which Katherine knew was another first.

She also kept in touch with Sol, making sure to keep him up to
date, reassuring him all was quiet and that she was safe at Alice's.

• • •

During Katherine's third week in Braydon, Mike McCusker
finally got the meeting with Marshall Livingston. As soon as the

three of them sat down together, it became clear the attorney had not wanted the conference to take place without Katherine and was glad she had been able to attend.

"Thank you for meeting with us, Mr. Livingston. You've obviously been doing a lot of work on this case. If I may, I have a few questions."

"It's good to see you, Katherine, and I'm happy to help. Fire away."

"I'd like to start with Alice Hawkins, the woman who brought me into this matter in the first place. How do you think she'll come out in all of this?"

"Alice is a fine lady, and I'd like to see her recover every penny she invested," Livingston said. "What makes this case atypical is that the bank has not yet been closed. While one vice president committed crimes that resulted in serious damage to the bank's balance sheets, and his conviction will surely bring the federal regulators down on the bank, the FDIC has yet to come in and seize all assets, much less officially close it. That's good news for our clients. As it stands, the FDIC doesn't have a claim to take its share off the top of any recovery."

Katherine took copious notes. "Understood," she said. "Could you please comment on the financial side—the likelihood of recovery and in what amount?"

"A bank policy expert I hired is of the opinion that the officers and directors committed gross negligence, and a forensic accountant estimates this cost the bank $30 million—52 percent of its tier-one capital—which is the true measure of any bank's financial strength," Livingston said.

Katherine looked at her notes. "Interesting. Tell me more."

"If assets based on deposits fall below a certain level, established guidelines are violated, and the bank can be declared insolvent. The FDIC can take over the bank, essentially making certain that depositors will be paid whole up to certain amounts. That is guaranteed by federal law. It does not, however, apply to investors, and the bank has not been declared insolvent."

"What about punitive damages?" Katherine asked. "They're usually triple, aren't they?"

"Yes, a jury can award up to three times the amount being sought. That gives us a lot of leverage for settlement."

Mike's eyes lit up. "Thirty-million dollars means they might award $90 million."

"Theoretically." The attorney reached in his desk and handed Mike a pamphlet that his firm provided to prospective clients. It listed the firm's major settlements. "As you can see, those kinds of numbers aren't generally in the cards. Juries are notoriously unpredictable."

He checked his watch. "Sorry, but I'm going to need to wrap this up. I have a deposition in a little while."

"We understand," Katherine said. "I appreciate your time. Speaking of settlements, on a scale of one to ten, how do you assess the probability for this one—and for what amount do you think this case might settle?"

"Can we go off the record on this?" Livingston asked.

"Yes, but only for this," Katherine replied.

Livingston nodded. "There are twelve people in the class action. If I had to make a guess about the amount of the settlements to avoid a trial, I'd be breaking out the champagne at $5 million for the class."

"Your fee comes out of that?" Mike asked.

Livingston shook his finger at Mike. "Young man, my firm puts up the money for all the investigators and a lot of other expenses most people know nothing about. Our third is nowhere near that when it's done. There are times when we barely recover our expenses. Every action brought doesn't produce a positive verdict. And until I tell you otherwise, this is all off the record."

"Agreed," Katherine said.

"Mr. Livingston, I wasn't trying to offend you," Mike said. "It's obvious I did, so I apologize. I'm just trying to get a handle on how much the Alice Hawkinses of this case can legitimately expect to see if this goes in their favor."

"If the investors recover half then they'll be doing well, but you have to understand everything I've told you. It could be more—or even much more—or it could be the bank is found insolvent, and there's no money to recover from the assets of those found guilty. There are a lot of pieces, and it could take years for non-liquid assets to be turned into cash. That's why a settlement is likely. So tell Alice she might get half her money back."

"She'd better put it under a mattress," Mike said.

Katherine stood up. "We've taken enough of your time, and again we thank you."

"It's always a pleasure to work with you, Katherine."

After thanking the attorney again, Katherine acknowledged that it had been a productive meeting. She discussed a few quick to-dos with Mike, and then headed back to Alice's house. Her mind was content, but the rest of her was restless. She decided it was time for a beer.

CHAPTER 53

A LITTLE AFTER HALF-PAST NINE in the morning, two huge men, each carrying a handgun, climbed out of a black Lincoln Navigator into an alley and walked past two dumpsters to the rear entrance of a small restaurant. The metal door to the back was locked. Boris, the slightly taller of the two, put his ear to the door and picked up the hum of kitchen equipment. Satisfied they had the right place, he pulled a lock pick from his jacket. In less than a minute they were inside.

The first person they saw was a short, pudgy, middle-aged man whistling as he stacked trays. What they did not see was the girl they had come for, but they figured she was probably up front waiting tables.

They expected to also encounter a cook at any minute, and their plan was for Oleg to hold a gun on both men while Boris snatched the reporter and rushed her out the back door and into the waiting SUV. Nobody had to get hurt as long as no one did anything stupid. Katherine needed to be kept alive for the long trip back to Brooklyn. Their boss had special plans for her.

Boris spotted a walk-in cooler and brought it to Oleg's attention with a quick motion of his head. Oleg nodded. Boris opened the cooler door, and the short man came over. Oblivious to the danger, he shouted, "No one to go in cooler! You can't go in there. Kitchen closed."

Boris raised his thick eyebrows at Oleg and motioned with his hands to stay calm. Johnny yelled over and over, "You not allowed. Leave Johnny's kitchen!"

"Anybody else here?" Oleg asked the short man, who said nothing in return. "Are you deaf?"

Johnny shook his head, his feet planted squarely as he stared at the two intruders, sweat pouring from his head and body.

"What's with this guy?" Oleg muttered.

Boris shrugged. "It doesn't matter. Put him in the cooler and find her."

"Find who?" Johnny asked.

"Katherine Kelly," Boris shouted. "Where is she?"

"She not here. She not here."

Oleg turned to Johnny, "We watched her come in here the last two days. We know she's here."

"She not here," Johnny said.

"She's here," Oleg insisted, grabbing Johnny's upper arm and squeezing.

"I told you to put him in the cooler. Let's go," Oleg said. "This guy is crazy." Of all the things Oleg could have said, that was the worst. Johnny jerked free of his grasp, picked up a stack of trays, and, from the top, started throwing them one by one at the men like giant, silver Frisbees.

Before Boris could say anything more, a tray hit him in the mouth, splitting his lip. He was trying to stem the blood and pull his gun when he heard somebody yell, "What's going on back there? Keep it down!" Johnny ducked under a ledge stacked with dirty dishes and yelled at the top of his lungs: "Bad men here, Miss Katherine! Bad men here! Go to Miss Alice! Johnny keep them away."

Neither Russian could bend down low enough to make it under the ledge and to the dining room without getting on their knees, which gave Johnny time enough to pick up a big pot of water he had been boiling for potatoes for lunch. When the hands of one of the men reached for him, he dropped the pot on them. It was impossible to tell if the screams were a result of hot metal or scalding water, but it was clear the profanity was Russian. Johnny climbed through the opening and ran straight to Katherine, who pulled him to her car.

• • •

Katherine drove to the house as fast as she could, using her Bluetooth to call Alice and let her know they were on their way and that she had one upset Johnny with her. Minutes later she pulled in the drive, and Alice helped Johnny out of the front seat and into the house. Inside, Alice and Katherine both made several attempts to calm him down. Nothing they said brought a stop to the crying. Alice looked up and whispered, "What happened? I've never seen him like this." In a low voice, Katherine gave her a rapid play-by-play, watching Alice's face grow grimmer with each word.

"Maybe it's time to call the police. Someone could have gotten hurt today," Alice said.

"I wanted to call 9-1-1, too, at first," Katherine said. "Then I realized on the drive over here that would just put more lives in danger. Somehow these gangsters figured out I'm down here. I just need a little time to figure out how—for all I know one of my phones is somehow being tracked by the Russians. I know someone who can help. I just have to reach him." She nodded at Johnny who had cried himself to sleep in Alice's arms. "I hate scaring Johnny; I hate that I have involved everybody else in this, most of all you."

Alice replied, "No time for feeling sorry about anything. Here's what I want you to do. Take my car and I'll keep yours. We'll straighten all this out later. Get your things in my car and go to Corey's—worse case his daughter Barbara maybe can hide you someplace. I have something I need to get."

They left Johnny asleep on the couch, and Katherine went upstairs to pack. After hauling her bags downstairs and putting them in the car, she went to the kitchen to find Alice. "I have everything packed."

"Good, take this." Alice said, holding out a small wad of bills to Katherine.

Katherine pushed it away. "I can't take money from you. I have what I need. My boss saw to that before I left town—but thank you."

"Okay, but please know it's here if you need me to wire it in the days to come. For now, take my car and get as far away from here as possible, but if you decide to fly out of an airport, just let me know where you left the car. I have someone who can go and get it."

"What if the Russians come here? What about you?"

"Nonsense. They're not interested in me, and they are going to think we called the police. I suspect they're going to be a lot more careful about what they try from now on. Besides, I have Buck and a few other tricks up my sleeve. Now scoot."

Katherine was not convinced, but Alice had her do-not-argue-with-me-young-lady look on her face, so she took a deep breath and headed for the front door. She passed Johnny still sleeping peacefully in the living room, with Buck on the floor beside him. Katherine could not help wondering when she would see them all again.

Alice must have read her mind because suddenly she reached up and gave Katherine a great big hug. "You be safe, dear," she said.

Katherine nodded and stepped outside, headed to Corey's and consumed by guilt.

• • •

Boris had been the unlucky recipient of the boiling water. With his blistered hands and wrists wrapped in kitchen towels like a box-er's, he had had no choice but to let Oleg take the wheel. His partner was now slowly driving up and down the streets of downtown Bray-don looking for a pharmacy. Eventually he had to settle for a conve-nience store—someplace they could get in and out of fast. They had no more pulled in than they heard the wail of sirens as the police responded to trouble at the Home Dairy.

Boris was too conspicuous to go inside, so Oleg did the hon-ors—yanking several tubes of burn ointment from the shelf, along with some feminine napkins and a half-dozen rolls of Scotch tape, the closest he could come to gauze and hospital tape. On his way out, Oleg pressured the woman at the register, already scared to death by the stranger's size and tattoos, to tell him where "Miss Alice" lived. Only after she gave an address from the phone book did he leave the store.

In the car, he told Boris the address, and then drove them back to the same secluded spot outside of town where they had parked while planning the best way to abduct Katherine with the least commotion. They agreed their second attempt would benefit from darkness. Meanwhile, Oleg applied the balm to Boris's hands and wrists. He wrapped the wounds again, hoping that anyone in the area would mistake Boris's howls of pain for an injured wild animal.

• • •

With Katherine safely incognito again and on her way out of town, Alice took stock of her situation. She had already taken Johnny home in Katherine's car, assuring him that all was well. Johnny was only too happy to believe her. She did not think the Russian gangsters, if that's what they were, would be able to track Katherine to her house; she also did not think she could write it off as impossible either. The men had managed to find Katherine at the café in a matter of days. She decided the best plan was to do nothing at all. What would they have to gain by hurting an old woman? Alice made herself a cup of Earl Grey tea and went to sit in her favorite reading chair. As always, she felt comforted with Buck at her side. The police would find no useful witnesses at the café, and they would most likely not bother to question Johnny, so she did not anticipate any police officers coming to her house for a follow-up.

• • •

It had taken them longer than Alice figured it would. The first knocks at the front door were loud ones, followed by a couple that threatened to splinter the wood. She hurried to the entrance to save her antique door.

"Good evening, gentlemen," Alice said in her sweetest southern voice as she opened the door with one hand keeping the other tucked under a shawl. "What can I do for you?"

The Russians shoved the door open wider, backing Alice up and into her house. Within seconds Buck was at her side, growling at the men. She pulled the dog back by the collar with her free hand and told the animal everything was okay. He sat but with his ears at full attention.

"Where is young Kelly woman?" Boris asked, rubbing the bandages on his wrists.

"Excuse me, to whom are you referring?" Alice replied. She saw the two Russians look at each other in apparent confusion. One of them opened his jacket, making sure she saw his handgun. "What is that, young man? A nine-millimeter Beretta?"

The Russians looked at each other and shrugged. "You know this gun?" Boris asked.

"My boss had many guns. Among other things, he was a hunter."

"Quit talk, lady. We know she is here. Her car is in back of your house. Garage empty. Where is Kelly?"

"She's not here, and I truly don't know where she is at the moment."

The larger of the two men moved toward Alice. Buck sprang to his feet, growling at the man, who took a quick step back. Not taking her eyes off the big Russian, Alice felt Buck stand and grasped his collar again. She heard a snarl building in Buck's throat. The dog was ready to lunge the moment she released her grip.

The other man said, "You have fine dog, lady. Is it worth bullet through his head to not tell us how to find Kelly?"

This game had gone far enough, and the threat to Buck told her it was time to use some of the skills she had honed acting in community theater.

"Oh, no, not Buck," she cried. "He's the only companion I have." As serious as the situation was, she had to hold back a chuckle at her overacting. She forced a tear. "If you must know, Katherine has gone to see Corey."

"And where can we find this Corey?" Oleg asked.

"Just north of Charleston. Route 703. After you come to Sullivan's Island, take the dirt road to Corrigan Yachts." Alice knew it would take them forever to find Corey's place, hidden away from civilization like it was, if they ever managed to find it at all. Regardless, Katherine would be far away by then. It didn't solve all their problems. Katherine couldn't run forever, and the Russians had made it clear they had sophisticated technology, unlimited resources, and people willing to do the heavy lifting. Still it would hopefully buy Katherine enough time to enlist the help of the FBI, or maybe, Sean.

"You write us directions," Oleg said.

"I will. Just don't hurt my dog." Alice forced another tear before taking Buck with her to the kitchen where she wrote out the directions on an index card. The route was accurate—what there was of it.

The Russians both gave her a couple of long, unsettling looks after she gave them the directions, but they did eventually leave. She was relieved to put the safety back on the little .38 Ruger automatic with the hollow-point bullets she had moved from under her wrap to inside her apron pocket while in the kitchen. Once she had it back in her gun safe, she called Katherine and told her what had happened. "Are you all right?" Katherine asked, horrified at what she had put Alice through.

Sensitive to the worry in Katherine's voice, Alice quickly reassured her. "I'm fine. You remember how hard it is to get to Corey's. That's where I sent them. Told them you were headed there. With the directions I gave them, I don't know if they'll ever find Corey's place, much less the ocean. Mercy, it's hard enough to get to with perfect directions. One thing for certain, Corey will give them a good workout if they do find his boatyard."

"Won't Corey be in danger?"

"Never."

Katherine thanked her and promised to call as soon as she was safely someplace far away. She glanced at the phone Sol had given her, knowing it was now the only number Alice had for her. Could it possibly have been discovered and the phone triangulated by the

Russians? It was not worth the risk. She decided she would do what Angelo had suggested and buy throwaways, which were virtually untraceable.

• • •

Boris and Oleg got to Sullivan's Island in an hour and a half, and then they argued with each other about where to go from there. They talked to various locals over the course of another three hours trying to get decent directions to Corrigan Yachts. Their efforts were hindered by their accents, even if folks had wanted to help. It was too dark to see any signs or turnoffs onto smaller roads. At one point, they were reduced to shouting obscenities at each other.

Boris had grown sick of the whole manhunt and resented their boss's strict orders not to hurt anybody in the course of the kidnapping. He would have liked to have put that pudgy café employee out of his misery and the old lady and her attack dog, too. In hindsight, he wondered if a dog qualified as "anybody."

If Boris and Oleg had their way, they would have gone in the middle of the night and taken Katherine Kelly from the old woman's house while everyone was sleeping. Sure, the dog would have gotten killed and likely the old lady, too, but they would have been in and out, and it could have been days before anybody found the collateral damage. But Baskhanov had said no. It had to be a clean extraction, as he called it. They were never even allowed to know who was actually issuing the orders.

It did not help that Baskhanov had not bothered to thank them more for locating Katherine so fast, though it had been sheer luck. In the course of an Internet search on Katherine, the Braydon bank article with her byline had popped up. Since they had nothing else to go on, Oleg had agreed it was worth a trip, and that was how they had ended up in the little town north of Charleston.

There, Oleg had overheard some old men in a diner yakking about the new waitress in town who was turning heads at the local café. It had seemed a good lead at first, but when he first saw her through his binoculars he was not sure she was the woman that they had confronted in New York. The more he watched her, however, the more he became convinced it was the woman reporter.

He snapped a picture and sent it to Baskhanov's tech crew in New York, and the men eventually matched it to Katherine's college graduation photograph. He did not understand why they couldn't get the go-ahead to just grab her, something they had successfully done dozens of times before in some of the busiest cities in the world.

"Stop bitching about what could have been. We must move forward. Keep driving," Boris said.

The next screaming match was about whether to go into Charleston and find a nice hotel and a good meal for the night. Oleg wanted *kasha*, maybe some beef stroganoff, and a couple of bottles of vodka. Boris thought a good steak would work and be easier to find. The other choice was to sleep in the car. Ultimately, they chose Charleston.

The next morning, after a quick breakfast, they drove back over the Arthur Ravenel, Jr. Bridge to make one final attempt to get directions from the locals. It cost them another hour. Finally, one old-timer, in-between puffing on his pipe and regaling them with stories about the fine boats built by Corrigan Yachts, drew a map to the winding dirt road that led to Corey's house.

Boris and Oleg followed the map to the big sign that read "Corrigan Yachts," but they weren't sure what to think of what they found: no cars, no people—just several big buildings, one with lumber stored inside, the other with what looked like a bunch of woodworking machines, and a third that contained a partially built wooden yacht.

They continued up the road to an old, two-story, wood-framed house. They knocked on the door; nobody answered. They looked through the windows and saw no one. Becoming more angry and confused by the minute, they followed a path to the waterway where they found a thin man with close-cropped white hair shining against his black skin. He was sitting in a wooden rocking chair watching the boats go by. Boris approached him and asked if he was Corey Corrigan.

"Don't see many up this early," Corey said. "Want some tea?"

The Russians looked at each other and shrugged.

"We're looking for Katherine Kelly. She is where to be found?" Boris asked.

"Oak."

Shrug. "Is she here?"

"There's the chair."

Boris tried again. "Who's here with you?"

"Barbara left."

"Who's Barbara?"

"I'm fine."

"You want me to apply a little pressure?" Oleg asked his partner.

"I want to blow his head off," Boris replied. "This whole thing is ridiculous. I do not know if this old man is screwing around with us or not."

"We could bust in the house and look around," Oleg said.

"Good house," Corey interjected. "My grandfather worked for Mr. Douglass, himself. Fine master turner."

"What he talking about?" Oleg asked Boris.

Boris shrugged and raised his hands. "Who knows?"

"Want some tea?" Corey asked. "See the boats."

"We're not going to get anything out of him, and I don't think anybody is in the house," Boris said. "Let's go back, look through every window we can. If there's nothing, then there's nothing."

"And we go back to boss, right?" his partner asked.

"I say, yes."

"Don't go. Sit. Have some tea," Corey said.

The two Russians walked away without saying good-bye. Corey, focused on the boats, did not seem to notice their departure. Back at the house, the men completed their check of the windows as fast as they could, finding nothing but frustration.

"This not good," Oleg said.

"For us, it's worse than that," Boris replied. "The girl must have circled back to Braydon. Where else could she go?"

"We've been there," Oleg said. "I hate that place."

"I have no love for this place either, but if we fail, we die," Boris said.

CHAPTER 54

TOMMY CALLED HARRY AT six o'clock in the morning. When he answered, all he heard was: "Now."

"Now what?" Harry asked, with sleep in his voice.

"You offered to help. Now's the time."

"Okay, Tommy," Harry said in a clearer voice. "What do you want me to do?"

Tommy explained his plan. "We have to move fast. How soon can you be at LaGuardia?"

"I'll call you right back. The Oompah Man is with you."

In a matter of minutes, Tommy saw Harry's call come in. He would be at LaGuardia at 10:24 a.m. sharp. Tommy would pick up Harry at the airport. Destination: Katherine's apartment in the Hamptons.

• • •

Harry managed an appreciative smile when the long, black limo with dark windows pulled up for him. The front passenger window slid down to reveal a big man in a black suit and another of equal size in a gray suit behind the wheel. Black Suit stepped out of the car, opened the rear door, and motioned for Harry to get in.

Harry complied and found Tommy waiting inside. "Nice ride, Tommy."

"You're on time," Tommy said, powering down the glass that separated the front from the back so he could give a few directions to the driver, including Katherine's address in the Hamptons. When they found neither Katherine nor her car at her apartment, Tommy directed the men to head to *Twin Forks Press*.

Shortly after noon, Tommy walked into the newspaper with Harry trailing behind. "I'm Tommy Greco and this is Harry," he announced, explaining to the receptionist that he was a friend of Katherine's father and here to talk with her boss.

Moments later Sol stepped into the lobby to introduce himself. "Come in, gentlemen. Let's talk in the conference room."

"This is the *situational*," Tommy said. "I know Preston Wilson. You're his daughter's boss. She's in trouble."

Sol nodded.

"I also figure you want to help her."

Sol nodded again.

"You also know she's missing. You can just keep nodding."

Sol smiled and nodded.

Tommy picked up his cell phone and called Preston, who answered on the second ring.

"Hi, Tommy."

"I'm with Katherine's boss. His name is Kaplowitz. I'm gonna hand him the phone so you can tell him that you're Katherine's father and that he has authorization to tell me everything he knows."

Tommy nodded to whatever Preston said and gave Sol the phone. They talked briefly, and Sol ended the call and handed the phone back to Tommy. Seconds later, Tommy's phone rang and he answered.

"I figured. Thanks." Tommy closed the phone. "Give me what you've got, Sol."

Sol quickly told them about Katherine's encounter with the Russians and how they had scared her into leaving town. He explained that he had given her two-months' worth of cash, an untraceable phone, a way to keep in touch, and directions to stay away until things cooled down. He said his understanding was that she planned to stay in Braydon, a town in South Carolina where she had been working on a series of bank fraud stories with a local reporter. Sol added that she had recently checked in and appeared to be all right.

"Untraceable is not unreachable. Can I have the number to the phone you gave her?"

Sol gave it to him.

"You've been good about exchanges of the *confidential*, Mr. K. And you helped my friend. You're a stand-up guy. I'm gonna give a *confidential* to you. I know some people, and I'm going to have a meeting and try to have an *accomodational*. You understand what you just didn't hear?"

Sol smiled. "Good luck, Mr. Greco. You, too, Harry."

"You can call me the Oompah Man," Harry said.

"Not the time or place, Harry," Tommy said. "We gotta go."

The men shook hands, and Tommy and Harry left. Back in the limo, Tommy gave the driver an address in Brighton Beach, Brooklyn. He explained to Harry that a meeting had been set up there for 3:00 p.m.

They sat in relative silence for the next two hours, although it did not escape Tommy's attention that one of Harry's legs had been twitching for thirty minutes and he could not seem to peel his eyes away from the tinted window next to him. Tommy knew Harry wanted to talk, but that was the last thing he wanted. He had things to go over in his mind, important things, things that could determine whether or not this day ended well.

"I know you're nervous," Tommy finally said, with a nod toward Harry's vibrating leg. "You can stay in the car."

"What about you?"

"It depends on how they play it. These guys are dangerous, but they have to be careful. They want what they want, but got to get it on the quiet."

"I don't want to stay behind. I want to go with you."

Tommy weighed the situation. Harry could be a loose cannon, but he admired his courage and commitment to the job.

"They know about me. They don't know about you. Let's see how it goes when we get there."

Harry sat back in his seat and continued to stare out the window as they headed to Brooklyn, muttering something under his breath that Tommy could not make out.

Brighton Beach looked decidedly different from the Hamptons. As their limo turned off the highway, down a street, and finally into an alley, the sound of broken glass and gravel underneath the tires made it clear they were far from Long Island. Harry craned his neck to see through the front windshield as the alley opened to a white, two-story commercial building on their left. There was a garage door on one side, and a steel door on the other. Tommy noticed a small, one-inch opening on the latter's upper section. Tommy tapped the dividing window with his knuckle. "This is it," he said.

The driver brought the limo to a stop. Frankie in the right front passenger seat got out, went to the door, knocked, said something through the opening, and the door opened. Two tall muscular men wearing black sweatshirts with their hoods up came out and followed Frankie to the limousine. They each took a place on either side of the right rear door.

Frankie gave the limo window a couple of sharp knocks. Tommy now instructed Harry to get out and stand silently by the car. He did as he was told, and the Russians searched him, finding no weapons. Frankie gave the door two more knocks. Tommy got out, turned his back to the men, and raised his arms. Again, no weapons.

Frankie, Tommy, and Harry followed one of the runners through the heavy metal door, where Frankie was instructed by a man he took to be a Russian to wait. He looked to Tommy, who nodded. The huge door swung closed and locked itself. Tommy's eyes had to adjust to the sudden darkness. There was no sunlight in the long hallway, only several individual, dull bare bulbs hung from the ceiling by cords. Watermarks stained the walls as the three men passed door after door. Another one of the Russians joined the men and led Tommy and Harry down a narrow hallway up one flight of metal stairs and into a large room.

Tommy scoped out the place. A massive red area rug covered the floor in an attempt to disguise the deteriorating state of the dilapidated building. Fluorescent lights lined the ceiling, and several chairs and a couch filled the center of the room, all facing a television mounted on the wall. Tommy noticed a couple of doors to his right, and one to his left. Everything was portable and designed to be packed and carried off at a moment's notice.

The Russian leading the queue stepped toward the door on the left, opened it slowly, peered inside, and closed it again. He told Tommy his boss was ready to see them and directed Tommy and Harry to follow him. Tommy nodded to Harry.

Inside, the Russian took his place by another big man near the door. Tommy quickly took in their new surroundings. The room was large and darkened by blackout curtains on the windows. One fluorescent ceiling light hung over a rectangular wooden table with a round, metal tray holding a bottle of vodka and four shot glasses. Behind it sat a short, broad-shouldered man in his sixties with tattoos on his fingers and a scar on his right cheek.

"So you're Greco," the man said, looking at Tommy.

Tommy nodded. "And you're Goremykin. You resemble your picture. You have a high position. Thank you for the meeting."

"I have information about your interest. What I need to understand is what can you do for me in return," Goremykin said.

"What I have to say is for your ears only. It's highly *sensitivenal*."

Goremykin stared at him so long another man would have looked away, but Tommy calmly met his gaze.

"I understand." Goremykin said. He said something in Russian to his two men who immediately stepped outside, forcing Harry with them. "We should talk alone."

Tommy considered his options. He knew his best hope to protect Harry—and to get them both out alive—was to show no weakness. "You must treat him well," he demanded.

"Of course," Goremykin said, "let us continue our discussion."

"Either we stand or we sit." Tommy said.

"Forgive me. Please, sit," Goremykin said, pointing to the chair.

"You, too, have some important friends, Mr. Greco. This meeting is most unusual. Would you like a drink?"

"Maybe later," Tommy said.

"Mr. Greco, again I ask, what can you do for me?"

"You know the circumstance. The reporter in question can't reach the witness against Baskhanov," Tommy said.

"*Ochevidetz*. The beholder," Goremykin said.

Tommy continued, taking note of the distinction. "Even if the reporter could reach the beholder, she couldn't force her to change her testimony."

Goremykin looked grim with a twisted smile.

"Here's how I can help." Tommy proceeded to explain the proposed arrangement, which involved not only the U.S. Attorney's office but also the U.S. Justice Department among various other federal and state agencies.

"There are many moving parts to this puzzle," Goremykin said.

"And the New York court is only one part," Tommy said.

"What is your interest?"

"Are you asking me what I want?"

Goremykin raised both of his hands and nodded.

"You stand down on the girl—forever."

"What does she mean to you?"

"I have not asked you about your *internalizations*. Either we have an *accommodational* or we don't."

Again, their eyes locked, with neither making a move or a sound. The silence was broken by loud Russian voices from outside the room. Goremykin's fist slammed the table while he shouted something in Russian. The next thing Tommy knew Goremykin's men were hauling Harry back in the room.

"What is it?" Goremykin asked.

"This man insists upon joining you. He's clean, but do you want him in here?"

Goremykin looked at Tommy, and then addressed the two Russians holding Harry. "I know nothing of this man. Take him away and have a discussion with him."

The two men nodded and Harry started to struggle. "Hang on a minute. I just—"

One of the Russian handlers pulled his gun and held it to Harry's head. Harry became docile as a baby as they walked him from the room. Tommy continued to calmly stare at Goremykin, slowly shaking his head.

"Is he one of you?" Goremykin asked.

"He's a friend of mine, and for your purposes, yes."

"Let's pay attention to what is at hand," Goremykin said. He reached for the bottle and poured a drink for Tommy and one for himself. "Now will you have a drink with me?"

"Not yet," Tommy said.

Goremykin laughed and slammed the table again. "We have a deal, Mr. Greco."

"Now I'll have that drink," Tommy said, picking up his glass. "I drink to your word."

"*Nasdarovje*," Goremykin said. And both men drank.

Tommy got up and strode to the door. Before opening it, he turned to Goremykin. "I am ready to leave, and I want Harry to leave with me."

Goremykin got up from the table, walked up to Tommy, and reached around him to open the door. Sticking his head out, he asked one of the men to escort Tommy to his car. Ignoring Goremykin's strongman, Tommy put up his hands and said, "We need to talk now—privately."

Goremykin waved the man off and closed the door.

"I came here unarmed and with respect," Tommy said.

"I need to talk with my men to better understand why that man is here. It may not be a problem, but we have to be careful. We will let you know."

Tommy looked deep into Goremykin's eyes. "My people tell me you've been in the cage—what I believe you call prison camps. You know the rules, and you know what happens when you break them. People here may think you're still in Russia. You said earlier there are a lot of moving parts. Harry *came* with me, and he leaves with me. That should be enough for you. Some of those parts are going to go very wrong for you if you screw this up."

Goremykin stared back at Tommy. Neither man moved nor said a word. Finally Goremykin broke into a friendly smile. "Please! We understand each other. Your man will leave with you and our agreement stands."

Goremykin flung open the door and nodded to the man on guard. Moments later Harry appeared, his face filled with fear, and Tommy and Harry were escorted to their car.

• • •

On the way back to LaGuardia, Harry did his best to get his blood pressure down to stroke level. "I thought the Oompah Man was a goner when they pulled me out of the room."

Tommy ignored the comment.

"What went on in there?" Harry asked.

"I'm not going to tell you, Harry. I like you and my *preferential* is for you to live. The odds of that happening are greater if you never speak of this again."

CHAPTER 55

KATHERINE WAS TIRED OF it all. Tired of worrying, tired of running, tired of not being able to be with the people she loved. She thought about Alice's suggestion that she fly somewhere no one could find her, but rejected the idea. She was tired of other people fighting her battles. It was time to stand and fight. She would drive back to Braydon, return Alice's car, and then go home. Or maybe she would spend a few days at the inn with Bobby. Whatever. What she would not do was run.

On the way to Braydon, one of Katherine's phones rang. Her heart stopped. Anonymous. She hesitated, took a deep sigh, and answered it.

"Hi, Kat. How's it going?"

Katherine struggled to remain calm. She looked for a way to pull off the road as she answered, "Hello, Sean."

"Where are you, baby? What's going on?"

"I'm just riding around enjoying the weather. It's beautiful where I am. Where are you?"

"Working on an assignment. You know how it is."

"Yes, I do—believe me."

"Kat, I'm calling because I'd like to clarify a point involving the investigation we're working on. We've been looking at various banks. I can't give you all the details, but I know that you've done extensive work on BNA. I'm wondering if you could tell me if you have found any connection between Bank North America and an offshore bank in Nevis."

Silence.

"Kat, are you there?"

"I am."

"Do you know anything about this? Maybe it came up in one of your investigations? I just want to confirm that there's a connection between BNA and a Nevis bank. It's important, Kat."

Silence.

"Look, I know you can't reveal sources in a story like this, but if there's no connection, then cough. If you remain silent, I'll know it's confirmed."

Silence.

"Thanks, Kat. I'd like to talk more, but I have to run. Hope to see you soon."

"Good-bye, Sean," Katherine said and hit the End Call on her phone.

Katherine had no idea what Sean's call was all about, but she had quickly made the decision to simply listen. As she drew closer to Braydon, she felt a wave of despair come over her, like she was drowning in dark waters. She thought about her grandfather, and how if he were there, he would have told her it was not a time to give up. Her phone rang again, this time the phone that Sol had given her.

"Hi, Sol. I'm so glad you called."

"Actually, it's Tommy Greco. I'm a friend of your father's. Sol gave me your number."

"Of course. Is my dad all right? Is Marcia okay?"

"Your father's fine. Marcia, too. I'm calling to tell you that you are okay also."

Katherine did not know how to respond. She decided to play it like she had not heard him.

"We've not had a chance to meet, but I've heard so much about you, Tommy—and your wife, Missy. And now you have a new daughter."

"We'll get together soon," Tommy said. "I'm in New York now. I'll take you to dinner. Forlini's in Little Italy. You'll like the food, and we can have a *celebrational.*"

"That's great, Tommy. It sounds like you have a lot to celebrate."

"So do you, Katherine. That's why I'm calling. Forget the Russians. They are no longer a threat to you. It's all been taken care of as of about an hour ago."

Katherine was trying to wrap her head around how Tommy had come to be privy to her problems with the Russian mafia. It all seemed a little much. "How . . . how is that possible, Tommy? Am I hearing this right?"

"It's more than possible. It's now a made *accomodational.* You can stop worrying about the Russians. Don't ask me more. Your dad thought you were in trouble. I was in a position to help. Beyond that, some things should not be talked about. Ever. You understand?"

"Completely. I don't know how to thank you, Tommy," Katherine said with a choked voice.

"That's not necessary," Tommy said. "Your father is a friend of mine and my wife's, and of Harry."

"Did Harry have something to do with this?"

"He was definitely there. As I mentioned, this matter is closed. No more questions." Tommy gave Katherine his phone number. "Call me when you're in New York and hungry. We'll have dinner." The line went silent.

• • •

Unknown to Katherine and to Boris and Oleg, they were all headed back to Braydon and less than an hour apart. Boris received a call from Baskhanov. The call was short. Boris turned to Oleg. "That was our boss. We are ordered to end the search for Katherine Kelly and come home."

Oleg let out a scream of joy that caused Boris to grab the wheel more tightly in spite of his injured hands. "I never be happier to get out of anywhere," Oleg said. "Everyone here is crazy."

Boris nodded like an oversized bobblehead doll. "I hate the South, too. I'm sick of this woman. I want to eat good food again. We go home."

• • •

Katherine had no more seen the words Call Ended flash on her phone than she called Sol so she could tell him about Tommy's news.

"My instincts told me he was the real deal. A rare thing today, I might add. What a relief. When will you be back in the office? These stories don't write themselves."

"I'm headed home via Braydon, so I can return Alice's car and make sure she's okay. I have a funny feeling she's not telling me everything about what happened after I left, though she sounded good on the phone. I also want to say good-bye to Mike McCusker, Mr. Livingston, and . . . some other friends of mine."

"You like that town, don't you?"

"I won't lie. The people are wonderful . . . and there's this guy. I have the attorney handling the class action checking out his family—not for me, for the story, but I have to be prepared for whatever he finds. I haven't had a chance to get back with him on it."

Sol laughed. "So you have an attorney checking out your dates now. I'm beginning to think we've had you on the investigative beat too long."

"Ha, ha—I'll admit I'm more than a little gun-shy after all the Sean business, but Bobby's family is definitely old South. I just want to be certain they had nothing to do with the crooked bank officers. Too many good people might lose their life savings, and even if the man I like had nothing to do with it himself, I'd never be comfortable with his family if they did."

"The sins of the father—"

"You got it." Both laughed.

"Have you been doing any thinking about Braydon on a more permanent basis?"

"Sol, are you firing me?" Katherine asked.

"Never. It's just that the newspaper's editor there likes your investigative skills. Of course so do I. He did, however, call me up this week to ask if he could talk to you about a possible job offer, which says a lot. Your life has been so upended these last few months, I thought you at least deserved to know all your options."

"You think I should move to Braydon?"

"I'm not telling you what to do. You may not realize it, but with your clips you could get hired by the *Times*, or better yet, *The Washington Post* or *Bloomberg* right now. If you're as fond of Braydon as you say you are, and the editor down there offers you a job, tell him you want to be assistant editor—and nothing less. I'd like to see you become a senior reporter someday, doing what you do for a lot of years to come, but I also can't help thinking about what you could accomplish with a team of reporters working under you. In the meantime, go see your father and Marcia, and Tommy if you can. We'll talk more about this later. Have a safe trip back."

"Wait, Sol. Before you hang up, I just want to say there's no way I can thank you for all you have done for me. You've been such a true friend—and a great mentor. I pray you haven't run with the faux key witness story."

"No worries. I decided after meeting Tommy, I'd wait."

"See you soon."

• • •

Katherine's next call was to Alice, who was overjoyed to hear that the only Russian she would be worrying about in the future was the expiration date on her Russian dressing.

"Your car is still intact," Katherine said, "and we'll both be back in Braydon by nightfall."

Her final call was to her father to check on Marcia. She breathed a sigh of relief when he said Marcia continued to improve. She told him her out-of-state assignment was over, and she would be home in a few days.

"I'm coming straight to the hospital to see you and Marcia," she said.

"Your voice sounds different," her father said. "Is there something I should know?"

Katherine smiled, and then promised she would explain everything when she saw him next.

CHAPTER 56

BETH WAS GLAD TO FINALLY have Harry back. It felt good to cook for a man again, especially one who enjoyed it. They cleared the table together and retired to the den to finish off the last of the bottle of wine Harry had brought.

She smiled as he took her hand. He looked as forlorn as a bloodhound. "I'm sorry I couldn't make it back sooner, Beth," he said. "Had something important I had to do."

"That sounds kind of ominous."

"You want the truth, pretty lady, it was." He had been struggling with what to tell Beth, especially in light of Tommy's admonition. He squeezed her hand and his gaze grew more intense. "There's only so much I can say. You're gonna have to trust me on this."

Beth nodded. "I trust you, Harry."

"I've talked with you before about Joe Hart. How I met him and what a friend he was to me and several others."

"Yes, I remember."

"One of those friends is a fellow named Tommy Greco. He and his wife, Missy, live in Nevada. He stepped up to help Preston and your daughter, and I felt I had to be there."

"Are either in trouble?"

"They're both fine now, but this is one of those times—and I'm serious as a heart attack—that I need you to listen to what I have to say and not ask questions."

"You're scaring me, Harry," Beth said.

"It was scary—big-time scary—but it's over now."

"So, that is where you've been, helping Tommy help Preston and Katherine?"

"It's more like I was there. Tommy did the heavy lifting."

"Was it dangerous?"

"Beth, I'm not answering any more questions. If we're going to have the kind of relationship I want—and I believe in my heart you want—it's got to be built on trust. I'll never lie to you, never, and I expect the same from you. I've learned certain things happen in life that just can't be talked about. This is one of them. I gave Tommy my word. Now I need yours."

Beth sensed a strength in Harry she never knew existed, a side of him she had never seen. She thought about all he had said for several minutes, took a deep breath, and then cupped his face in her hands and kissed him deeply.

"I do trust you, Harry, and I love you."

The look on Harry's face was priceless. Beth refilled his glass and moved closer to him. "I told you in one of our conversations that sometimes I don't like myself very much," she said, her thigh now touching his. "I didn't tell you why."

"You don't have to tell me why."

"I want . . . I need to tell you. And I need to hear myself telling you." Beth set down her wine glass, put both her hands on Harry's forearm and started, "When I was twenty-one . . ." and she didn't stop until she had told him the story about Katherine's conception.

When Beth finished, she got up to let Hailey in. Harry stood, too, and embraced her. "You don't have to tell me anything more. As far as I'm concerned the past is the past and good riddance."

Beth sat back down on the couch and motioned for Harry to join her. He sighed and did as directed. Beth took a few more sips of wine before she continued. She told Harry about meeting Preston in the hospital and their one date.

Harry put his arm around Beth and drew her close. "Beth, you've no reason to feel ashamed about this. There are so many other choices you could have made. What matters is you put your life aside and put your baby's first."

"For twenty-three years, I didn't tell Kat the truth—or my parents, for that matter."

"You keep gettin' mad when I say something, but you got to let me speak for a minute. You raised a beautiful and smart daughter anyone would be proud of and that I know your father adored. You're being way too hard on yourself for no reason that I can see."

Beth moved away from Harry and said, "You're not going to feel so friendly toward me when I tell you the rest. I never told Preston about Katherine."

Such a sadness came over his face that Beth knew he was putting himself in Preston's shoes and thinking about what it would be like to have a child but never know it.

Beth soldiered on. "I finally made the call but only because Katherine forced my hand. She was finishing journalism school and already showing signs of becoming a heck of a reporter. I knew her first investigation would be to find out who her father was. It was the one question all her life I had failed to answer.

"I told Preston about Katherine, and that she would've found out sooner or later. I thought it would be better if he knew so he could be prepared."

Harry sat up a little straighter. "What did you tell Katherine?"

"She figured out that Larry, the man I had said was her father, couldn't possibly have been her dad. She confronted me, and that's when I told her that Preston was actually her father."

"So in the end, you told the truth to both your daughter and her father. What's wrong with that?" Harry asked.

"What's wrong is that I was not honest with either of them from the beginning. As the song goes, 'what do you think of me now'?"

"I think the wine's gettin' to you, and you're emphasizing the wrong lyrics. The song also says 'time has come—stage is set.' I don't give a darn about any of this. I made my peace as far as your history with Preston. Yes, I knew he only recently learned from you that he had a daughter. I also needed to know he wasn't somehow still interested in you, or vice versa. Now I'm gonna tell you something I shouldn't: Preston doesn't just love Katherine, he cares about her mother. He considers you both family, and he told me, even if he lost his business in this legal mess he's in, he'd do whatever it took to find the money to get the best eye treatment for you that could be gotten anywhere in the world."

Beth started to sob as Harry drew her head to his shoulder.

"Nothing to cry about, little lady. I know he wishes he had known about Katherine earlier; he also understands what a difficult position you found yourself in. He's not mad at you. I'm positive of that. In fact, no one could be happier about us than Preston when he learned we were seeing each other. We're keeping the love in the family."

He gave her his best Oompah Man smile, and Beth could not help but smile in return. A few moments passed; she reached for his hand and grew serious again.

"Since we're being bedrock honest with each other, I have to tell you, Harry, I worry about you being bipolar. I know you can't help it. The problem is, I don't know if I'm strong enough to handle your ups and downs and my own medical problems."

"I'm managing my situation quite well. You don't have to take care of me. You need to take care of yourself." Harry paused. "Sorry, that came out wrong."

"It didn't come out wrong at all. I always do that."

"Do what?"

"Take care of myself first. Run away from men every time they get too close. I've become a prisoner in a cell built with bars of guilt. It's a shame you're not a cowboy singer—that would make a good country-western lyric."

Harry rolled the last of his wine around in his glass. "What's it called when married couples fight and then make up?"

"I don't know. Reconciliation? Conciliation?"

"That's it, that's it," he said. "You need to reconcile with your past and get to a place where you feel about you, the way *I* feel about you."

"Harry, that is the sweetest, kindest thing anybody has ever said to me."

Harry put both of his arms around Beth and pulled her close. She laid her head on his chest. She could hear his heart thump, and she could feel hers beating with happiness, too.

"Maybe at last I'm safe," Beth said. "Safe from myself. Safe from my guilt. Safe from all my past mistakes."

"I'll tell you what, little lady. Maybe this is one roller coaster worth riding, and the prize will be your key out of prison."

CHAPTER 57

KATHERINE'S REUNION WITH ALICE AND Buck was nothing short of marvelous. They talked into the night and devoured cookies, with Buck having his share. The dog followed her to bed, curling up at her feet. She slept better than any other time she could remember.

In the morning, she met with Mike McCusker and later that day with Mr. Livingston, who provided an update on the status of the class-action lawsuit against the bank. She thought about stopping by the inn to see Bobby, but her desire to get back to New York was too strong. She couldn't wait another minute to see her father, Marcia, and P.J., not to mention Sol and Susan. Besides, she knew she would be returning to Braydon soon.

Katherine and Alice had a quick lunch at the Home Dairy so she could say good-bye to Johnny.

Next, she sought out Mr. Niemeyer, who was filling in as cook that day, to apologize for all the problems she had caused him and the café and to thank him for allowing her to be a small part of the great Home Dairy.

Then it was time to go.

She paid the check and stepped outside to the street with Alice. Suddenly, she was too choked up for words. What was there to say?

"There will never be good-byes between us," Alice said, reading her mind. "You once told me that you wished you had met Joe Hart.

I want you to know that I believe that you hold him in your heart, Katherine. There is no higher praise in my book."

• • •

Katherine drove back to New York, singing along with the radio all the way. She had planned no calls to anyone, just to enjoy the ride. Her euphoria lasted for five straight hours and ended with the buzz of a cell phone. She looked to see who it was from and blanched when she saw Anonymous. Her first instinct was to ignore it, but she knew any self-respecting reporter would take the call. She picked up the phone.

"Hi, Kat. How you doing?"

"I'm doing great, Sean. How are you?"

"I'm fine, just curious about something."

"About what?" Katherine asked over the music blaring in the background.

"Why you threw me a curve ball."

"For the record, on the off-chance you're recording this, I don't know what you're talking about."

Sean was silent for a moment, and then he asked, "Where are you now?"

"I'm on my way back to New York. Why?"

"I need to see you. Have a lot I would like to say to you, and I don't want to do it over the phone."

"I can understand that," Katherine said.

"Please, Katherine. I'll come to where you are."

"I'm still a good two hours from Washington. Let's see . . . My GPS says I'll arrive at six-fifty. I'm spending the night at The Hampton Inn in Alexandria."

"Great. I'll meet you there. There's a steak house in that area. Could I take you there for dinner?"

Katherine felt herself slipping back into a place she didn't want to be. "Honestly, Sean, if you must know, I just don't want to see you or talk to you."

"Come on, Kat. You have to eat," Sean said.

"You can come if you want, but it'll be at your own risk."

"I'll take that risk," he said.

By the time Katherine checked in and freshened up a bit, Sean was in the lobby. She greeted him but kept a polite distance.

"Thanks for seeing me," he said.

"What do you want?" Katherine asked sharply.

"Could we go to your room and talk?"

"No."

Sean threw his hands up in defeat. He stood thinking for a moment, and then turned to Katherine and said, "Let me see if I can find a quieter spot. Wait here, please." He disappeared around the corner for several minutes, only to return with a smile on his face. "The concierge says the indoor pool is open and all but deserted today." He led Katherine down one hallway and then another before the smell of chlorine hit her nostrils. He held the door open for her, and then motioned for her to take a seat at one of the tables by the pool.

"Okay, you have my undivided attention. Why don't you start by explaining why you deceived me," she said, her voice rising to a shout.

"I'll try. I just need you to promise me that this conversation will always remain between us."

"My word's not the one in question here," Katherine said, folding her arms, "but, yes, I promise."

"Although I can't give you the details, I've been working on an intensive, high-level security matter for several months. Our Secret Service team has been working with the FBI and CIA. You've written about fraud in one of the banks that's been a target in our investigation. As you know, I was ordered to tap your phone and report any information that might help with our case."

"How would I know that?"

"I tried to tip you off several times," he said softly, laying his hands on the table. "I had to be careful. The Service reads the transcripts."

"Do you mean the reference to Susan?" Katherine asked, looking at him warily.

"That was one of them. This goes all the way back to the conversation we had last November when you asked me for help on your case. I told you then I couldn't get involved because I worked for the Service. I can't count how many times I haven't been able to talk about something, or tell you where I was, for that matter. I didn't make those things up. It's part of the job. I also didn't create the conflict with the bank. You did. And then the situation became more complicated when your father's CFO went and got into a business deal with the same bank. Then the Russian mafia got involved, including a Russian developer we'd been looking at as part of a much-larger investigation. The good news is the investigation is over. The better news is you're out of danger."

"You know about that, too?" Katherine asked, raising an eyebrow.

"Yes."

"Did you make that go away?"

"No, you had a guardian angel for that one."

Katherine looked deep into Sean's eyes. Over the past few months, she had grown to almost despise the man sitting before her, but now she wondered if her problems had actually been with the mission, not the man.

"You may be surprised to hear this, Sean: I do understand. There are things that I, too, can't discuss because of my job. I must tell you that I have real trouble accepting the fact that for months you have been part of a fishing expedition involving my family. You've also been spying on an American journalist who has done nothing wrong. Why didn't you just bring me in and question me?"

"If it involved your source, would you have disclosed it?"

"Absolutely not."

"And then, we would have gotten a court order, and you would have stood on principle and gone to jail for contempt—and neither of us would have been any closer to catching the bad guys. That didn't seem like a productive path for us to take."

"So I should thank you because I'm not in jail?" Katherine said, her voice rising.

"Come on, Kat. We're coming to the problem from two different places. That doesn't make me wrong and you right. When I first met you, you told me that you admired that I was going after the bad guys. That's what we do."

"I'm not one of your bad guys!" Katherine shouted. She could feel her cheeks burning and her pulse quickening as she tried to make him understand.

Sean put his hands up to try to shush her as her voice echoed loudly off of the tall, glass windows that encircled them.

"Things aren't as simple as they were when I was doing advance work with the Service," he said. "We're dealing with a sophisticated and lethal enemy. Every day, every hour is a battle to keep them from getting ahead of us, or worse, breaching our security, discovering our deepest secrets so they can sell them to our enemies. I never wanted to hurt you, Kat. I'm trying to protect you, and our country."

"I know you believe that. I just don't accept that we have to sell our souls to do it. What have we gained if we lose what makes this country great in the process? You feel you've got to be better than the bad guys at what they do, beat them at their own game. Is that a fair assessment?"

"Right."

"That's the point, Sean. It's not right. It's wrong. I understand your rationalization for doing what you do. I just wonder, where do you draw the line? When does your conduct become the same as the conduct of the people you're fighting? You want their secrets. They want our secrets. You go dark and deep to get theirs and then try to figure out how to keep them from getting ours."

Sean looked like he was going to say something then thought better of it. Katherine stood up.

"How can I ever trust you? If I can't trust you, how can I love you? That's the question I have to answer." Angry tears welled in her eyes.

"If you'll sit down and listen I'll tell you how. Give me a chance to re-earn your trust. This case is over. I've followed orders and completed my assignment. I've asked for, and received, a transfer back to the protection unit. I was doing advance work when we first met. You didn't seem to have any problem with that."

"Still, you can't promise me that you won't ever lie to me or deceive me again, can you?"

"No. I can't take the secret out of the Service. What I can promise you is that if I can't tell you what you want to know, I'll say so. I'll also share as much information with you as I can about my assignments without violating my code of service. I trust you and I want you to be able to trust me," Sean said.

"You make it sound so easy, but you just don't get it. My heart's been fighting with my mind for months over you. My mind tells me not to trust you. My heart tells me to separate what you do from who you are and to love you. I'd like my mind and heart to be in unison."

Sean's head dropped into his hands. When he lifted it back up, he nodded in understanding. "Well, think it over, and as you do, I'd ask you to keep three things in mind. First, as a reporter, you're going to someday be asked to keep a secret or protect a source in a situation that is not clearly black or white. I want you to know that I'll stand by you in those times and trust why you have to do it. Second, I never intended to hurt you. I kept quiet about our relationship because it was a conflict of interest, but I knew that if I wasn't the one watching you, I couldn't protect you, either."

Katherine thought about that for a moment and said, "You're right, Sean, we're coming from two different places. You're looking for forgiveness—or at least you should be—and ultimately, a resolution, but if there's going to be a you and me, together, we have to find a path to reconciliation."

"You're the journalist, not me, but aren't you're getting tied up in semantics?"

She looked up at the glass ceiling; she could almost see the sky. "It might be semantics to you, but the distinctions are important to me." Was she expecting too much? He was trying. Why couldn't she bring herself to forgive him? Katherine looked at Sean, fighting back tears. "By the way, what's the third thing?"

"The third is I love you." He stood and kissed her gently on the forehead, and then turned and walked away.

Once again, Katherine was back at the enduro motorcycle race where she had met Sean, looking at the back of 6A as he disappeared.

• • •

The rest of her trip home went smoothly. Katherine arrived at her apartment before noon the next day, unpacked, freshened up, and drove into Manhattan. She parked her car at her father's, then caught a cab to the hospital. The door to Marcia's room was half open, and she could see Marcia talking with Preston. She knocked softly.

Preston turned around and looked at Katherine. "I didn't see you there," he said.

"I hope I'm not interrupting," Katherine said.

Preston shook his head and motioned her in. "We were just talking about Harry's visit and all that he has going on."

"I had no idea that Preston and Harry had been talking every other week for some time," Marcia said. "I didn't think he'd been in touch with Harry since the funeral."

Preston gave Katherine an update on how well his wife was doing, and then he mentioned that he had yet to have lunch. He suggested Katherine sit with Marcia while he ran down to the cafeteria.

"Can I bring you back anything?" he asked his daughter.

Katherine shook her head, and as her father left the room Marcia motioned for Katherine to sit in the chair closer to her.

"I've wanted to talk with you for so long," Marcia said. "Preston told me you've been by often to check on me, and I'm so thankful for your concern and for your keeping Preston company."

"I'm glad I'm here and that we're able to talk again. You look wonderful, and I promise I'm not just saying that."

"I feel much better. Again, considering. My doctor tells me the more I talk and move even the little that I can, the better. I tire fast but I'm alive. I have so much to live for that I can't give up now."

"You surely can't. It would break Preston's heart," Katherine said. "He's barely left your side since the accident, and only then to make sure P.J. was okay. You're his whole world, you know."

Marcia blushed like a schoolgirl. "A lot of men would have taken one look at me, and turned and run," she said.

"But not Preston," Katherine said.

"No, not Preston."

A small smile played about Marcia's lips as she looked up at Katherine. "I know it sounds crazy, but this thing has also brought Preston and my parents closer, although that's something of an understatement."

Seeing the puzzled look on Katherine's face, Marcia then shared something Katherine had been completely unaware of—that her parents had never approved of her marrying Preston and had always dealt with him at a distance.

"Both have made a 180-degree change in attitude," Marcia said. "I don't think either of them would trade him for a crown prince after all this . . . but enough about me, I hear you've been on an important, secret assignment. Tell me all about it!"

Katherine gave a vague winding account of a work in progress, a story that did not even ring true to her as she was saying it. She decided to cut it short. "It didn't work out as intended, so that's why I'm back early." At least that part was true.

Marcia smiled as Katherine finished her tale, and her eyes were knowing. "When you come as close as I have to dying, and you're lying in bed looking at a long recovery, you can't help rethinking what life is all about. Your focus becomes crystal clear about who loves you, who your friends are, and what matters. I've made a lot of mistakes—particularly in relationships," Marcia said. "I realize that now."

Confused, Katherine wondered if it was Marcia or the medicine talking. Still, Marcia was saying exactly what she needed to hear.

She inched closer so as not to miss a word as Marcia's voice lowered and continued: "I'm telling you this because in some ways we're a lot alike. You're detached just like I've become. Your best friend's an alcoholic who depends on you. From what you've told me, the men in your life are problematic or absent. If you're like me, you feel alone more often than you would like. You and I both need to work harder at building meaningful relationships. I've come to realize in here that they are what matter most."

Katherine was stunned—she could not believe Marcia was using one of their first visits since her recovery to lecture her. "I don't think that's fair," Katherine said, knowing she sounded defensive. "You don't know me or my friends, much less anything about my love life. Why would you say that to me?"

"I've had enough training to see the patterns, Katherine. I don't mean to overstep, but I care about you and it's not a good picture. Where's my friend, Ann? Once upon a time, she would have been here in a New York minute. Now, when I needed her most, she hasn't even bothered to call, much less come to see me. Yet, she is the closest thing I have to a best friend. Bill and Mary came, but not Ann. I fault myself for that."

"You may be judging her too harshly. Ann bawled her eyes out when I called her about what had happened."

"Don't let me off the hook, Katherine. What I need to do is be honest with myself and work on changing me. That's why I had started seeing a therapist again, and as hard as I'm being on myself, I also think you could benefit from seeing someone. Just don't walk into an explosion on the way."

Marcia's vulnerability released something in Katherine. With a choked voice, she said, "I feel like I already have. I learned I couldn't trust the man I loved. He says he loves me but then why do I feel neglected and betrayed? Why does it feel like he always puts work before me? He obviously has a different agenda. He was the first man who gave me that special feeling. That fire."

"Oh, now that's a topic I know something about," Marcia said. "Surely, you know that has been a running issue with Preston and me. Let me save you and your fellow a little time: you are also married to your work—maybe both of you need to give a little. Are you hearing what I'm saying? I apologize if I've been too direct, Katherine. It's going to take time, for both of us. Maybe a year from now we can have this conversation again and compare lives."

Marcia smiled in a way that made Katherine believe they could develop the kind of friendship she'd hoped for from the beginning.

Katherine wiped her eyes. "You don't mince words, do you?"

"I like to think true friends tell us what we need but maybe don't want to hear," Marcia said, "and I'd like us to be friends."

"I would, too," Katherine said, appreciating once more how fast life could change. She had walked into this hospital room to comfort someone who was almost a stranger, and she would leave knowing she and Marcia finally had the start of a real relationship.

Marcia squeezed Katherine's arm just as Preston walked into the room, a big smile on his face. "Looks like you two had a good talk."

• • •

Back home, Katherine called Susan, and they chatted. It was a nice and welcome break from what Katherine had been through. She ordered a pizza, and when it arrived she settled on the couch with a cold beer. That was when she noticed the flashing light on her answering machine. She pressed the Play button and a man's voice filled the room: Please call. The blunt brevity of the message sent a slight chill through her body. She dialed the number on the message; the editor of *The Braydon Constitution* picked up on the first ring.

"Thanks for returning my call, Katherine. I'll get right to the point. You're a good reporter, with depth and great instincts. We need you here. I'd like you to become our assistant editor. We can talk about salary and benefits at your convenience, but I can promise you that you'll like the package."

"Wow," Katherine said, "I was expecting bad news or another crisis. Thank you, it's a wonderful offer. I don't know what to say."

"I'd love it if you'd say you'd take the job, but you don't have to give me an answer tonight. Think it over. I'll just end this call by saying that we would be fortunate to have you, and I don't mean just the paper. You've made a lot of friends in Braydon."

"I appreciate your saying that, more than you know. I will, of course, think it over. Honestly, I'd like to talk with Sol first. Do you mind if I tell him about your offer?"

"Not at all. He's a good man, and he knows we're interested in hiring you."

"I'll get back to you as soon as I can," Katherine said. She reached Sol on his home phone.

"What's up, kiddo?"

"I've been offered the assistant editor position in Braydon."

"Congratulations. When do you start?"

"I never stopped."

"Meaning what?"

"Meaning I never stopped working for you and with you. I don't want to stop now. The assistant editor position is a great offer, and I do like Braydon, but I love New York—and I know I can put up with you."

They both laughed.

"You have other options besides putting up with me. I'm serious about the *Times*. Why don't you give that a shot?"

"Why not instead you have a talk with Chuck, sort of a realignment conversation, and see if you can find an office for me with a little more room and privacy."

"Why don't you leave management to me? The office is not a problem; neither is Chuck. He's decided it was time for him to explore other opportunities. He's looking at magazines and thinking about writing editorials. Maybe the next great American novel."

"Why didn't you tell me about that?"

"Because you would have worried that I needed you, and I didn't want you staying out of a sense of obligation."

"You do need me. More importantly, I need you. Apart from the mighty mentor award, you've been the best boss and friend I could ever hope for. I'll never forget how you were there for me when the chips were down."

"Okay, okay. Enough. You've made your argument and won your case. Your new office will be waiting."

CHAPTER 58

THE SUN WAS STILL HIGH IN THE SKY by the time Katherine reached Saint Luke's. It was her favorite time of year, sidewalks and balconies were decorated with flowers, and the days were not only getting longer, they were also getting hotter. It made weekends much more pleasurable. Her visits to the hospital had become less frequent with Marcia now in rehabilitation. Preston was the only cheerleader Marcia needed. Katherine had been happy to let her father do the honors, and that was a relief. The frequent four-hour round trip had been taxing.

She stepped off the elevator and into the rehabilitation center, giving a quick wave to the nurse at the front desk. She found Preston and Marcia sitting at a table together talking. Katherine marveled at how fast the world could change, yet how some things never did. It was hard to miss how much the two people in front of her were in love, as they leaned in close like college sweethearts.

Marcia was the first to spot Katherine, and her smile seemed to widen further. Her father saw Katherine and jumped to his feet.

"Hi, sweetheart," he said, giving her a hug. Katherine responded in kind before leaning over to give Marcia a kiss on the cheek.

"We weren't expecting you today," Marcia said, taking a last sip of bottled water.

"I just thought I'd come into the city and surprise you both," Katherine said.

Marcia gave her a look through narrowed eyes but before she could say anything, Preston asked if she would like him to get her some more water.

"Yes, dear. I never thought learning to walk could be so hard. That must be why we leave it to toddlers," Marcia said, holding onto his hand for a moment before he walked away. "So, Katherine, are you going to do it?"

Katherine gave her a startled look before flopping down into a chair at the table. "When did you become a mind reader?" She made a funny face. "Everything as a journalist is telling me not to, but everything as a woman is telling me to take a chance and go for it."

"I knew there had to have been a reason you stopped by," Marcia said. "You know, besides me."

Katherine feigned hurt. "You know I follow your progress like it was my own. Can't visit you enough. Phone calls just don't do the trick."

"I know, I know. I was just teasing. You're here too often as it is for a professional journalist." Marcia's smile faded. "Do you know how you're going to do it?"

"Not so different from what you and I are doing right now. I've already made the arrangements. It's just not at a hospital."

"I should hope not. Hospitals are not the best for that sort of thing, though I suppose it wouldn't hurt for there to be doctors nearby if things took a turn for the worse."

They both laughed as Preston returned with the water. He broke the seal and unscrewed the cap before handing it to his wife.

"I have to be on my way," Katherine said, standing up.

"So soon?" Preston objected with a frown. "You just got here."

"I'll stop by your place tonight before I leave the city, Dad. I'm meeting somebody."

Preston stood up to give her a hug, but Marcia reached out and lightly grabbed Katherine's hand first. Katherine and Preston both looked questioningly at her. "You know," Marcia said firmly, "even if this turns out to be a huge mistake tomorrow or ten years from now, your father and I will always be here for you."

"Thanks," Katherine said. "It means a lot to have someone who cares about these decisions as much as I do."

"Wait, what's going on? What mistake?" Preston said, flustered. "What could I possibly have missed in sixty seconds?"

The two women laughed, and Katherine said, "She'll tell you. I'm late."

• • •

With Casey's brilliant financial skills and Alex's wonderful back-up, it was looking more and more like Wilson Holdings was on the mend. The Charlotte bank had kept the lines open and all accounts were current; they had decent surpluses in all but one store, and its shortcomings were seasonal and easily covered. And that's why Preston found himself whistling loudly as he walked up to the entrance of his Manhattan dealership. Before he could open the door, a thin man wearing a cheap suit approached and asked if he was the Preston Wilson who resided at 725 Fifth Avenue in New York City. When Preston said yes, the man handed him a white envelope and replied, "Mr. Wilson, you've now been officially served."

Preston called Barry Snyder. Before Preston could say a word, Snyder asked, "You got it? The subpoena?"

"Yes. And I'd like—"

"Come right over."

After a few pleasantries, Snyder said, "I was picking up the phone to call you when you called. I just received the trial date a couple of minutes ago. The prosecution has arranged a nonjury trial, and the defense counsel, to my surprise, has agreed."

"There have been so many delays, I was beginning to wonder if this thing would ever get to court."

"It's definitely on now."

Preston looked at his name on the subpoena. "What does any of this have to do with me?"

"The U.S. attorneys want to make sure you're present. Either they want to call you as a witness, or they want to cross-examine you if one of the defense attorneys calls you as a witness. My guess is the prosecutors want you to be their witness against Disley."

"You think this is because I told the FBI about Disley?"

"That's my gut. I know you're not paying me to 'suppose' things; however, we seldom get much to work with ahead of time."

"If they knew I was going to help them, why did they have to subpoena me? Why not just ask me to come?"

Snyder gave Preston a coy grin. "Because you could change your mind. In that situation, they would then call you as a hostile witness."

"What exactly is a hostile witness?"

"One who may be cross-examined—the prosecution could call you to the stand, ask leading questions, and cross-examine you," he said.

Preston threw up his hands. "Will this ever be over—am I now more at risk?"

"There's always exposure of some sort in this kind of case. I'll bring a motion before the judge that you be granted immunity from prosecution. Then you can testify without fear of being indicted."

"You think the judge will go along with that?"

"Ordinarily, yes, but here, it's fifty-fifty. The prosecution may argue against granting you immunity because you're an unindicted co-conspirator. That may be enough for the judge to refuse my motion."

"I hate that damn phrase," he said. "If the judge refuses, then what happens?"

"Then you plead the Fifth."

"Why would I plead the Fifth if I'm going to testify against Disley? He's the thief. All I did was own the company and stupidly give him the access codes to the bank accounts."

"I know it sounds crazy, but you still run the risk of being indicted. It all gets down to how zealous the prosecutors are about pursuing a conviction. You're a lot juicier morsel than Disley. The prosecutor might insinuate that you gave Disley the codes knowing he'd take the money and give some of it back to you. For all we know, he might have set up one of the Caribbean accounts with your name on it."

"I feel like we're going in a circle, but I won't plead the Fifth and I won't ask for immunity."

"That's not smart."

"This whole case isn't smart as far as I'm concerned. I voluntarily talked to the FBI, told them all I knew, and asked for nothing in return. You never advised me that you thought I'd done anything criminal. I'm sorry for the way I'm sounding, but this is way beyond anything I've even remotely considered."

"I don't like telling you this, Preston, but if the prosecutor sees an opening, I'm certain you'll be charged with something."

"Then why haven't they?"

Snyder sighed. "Preston, what do you have to lose by asking for immunity?"

"My reputation has been tainted enough, which no one seems to understand. Asking for immunity implies that I've done something wrong. Pleading the Fifth shouts it. My managers have been killing themselves to smooth over what's happened already, and all but one of my stores are improving. But with a bad shot of publicity, there's no way Wilson Holdings can recover. I wouldn't even buy a car from me."

"So what do you want me to do?" Snyder asked, sounding more peeved than resigned.

"Call up the prosecution and tell them I'll be there, with or without a subpoena."

"Okay." There was a long pause. "This should be interesting."

• • •

Katherine parked on West Fourteenth Street, put some money in the meter, and began walking. She made a left on Washington. She could see the hotel, with the unused, elevated railway line running straight through it, some twenty-five feet in the air. The tracks had been converted into the High Line, a favorite neighborhood park. However, that was not where she was going. She crossed the last intersection, following the boisterous noise emanating from the Standard Biergarten.

The huge beer hall was a gathering place for young people on the weekends, and its ceiling was the railway floor above. It was just the kind of urban color that she loved and why she could never move to Braydon. Towering in front of her stood a collision of old and new, too interesting to ignore.

The beer garden was busier than it had been on her last visit. Manhattanites must be desperate to leave the cold behind.

Katherine navigated past the hostess dressed like a German beer girl and continued into the hall. It was loud, but that was what she had counted on. The long tables were emptier than the rest of the restaurant where games were played. Looking around, she saw Sean sitting by himself in a white T-shirt, holding a half-empty mug. He looked a little down in the mouth as he stared at his brewski.

She casually walked over to his table and said, "That's not going to refill it."

Sean looked up at her.

"I'm going to keep on trying," he retorted.

Katherine could see relief on his face. "Can I sit down?"

"Please." He looked around and said, "I ordered one for you, but I don't know where the waitress is."

"That's fine."

They looked at each other for several moments before Sean said, "It's been weeks. I wasn't sure if you were going to call."

Katherine sighed. "I wasn't sure if I was going to, either."

"Why did you?"

"A . . . friend of mine talked me through it."

"You didn't—"

"No, I didn't say anything I shouldn't have," she reassured him, as a bouncy waitress in a short skirt set a cold mug of yellow beer in front of her. "Thank you."

They stared at each other for a few more seconds after she flounced away.

"I can't say I liked the way we ended things the last time we saw each other," Sean said.

"Then why did you leave the way you did?" Katherine asked, leaning forward across the table.

"You were yelling."

"I was offended."

"I drove three hours to see you that night, and you barely batted an eyelash at me. I bore the brunt of your anger for ten minutes then drove three hours back in the opposite direction."

Katherine grimaced. She had felt badly about that when she thought about it later. She took a sip of beer.

"Kat," he said, and put his hand close to hers. "Someone once told me that when a person loves you and proves it, you should hang on. If you let go, you're making a mistake that you may never get to undo. As we grow older, the fact that someone can't wait to see you every day is a blessing. The chances of finding somebody like that is uncommonly rare."

She raised her eyebrow at him. Not another lecture, she hoped.

"What I did—for you—could be considered treason by some people I work for at the Service."

"Then why *did* you do it?" she asked him, looking away.

"Because I know you're a woman of morals and that we were on the same side, as much as you don't want to admit it. And because . . . I knew that somewhere deep in your heart, you love me just as much as I love you."

Off in the distance a group of table bowlers howled in joy. Maybe somebody had won.

"It was something I couldn't deal with at the time, Sean. I'm a journalist, and you were Big Brother spying on me. You're right. I was falling in love with you, and that's what made it worse. Had it been anybody else, it would have been a flesh wound. Because it was you, it was a knife through the heart."

She began to feel a lump forming in her throat, so she took another swig of beer to hide it. Sean must have noticed because he changed the subject to a lighter topic.

"So, how do you know this place? You're not the type who enjoys crowds."

The answer was one she had hoped to avoid, but she was prepared to answer. "I was set up on a date here." She could see Sean's face turn serious. "I stood him up, though. I couldn't get you out of my head. It was too soon."

When she looked back up at him, she was touched at how hopeful he looked. "Then I met him here a few days later to apologize in person."

"Was he good looking, at least?"

Katherine grinned. "Not really."

He squeezed her hand as they laughed. "You know I'm willing to give this another shot. Nothing has changed on my end. I would still drive six hours to see you for ten minutes."

She looked into his eyes for a second before she said, "On one condition—you promise to tell me when you're spying on me?"

"In my new position, I wouldn't be asked to."

She squeezed his hand back. "Then I'm willing to give it another shot, too."

CHAPTER 59

PRESTON AND HIS LAWYER arrived at the courthouse a half-hour early. Courtroom 709 was just as imposing as Preston had expected: A high judicial bench with a large brass seal above it on the wall. Another tier for the court clerk. A place for the stenographer. Dark, paneled wood everywhere. A long, two-row jury box. Two tables for the lawyers and litigants. And seating for the public was separated from the proceedings by wooden dividers with gates.

Attorneys for the prosecution and the defense were already at their tables, reading notes, shuffling papers, and talking amongst themselves and their assistants, who sat behind them in the first row of benches. The court clerk was at his station, a uniformed officer stood at the ready, and the stenographer was already flexing her fingers.

At precisely nine a.m., an officer of the court commanded everyone to rise, and U.S. District Court Judge Albert Goldman strode to the bench and took his seat, quickly instructing everyone to take his or hers as well.

Snyder whispered to Preston, "Judge Goldman is an experienced, no-nonsense criminal law attorney. He's been on the bench fifteen years, and he's never been shy when it comes to publicity for himself."

After a brief statement from the court and some preliminary motions made by the defense attorneys, Judge Goldman asked the prosecuting attorneys if they were ready to proceed. Before they could answer, one of the defense attorneys asked if he could approach the bench. The judge nodded. Gil Gillespie, Mark Conners, and Carol Martin, led by the middle-aged, beefy defense lawyer with glasses, gathered in front of the judge. What followed was an intense, heated discussion that ended with the judge announcing a brief recess.

"What's going on?" Preston said.

"Not sure. Sit tight, and I'll try to find out." Snyder caught Carol Martin in the hallway just as she was leaving the courtroom. "What's this all about?"

"I only have a second. Baskhanov's lawyer just told the court he now wants to accept our plea offer. Gil told him it was too late. It got a little bumpy, so the judge gave us fifteen minutes to hash it out. I've got to go. I don't want them to start without me."

Snyder returned to Preston and told him what Carol had said.

"Can he still do that?"

"Yes, if the prosecution consents. Apparently they're playing hardball. It's tricky. What they've wanted in exchange for the plea is to control Baskhanov's testimony against the bank and Disley. He pleads guilty and the case against the other people involved in the fraud could fall apart. Even Disley could walk. The prosecution could still call Baskhanov, but they couldn't compel him to tell the truth—about anything. What I don't understand is why a man like Baskhanov would cave. It doesn't make sense."

"So what happens now?"

"We'll know in a few minutes."

Everyone eventually returned to the courtroom, and the judge called all the attorneys back to the bench. After a brief discussion, the lawyers returned to their seats. The judge said, "Mr. Baskhanov, please stand with your attorney." As ordered, Mikhail Baskhanov, whom Preston thought had the natural hair of a piece of shag carpet, and his lawyer stood. "This court has been informed that you desire to plead guilty to all charges against you. Mr. Baskhanov, do you in fact desire to plead guilty to all the charges?"

"Yes, your honor," the attorney said on Baskhanov's behalf. "My client pleads guilty to all charges."

"Let me ask you, Mr. Baskhanov, and I want you to answer this question and not your attorney: How do you plead to violation of Section 1443 of the United States Criminal Code, conspiracy to commit bank fraud?"

"Guilty, your honor," Baskhanov replied, without the slightest hesitation.

"Do you make this plea after full advice by your counsel?"

"Yes, your honor."

"Do you make this plea voluntarily, without any promises made to you of any kind?"

"Yes, your honor."

"Do you understand that making this plea will result in the court finding you guilty of this charge?"

"Yes, your honor."

"Do you understand you may be sentenced to prison for the rest of your life?"

"Yes, your honor."

The judge proceeded to question the defendant as to his plea for each of the specific charges that were brought against him in accord with the criminal complaint. With each one, the judge painstakingly asked him if he understood what he was pleading to, what it meant, and whether he was doing so on the advice of his counsel. The judge followed those questions by asking Baskhanov's counsel on the record if that was his advice to his client. When this was concluded, the judge accepted his guilty pleas on all counts and ordered the defendant taken into custody, pending pre-sentence investigation. Then the judge ordered another brief recess.

People shuffled out of the courtroom. Preston, jaw agape, asked Barry Snyder, "What the hell just happened?"

"Apparently the prosecutors stonewalled Baskhanov and his attorney, and they just folded. It's highly unusual for a guy to plead guilty to everything. I don't remember when I've seen a defense lawyer let that happen. Especially when they'd already offered him a plea. I don't know why on earth the defense waited. I've been doing this a long time, and I've never seen anything like it."

"The plea helped the prosecution, right?" Preston asked.

"Yes and no. They got Baskhanov, but if he clams up, like I said earlier, they have to prove there was a conspiracy to commit bank fraud between him as the developer and Thompson, Bowers, and Disley. Without Baskhanov, the prosecution will have a tough time. I surely wouldn't want their case. This is why I don't understand letting the Russian plead. But, more importantly, I don't know why he did it."

Preston nodded, trying to get his head around this latest development.

"I'll tell you one thing," Snyder said, "I think this case is going to move a lot faster than anyone imagined. I mean rocket speed."

Everybody filed back into the courtroom, and the judge instructed the prosecution to proceed. Gil called Maria DeSanto first, who described the scheme her supervisor Stacy Bowers had orchestrated, meticulously detailing the manufactured appraisals, the phony financials, and the fabrication of the bank's transactional processes.

The next portion of Gillespie's questions for Maria DeSanto dealt with Baskhanov, and how the developer had approached the bank in connection with his stated purpose of obtaining financing for the real-estate lots. She provided a comprehensive description of the real-estate project and how Bowers had conspired to finance the purchase of the lots through loans from the bank, secured with collateral provided by Baskhanov's shadow corporations.

His examination continued until the court declared a recess for lunch. After the recess, the questioning of Maria DeSanto continued. After two more hours, the prosecution turned her over to the defense.

Austin Disley's attorney, Anthony Spagnello, went first, deftly questioning Ms. DeSanto for more than an hour, probing what she knew and what she had done. He asked sharp questions about whether she thought her immediate supervisor, a woman under Stacy Bowers, was wrong in what she had done. When she said yes, he asked her why she had then failed to confront her. After all, De-Santo knew they were bogus documents, and yet her supervisor had accepted them. Had the prosecution promised her they would not arrest her if she testified against Bowers, without any interest in this other subordinate? She admitted such a deal had been struck. She would be granted complete immunity in return for her testimony against Bowers. The other person was never discussed, beyond a few passing comments.

Spagnello went in for the kill. "Do you know Austin Disley?"

"No."

"Had you ever heard of him before this case?"

"No."

"Did you ever see his name involved in anything or in any way with Bank North America?"

"No."

"Do you have any personal knowledge of any conversation between Mr. Baskhanov and Mr. Disley?"

"No."

"Apart from anything you've learned from discussions with the prosecution—which I do not want you to talk about—do you know of anything *based on your personal knowledge* that would indicate Mr. Disley was part of a conspiracy to defraud the bank you work for?"

"No."

"So you personally don't know why Mr. Disley is a defendant in this case?"

The prosecution objected to that question, which the judge sustained. Maria DeSanto had no need to answer—her face did it for her. Spagnello smiled. "I'm finished with this witness, your honor."

The court was adjourned until the following morning.

Chapter 60

COURT OPENED THE following morning with Carol Martin as the attorney handling the case for the prosecution. She called Robert Reynolds to the stand. He told the court about Disley's plan to help BNA by offering the developer five luxury cars at wholesale. He said the developer claimed it was needed to put the scheme over the top. He mentioned how aggressive Baskhanov had been, insisting that the dealership also take his fleet of five Cadillac Escalades in trade at three times their Blue Book value. Even though his role was a small component of the entire plot, Reynolds's testimony was compelling and damaging to Austin Disley, as it clearly linked him with the conspiracy and fraudulent elements of the case.

At least until Spagnello went to work again. He started by asking if Reynolds had also made a deal with the prosecution in exchange for his testimony. Reynolds admitted he had. Then he grilled Reynolds about how long he had worked for Wilson Holdings when the aforementioned actions had allegedly occurred. He said it had been only a few months. Had he been fired at any prior jobs? He had. Did he have personal knowledge of Disley's talking with anybody at the bank? No.

Spagnello's assault continued for more than an hour, prying from Reynolds any and everything he knew, which ended up being not much. When he was finished, it was as though Reynolds had barely worked for the dealership and would have had trouble

411

finding the showroom's restroom. Carol Martin's redirect was as ineffective as it was short, and Reynolds was excused.

Martin next called Preston Wilson to the stand. For Preston, being called to testify against Austin Disley was on par with being put in front of a firing squad. You could prepare for it all you wanted to, but it was never the same once you got there. In the few seconds needed for him to walk from his seat to the witness chair, a spate of memories involving Disley flashed before him. When it ended, all that remained was the commitment he had made to his friend to stand by his side—no matter what—his way of paying him back for having helped to save his father's life.

In the witness chair, he tried to get comfortable, but it all seemed so surreal. He could barely concentrate on Carol Martin's questions, an inordinate number of which seemed to be about his background, Wilson Holdings, each store, and his relationship with BNA. Finally, she turned to the topic of Disley. Preston described their relationship as boyhood friends dating back to their boarding school days at Hotchkiss. He talked about Disley's coming to him for a job about two years earlier, and how he had hired him to assist Casey, and when Casey left, how he had become CFO of the Manhattan store and Wilson Holdings.

"Then what happened?" Carol asked.

"Late last year, I learned he'd been arrested for conspiracy to commit bank fraud." As he spoke, Preston looked at Austin, who still wore the expression of a clueless puppy—unaware of what was coming, but sensing something bad was about to happen.

"What did you do when you learned about his arrest?"

"I fired him."

"Your company leased its real estate for the Manhattan store from BNA. Correct?"

"Yes."

"BNA also supplied your inventory financing. Correct?"

"Yes."

"And that bank is still your landlord and floor-plan provider?"

"Yes. Capital lines, too," Preston testified.

"So you have a close relationship with BNA?"

"We do."

"And Disley was aware of that as CFO, correct?"

"Of course."

"Is that a yes?"

"Yes."

"Do you have personal knowledge of any activity by Disley that would indicate he committed fraud with BNA?"

Preston said nothing, so Carol repeated, "Do you have personal knowledge of any activity by Austin Disley that would indicate he committed fraud with BNA?"

"Not . . . directly."

Carol gave Preston an "I could kill you" glare, and then proceeded to have him explain Alex Herman's role at Wilson Holdings for the court. Being careful not to lead Preston, she asked, "Can you explain any transactions that Mr. Herman brought to your attention—anything that went on at your Manhattan dealership involving Mr. Disley—which you found unusual?"

"Yes. Alex discovered that five luxury cars had been sold at wholesale—and none were included in the stores' gross sheets, and he also uncovered the buyback of the five Escalades."

Carol asked Preston about the meaning of wholesale in the automobile industry and the negative impact on his dealership as a result of selling five highly expensive cars without any profit. Then she asked him to explain the impact of buying five cars at triple their value—and why a dealership would try to avoid that at all costs as well as how that could upset the franchisors.

"More importantly, how did it go undiscovered?" she pressed.

"We learned later that Robert Reynolds had kept this from our bookkeeping department by repeating Disley's story that it was something upper management wanted to do to help its relationship with the bank. It was all absurd and untrue, just as Mr. Reynolds testified."

"Did Mr. Reynolds have the authority to make the decision without Mr. Disley's approval?"

Preston glanced at Disley saying, "I don't know."

"You don't know?" Carol demanded. "Aren't you the CEO of the company?"

"Ms. Martin, I don't know if Mr. Reynolds made the decision on his own or if Mr. Disley knew about it."

"I didn't ask you that."

"Your Honor," Snyder interrupted, standing. "Ms. Martin is badgering the witness."

Judge Goldman stared down at Preston.

"I want to hear what Mr. Wilson has to say. I'll allow the question. Objection overruled."

Carol's voice this time was more modulated. "Mr. Wilson, did Mr. Reynolds have the authority to make the decision to sell the five cars at wholesale?"

"No, he didn't have the authority. That doesn't—"

"That's all for now, Mr. Wilson. Besides firing Disley, what else, if anything, did you do after you learned of the unauthorized transactions?"

"I called the FBI and told an agent what had happened. He asked me to meet with him and his associate. I did, I explained everything I knew, and I answered all of their questions."

"This doesn't seem like a case for the FBI. Why wasn't that handled internally?"

"I was concerned there might be something going on with Austin and BNA. I couldn't take that risk. While my business has had bank issues in the past, our relationship with BNA since has been quite good, and I couldn't take the chance of jeopardizing it. I was determined that Wilson Holdings would not hold anything back."

"If Mr. Disley is found not guilty of any crime in connection with BNA, would you rehire him?"

"Absolutely not," Preston's answer was fast that time.

"Why?"

"Because he clearly didn't do what he was hired to do."

"He's your lifelong friend."

"Yes." Preston turned his eyes to Austin, this time not pulling away. "He will always be my lifelong friend, but I can't let him or anyone else ruin my business. That would not be fair to my family or my employees."

"And you've testified today voluntarily?"

"I was subpoenaed, but I would have testified anyway."

"Have any promises of any kind been made to you in exchange for your testimony?"

"No, nor did I ask for any."

"No further questions," Carol said.

"Your witness, Mr. Spagnello," the judge said.

Spagnello rose and said, "I have no questions, Your Honor."

The smile that had started to form on Disley's face turned to the pained look of someone who had just had a tooth extracted without anesthesia.

The judge pounded his gavel, and Disley began an animated exchange with his attorney.

"You're excused, Mr. Wilson," the judge said, glancing at Disley and Spagnello as their discussion grew louder. "We will take a fifteen-minute recess."

"Are you still upset with me for not seeking immunity?" Preston asked Barry Snyder as they left the courtroom with Disley and Spagnello still going at it.

"No," Snyder said, patting Preston on the back. "You were entitled to make that decision. And I think your testimony went well. Carol Martin never asked you about what you did or didn't do to supervise Disley—what you knew or should have known. She just touched on the outer walls so she wouldn't look bad, and she was pretty pissed at you, so I admire her restraint. She gave you a platform to tell your story any way you wanted. She left it to Disley's lawyer to go after you."

"Why didn't he?"

"Probably because he doesn't believe his client."

"Does that happen often?" Preston asked, finding Snyder's observation unbelievable.

"I think it did today."

When the trial resumed that day, Baskhanov, who had nailed Thompson, was called to the stand, and he confirmed all that Reynolds had said, testifying explicitly about the part Disley had played in the scheme. His testimony appeared to put a lock on the conspiracy and the roles the bank and the developer, as well as Reynolds and Disley, had played.

Even though Preston's testimony in the end had not been as damaging to Disley as Barry Snyder had anticipated, the prosecution carried forward like it had the wind at its back. Carol Martin recalled Thompson, and his testimony clearly harmed Disley. Thompson's attorney's cross-examination was intense and exhaustive, trying to further the contention that Disley was at fault rather than his client.

The court, being presented with no further witnesses, directed counsel to make closing arguments. The defense attorneys went first, with Thompson's making a long and involved argument to demonstrate his client's innocence.

Then it was Spagnello's turn.

Snyder leaned close to Preston and said, "This should be interesting." He let out a brief chuckle. "I think the judge knows that Spagnello doesn't believe Disley."

Spagnello began his argument by telling the judge that Disley had believed he was helping the company by doing the bank a favor—and that's why he had arranged to have the cars sold at wholesale as a way of securing the developer's business. Then he told the court it was his client's position that he had never stolen any money from the company but only taken what he was entitled to as severance pay, an amount befitting any high-ranking corporate officer upon leaving a company. When Spagnello finished, the judge asked, "Why didn't your client ask for a jury trial?"

"I fully discussed that with my client, Your Honor. He decided he would put his faith in the court."

Snyder nudged Preston in the arm. Carol Martin told the judge that she felt no closing argument to be necessary. She, too, would put her faith in the court. Then she looked at Spagnello and smiled, which he returned in kind. Preston thought he detected a quick wink thrown his way, but then dismissed it as pure fantasy.

The judge told all present that he would reserve his decisions, and court was adjourned.

• • •

On the way back to the U.S. Attorney's office, Carol and Gil walked in silence, carrying their scuffed and bulging briefcases. They passed one of Gil's favorite Irish bars. He stopped, looked at Carol, and looked back in the window.

"A Blue Moon sounds good," Carol said, and followed Gil to a small table in back. "We nailed it."

"I don't see another outcome," Gil said. "Nice job."

"There's one thing I don't get. Why did Baskhanov lie down? More importantly, why did he then cooperate with us on the stand after he pled guilty without a plea bargain?"

"I hate to tell you this, Carol, but our play was performed off Broadway. What we've done with BNA is only the tip of the iceberg."

"You're telling me this now?"

"I'm *not* telling you this now—or ever—but one of my good friends in the FBI has *not* told me that his unit, together with the Secret Service, is about to make a move against a number of high-level Russian criminals who have compromised several U.S. banks, including BNA and J.P. Morgan—hacking, money laundering, identity theft in the billions—we're talking major financial crimes. Baskhanov is a two-bit player caught up in a much larger game."

As they ordered beers, Carol considered the implications. "I still don't get the connection to Baskhanov."

"It's simple. They flipped him," Gil said. "They're going to be talking to the judge privately. Instead of serving time, Baskhanov is going to work for the NSA and CIA in Russia to get the kingpin, or so I'm *not* told."

"Then we're not done with BNA?" Carol asked.

"*We* might be done, but the NSA isn't."

CHAPTER 61

A T THE END OF EACH trial day, Preston had made the trip uptown to the rehab hospital to bring Marcia current on the events of the day. Naturally, she was worried about the proceedings, and he had wanted to ease her concerns the best he could. So far she'd been pleased to hear that his attorney felt it had gone well in all respects, and that he expected an early decision. He had confided in her that he had done what he could not to harm Austin with his own testimony, but that the case against his friend was rather compelling, and he thought Austin would be doing time for his crimes.

What he did not tell his wife was he just hoped it would not be too severe. Preston had already paid back the money Austin had lost on the five cars, and he was working out a plan with Casey to see that the eighty grand would eventually be returned to each store out of his share of the company's future profits. He had been the one to bring the fox into the henhouse, and he was taking full responsibility for the half-million his friend had cost the business.

Three days after the trial ended, Barry Snyder called Preston to tell him that the judge had rendered his decision. Baskhanov, who had already pled guilty, would be going away for twenty years. Reynolds was found guilty of one misdemeanor. Thompson and Disley were found guilty on all the bank fraud and conspiracy to commit bank fraud charges. However, Disley, who could also have been found guilty of grand larceny, misrepresentation, and fraud related to all the counts involving Wilson Holdings, received a huge break. Baskhanov's refusal to testify against Thompson had put a damper on the prosecution's case against the bank executive. Carol Martin had convinced her co-counsels that someone else needed to testify against Thompson, and after scrutinizing the options right down to the most minute details, the only person left was the one with the most to lose—Disley.

Spagnello was later heard to say that he had never been more shocked than when Carol Martin came to him with an offer for Disley's testimony. What had started out as a proffer to not try Disley for misrepresentation and fraud involving Wilson Holdings, ended up with Spagnello's having the grand larceny charges dropped as well. Disley now believed Spagnello to be the greatest attorney alive, completely unaware that he had won by default.

To Spagnello's credit, regardless of how much he disliked his client, once he sensed the prosecution's weakness, he had gone right for the jugular. When Preston learned the grand larceny charges had been dropped against his old friend, a great weight was lifted from his shoulders, as it meant he wouldn't have to testify against Disley. The specific sentences for each defendant would be handed down later.

Barry Snyder's call had come in while Preston was in Marcia's room at the rehab facility. "So, it's finally all over," Preston said, wanting to jump for joy despite his regret that the judge had lowered the boom on Austin.

"Thank you for all you've done, Barry."

"You're welcome. It's been a pleasure representing you, and I mean that."

As Preston hung up the phone, he was grinning so hard it hurt. It did not take Marcia long to realize it was the good news for which they had waited so long.

"You've got to call everyone," Marcia said.

"It'll be in the papers," Preston said.

"Make the calls," Marcia said, giving him a funny glare that made him laugh.

Preston started with Casey and Alex, and then he called Katherine, who said she would call Beth, as her mom would want to know. Then he called each of the Collectibles.

"Please also call my mom and dad and tell them," Marcia said.

Preston had a brief pang of guilt at not having placed them toward the top of the list, but his oversight had been out of habit, not intent. He told Marcia he was stepping out for a minute to get some fresh air and he would be right back. Outside the hospital, he headed to the nearest neighborhood market and bought the best bottle of champagne he could find and a couple of plastic flutes. He hid it all in a bag and went back to the hospital.

Sipping champagne, Preston and Marcia talked and laughed as they relived the ups and downs of the past year. At this very moment, neither could recall a time they had been happier in their marriage, save for when P.J. was born.

• • •

Katherine had been at the newspaper when Preston called, and she immediately ran to Sol's office to give him the verdict. Then she called her mother. Then Susan. She was too excited to do much work, but there was something she felt she needed to do. She poked her head back in Sol's office and asked for a few days off so she could go to New York and see her father. Sol just flashed her a thumbs-up, and she was out the door in a whirl of motion. In Manhattan, she did stop by to see Preston and visit Marcia in the hospital, but two days later she was sitting in Barry Snyder's office.

"You wouldn't tell me what you wanted," Snyder said, "but since you're Preston Wilson's daughter, I agreed to see you. So, Ms. Kelly, what can I do for you?"

Katherine smiled. "First, thank you for all you've done. As you can imagine, we're all thrilled about the verdict. That said, I'm worried about my father remaining an unindicted co-conspirator. I've been studying up on the topic—and I'm no lawyer—but it looks to me as if he could still be indicted. Am I right?"

"That's highly unlikely," the attorney said, with a raised eye-brow.

"Then why not have him released, if only for peace of mind? I worry that he could still be brought in as a suspect down the road."

"Ms. Kelly, I couldn't get that rescinded if I wanted to. It's entirely up to the U.S. Attorney's Office."

"Who would that be specifically?" she asked.

"Probably Carol Martin, or her boss, Gilbert Gillespie."

"Where would I find him?"

Snyder leafed through his lawyer's handbook. "One Hogan Place, in Saint Andrews Plaza."

She shook hands with Snyder and left. Katherine walked to the subway and took the first appropriate train. She was there in half an hour, and as luck would have it, Gil Gillespie was in, and he agreed to see her—not as Preston's daughter, but because she identified herself as a reporter interested in doing a story on him as a follow-up to the bank fraud case.

"It's nice to meet you, Ms. Kelly," Gillespie said as she entered his office, syrup dripping off each word. "Have a seat. Would you like a soda or a bottled water?"

"No, I'm fine, but thank you. I want to congratulate you on your victory in the bank fraud case. You put a lot of crooks behind bars."

"Have you been covering the case?" the prosecutor asked.

"I've been covering it from a different angle."

"What angle is that?" he asked.

"My father's. I'd like to ask you to authorize the release of Preston Wilson as an unindicted co-conspirator."

Gilbert hesitated. "Why would you ask me to do that? Maybe more importantly, why would I do that?"

"Because I understand he testified voluntarily on behalf of the prosecution. He did, didn't he?"

"Yeah, kind of."

"I don't understand."

"He didn't exactly . . . don't worry about it. Yes, he testified for the prosecution."

"Then in the interest of justice, which is what I understand your position as prosecutor is all about, it would seem fair to release him—remove the cloud he's been under, restore his reputation."

"Why are you so interested in this?" he asked.

"He's my father. He has done nothing wrong. I know it and so do you."

"Are we on the record?"

"Do you want to be?"

"I'd rather not."

"Then we're not. Will you release him?"

"It's not our policy, generally, to do that in a situation like this. Still, you have no cause to worry. It's unlikely we would ever ask that he be indicted."

"Is that a yes or a no?"

"It's a polite no." He gave Katherine an obviously fake smile.

"Then let me give you a polite response as well." Katherine came forward in her chair. "I've written an article about prosecutorial abuse, particularly in the area of unindicted co-conspirators. It includes all the motives for prosecutors to list someone in this category, including as a means to pressure them, threaten them, and gain an unfair advantage. I've got the statistics for those listed as unindicted co-conspirators versus those who are actually indicted. I've got pages and pages of statements from lawyers, judges, and others decrying the abuse. And you might like to know that you will be featured as the prosecutor who best illustrates that abuse. I'm expecting the story to go national with a lovely photo of you, of course. That is, unless you decide to have him released."

"Are we still off the record?"

"Absolutely. But the article won't be." Katherine observed Mr. Gillespie as he weighed his options and added, "I understand you have a desire to be attorney general one of these days. These convictions all help, don't they?"

Gillespie's countenance no longer held a smile, even a forced one. He got up from his chair and stood directly in front of and over Katherine. "I'm not a man who's intimidated by threats; however, I don't happen to think your father was guilty of anything. If I get the release, how will I know that you won't write the article anyway?"

Katherine stood, and while she was several inches shorter than Gillespie, they were no more than a foot apart. "Because you're smart. If you grant the release, your name and your office won't appear anywhere in the story. Also, you'll be able to sleep at night knowing you did the right thing."

Gillespie stepped behind his desk. "All right. Preston Wilson will be sent a copy of the release as soon it's issued. For the record, I am doing this on my own volition."

"Of course you are. Thank you, Mr. Gillespie. I'll keep my part of the bargain."

They shook hands knowing full well who had won the battle, and the victor was next seen whistling in the elevator with a smile on her face.

CHAPTER 62

KATHERINE BARELY MADE it outside before she started punching Preston's number in her phone. She caught him at the dealership, told him she had some news, and asked if she could swing by.

A half-hour later, she rushed into his office. Preston got up from behind his desk and gave his daughter a warm hug.

"I just met with Gil Gillespie," Katherine said.

Preston's face fell upon hearing the prosecutor's name. "Why? I thought you had some good news."

Katherine smiled broadly.

"I do—I just got Gillespie to drop the unindicted co-conspirator charge. He'll be sending you a letter. You're free."

"How? How did you do it?" Preston asked.

Sitting down on the closest chair he could find, Preston had a look of shock on his face.

"Let's just call it journalistic persuasion," Katherine said.

Preston sat motionless, head down, eyes moist.

"Dad?"

No response. "Dad, are you okay?"

"Yes," Preston said, warm tears rolling down his face. "I've never been more okay, and never been more thankful, and, for the record, I've never been more proud. What an amazing young woman you are."

He rose and gave his daughter a soft kiss on her forehead. "You did what no one else could, and you did it just for me. I love you."

• • •

Three days later, Preston walked into Marcia's hospital room only to find his wife missing. He had come bearing gifts—a bottle of cold Tattinger's and two champagne glasses. He found her in the rehabilitation gym, walking with the help of two therapists. She smiled and waved at him. "How do you like this? I'm getting pretty speedy."

"I love it," he said. "You'll be running laps pretty soon."

He motioned for her to join him on a nearby bench, and with the help of the aides she was soon sitting by his side. He pulled out the release from Gillespie and handed it to her.

"How do you like that?"

She looked over the document and then looked at Preston. "You and I have talked about this many times, and you said Snyder told you it would be up to the U.S. Attorney. They almost never drop these. I thought we were never going to be rid of it. How in heaven's name did you pull this off?"

"I didn't. Katherine did. She told me about it a few days ago, but I didn't want to tell you until I had the actual letter in my hands. You know what this means, Marcia."

Marcia nodded, and the smile that spread over her face was one of pure joy.

Preston looked at Marcia. In a barely audible voice, he said, "I have my reputation back. More importantly, I have my family and my friends. I've got a hold on what matters and I've let go of what I can't control. The clouds are gone, replaced by gratitude."

EPILOGUE

WHEN MARCIA WAS ABLE to leave the hospital for good, she and Preston sold their apartment at Trump Tower and moved to their modest ranch house in the Hamptons. They found they loved sitting on the porch and smelling the fresh ocean breeze. P.J. loved the freedom a home with a yard provided. Now he could have a puppy, and having someone to play with was as easy as walking next door. Preston's business was also back in the black. In fact, Wilson Holdings, with Casey in charge, was headed for one of its best years in ages.

Alice's class action suit was settled for more money than anyone had imagined—nowhere near 90 million but almost double everyone's investment, and that was after Marshall Livingston's third came off the top. Alice put half of her seven-figure share of the settlement in a stable retirement fund. Then she sent sizable checks to Tommy, Missy, Harry, Corey, Johnny, and Preston with a much larger check to Katherine, because without her, there would not have been a settlement. When she finished distributing the money, she thanked Joe, as she did every day, positive he was smiling down on her and all the Collectibles.

Harry and his Oompah Band continued to be in demand, and now with Beth sharing his home, he was happier than ever. Beth's spirits continued to improve, and Harry's even more so. Preston had asked a doctor friend to do some research, and as a result, Beth was scheduled for an appointment in Cleveland, with one of the world's leading specialists in macular degeneration. Preston insisted on paying the travel expenses for both her and Harry, as well as all the doctor bills. Beth knew she would never see normally again, but thanks to Preston's intervention she would likely never go blind either.

Justice was served thanks to Judge Goldman, who handed down the following sentences: Thompson and Baskhanov, twenty years in a federal penitentiary; Reynolds, one year; Bowers, seven years; and Disley, ten years on the conspiracy charge. The judge also ordered Disley to pay Wilson Holdings back the four-hundred-thousand dollars. Preston hired a lawyer to see if Disley's verdicts could be appealed. There was no way to tell if it would produce a different outcome, but the process was in motion, and Austin had sent Preston a letter apologizing to him and thanking him for his friendship.

In a move that shocked everyone, except Baskhanov and one other high-ranking official, before the Russian could enter the federal prison system, the U.S. Justice Department had him deported back to his homeland. The NSA decided he would be more beneficial to our country there.

As for Katherine, well, she became one of the youngest editors in the history of the *Twin Forks Press*, but only after Sol agreed she could continue to also report and write. Sol still worries that he will lose her someday to the *Times*, but he takes consolation in the fact that she'll probably win him a Pulitzer before she goes—that is, if he can keep her off the dirt bike tracks long enough to finish her latest investigation.

Preston, Marcia, P.J., and Katherine have sent an invitation to their friends, including all of the Collectibles, old and new, to celebrate Labor Day at their home in the Hamptons. Would you like to join them?

ABOUT THE AUTHOR

An attorney and former judge, James J. Kaufman lives with his wife, Patty, in Wilmington, North Carolina. The author of several works of nonfiction, he is also the bestselling author of *The Collectibles* and *The Concealers*. *The Conciliators* will be released September 2015. Visit the author at his website, www.JamesJKaufman.com.

General Book Club Questions
for *The Conciliators*

1. This novel begins with two quotes, one from Ralph Waldo Emerson and the other from Winston Churchill. What were your thoughts when you first read these quotes? How would you apply these quotes to the characters, beginning with Preston, Marcia, and Katherine?

2. The Prologue presents a bridge between the end of *The Concealers* and the beginning of *The Conciliators*. Did you find Preston as presented at the end of *The Concealers* and in the Prologue the same man at the end of this book? If so, why? If not, what were the material changes you observed? What do you believe drove those changes?

3. Why the title *The Conciliators*? Did the term "the conciliators" have any particular meaning to you before you read this novel? After? Describe your feelings about conciliation, reconciliation, and how those feelings interact with what you see as the theme of *The Conciliators*. Can you identify specific characters as conciliators in this novel? Who are they? Why did you pick them?

4. Do you feel Austin was justified in what he did? Do you believe, in the end, Austin was treated fairly? Was justice achieved where he was concerned?

5. What did you feel about Preston's reaction to Austin's behavior throughout the novel?

6. Do you feel that Preston, Marcia, Katherine, and Beth changed during the course of this novel? If so, how and why?

7. Has Preston now fulfilled the commitment that he made to Joe Hart? If so, when and how?

8. How would you describe Katherine's relationship with Susan? Is she her friend? Is there another way you would describe their relationship?

9. How do you feel about Katherine's relationship with Sean? Would you have taken her position with Sean at the end? Describe the distinction she made between resolving and reconciling issues. What did you feel about Sean's attitude toward Katherine at their meeting in Alexandria? Would you have acted the way he did? Why or why not?

10. How would you describe Preston's relationship with each of the collectibles at the end of the book as contrasted with the beginning of the book?

11. What, if anything, do you believe Marcia learned about life after her near-death experience? Have you, or do you know any person, who has undergone such a change in near death or extreme adversity?

12. What was your reaction to the conversation between Harry and Preston after the funeral?

13. What impact did Tommy and Missy have on Preston?

14. Did Katherine breach any journalism ethical responsibility? If so, when and how?

15. Should Katherine have disclosed her relationship with her father in her first story involving the arrest of Austin Disley?

16. Now that you have finished *The Conciliators*, Book Three of the trilogy, do you feel that Katherine made the right decision by turning in the story and continuing with it? Why or why not?

17. Were you satisfied with the end of this trilogy? Why?